HARVEST OF THE
COLD MONTHS

HARVEST OF THE COLD MONTHS

The Social History of Ice and Ices

ELIZABETH DAVID

Edited by Jill Norman

VIKING

VIKING

Published by the Penguin Group
Penguin Books USA Inc., 375 Hudson Street, New York, New York 10014, USA
Penguin Books Ltd, 27 Wrights Lane, London w8 5tz, England
Penguin Books Australia Ltd, Ringwood, Victoria, Australia
Penguin Books Canada Ltd, 10 Alcorn Avenue, Toronto, Ontario, Canada m4v 3b2
Penguin Books (NZ) Ltd, 182–190 Wairau Road, Auckland 10, New Zealand

Penguin Books Ltd, Registered Offices: Harmondsworth, Middlesex, England

First American edition
Published in 1995 by Viking Penguin,
a division of Penguin Books USA Inc.

1 3 5 7 9 10 8 6 4 2

Printed in Great Britain by Butler & Tanner Ltd, Frome and London

ISBN 0-670-85975-4
CIP data available

Printed in Great Britain

Contents

Editor's preface

Soon after finishing *English Bread and Yeast Cookery* in the mid 1970s, Elizabeth David started researching early ice-cream recipes and the links between Levantine sherbets and the sorbets and ices of Europe. This led to study of the elaborate banquets and other festivities at which ices and ice-chilled fruits and delicacies were served, often against a backdrop of table decorations and dishes which were themselves fashioned out of ice. She wrote a number of articles on early ices and sorbets before transferring her interest to the role of ice and snow as both luxury and necessity in the warmer countries. Long an avid reader of the books of early travellers, she traced descriptions of storing snow and ice for summer use and of ancient ways of making natural ice across the whole of Asia, from China to Turkey, and in the Middle East and southern Europe.

She then turned her attention to the seventeenth-century inventors and scientists, members of the Royal Society and their European counterparts, who had experimented with freezing and producing cold by artificial means. From there her historical researches extended to the world-wide trade in harvested ice, to the nineteenth-century commercial development of artificial ice and to the practical application of the new ways of freezing, first by the *limonadiers* and confectioners and later in agriculture and industry, to open up ever more distant markets for their produce.

Whenever a particular aspect had been investigated to her (always temporary) satisfaction, that section of what was to become a social history of ice and ices was written up, and the sources used were listed.

Most of her research stopped at the early years of this century, the time when the harvesting, carriage and storage of natural ice had become all but obsolete trades. The essays collected here were mostly written by the mid 1980s, when ill-health and decreasing mobility made research trips, even visits to libraries, more and more difficult. Notes for chapters on early mechanical refrigeration, on ice-cream parlours and soda fountains, on ice houses, never reached the stage where Mrs David was satisfied she had enough of the answers. I have added a few notes on early ice pits and a sketch of the development and use of ice houses in an Introduction. Some knowledge of their importance and the manner in which they functioned may be useful for understanding the rest of the text.

Acknowledgements

I am grateful to Sylvia Beamon and Susan Roaf who allowed me to draw on their *Ice-houses in Britain* in preparing the Introduction. Dr Suzy Butters contributed much of the documentation for text and illustrations for the chapter on Florence. Audrey Coe kindly lent a copy of the unpublished Leftwich Chronicle. Jenny de Gex provided some essential last minute picture research. Annie Lee did a meticulous job of copy editing.

Special thanks to Paul Breman who spent weeks sifting through boxes of papers to ensure that none of Mrs David's original notes were overlooked, then checked references, corrected proofs and generally kept the whole project on track. And to Sasha Breman who typed and retyped, corrected proofs and dealt with most of the correspondence.

Thanks are due to the following persons and institutions for permission to reproduce illustrations:
Index, Florence for the Boboli Gardens (p. 10)
The National Museum of Denmark for the zinc bottle (p. 22)
The Wellcome Institute for the portrait of Latini, L14343, (p. 142)
The Warburg Institute for the portrait of Della Valle (p. 190)
Elisabeth Beazley for the ice houses of the Iranian plateau (pp. 207 and 208)
The National Maritime Museum, for Unloading ice at Great Yarmouth (p. 235)
The Museum of London for the Billingsgate fish market (p. 241)
The British Library for the ice pits at Allahabad, V10244, vol. 1, p. 76 (p. 249)

Felicity Kinross and R. A. W. Guest for the illustrations on pp. 293 and 349

Archivio di Stato, Firenze: Santa Maria Nuova, 694, c. 3 for the map of the Olmo estate (pl. 1)

Phillips, fine art auctioneers, for *La belle limonadière* (pl. 4)

Hobhouse Fine Art for the abdar cooling water (pl. 5)

Giraudon/Bridgeman Art Library for The Oyster Lunch, Musée Conde, Chantilly (pl. 12)

J.N.

Introduction

We do not know for how many millennia man has exploited the preservative properties of ice, but the earliest recorded ice houses were built at Mari beside the Euphrates river in Mesopotamia almost 4,000 years ago. In *The Ice-houses of Britain*, Sylvia Beamon and Susan Roaf note that cuneiform texts describe an ice pit twice as long as it was deep (12 m by 6 m) and lined with tamarisk branches. The ice supply was well guarded, but demand was such that it was almost sold out three days after reaching the city. It was used by the rich to cool their wines and other drinks.[1] There is confirmation in *Proverbs* (XXV:13) of the custom of preserving snow and the value placed upon it: 'As the cold of snow in the time of harvest, so is a faithful messenger to them that send him: for he refresheth the soul of his masters.' And in the Shih Ching, *c.* 1110 BC, we learn that the ancient Chinese were accustomed to harvesting and storing ice for the summer months (see p. 227).

The Greeks and Romans adopted the use of ice houses and the habit of cooling their drinks from the Middle East. Snow was sold in the markets of Athens from the fifth century BC and according to Pericles was widely used by ordinary people and soldiers as well as by the nobility.[2] A piece of ancient gossip about Diphilus, the comic playwright (355–288 BC), is recounted by Athenaeus:

Once upon a time Diphilus was invited to Gnathaena's house, to dine, so they say, in celebration of the festival of Aphrodite ... And one of her lovers, a stranger from Syria, had sent her some snow ... the snow was to be secretly shaken up in the unmixed wine; then she directed the slave to pour out about a pint and offer the cup to Diphilus. Overjoyed, Diphilus quickly drank out of the cup, and overcome by the surprising effect he cried, 'I swear, Athena and the gods bear me witness, Gnathaena, that your wine-cellar is undubitably cold.' And she replied, 'Yes, for we always take care to pour in the prologues of your plays.'[3]

Chares of Mitylene, in his *Records of Alexander*, described how to store snow in pits. It is said that when Alexander conquered Petra in 837 BC he had thirty pits dug, filled with snow and covered with branches of oak.[4] Plutarch described a similar procedure in which the pits were covered with straw and coarse cloth.[5]

In *The History of Ancient and Modern Wines*, published in 1824, Alexander Henderson affirms:

The Romans adopted the same mode of preserving the snow, which they collected from the mountains, and which, in the time of Seneca, had become an important article of merchandise at Rome, being sold in shops appropriated to the purpose, and even hawked about the streets ... At first the only mode of employing snow was by fusing a portion of it in the wine or water which was to be cooled; and this was most conveniently effected by introducing it into a strainer (*colum nivarium*), which was usually made of silver, and pouring the liquid over it. But as the snow had generally contracted some degree of impurity during the carriage, or from the reservoirs in which it was kept, the solution was apt to be dark and muddy, and to have an unpleasant flavour from the straw: hence those of fastidious taste preferred ice, which they were at pains to procure from a great depth, that they might have it as fresh as possible ... A more elegant method of cooling liquors came into vogue during the reign of Nero, to whom the invention was ascribed; namely, by placing water, which had been previously boiled, in a thin glass vessel surrounded with snow, so that it might be frozen without having its purity impaired.[6]

All around the Mediterranean, snow from the mountain ranges was carried to the ice stores of the cities. The Mamluk kings of Egypt had snow shipped from Lebanon to Cairo in the thirteenth and fourteenth centuries. In Spain there are records of snow pits being dug on the order of Carlos III of Navarre (1387–1435). A pilgrim to the Holy

Sepulchre, Canon Pietro Casola of Milan, arrived in Jaffa on a Venetian ship on 24 July 1494. A party of Moors brought gifts to the captain, including a large sack of snow. 'It was a great marvel to all the company,' recorded Canon Casola, 'to be in Syria in July and see a sack of snow. It was also a comfort to many, because some of the snow was put into the water – which was hot – and cooled it.'[7]

The earliest modern documentation of the ice trade in Italy dates from the fifteenth century. Much of the early ice gathering was on a small scale, as people collected ice from ponds and stored it in pits. By the seventeenth century a substantial ice industry had developed in the Lessini mountains in Friuli, and ice was sent overnight by cart to the wealthy citizens of Verona, Venice and Mantua.

At this time many estates had their own ice houses and ice ponds. A detail from the 1693 manuscript map of the country estate at Olmo of the hospital of Santa Maria Nuova in Florence shows the ice ponds and ice house situated quite near to the *fattoria* or main house. The estate was large; it comprised twenty-four farms and areas of woodland in addition to the part shown (see pl. 1).

In Rome, noted Père Labat in 1730, snow was preserved, not ice. Ice was scarcely known in the Roman Campagna, he said, and in some years snow was rare, lying only a few hours when it was gathered quickly and carried to the ice houses.[8] A useful account of Italian ice houses is found in *Remarks on the Antiquities of Rome and its Environs* by Andrew Lumisden. Although the ice house he describes is very large, it was constructed in much the same way as the one John Evelyn wrote about to Robert Boyle, which is shown on p. 3.

A little above Rocca di Papa (on the ancient Mons Albanus) is a plain called Hannibal's Camp. It is here that the snow is collected annually for the use of Rome. On this dry plain they dig pits, without any building, about fifty feet deep, and twenty-five broad at the top, in the form of a sugar-loaf, or cone. The larger the pit, the snow, no doubt, will preserve the better. About three feet from the bottom they commonly fix a wooden grate, which serves for a drain if any of the snow should happen to melt, which otherwise would stagnate, and hasten the dissolution of the rest. The pit thus formed, and lined with prunings of trees and straw, is filled with snow, which is beat down as hard as possible, till it becomes a solid body. It is afterwards covered with more prunings of trees, and a roof raised in form of a low cone, well thatched over with straw. A door is left at the side, covered likewise with straw, by which men enter and cut out the ice, for such it becomes, with a mattock. The quantity daily demanded is carried to Rome, in the night time, in carts well covered with straw. It is found by experience, that snow, thus pressed down, is not only colder, but preserves longer, than cakes of ice taken from ponds or ditches.[9]

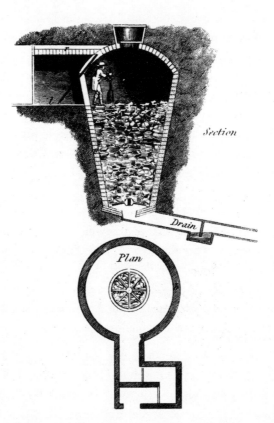

Section and plan of an ice house from *The Cyclopedia or Universal Dictionary of Arts, Science and Literature*, Rees, 1819. Small quantities of ice could be added through the opening in the roof. A cartwheel effectively blocks the entrance to the drain. The angles between the entrance and the inner doors (see plan) prevented warm air entering. The passage could be filled with straw to increase insulation.

The nobility and clergy of France also appreciated the preservative and cooling properties of ice and snow. Ice pits were dug in the grounds of châteaux and palaces, abbeys and monasteries. A thirteenth-century ice house has been excavated at Vauclaire Abbey in Aisne. Henri III was satirized, among other things, for his excessive use of ice and snow, and by the time Louis XIV made extensive improvements to Versailles in the third quarter of the seventeenth century at least two ice houses had been built to supply the needs of the court. By the end of the century it had become customary for rich and poor alike to use ice; in 1701 a royal edict brought in regulations to prevent its unauthorized sale at excessive prices in Paris and throughout the provinces.[10]

In England at that time only the most wealthy could afford ice. James I had had two brick-lined snow pits (as they were then called) dug at Greenwich between 1619 and 1622, and another was made at Hampton Court in 1625. At the restoration of the monarchy Charles II, who had spent much of his exile at the French court, ordered ice houses to be built in Upper St James's Park in 1660. They were mentioned by Boyle in the same paper to the Royal Society as Evelyn's description of the Italian ice houses. The court followed the fashions set by Charles, and the use of ice was no exception – so ice houses were constructed at their London mansions and at their country estates.

On the accession of William and Mary in 1689 a list of incidental expenses allowed to servants at St James's Palace included an item of £91 5s. to the 'Yeoman that keeps the Icehouse, for filling the Ice-houses, and all necessaries if found needful', and this same 'yeoman and keeper of ice and snow', one James Frontine, was paid £5 0s.0d and £55 0s.0d board wages per year.[11]

These early ice houses were pits sunk in the ground and thatched with straw, and were expensive undertakings on account of the digging. Initially snow pits were lined with clean straw, and layers of ice or beaten snow about a foot thick were interspersed with straw. Any empty space was also filled with straw and a grate in the bottom of the pit allowed melt water to drain away. Later ice houses were lined with brick. The brick structure continued above ground as a dome with a passage leading to the door. The ice houses were egg-shaped, the pointed end in the earth and the larger end rising above ground level. In the *Gardener's Dictionary* of 1768 Philip Miller emphasized the importance of locating an ice house in a dry situation, avoiding the shade of trees, and suggested a raised position to allow easy drainage.[12]

During the eighteenth and nineteenth centuries the *nouveaux riches*, with wealth from empire, industry or the spoils of war, bought country properties, built sumptuous houses and laid out gardens, complete with ice house. These were often far grander affairs than the snow pits of the Stuart period and sported showy façades: Egyptian and Grecian temples, Gothic grottoes, Chinese pagodas and rustic cottages dotted the parks of the rich, though a few preferred to landscape their ice houses and planted shrubs over them, as did Joseph Paxton when he was head gardener at Chatsworth in the 1840s.

Ice was also stacked, particularly on small estates and dairy farms.

York ice house, constructed in the early 19th century and restored circa 1980. Photograph: Elinor Breman.

The ice-stack is made on sloping ground close to the pond whence the ice is derived. The ice is beaten small, well rammed, and gradually worked up into a cone or mound 15 ft high, with a base of 27 ft, and protected by a compact covering of fern 3 ft thick. A dry situation and sloping surface are essential with this plan, and a small ditch should surround the heap, to carry rapidly away any water that may come from melted ice or other sources.[13]

By the end of the eighteenth century large ice houses were built in the towns and cities. Most were privately owned and built for the fishing industry or the confectioners (see p. 310), and were extremely expensive to construct. According to the architect John Papworth, writing in 1818, 'Small ice wells may be executed at a very moderate expense, provided the means of drainage is easily obtained; in London residences, on this account, they would be formed without difficulty in the vaults', whereas for confectioners whose trade demanded spacious ice reserves, 'the formation is proportionably expensive ... in several cases, where the site and other circumstances have been unfavourable, the expense of one of these depositories of ice, have been almost incredible'.[14] The spread of the railway network meant that ice imported from America and Norway could be transported from large depots at ports and in cities to country estates as well as to urban dwellers and industry: ice became available to all.

Jill Norman
February 1994

Florence

Snows of Yesteryear

In June 1581, Michel de Montaigne was staying in Florence. 'It was so hot,' he recorded in his journal, 'as to astonish even the natives.' Two days after the St John's Day midsummer festivities, he dined at the house of Signor Silvio Piccolomini and wrote, 'it is customary here to put snow into the wine glasses, I put only a little in, not being too well in body'. The Trebbiano wine, of which he had drunk 'a great quantity when heated by travelling' was sweet and heady and had given him a horrible migraine.[1]

Montaigne, who did not frequent the court of Henri III, the effeminate reigning monarch to whom the introduction of snow and ice – and forks – to refined French tables is usually attributed, and who does not on any previous occasion mention snow-chilled wine, was nevertheless quite unsurprised by the Florentine custom. No doubt he had heard of it many times, and as a man steeped in classical writings he would in any case have been perfectly conversant with the frequent references in Greek and Latin literature to the storage of snow, and to its ancient usage for the cooling of wine and water. He could not, for example, have failed to know the story of Nero having his drinking water boiled before it was put into flasks to be cooled in snow, nor of Seneca's slightly shocked affirmation that in his day people went so far as to use ice as well as snow, nor again of Pliny's denunciations of the degenerate custom of turning the seasons upside down by those people who in summer used the snows of winter to chill their wine. Evidence of the contemporary use of snow by the Florentine gentry had also been forthcoming for Montaigne when he and his party, after riding from Bologna to Florence, had visited Pratolino, the Grand Duke Francesco's summer residence about nine miles distant from the city and two miles off the Bologna road. It was November 1580, and here in the grounds of the villa they saw 'some very wide holes in the ground where they keep a large quantity of snow all the year round; and it is placed on a litter of broom, and then all this is covered, up to a great height, in the form of a pyramid, with thatch, like a little barn'.[2]

The section of Montaigne's *Travel Journal* in which his visit to Pratolino is recorded was in fact written by his French secretary, and although perhaps dictated by Montaigne himself, conveys a rather confusing description of what the Italians at this time usually called *bucche di neve*, snow holes or pits, rather than stacks as implied in the Frenchman's phrase. Snow stacks built up from ground level and finally covered with a thick layer of straw or dried rushes were in fact fairly common in Europe, and the method was perfectly effective in preserving the snow,* but I think that what Montaigne and his party saw at Pratolino was more likely to have been a series of snow pits with protective straw-thatched roofs, looking in outline somewhat like wigwams but with a porch and a door at one side leading into an antechamber from which a ladder or steps gave access to the snow store. This would tally both with the Montaigne description and with the illustration of a contemporary Danish ice house in the grounds of Lundhov, Frederick II of Denmark's manor house near Helsingfors (more familiar to us as Elsinore), reproduced in pl. 2. John Evelyn's diagrammatic illustration of a snow pit such as those he had investigated when he was in Italy in the 1640s shows similar characteristics, with its high pyramid-shaped thatched roof and lantern pole, although this does not protrude through the roof to give the wigwam-like profile so striking in the Danish ice house.

The Grand Duke Francesco's delightful villa at Pratolino had been completed in about 1571, while he was still Grand Prince. The villa and grounds, initially intended as a residence for Bianca Cappella,

---

* As far back as the third century AD the Emperor Heliogabalus (AD 204–22) had had 'snow mountains' built up in the grounds of his villa near Rome.

An illustration of an Italian ice house as described by John Evelyn. Evelyn wrote his description for Robert Boyle who incorporated it as an appendix to a paper of his own. The illustration is from *The Works of the Honourable Robert Boyle*, Vol 2, 1744.

Francesco's Venetian mistress of long standing, eventually his second wife, were designed and built by the young Bernardo Buontalenti, one of the most remarkable Florentines of the latter half of the seventeenth century. A multi-faceted genius, Buontalenti was architect, costume designer, dazzling master of mechanical waterworks and hydraulic engineering, impresario of the Medici feasts, festivals and fireworks, and still believed by some to be the inventor of ices. The roots of this belief, it now appears an entirely erroneous one, can be traced to Buontalenti's construction of ice houses not only at Pratolino, and in the Granducal Boboli Gardens, but around the walls of Florence itself. These latter ice houses were for the public sale of ice and snow and were not constructed until some thirty years after the building of Pratolino, by which time Buontalenti had himself obtained a concession from the Grand Duke Ferdinand I, brother and successor of Francesco, for the supply of snow to the people of Florence. Buontalenti's snow monopoly lasted until his death in June 1608, and somehow, no doubt via the familiar linguistic misinterpretations of later generations, his name, already associated by his contemporaries with the much-increased popular use of ice and snow in Florence, subsequently became attached equally to the invention of ices, it being a curious truth that food historians, of whatever nationality, rarely trouble to distinguish between ice and ices.★

That the obviously increasing use of snow-chilled wines and beverages by the Florentines during the latter decades of the sixteenth century can be attributed solely or even mainly to the construction of Buontalenti's ice houses seems to me debatable. Certainly they must have helped to spread the habit and familiarize it to many who would not or could not otherwise have used snow and ice so freely, but at the same time the usage was on the increase everywhere in Western Europe – with the exception, that is, of the British Isles – and the part played by the Florentines and their Medici rulers was just one manifestation of a general movement. That part does, however, have some very particular points of interest that are worth looking into.

The Florentine love of iced wine goes far back, at least as far as the fourteenth century, when there is a pointed allusion in the chronicle of Donato Velluti, who in 1345 or thereabouts headed an embassy from the Republic of Florence to Mastino della Scala, lord of Verona. Very special honours were accorded the ambassadorial party. Della Scala in person rode two miles outside the town to greet them, they were lodged in a nobly furnished house and were attended by many knights and other good gentlemen; morning and evening the tables were most nobly set out, there was *molto ghiaccio* to chill the wine (it was the month of August), confectionery and wax candles without count. Their horses were stabled and fed, 'all without ourselves having to spend one florin'. A further reference at about the same period occurs in a description of a fourteenth-century Tuscan feast and 'barrels of white Tuscan wine In ice far down your cellars stood supine; And morn and eve to eat in company of those vast jellies dear to you and me'. No doubt those 'vast jellies' required the use of snow to set and keep them cool as much as the Tuscan wine needed chilling.[3]

Now, returning to the days of the Grand Dukes, which began in 1569 when Cosimo I was granted the title by Pope Pio V – he whose

---

★ In English usage of the nineteenth century there was a common lack of distinction between ice for cooling and ice meaning ices as refreshments.

private cook was Bartolomeo Scappi – we find signs of a growing preoccupation with the construction of snow pits, the supplies of snow to fill them, the purchase of massive silver wine coolers with inner containers for snow, and other small but significant manifestations of a trend towards the more efficient cooling of drinks and a more regular provision of snow.* In 1570, for example, a new wine cooler was acquired by the Grand Duke Cosimo's butler, Michele Biscaino, and was recorded in the Wardrobe Accounts for that year as 'a large silver wine cooler with an inner vessel, to hold snow, and with, for feet, three tortoises'. This was inventoried at a weight of 25 lb 17.3 oz (evidently for precious metals the Florentines were using the so-called heavy pound of 28 oz rather than the more usual 12 oz pound). In the same Debtors and Creditors books of the Wardrobe Accounts for the years 1570 to 1574 a second 'very large wine cooler' is recorded, and this one had figures and serpents for handles, and 'within, a vessel to hold snow', the feet 'four eagles' claws holding four balls filled with gilded stucco', presumably a reference to the Medici coat of arms. The weight of this great wine cooler was 28 lb 7 oz, and the gilded stucco weighed 27 lb 18 oz; it was consigned on 12 June 1570 or 1571 – the precise date was not filled in – and paid for in August 1571.[4] Possibly this latest acquisition was in readiness for the midsummer festivities of St John's Day, when the Grand Duke's palace was traditionally thrown open to the public, and food and wine were freely offered to all comers.

By 1571, the Grand Duke Cosimo had already delegated many of his duties to his heir, Prince Francesco, and it was in 1574, the year of the latter's succession, that there appeared in Florence the first Italian translation of the Spaniard Nicolas Monardes' curious and original

---

* For previously unpublished information concerning the snow and ice provision for Florence during the latter part of the sixteenth century I am much indebted to Dr Suzy Butters of Manchester University, who has most generously communicated to me many notes on and transcriptions of original documents made by her in 1969 in the course of research in the Medici archives for a study of Bernardo Buontalenti and his work. In my references for these pages those given to me by Dr Butters are initialled S.B. For the interpretation put upon them, both linguistic and historical, I take entire responsibility.

little treatise on snow and ice and their uses in the treatment of various illnesses as well as for the chilling of wines and other beverages. This *Libro de la Nieve* had originally been published in Seville in 1571 together with the second part of Dr Monardes' work on the plants and medicines of the East Indies (which included North and South America) at that time being brought to Spain. This, although an important work, was not translated into Italian until 1589,* and *The Boke Which Treateth of the Snow,* which ran to only twenty-seven pages, was in intent an exercise in propaganda for the more widespread use of snow and ice in hot climates, and in particular for the establishment of a regular supply to Seville, Monardes' native city.

The full title of the little-known 1574 Italian translation of the *Libro de la Nieve* was *Trattato della Neve e del Bere Fresco, raccolto da G.B. Scarampo e ridotto in lingua toscana.* The publisher was Sermartelli, Florence. At a time when the members of the medical faculties of Europe were almost unanimous in their condemnation of the growing practice among the rich and fashionable of drinking their wine, water, and sweet beverages chilled with snow, a doctor who campaigned for the greater availability of snow and who advocated its use in the treatment of fevers and many other maladies was news indeed. It is hard to believe that the publication in Florence *in lingua toscana* of the Monardes tract was a chance happening. Was it sponsored by Francesco while he was still Grand Prince? It surely would have suited him to see the treatise made available to all literate Tuscans. Not that he himself would have had any problems with the Spanish tongue. His mother, the beautiful Eleanora of Toledo, who had died in 1562, had been the daughter of Don Pedro, Marquis of Villafranca, Spanish Viceroy of Naples, and her children were certainly conversant with the language. It was simply that the promotion of the use of snow in his domains would have been good policy. There were always snow-harvesting concessions to be sold, taxes to be levied, the State's coffers enriched. In addition there were Francesco's own tastes to be taken into consideration. Here was the chance to refute Italian medical disapproval of what appeared to the physicians to be a highly

---

* This translation included another Italian version of the *Libro de la Nieve.*

undesirable and indeed dangerous indulgence. The Monardes treatise must have infuriated them.

The reaction of one of Grand Duke Francesco's own doctors, Piero Nati of Bibbiena, was to compose his own treatise on the subject of 'the injurious custom of drinking iced wine', in which he blandly asserted that the Florentines made little use of snow owing to the abundance of excellent, pure, and naturally cold water available from the large number of wells in the houses of the city throughout the summer, ample for everybody to cool their wine and fruit with. Here he was referring to the custom of diluting wine with water when it was poured into the glass, at the time general practice in Italy, France, and Spain, although not in the German States. He went on to comment on the current acceptance of the opinion expressed 'by many' that snow is not injurious but good and healthful. He wags his finger at those who have taken to using it 'universally', opening public shops all the year round, 'following perhaps the example of those cities which pay greater attention to such refinements than they should, unless truly the weather is hotter, the air more unhealthy, and good cold water lacking'. These words were without doubt a retort to the Spanish author of the *Libro de la Nieve* and a scarcely veiled reproof of the Grand Duke, with his Spanish sympathies and closely maintained relations with the Spaniards of Naples and Sicily. As for Nati himself, he recognized that warm wine was disagreeable, but he advised moderation, a middle course. He liked his wine cool, he said, but not made freezing with snow. Openly attacking those 'learned and wise persons who praise the use of snow for chilling wine and who have even written publicly of it, producing in confirmation of their views the testimony of many worthy authorities, Latin, Greek and Arab', Nati proceeds to quote passages from the very same authorities deploring and condemning the practice of drinking iced and snow-chilled wine.

It is of course quite true that Monardes had been highly selective in his choice of quotation and that his purpose was biased. So, equally, were Piero Nati's, and it was indeed quite easy to make Hippocrates and Galen, Pliny and Varro, express totally contradictory opinions. But when Nati pulled from his hat a modern authority in the person of 'Montano, famous physician to the illustrious S. Galeotto Pico della Mirandola' he had quite a trump card. In the year 1550, Nati said, Montano had blamed Pico della Mirandola's custom of drinking iced wine for the indisposition he had been suffering, for 'this custom of Princes of wishing too delicately and too exquisitely to enjoy that which gives them pleasure, also does them much harm and brings the course of their lives to a premature close'. With a good deal more in the same vein Nati brings his *breve discorso* to an end with the reiteration of his advice that drinking cool should not mean drinking with snow or ice, but simply with the use of naturally cold water, and that equally the fruit eaten at the best tables, which are cherries, plums, melons, figs and grapes, should be cooled with the same cold water.[5]

Piero Nati's reproof to all snow and ice advocates appeared in 1576, two years after the Italian version of *The Boke Which Treateth of the Snow.* Similar treatises continued to appear, in Italy, Spain, France, and nearly all western European countries, for a century. As late as 1702, Louis Lémery, the French chemist and author of *Traité des Aliments*, published a warning of the dreadful consequences of drinking iced beverages reminiscent of today's newspaper articles on the perils of smoking. Piero Nati, however, and all the physicians who followed him into his particular pulpit, were fighting on a losing side. The Grand Duke Francesco, it goes without saying, paid no heed to medical warnings. Both he and his brother, Ferdinando, who was a Cardinal living mainly in Rome, were firmly committed to the use of snow and concerned themselves personally with ensuring adequate supplies. On 21 November 1577, for example, just three years before Montaigne saw the wide holes stacked with snow at Pratolino, the Grand Duke writes from Florence to Benedetto Uguccioni, superintendent of building at Pratolino, saying that now the snow has come he should start filling the *buca*, the pit, and that he should take it from the nearest source rather than sending to fetch it from far away, and when it is packed it is to be well sprinkled with water to harden it. Next day Uguccioni replies politely to the Grand Duke that he will attend to the packing of snow in the *conserve*, the repositories (the Grand Duke's officers of the household always refer to the *conserve* or *conserva* rather than to *bucche* or the *buca*), and that this will be done with all the diligence commanded by His Serene Highness. However, he has not yet been able to do it because there has been so little snow and what there was was 'very watery'.[6] Again in 1582, on 12 February, Uguccioni writes, this time to the Cavaliere Serghuidi, the Grand Duke's secretary, that at Pratolino all goes well, but in the *Conserve della Neve* it has not yet been possible to put any, for there has come so little.[7]

In 1583 Cardinal Ferdinando bought for himself the Villa Ricci in the Pincio, the palace still known today as the Villa Medici. Here he probably had a more conveniently situated snow store constructed in his own grounds, something such as the great Vignola had designed when he built the Villa Giulia for Pope Julius III in the 1550s. There a decorative grotto in a hill in the grounds of the villa close to the Tiber concealed a large vaulted underground snow store.[8] This provided a practical solution to the problem of bringing snow in daily loads from a pit in the hills, a system attended by a variety of hazards. Snow was a precious commodity and the diversion and robbery of a load or two evidently a fairly common crime. Among Cardinal Ferdinando's letters preserved in the Medici archives is a copy of a paper addressed to the Rome Chief of Police and all other personages of whatsoever rank or condition, giving notice that Ottaviano da Burrino, his muleteer, and the muleteer's boy, are bringing two loads of snow per day to Rome, are not to be molested in any manner whatsoever, nor the snow to be taken to any other place whatsoever, 'for it is for our use'.[9] Dated 24 July 1571, the Cardinal's pronouncement serves to demonstrate the cumbersome procedure entailed when snow had to be brought from a distance. In the heat of a Roman July the melting of a large part of the precious loads carried by the mules was as much a hazard as was their diversion to some other snow-hungry noble lord, church dignitary, or state official who would pay good money for a supply on a day when the weather was stifling and he was faced with the disgrace of offering warm wine to his guests. It seems obvious enough that by constructing capacious ice or snow stores in the gardens of their city palaces and suburban villas the Romans and the Florentines could bring in their snow during the winter months, when it was plentiful and while there was far less danger both of diminution by melting and total loss by theft; from about the 1570s on, this system appears to have been the most generally in use in the great Italian cities.

In Florence the newly refurbished Pitti Palace, bought in 1549 by Eleanora of Toledo from the Pitti family, had snow-cooled wine cellars underneath Ammannati's Grotto, and in the Boboli Gardens behind the Palace, a grotto excavated out of the side of the high hill, the *collina* or *monte di Boboli*, with an ice house underneath, was the work of Buontalenti, who had been in charge of the garden designs in the days of the Grand Duchess Eleanora and was still working there in 1576 for her elder son Francesco, now Grand Duke. It was in that year and indeed the very one in which Piero Nati published his anti-snow treatise that the Boboli grotto was made for Francesco. At about the same time, prompted perhaps by the heat of a Tuscan summer, he became interested in discovering how Turkish sherbets were made, and wrote to Mafeo Veniero, of the great Venetian family, that it would give him much pleasure if Veniero would send him the *ricetta delle*

The ice house in the Boboli Gardens: the loading door.

sorbette, the receipt for sherbets, and the manner of making the best and most noble of Turkish potions and beverages,[10] clear enough evidence that, legend notwithstanding, sherbet drinks had not yet at that time reached Florence and that the Medici family certainly did not, as has been asserted by more than one Italian food historian,[11] possess the 'secret' of making *sorbette* in the sense of water-ices or even of the perfumed and ice-cooled beverages of Turkey and Persia.

What the Grand Duke did with his sherbet recipes, or if indeed he received them from Mafio Veniero, it would be interesting to know. Perhaps that information will one day come to light. Meanwhile we do have knowledge of a favourite beverage concocted, it was reported, by the Grand Duke himself. Describing his addiction to highly spiced, heating, and indigestible food, and his drinking of many kinds of wine such as malmsey from Candia (Crete), sack from Spain, Lacrima from Vesuvius, various wines from Tuscany and Corsica★, all with snow, one of his contemporaries, Gianvittorio Soderini, refers to a mixture of white grape must poured boiling over *latte infrigito*, iced milk, and drunk by the Grand Duke 'at strange hours'.[12] This was an allusion, no doubt, to the long days and nights Francesco spent in his laboratory in the Palazzo Vecchio studying chemistry and making scientific exper-iments, evolving new methods of glass-blowing and of making por-celain, activities viewed with hostility by the Florentines, who believed that he was manufacturing poisons for Bianca Cappella, who was much disliked and therefore inevitably suspected of being a witch. As for the icy-hot milk and grape must drink, it sounds like an innocuous enough concoction, probably drunk as a pick-me-up, and hardly the sinister tipple hinted at in the account.

I have read also of a frozen milk, egg-yolk and malmsey drink invented by the Grand Duke Francesco. I think it would be a mistake to make too much of this unauthenticated report. However, in the 1580s Giambattista Della Porta was experimenting with the freezing of watered wine by immersion and agitation of the bottle in a bowl of snow and saltpetre, and by 1589 when he published his new edition of *Magia Naturalis*, he had succeeded in doing so to his satisfaction (see

---

★ At this time under Genoese rule.

p. 70). Francesco, given his many contacts with Spanish Naples, and, more importantly, his very serious interests in science and chemistry, could without doubt have learned about Della Porta's freezing experiments well before his death in 1587, and it was clearly the kind of experiment which would have appealed to him. But if indeed he possessed this new knowledge, we have no evidence to confirm that he used it.

When in 1587 Francesco and his Bianca died within hours of each other, their deaths inevitably, and for long after, attributed to poison,★ it was Cardinal Ferdinando who succeeded his brother as Grand Duke. A new era of Florentine life was inaugurated by Ferdinand I. Relinquishing his Cardinal's hat the year following his accession, in 1589 he married Christine of Lorraine, daughter of Henri, Duke of Lorraine, and through her mother, Claude de Valois, granddaughter of Catherine de Medici. The wedding festivities, spread over a period of six weeks, from 5 May to 15 June, were the excuse for an unparalleled display of Medici opulence. As was customary for such festivities, armies of architects, designers, sculptors, painters, artists and craftsmen were kept busy for months beforehand constructing and decorating triumphal arches, organizing processions and parades, devising ballets, theatrical spectacles, musical dramas. There were to be magnificent banquets, extravagant displays of sugarwork and confectionery, fireworks on an unprecedented scale, 2,000 foreign guests lodged in the city and maintained at the expense of the Grand Duke, receptions in the Boboli Gardens, and for one of the most daring spectacles of the whole six weeks, a mock naval battle fought in the flooded courtyard of the Pitti Palace. This of course was devised and stage-managed by the water-engineering genius Bernardo Buontalenti, also responsible for the invention of new and spectacular stage machinery, gorgeous costumes, fabulous fireworks.

It was the first of the series of great fêtes held by Ferdinand in the twenty-two years of his reign, the most famous of all, designed to impress all Europe, being the festivities held in October 1600 to celebrate the marriage of his niece Maria, younger daughter of

★ But in reality almost certainly from the effects of acute malarial fever.

Francesco, to Henri IV of France. On the day of the marriage ceremony (Henri, much indebted financially to the Medici, had agreed to divorce his childless first wife, Marguerite de Valois, and to marry Maria, but did not care to absent himself from France to attend the wedding in person), Buontalenti once more excelled himself in the invention of mechanical marvels to astonish the wedding guests. As the colossal wedding banquet drew to a close, an automatically propelled table moved from in front of the new Queen of France, her uncle and their guests, to the two side walls of the great banqueting room, where it transformed itself into two fountains adorned with gold relief and precious stones, to be replaced by another table which rose through the floor, fully set with one of the fantastic desserts, at the time regarded as the very summit of splendour, in which everything, from the goblets and dishes to the napkins and knives and statues, was fashioned out of sugar. No sooner had the guests finished nibbling at their confectionery than the lights were extinguished, and with a realistic clap of thunder two pillars in the great hall opened out into two grottoes lined with brilliant gems. From one grotto stepped a young girl dressed as Juno, complete with sceptre, crown, and peacocks, from the second Pallas Athene with a rainbow on her head. When the goddesses had delivered a song in honour of the nuptial pair they vanished into their grottoes, the lights were relit, and in the place of the royal confectionery table appeared another, this time set with glittering crystal and shining mirror glass. This table, in turn, so the report assures us, was transformed as if by magic into a garden with shrubs, paths, fountains, flowers, fruit, statuettes of nymphs and shepherdesses. Tame singing birds hopped about the garden, and the new Queen was able to take them in her hands and distribute them among the ladies present. A pretty picture. Buontalenti was congratulated on his wondrous inventions, but from the Papal Legate and the French Minister there was headshaking. It had all smacked rather too much of the supernatural. In order to quieten them down and reassure them that no sorcery was involved, the Grand Duke explained to them how the transformation scenes had been worked.[13]

Buontalenti's ice pools

Bernardo Buontalenti, inventor of so many magical fantasies for ceremonial occasions, had also been the creator of many rather more
lasting works. For the Grand Duke Francesco he had created the
entrancing Pratolino with its gardens and grottoes, its fountains and
lakes, its myriad waterworks which had so impressed Montaigne and
his party, and of which in the 1640s John Evelyn was to record that
there was 'a large walk at the sides whereof gushes out of imperceptible
pipes, couched underneath, slender pissings of water that inter-
changeably fall into each others Chanells, making a lofty & perfect
arch, so as a man on horseback may ride under it and not be wet with
one drop ... this Canopi or arch of water was mithought one of the
surprizingst magnificences I had ever seene, & exceedingly fresh
during the heate of summer'.[14] For the Grand Duke Ferdinando
Buontalenti had remodelled and adorned the Villa Artemino, a
delightful hunting lodge west of Florence and beyond the town of
Signa; he had transformed the medieval castle of Petraia into a magnificent country villa with yet another splendid garden; he had
designed the Belvedere Fort overlooking the city of Florence, worked
on the Galleria of the Uffizi and on the Boboli Gardens, constructed
a new harbour at Livorno to replace the old one at Pisa, now almost
silted up, and had been responsible for many new fortifications and
waterworks.

The more we hear of Buontalenti's activities, the more we come to
know of his inventive genius, the better we understand that this
remarkable man was far from being above designing comparatively
lowly domestic necessities such as dairies, wine cellars, kitchens, and
ice houses. Michelangelo after all had not been too grand to sculpt
such utilitarian objects as marble mortars for the kitchen nor to turn
aside from work on his Hercules to fashion a statue out of snow to
please the youthful Piero de Medici, son of Lorenzo the Magnificent.[15]
That Buontalenti, like his former master the Grand Duke Francesco,
may have dabbled in artificial freezing experiments we may strongly

suspect, but we have no evidence to support such a premise. What we do know for certain is that towards the end of the sixteenth century, when he was in his late sixties, Buontalenti had understood that to Florence and the Florentines snow and ice were increasingly necessary commodities and that an assured supply of one or both could not but be the basis of a lucrative business. Everyone with aspirations to comfortable and elegant living now had a private snow store in the grounds of their town mansion and country villa, or in the hills close to the source of supply. According to Dr Pisanelli in his *Trattato della Natura de Cibi, et del Bere*, or *Treatise on the Nature of Foods and Beverages*, published in 1584, it had then already been twenty-five years since the use of snow in summer had been introduced in Sicily, and there every poor artisan now wanted snow as he wanted bread and wine. In Florence, too, a supply of snow was soon to become a necessity to the common man as well as to the gentry and the nobility. The men who ensured that all would be able to buy snow when they needed it were the Grand Duke Ferdinando and Bernardo Buontalenti.

In 1598 Buontalenti had petitioned the Council of Eight, administrators of Tuscany's financial affairs,* for the sole concession to bring snow into Florence and to sell it from his own *bucche* or snow pits. The concession was granted with effect from June that year. Already by the 14th, however, Buontalenti was writing to an official, Lorenzo Usimbardi, complaining that his monopoly had been violated. Referring to the Grand Duke, he recapitulates how 'His Serene Highness has made me a grace of the snow, that none may bring snow into Florence as from the first of June, and that any others who go to my snow pits will be condemned to a fine of 25 *scudi* and two strokes of the rope ...' His complaint is that he has caught a certain Cosimo at Porta alla Croce with a load of snow which he is taking to Alessandro Orsini, Duke of Pittigliano. Orsini is claiming that he has had permission from Usimbardi last year to use the snow for his own purpose. Buontalenti can't believe that Usimbardi did any such thing. He is therefore writing personally to Usimbardi before putting the matter

* There were then two Councils of Eight, the first being concerned with the defence of the realm and foreign policy.

to the Grand Duke for settlement of the affair. He adds that all this is bad for the snow business and will ruin his profits.[16]

Buontalenti was a man who had always spent everything he earned on further research and experiment. In the time-honoured tradition of inventors and innovators he had saved little for his old age, and had a large household to maintain. His snow income was to be a regular addition to his earnings as the Grand Duke's Superintendent of Public Works. Reading between the lines of his complaints against Orsini, one senses that Buontalenti suspected Usimbardi of perpetrating a piece of common trickery on him, more than likely of having accepted a bribe and turned a blind eye when the 'said Cosimo' raided his snow store. How the matter was settled we do not know, but soon there are more interesting developments, and unfamiliar terms begin to appear in the official correspondence concerning the construction or maintenance of the public and private snow stores. In 1603 an official of the *Parte*, a body roughly equivalent to an office of works but responsible also for the issue of various commodities such as wood and certain building materials, mentions for the first time the construction 'with all possible speed' of a *buca da diaccio* at the bastion of the Porta San Gallo; not only is there to be a new ice pit, but this ice pit is for the Grand Duke, it is to be large and capacious, but if any damage be done to Bernardo Buontalenti (who already had a snow pit at the San Gallo bastion) it is to be made good, and in order to gain easy access to the ice pit the workmen are to construct a bridge of two girders across the bastion, and it is to be situated as near as possible to the *peschiera del diaccio*, the ice pond, so that it [the ice] may be easily carried, i.e. from the pond to the pit.[17]

These references to an ice pit and an ice pond are significant changes. I think that Buontalenti, the great water engineer, had now turned his attention to the making of special reservoirs conveniently sited for the creation of ice and the elimination where and when possible of the necessity to supply Florence with snow from the surrounding hills or from even higher up in the Appenines. That method was unsatisfactory on several accounts. Before the snow could be transported, much work, beating down and compressing the snow into bales, was involved, the journeys were long and slow, there was the ever present risk, as we have seen, of robbery, and should there be delays or a sudden spell of warm weather, of disappearance of the precious snow owing to unavoidable natural causes. Ice naturally frozen on the spot, where it could be lifted from the ice pool and carried straight to the ice house, would undoubtedly be preferable. Given that so many people were in the habit of putting snow directly into their wine, ice would have had the added advantage of being clear and clean and altogether more appealing to the eye as well as more hygienic, for it appears fairly certain that, like the ice reservoirs of Persia, the Florence ice ponds were man-made, and initially created by an irrigation expert in the person of Buontalenti. He, of course, may well have known of the Persian methods, but to so experienced a water engineer and so ingenious a man it would hardly have been difficult to work out a system for himself.

Henceforward, in Florence, it is of ice pits rather than snow pits that we hear, and terms such as *conserve di acqua per diacciare*, ice reservoirs, and *laghi di diaccio*, ice lakes, begin to recur. In October 1605 we find Buontalenti building another ice well at the San Gallo bastion, and rushes for lining or covering it are to be provided by the *Parte*.[18]

Only a few weeks later, on 10 January 1606, writing an infinitely sad letter to the Grand Duke, who is staying at his villa at Poggio a Caiano, Buontalenti tells Ferdinando that he is old and infirm and since his fall in the Galleria he has never been right again, that he has fifteen mouths to feed, including four nieces and three nephews, and he is lacking two *moggia*, bushels, of grain to live on this year.[19] He makes no reference to his ice revenues or to any new ice houses or other projects. Two and a half years later, in June 1608, he died aged seventy-eight, just a few weeks before his friend and colleague the great sculptor Giambologna, with whom he had collaborated on so many projects for the glorification of the Medici Grand Dukes and the beautifying of Florence.

The Grand Duke Ferdinand did not pass on to Buontalenti's heirs the ice concession and the annual pension of 210 *scudi* which went with it but granted them to a man named Francesco Paulsanti, who had previously had some connection with the ice business and the construction of ice pits. Possibly he had been Buontalenti's assistant. On 12 December 1608, six months after the latter's death, Paulsanti writes to Raffaello Carnesecchi, *Provedatore* or Purveyor to the *Parte*, whose functions seem to have been approximately those of a Quartermaster General, to inform him of the Grand Duke's gift and to say that this includes the concession on the Bastion of the Zecca, the old Mint. Around the bastion, Paulsanti writes, the ground is in need of preparation for the *conserva di acqua per addiacciare*, the water reservoir for freezing; for this work he will need twenty men, and it will take two days.[20]

Evidently the Florence ice business was growing. For twenty men to spend two days on preparing the ground for a reservoir, the area it was to cover must have been quite extensive, and anyway by 21 December it is freezing, sufficiently so to fill the ice pit, and furthermore in Paulsanti's view the *fossetto*, the trench or moat, which runs from the Porta alla Croce the length of the wall as far as the Arno, should be cleaned out and somewhat enlarged. Whether this *fossetto* was an ice trench or an irrigation channel of some kind is not clear, but most probably the latter. From a further communication on the 31st we learn that this was a propitious period for the ice and snow harvests. Paulsanti was requiring men to pack both ice and snow for Florence, for Pratolino, for San Casciano, where there are ice and/or snow pits.[21]

In 1609 the Grand Duke Ferdinand died and was succeeded by his son Cosimo II, who only a year earlier had married Maria Maddalena, Archduchess of Austria. In 1620, still only thirty years old, Cosimo too died, leaving his ten-year-old son to reign for fifty years as Ferdinando II. At some time during the reign of Cosimo II, he and the Grand Duchess Maria Maddalena had evidently taken back some of the ice house concessions and in 1618 were using the two on the bulwark outside the Porta San Gallo for the supply of the royal household, and three years after the young Grand Duke's death, his Grand Duchess is recorded as having given an order for the tower which stood between Pinti and San Gallo to be used as a *conserva di diaccio*.[22] Porta Pinti was on the eastern wall of Florence, midway between the Porta San Gallo and the Porta alla Croce. The tower, an old watchtower perhaps, was a curious choice of ice house on the part of the Grand Duchess, but there was an area of flat country around Pinti, and there may have been a suitable site for an ice reservoir. Could the tower have been the one seen in van Asselt's tapestry, woven in 1643 for the Medici and depicting the harvesting of ice outside the walls of an Italian city, and now hanging in the Palazzo Medici-Riccardi? I doubt if towers converted into ice houses were a commonplace.

The 'Quinta Essentia'

In the composition of a true beverage
Snow is the fifth element.
He is mad who without snow
Thinks to receive a satisfied guest.
Bring then from Vallombrosa
Snow in God's plenty:
Bring from every hamlet
Snow in heaps
And you Satyrs
Leave your jigging and chattering
And bring me ice
From the grotto under the Boboli hill.
With long picks
With great poles
Shatter
crush
crunch
crack, chip
Until all resolves
In finest iciest powder,
To cool my drink,
To refresh my palate,
Or I shall die of thirst,
For warm wine I cannot swallow.[23]

I do not know if Francesco Redi's famous poem *Bacco in Toscana*, written in the 1660s, has ever been published in English translation. If there is such a translation I have not found it, so have myself done the best I can to convey something of Redi's bubbling, fizzing, joyful singing. Compared with his bewitching and infinitely expressive seventeenth-century Italian words, my twentieth-century English ones can hardly be other than plodding and pedestrian. A sequence such as *Dirompetelo, Sgretolatelo, Infragnetelo, Stritolatelo* conveys the cracking, splintering, shivering, crushing, crunching of ice, and Redi's own relish in the sounds, to a far finer degree than I can ever hope to achieve. Here are some more lines in my necessarily very free translation:

> Wine coolers and ice flagons
> Stand ready at all times
> With spotless glass flasks
> Stoppered, clasped fast in the rime
> Of the crystalline snows.

Redi's ice flagons are interesting. He calls them *cantinplore*, a word derived initially from the Greek but which came to Tuscany from Spain in 1543, the Spanish version being *cantimplora*, meaning singing-sobbing, from the sound made by the air trapped in the cylindrical ice pocket which was an integral part of this type of flagon. Since Redi himself explained the term and described the vessel at some length I quote his words:

In Tuscany the *cantinplora* is a glass vessel which when filled with wine has in the centre a hollow in which to put pieces of ice, or snow, for chilling; it has a long thick neck which rises from one side, in the manner of a watering pot. Today it is not much used, and at the Court they call *cantinplore* those silver or other metal vessels which hold one or more *bocce*, glass flasks with a fat round body and a long narrow neck which serve for the chilling of wine or water with ice.

Here it should be explained that Francesco Redi, born in Arezzo in 1626, was physician to the Grand Duke Ferdinand II of Tuscany and at the same time one of the most distinguished members of the

A pair of Irish decanters with lozenge stoppers and the most unusual feature of an ice pocket entering the decanter from the side, 27 cm high without the stopper. Circa 1780. From the catalogue of the Wine Trade Loan Exhibition of drinking vessels held at Vintners Hall, London in 1933

Accademia della Crusca, the institution founded by the Grand Duke Francesco in 1583 with the aim of safeguarding the purity of the Tuscan language. The name *Crusca* derived from the bran left after the sifting or bolting of flour, and accordingly the members of the Academy met to discuss the origin and to pronounce on the worthiness or otherwise of every word to be included in the dictionaries which they compiled and every few years revised.

The solemn sessions of this august body must have been much enlivened when Francesco Redi started reciting his improvised verses in praise of Tuscan wines to the assembled members. It was these verses which, continually added to and reworked from 1666 onwards for the next nineteen years, finally emerged into the light of day as *Bacco in Toscana* in 1685.

When his poem was published, Redi's annotations on his own verses filled nearly 300 pages to the thirty occupied by the lines themselves, and when discussing the meaning, significance and origin of words he is no less fascinating than when he is letting off the crackling fireworks of his poetry.

Returning to his Spanish *cantimplora*, Redi quotes Sebastiano Covar-ruvias and his *Tesoro della Lingua Castigliana* as saying that 'this is a copper carafe with a very long neck for chilling water or wine buried in snow, and it is agitated in a pail filled with snow, a thing very well known and used in Spain everywhere.' He appears to be describing the bottle depicted by Dr Blas Villafranca in his 1550 work on saltpetre cooling methods (see pp. 67 and 71). 'It is called *cantimplora* because

A zinc bottle with a silver neck, 39 cm high, of Indo-Persian origin. It was acquired for the Royal Kunst Kammer in Copenhagen before 1741.

Another early version of a cooling device, Scacchi's frigidarium, 1622, was in fact one part of an ingenious system that could be used to cool or heat beverages. The jar (E) was filled with snow, and put into the container in the centre (B). Bottles (F) containing the wine or water to be cooled were put in on either side (C).

the water or wine inside it, by reason of the air trapped in the neck makes two different sounds, some low, others high, some glad, others sad, so that it appears to sing and sob simultaneously. For the same reason the French call *chantepleure* a certain type of bucket and watering pot which they use for watering gardens.'[24]

Evidently then the Spanish and Italian *cantimplora* could be quite a variety of different vessels, but one always in some way connected with the chilling of wine and/or water.

It is an inviting scene which Redi plucks out of the air, a scene in which frosty, round-bellied, short-necked glass wine flasks are packed in assorted snow-filled silver wine coolers, and elegant flagons embodying their own ice compartments stand arranged on a tiered buffet in a shaded arbour of some delicious Florentine garden. Why, though, did he call snow the fifth element? It was simply that to the Tuscans to say that something was the fifth element meant it was essential, *necessarissima*, and in the distant past both Florence and the Florentines had been so-called, first when Boniface VIII, at his coronation in 1294, had remarked in open consistory and for the benefit of the twelve Florentine ambassadors present that 'among things human the Florentines are the fifth element', and later on when the fourteenth-century poet Antonio Pucci called the city of Florence the *quinto elemento*, an echo probably of the 'quinta essentia' of the alchemist, the quintessential ingredient. To Francesco Redi, then, it was snow to chill his wine which constituted the *necessarissimo*, the fifth element. As for the ice from the grotto in the Monte di Boboli, Redi explains that in one of the little hills in the Grand Duke's garden there was an ice house for cooling those wines which in the summer were stored in the grotto under the said ice house. This same ice house was described by Richard Lassels, author of *The Voyages of Italy* (1670). When he was in Florence in the 1660s Lassels inspected the Palazzo Pitti, saw the Grand Duke's bedchamber and his collection of 'curious Thermometers or Weather Glasses', and in the gardens remarked particularly on the Grand Duke's 'curious Ice-House and coole cellar under it, where the melting Ice dropping downe upon the Barrels of Wine, refresh it so exceedingly, that in all my life I never drank so coole as I did at the Tap in the Cellar'.[25] Presumably there were pipes which conducted the ice-water down to the cellars below.

It is somehow poignant to discover that late in life the joyous and witty Redi turned from his celebrated hymn to the wines of Tuscany to the composition of one in praise of all kinds of water. He called it *Arianna Inferma*, *Ariadne Ailing*, but left only a few fragments when he died in 1698. In *Arianna* he was putting the praises of water into the mouth of Ariadne, who is suffering from a fever and a burning thirst, and who demands snow and ice for her water just as Bacchus does for his wine, and Redi in fact repeats his passage about the wine coolers, the *cantinplore*, the *cantinette*, the glass flasks, the crystalline snows, and here too in this charming fragment he describes eating a *sorbetto*, and now at last it *is* being eaten rather than drunk: *oh come scricchiola tra i dente, e sgretola*, he says: oh how it crackles between the teeth and dissolves, now in the mouth, then down the gullet, and slips cold, cold, right down to the stomach. Redi was, I think, experimenting with the passage and one following, also concerned with a description of ices, for numerous alternative lines were found in his papers by his editors, two learned abbots who had both been his friends and who prepared and annotated his collected works for publication. Descriptions of the ices of this period are far from common, so it is worth discovering what Redi has to say about them. First comes 'this finest frozen snow, rising from the rims of the goblets in hillocks', then it is 'this delight, fair, adorable, beautiful, with its name so charmingly expressive, called in the public shops fresh *pappina*', meaning pap in the sense of something being eaten with a spoon. Over a century later a *sorbetto* composed of cooked milk and 'other ingredients' was still known as *pappina*, but seems to have been, as Redi said, an ice-cream vendor's term rather than one of the professional confectioner. Redi addresses the doctors, 'Oh, if the more expert among them would only give these *pappe* to their patients, those ever-open hospitals could be kept ever-closed, and that poor old Charon could slumber on his barque on the shore of Acheron.'[26]

It was early days to be advocating the use of ices in the treatment of the sick. Not until half a century later do we hear of French doctors prescribing them or advising their patients to order them from Dubuisson, proprietor of the old café Procope in Paris, and it was only in the 1780s that the Neapolitan doctor Filippo Baldini came out with his book in praise of *sorbetti* and what he considered their many medicinal and tonic properties. As a physician, one wonders if Redi, so vastly different a man from Piero Nati, his predecessor of so long ago, had been trying out ices in the treatment of his patients or whether he had found them beneficial in the alleviation of his own infirmities. Those are speculations, but a point which emerges from his lines as a certainty is that more than once Redi refers to ices and *sorbetti* as novelties and to recipes for them as mysteries, with their many ingredients, so delicate, sweet, new, elegant, that the formulae are positively majestic in their gravity. To those who swallow them and to those apothecaries who make them they have now become archi-delicious, and what is more important, useful. With a sharp dig at the apothecaries, a body of practitioners who at the period were often under attack both from the medical profession proper and from the general public, Redi the physician remarks that were these delicacies useless, in other words unprofitable, the apothecaries would find them odious no matter how delectable they might be.

The container used by the Accademia del Cimento for their freezing experiments.

Later, following the repetition of his lines about the snow-filled wine coolers standing at all times in readiness, Redi gives Ariadne in her delirious thirst a vision of *aloscia,* a popular Spanish mixture of honey, water and spices, much drunk in the summer, and of a whole lakeful of *candiero.*[27] The latter delight was also mentioned in *Bacco in Toscana,* and Redi himself explained it. It was, he said, a kind of beverage *modernamento inventata,* and his friend the illustrious Conte Lorenzo Magalotti had written a detailed description of it in verse. It turns out to have been a kind of semi-frozen custard, and Magalotti, who had been Secretary to the Accademia del Cimento and had recorded all their freezing experiments made in the 1660s,[28] gives a nice verse recipe for this 'modern' invention. There was nothing particularly modern about the mixture itself, so the novelty was in the freezing.

Here are Magalotti's directions in my translation:

Egg yolks barely cooked/ Beaten in a spotless porcelain,/ And if you want something sovereign/ When they are beaten, and frothy/ Then put sugar/

Rather more than a pinch/ Take a large *bucchero* [clay vessel]:/ Don't do it timidly:/ A little musk, and amber in plenty,/ Twenty or thirty jasmine blossoms/ Pare a couple of small lemons/ Just to rejoice the palate:/ Then leave it to stand/ To rest,/ Until the aromas are all extracted:/ Then with deliberation (An important point!) Separate and detach/ One by one/ The white petals of the jasmine:/ And the green parings/ Of the lemons:/ Then thin with water/ With much water,/ And pour it all from one basin to another/ Until you see/ It has all incorporated/ Mixed and mingled/ This smooth-scented/ Delicate soup/ Truly worthy of Cyprus:/ Through the finest cloth sieve/ You now strain it.

At last we come to the really exciting part. You are to put in a gilded *cantinplora* – yes, again – the most translucent crystals, born of turbulence and the icy caves of Vallombrosa. Pound, chop and pulverize them, and crush cooking salt too. You are to spray the mixture and before long you see that the crystals change into pearls, and from frost into snow.

At midday, thirsty from this work, pack a good portion of it round the *sorbettiera* and when you perceive a pearly frost adorning the outside of this vessel you take a clean silver spoon, promptly detach and redetach the frozen parts, for they will refreeze in a moment, until stirring hard, hard, this with the other, *tra gelato, e non gelato*, from frozen and unfrozen, it little by little becomes like thickly coagulated milk.

> And it is called Candiero:
> Thus was it named by the Sicilian
> Who erstwhile made it to quench the thirst
> Of the Signor di Carbognano.[29]

That name *candiero* is quite a curiosity. The modern *Grande Dizionario*, citing Redi, defines it as a beverage based on eggs, milk and sugar, and concludes that the word comes from the Spanish *candiel*, meaning *zabaglione*. The 1688 edition of Florio's Italian-English dictionary, however, has the verb *candere* (not to be confused with *candire*, to candy) meaning to shine white, to glitter bright. That would be a beautifully appropriate description for an ice, but I suppose we must accept the *zabaglione* definition, however unlikely it may seem. Florio, by the way, translates *zabaglione* or zabaione as 'a cawdle', and that of course was very much what it was – a warm, sustaining drink – before it reached the menus of international Italian restaurants as a showy little dessert demonstrating the waiters' skills with an egg-whisk. Less picturesquely, the modern Cassell's translates *zabaglione* as 'egg-flip with wine: custard mixed with Marsala'. To Redi and Magalotti in the second half of the seventeenth century I rather think it was more like a very lightly cooked custard baked 'between two fires' than the frothed-up confection we know today. At any rate, in the *zabaglione* recipes given by Bartolomeo Stefani in *L'Arte di ben Cucinare* (1662), that was the method of cooking directed, and he did add pine-nut or melon-seed milk, the first for people going out early in the morning or for a long day's hunting expedition, the second for convalescents, milk in these cases meaning the pulverized nuts or seeds steeped in water and wrung through a cloth. A century earlier, Scappi's *zabaglione*, consisting of egg yolks, wine, chicken broth, sugar and cinnamon, was cooked in a long-handled shallow saucepan called a *bastardella*, more commonly used for the hash of chicken, almonds, and broth called *biancomangiare*.

It has been appropriate here, I think, to devote a certain amount of space to the varying and changing meanings of names such as *cantimplora*, *candiero*, and *zabaglione* because to Francesco Redi and to Lorenzo Maga-lotti, also a member of the Crusca Academy, these matters were of so much concern. If only Redi had lived to finish and annotate his *Arianna Infirma*, or had chosen to comment on his friend Magalotti's verse formula for the preparation and freezing of *candiero*, we should know a great deal more about the early history of Italian ices than we now do. He might for instance have revealed who that Sicilian *candiero*-maker was and who his master the Signor Carbognano, he might have told us when it was that *sorbetto* the sherbet drink started turning into *sorbetto* the ice. He disparages the former in *Bacco in Toscana* as *bevande da svogliati*, beverage of the listless, the bored, but in *Arianna* makes his heroine demand that at least her useless attendant let fall into her mouth the *rugiada congelata*, the red ice of the *sorbetto* (in *Bacco, rugiada* is unwatered red wine), and upon this line Redi's editors commented that as well as the *sorbetto* for drinking the name is applied to the grains of frozen waters which float in the form of hailstones.[30]

How commonly used and understood the term *sorbetto* may have been in Redi's day, whether as an iced drink or a half-frozen one, or both, is hard to determine, but one certain point about it is that the Crusca scholars did not accept the word as belonging to the language and did not include it in their *Vocabolario* or Dictionary of 1686 nor that of 1691. Giovanni Torriano, who in 1688 updated John Florio's 1611 English-Italian Dictionary or *Worlde of Words*, was not so exclusive. He translated *sorbetto* as 'any kind of supping broth; also a kind of drink used in Turkey, made of Lemonds, Sugar, Corrans, Almonds, Musk and Amber very delicate called in England Sherbet'. This entry was new since 1611, and Torriano made no reference to frozen sherbets. He did, however, give an entry for *gelato* as 'frozen, congealed, gellied'. This too was an entry new since 1611, and although it does not yet appear as a noun it is not without relevance to the story of ices, because when translating seventeenth-century and indeed earlier culinary Italian it is all too easy to fall into the trap of supposing that *gelato* meant something frozen or congealed when in fact it meant 'gellied'.

How the ice-mad gentlemen of Ferdinand II's court, men like Redi and Count Magalotti, must have delighted in the glittering display of ice goblets, ice fruit bowls, ice pyramids and the mountains of ice and snow broken up for chilling the fruit and cooling the jellies when the Medici gave the series of great feasts celebrating the marriage in June 1661 of the Hereditary Prince Cosimo and Princess Marguérite-Louise of Orléans. It was the very apogee, the ultimate, the fifth element indeed. No wonder English travellers like Sir John Reresby and Richard Lassels remarked with some surprise on the Italian addiction to ice. 'In the summer the meanest person seldom drinks his wine without having it cooled either with ice or snow, which is preserved in places for that purpose underground, and sold publicly in the markets,' said Reresby,[31] who was in Florence, Vicenza and Venice in 1657, and Richard Lassels at about the same time was recording that 'for their Wines they use Snow or Ice, which they keep all Summer; they that are much us'd to this way will not in this Country, even in Winter, drink without Snow'.[32] Even the Florentines themselves were sometimes surprised at the way everybody wanted ice all the year round. '*Questa delizia*, this pleasure has taken such a hold that many people use it continually, even in winter,' wrote Tommaso Rinuccini in the record he kept in Florence in the 1660s.[33] Buontalenti and those who followed him in the ice business had done their work well, and that work had not been forgotten. When the two abbots, Anton Maria Salvini and Giuseppe Bianchini, came to annotate Redi's *Arianna Infirma*, they recalled to their fellow Florentines the debt they all owed to 'the invention of the art of so delectably conserving snow and ice for the summer, as we do it now, attributed to the fruitful discoveries made by ingenious Florentines in the person of Bernardo Buontalenti, who as a reward from the Grand Duke Ferdinando I, was given for his lifetime the income he derived from the sale of that which Redi called the fifth element'.[34]

Times and Florentine tastes have changed. Where are the snows of yesteryear? On a sultry September evening in 1981, sitting at a pavement table outside an expensive Florence café, I found it impossible to obtain a glass of chilled wine. The waiter disappeared for fifteen minutes before returning with three or four cubes of ice already half-melted in a tumbler. The following evening, in the little town of Castellina in Chianti, the proprietor of the smartest café in the place was dismayed when asked for ice. He did his best. Taking the ice tray from a very small refrigerator behind the bar, he spent five minutes extracting four cubes of ice. They appeared to frighten him. Very gingerly, with sugar tongs, he dropped two of the precious cubes into each of our glasses. Francesco Redi would have improvised a few sparkling verses to mark this odd little incident. I can only echo Boileau's famous 'What no ice?' 'In this weather? Oh, the disgrace!' But the point was that the proprietor of that busy little café didn't in the least suppose that to have no ice for his customers constituted any kind of disgrace. Indeed it was clear that the Tuscan addiction to ice – I do not mean ice-cream – is a thing of the past.

Shine White Diamant Ice

To Richard Lassels, Italy in the 1650s and 1660s seemed to be

Nature's Darling, and the Elder Sister of all other countries . . . in Lombardy and the Campania Ceres and Bacchus are at a perpetual strife . . . she by filling his barns with corne; he by making the cellars swimme with wine . . . other parts of Italy are sweating out whole Forests of Olive-trees, whole woods of Lemmons and Oranges, whole Fields of Rice, Turkey wheat, and Musk-millions . . . it abounds also in silks and silkwormes . . . and for the feeding of them they keep a world of Mulberry trees whose leaves are the food of those little wormes . . . It's rich allso in pasturage and cattle, especially in Lomberdy, where I have seen cheeses of an excessive greatnesse and of a Parmesan goodnesse. The surface also of the earth is covered with many curious simples and wholesome hearbes: Hense so many rare essences, cordials, parfumes, sweet waters and other odoriferous distillations so common here, that ordinary Barbers and Landresses will sprinkle them in your face and parfume your linnen with them, over and above your bargain . . . Hense none of the meanest things to be seen in Italy are some of the fondaries or stilling houses of the Great Dukes of Florence, the *speciarie* or Apothecaries shops, of the Dominicans of S. Marco, and of the Minimes of Trinita di Monte in Rome . . .

In Florence, turning from Nature's bounty to the wonders and riches of the Medici palaces, gardens, art galleries and treasuries, Lassels is privileged to see the 'chambers of the Great Duke's appartiment' and finds them 'most sumptuous'. He is shown the Great Duke's Argentaria or Plate and is awestruck by the

greate square room with twelve great cupboards as high as the room, all set with silver and gold plates, dishes, forks, spoones, knifs with a world of other rich vessels set in gold. In another cupboard they shewed me the four great sylver bedposts enameld here and there, and set with polished stones of divers colours: they were made for the new Great Princesse, daughter to the late Duke of Orleans.[35]

That new 'Great Princesse' was Marguérite-Louise, sixteen-year-old daughter of Gaston, Duke of Orléans, and first cousin of Louis

XIV. The Medici celebrations on the occasion of her marriage to Cosimo, heir of Ferdinand II, Grand Duke of Tuscany, reached their climax in June 1661. The silver four-post bed was ready for the arrival from France of the young Princess, already married by proxy in Paris two months previously. Since that 17 April 1661, when the bells of Florence had rung for three days, the festivities in the Tuscan capital had continued relentlessly, regardless of the Grand Prince Cosimo himself, lying ill with measles and unable, or unwilling, to rouse himself from his bed. Princess Marguérite-Louise, equally disinclined for the marriage, was on her way to Livorno by sea, escorted by her new uncle-in-law, Prince Mattias de Medici. In Florence the assembled Medici awaited the bride. Banquets and collations and theatrical spectacles were planned. Dressmakers were embroidering a cloth of silver dress, jewellers fashioning a massive diamond and pearl chain, and milliners creating a lace headdress to be worn by the bride for her solemn official entry into Florence with her husband. Silver trappings and white plumes were in preparation for the adornment of the four white mules which would draw the Princess in an open litter through the streets, and under the triumphal arches now being raised all over the city. The Medici, in short, were out to show French royalty what Florentine magnificence really meant.

There had already been one great banquet on 5 June, at which the sixteen sugar paste *trionfi* had represented the rivers Seine, Arno, Rhône and Danube, the four seasons, the four elements and four kinds of chase, a boar hunt, a roe-buck hunt, a lion hunt, and a hunt with falcons. One hundred different dishes, not counting the confectionery, had been served, and 350 napkins folded and pleated into ornamental shapes. Now the preparations for the great *merenda* on the 10th and another on the 15th were in train. Confectioners were rolling out acres of marzipan paste and carving it into the fleur-de-lis, the lions, and the double-headed eagle of the bride's arms, fashioning and colouring the gold-lily-emblazoned azure ball and the five red ones of the Medici. The leopards of France, the lion and lily of Florence, lions, lilies, roses and castles of Aragon and Castile and Leon, the oaks of the Della Rovere, family of the reigning Grand Duchess Vittoria, were being made out of pastry and sugar work, gilded and silvered.

The cooks were boiling cauldron upon cauldron of calves' feet and jelly, wringing sackfuls of beaten almonds through tammy cloths to make almond milk for blancmangers of shredded capon breast stiffened with rice starch and set in moulds fashioned in heraldic shapes – lilies, lions, the *fascie* of the Medici. Supplies of new asparagus, the little spring mushrooms called *prugnoli*,[36] preserved truffles, green almonds, sweet young fennel, melons, cherries, were pouring into the Medici larders. Boxes of quince and peach pastes from Genoa, Siena, Valencia, dragées, comfits and *calicione*★ from Foligno and Spoleto were piling up in the palace confectionery. The Grand Duke's distillers were working overtime to produce enough sweet waters, essences, syrups, liqueurs and perfumes to last for the rest of the month, the resources of his ice houses were raided for blocks of snow and ice to keep the table fruit fresh and cool, his herb gardens for young salad plants and artichokes, his orange and lemon groves for fruit to make lemonades, for huge citrons to be carved into coronets and crowns, and for oranges to garnish every second dish. The butlers were pleating and folding starched cambric napkins into new and ever more extravagant fantasies, birds, beasts, ships, arches, colonnades, cascades, to decorate the banqueting tables and dazzle the guests.[37] The keeper of the Grand Duke's *argentaria* was giving out *compote* dishes and chargers and fruit dishes for biscuits and sweetmeats and salads; fluted silver moulds were being made ready for the ice and fruit pyramids which would be frozen to make the showpieces of the cold first service of the Grand Duke's banquet on the 15th.

It was Cardinal Mazarin who had decreed the Tuscan marriage for Princess Marguérite-Louise. It was said that Mazarin had papal ambitions. As allies the Medici cardinals – at the time there were two – would be valuable to him at the next conclave. But in 1660 Alexander III, the former Cardinal Fabio Chigi of Siena, was only sixty. It seems unlikely that Mazarin, two years younger but in ailing health, can really have hoped to succeed Pope Alexander. In the event, Mazarin died in March 1661, while Alexander survived until 1667. Perhaps the

---

★ Small almond cakes, like the *calissons* of Aix-en-Provence.

young Orléans Princess, still officially in mourning for her father who had died the previous year, hoped that Mazarin's death would free her from an unwelcome marriage and dreaded exile in a foreign country. If so, she was horribly mistaken. With Mazarin's death Louis XIV had taken the reins of government and diplomacy into his own hands. Henceforward the King was the State. Himself only twenty-three and very recently obliged to submit to a political marriage with the unprepossessing Infanta Maria Teresa, he listened kindly to his cousin's pleas – and firmly rejected them. His word had been given to the Grand Duke, they had exchanged gifts, he could not lose face by breaking the contract, Marguérite-Louise must accept her fate. So the young girl who had been brought up in the hope that she might marry her cousin Louis and become Queen of France, and who had now conceived an adolescent passion for another first cousin, Prince Charles of Lorraine, was on her unwilling and unhappy way to Florence, never at any time to be reconciled to her marriage.[38]

As Marguérite-Louise and her retinue approached the port of Livorno in the royally decorated galley provided by the Medici at a cost of 50,000 *scudi*, the ageing Cardinal Carlo de Medici, Mazarin's contemporary and great-uncle of the young Grand Prince, feasted with family, fellow cardinals and prelates in Florence. Born in 1596, sole survivor among the nine children of Ferdinand I and Christine of Lorraine, now Dean of the Sacred College and one of its most influential members, Cardinal Carlo (not, by the way, to be confused with Cardinal Giovan Carlo, his nephew and the Grand Duke's brother) was a genial prelate who enjoyed worldly pleasures, drank choice wines and kept a sumptuous table. With an annual income of 10,000 *scudi*, the run of five villas, and attentive friends, nieces and nephews to seek out for him the best produce of Italy and the most luxurious imported delicacies, the finest Padua hams, the best Parmesan cheeses, chocolate from the Spanish colonies, cartloads of Corsican oysters brought from Livorno, the costliest essences and perfumes from the Medici distilleries, were among many luxuries enjoyed by the Cardinal. He appreciated beautiful books and indulged a passion for hunting. When the new Grand Princess arrived, rebellious and fiercely hostile to Tuscany and all its people, the convivial Cardinal took trouble to make himself agreeable to her. He proved to be one of the very few members of her new family with whom she was able to establish and maintain a friendly relationship.[39]

The *merenda* given by the Cardinal on 10 June 1661 as part of the wedding celebrations was recorded by Venantio Mattei, a steward whose native town was Camerino in the Marche. Although Mattei's book, *Teatro Nobilissimo di Scalcheria*, published in Rome in 1669, was dedicated to Cardinal Giacomo Rospigliosi, nephew of Pope Clement IX, and evidently his lord and master at that time, it is clear that in the summer of 1661 he was taking part in the organization of the Medici festivities. He records, at length, four feasts given in connection with the wedding. Very probably, since he also records many dinners and banquets in Rome, he was in the old Cardinal's service there, moving on to Cardinal Rospigliosi after Cardinal Carlo's death in 1666. Whichever household it was that he presided over, Mattei left a valuable record of the manner in which Florentine and Roman banquets, and as a contrast, some quite modest dinners and suppers, were served in the middle years of the seventeenth century. Sometimes, as in the case of the Medici feasts, the choice of dishes set before the guests was as wondrous as their content. A *merenda* in those days was usually a light repast served between afternoon dinner and late evening supper. The Cardinal's *merenda* was a festive one, however, and the food could scarcely be described as light, the first cold service from the buttery or pantry alone consisting of thirty-five separate dishes. Many of these were, it is true, purely ornamental, others were pretty trifles on small round silver plates, dishes of butter worked into fanciful shapes, sugar baskets filled with comfits and little biscuits in whirls and twirls and rings. There was a great deal of ice and snow about, some of it natural and some of it artificially frozen into goblets and fruit dishes. The trick of making these things, discovered in the early 1620s and described on p. 56, by the 1660s had developed into something of an art. In the heat of a Florentine June all that sparkling ice and snow must have been a welcome and beautiful sight.

Among the more serious and substantial of the cold dishes prepared in the pantry for the first service of the Cardinal's reception was the medley called a *capirottata*.[40] That day, this variable dish was composed of young roast chickens and larded and roasted capons, carved and set upon the dishes with slices of roast sweetbreads, small birds in *daube*, slices of salted pigs' cheek boiled and fried golden, and *mortadella* cooked and sliced. The whole affair was covered with a sauce of verjuice 'made somewhat thick' – in other words a sweet-sour syrup – and decorated with egg-yolks cooked whole in sugar, with slices of carved lemon all around. Ice under and over the dish ensured that it would be *freddissimo*. Hams cooked in wine, milk and water, two to a dish, were stuck with little pieces of cinnamon and whole cloves, set upon napkins and decorated with flowers and carved, gilded bay leaves; a Genoese pie, filled with cooked and uncooked egg-yolks, candied sweetmeats, butter and sugar, was festooned with a pistachio sweet-meat, which sounds something like an oriental Turkish delight made in long sausage-like strips; a dish of small flat omelettes in three layers, spread variously with capers, pitted olives, marzipan paste, and every sweetmeat in the repertoire plus fennel seeds, pistachios, sugar and cinnamon, was garlanded with egg fritters, the topmost omelette strewn with more sugar and cinnamon, lemon juice squeezed over the whole; another pie, made in the shape of the letter S, consisted of several layers of the rich and sweet short pastry called *pasta frolla*, with fillings of candied citron, pistachios, cooked egg-yolks, marzipan paste, slices of lean ham, a hash of roast capon breast, roasted sweetbreads and whole verjuice grapes; sugar and cinnamon completed the mixture, and the carver sliced the pie crosswise so that each slice presented a mosaic of several colours arranged in orderly fashion.

Among the jellied dishes were roast guinea-fowl split to represent the Imperial eagle, the breast stuck with pine-nuts arranged like flowers, the head and neck also split, the whole covered in jelly and decorated with more jelly in several colours, the two heads crowned with coronets of sugar paste picked out in gold; pigeons in *daube* in the Catalan manner, the breasts larded, first half roasted then stewed in muscatel wine with lemon juice, powdered *mostaccioli* (spiced and musk-scented biscuits), and pounded candied citron, this sauce to be reduced to a jelly-like consistency and poured over the cold pigeons, the dish garnished with ten rose-shaped tartlets filled with five different sweet jellies, red quince, bitter cherry, white quince, green grape and plum, the jellies stuck with little candied cinnamon sticks and pistachios, the tartlets then covered with marzipan paste in the shape of the Grand Duchess's oak tree, with a sugar icing flecked with gold.

Less daunting dishes were *marzolini*, the fresh spring cheeses of Tuscany, served in halves (they weighed about 24 oz each), three halves to a dish, set on napkins decorated with flowers and carved gilded bay leaves; and an almost modern nursery dish consisting of a sop of cantucci or Pisa biscuits,* steeped in muscatel and lemon juice, arranged in an Imperial dish (an extra large charger) with a covering of orange segments, split green almonds, tender sweet fennel, and dice of candied citron with, of course, sugar over. 'Have a care', notes the steward, 'that all be *ben freddo*', very cold, 'with ice under and over'. There are bowls of round, musk-scented comfits and Siena peach sweet-meat, sugar paste lilies with covers, concealing ribbons and laces for the princesses, a dish of blancmanger in the shape of a lion's head, decorated with the Medici lilies and balls, a charger of Genoa sugar plums, a plate of olives, decorated with coronets and figures of carved citron, a royal salad with figurines, crowns, the *fascie* and lilies of the Medici, and the tender green salad leaves called *insalatine*. (These ceremonial salads were usually left on the table throughout the main part of the meal and dressed only during the third or fourth service, but in this case Mattei notes that it was for a first dish.) A plate of butter in the shape of a lion with a raised paw represented one of the heraldic devices in the arms of the *Serenissima Sposa*, the bride; there was a confectioners' fantasy of marzipan eggs, some whole, some in halves, the whole ones filled with small ribbons or favours for the ladies, the halves coloured yellow like yolks, and another one of small sugar baskets filled with pistachio nougat and flecked with gold leaf. A dish of verjuice jelly was decorated with sugar figurines alternating with more jelly of several colours, there was a charger of candied pistachios, and one of pears in syrup with a complex decoration of sugar rings filled with *ova miscide*, a little trifle of egg-yolks beaten with rosewater, cooked in clarified sugar and squeezed through a syringe into lozenges or *vermicelli*. These were to alternate with oaks made of pistachio paste flecked with gold.

---

* Rusks made from rich light bread, sliced and rebaked.

It all begins to sound like some monstrous tea-party for overfed children – and there were six more services to come. The fresh fruit and the ice and snow at least did something to cool the atmosphere, rest the eyes and revivify the spirits of the guests. Fruit, in fact, was probably what the company mainly ate of that huge cold spread. Italians were brought up to eat fruit at the beginning and at the end of every meal. Doctors approved of the practice, although they were dubious about 'cold' fruits such as melons and plums. By this time medical approval extended – at any rate at the Medici court – to the custom of eating all fresh fruit half frozen in snow and ice during the summer months, and even when it didn't, that was what fashion now decreed. Anyway, people argued, the ice helped to preserve the fruit from 'corruption', so iced fruit they ate, whatever their physicians had to say about it.

At the Cardinal's table that 10 June a dish of strawberries was served with ice under – by which Mattei usually meant that the ice was in a separate dish – and sugar over. Apricots were served in ice *tazze*,* with flowers and leaves; green almonds in ice *tazze*, with garlands of myrtle and flowers; pears in ice *tazze*, with flowers and leaves; sweet cherries with leaves and ice (had the *tazze* run out?), sweet-sour cherries with leaves and flowers; sweet fennel with flowers, leaves and ice; and pyramids of ice, with divers sorts of fruits.

Those pyramids of ice and fruit figure a number of times in Mattei's banquet lists. Once he mentions that they are two and a half palms high – about 22 inches – and once, for another of the Medici wedding feasts, he says that they may be frozen in *catini d'argento scannellati* – literally deep silver basins, channelled or fluted – and will make a fine show. I think Mattei's fluted basins must actually have been moulds specially made by the Grand Duke's silversmiths. Covers would have been necessary before they could be set in the freezing tubs. The salt can have done little good to the silver, but in a world where your

* Not necessarily the shallow, stemmed cups known to the English-speaking art world as tazzas, but bowls, vases, dishes, or drinking cups of unspecified shape and size. In Italian, the term also covers the marble or stone basins of fountains. It is also a term used in metal casting or smelting in moulds. This may have been the sense in which Mattei was using it. See the description of how ice vessels were made, p. 56.

employers owned sets of solid silver tables and cabinets and gave their children jewel-encrusted silver bedposts for wedding presents, of what account were a few new silver basins every now and again?

Eventually, as we know, moulds for ices were made mainly of pewter, and the manner of setting fruit in pyramid moulds, three-quarters filling them with water, covering them and freezing them in ice and salt, we also know. Directions of a rather muddled nature appeared in a *Recueil de Curiositez Rares et Nouvelles* published in Paris in 1674 – a medley of Curiosities and Secrets collected by the Sieur D'Emery[41] – and a much more explicit one by a French professional confectioner and distiller called Audiger, whose *La Maison Réglée* appeared, also in Paris, in 1692, see p. 100. Audiger, incidentally, had learned some of his skills in Rome, in 1659 and 1660, at just about the time that Mattei was practising as a professional steward. We know from Antonio Frugoli that ice pyramids as centrepieces were already appearing in the 1620s and from John Barclay that ice dishes and goblets were beginning to be known at about the same time. Forty years on the art had clearly reached a high degree of reliability. In the palaces and villas of the Medici – Cardinal Carlo's Florence house was the Casino in the Piazza San Marco, built by Buontalenti, but his banquets were given mainly at the Villa Careggi or the Villa Caffagiolo out in the country – the ice specialists must have had plenty of room for large freezing tubs, and the use of quantities of the required double moulds for creating the ice banqueting vessels. In capacious ice-cooled cabinets relays of the prepared goblets, bowls and fruit dishes could be held in reserve, so that any which threatened to melt on the dinner table could be quickly replaced. The same would apply to the spectacular ice and fruit pyramids. So long as the operator remembered to leave enough space in the mould to allow for the expansion of the water as it congealed, the actual freezing of the pyramids was no problem (although turning them out must have been a horribly tricky business). It must be noted, though, that these were not ices but just plain ice. No sugar was involved. That is a key point to remember. The effects of sugar in a mixture to be frozen were still very imperfectly under-stood, and the high proportions of sugar syrup in the sherbets, lem-onades, and all the tribe of sweet waters of those days made them virtually impossible to freeze – indeed a sweet snowy mush was just what was intended and expected. Magalotti's *candiero*, it will be remembered, was *tra gelato e non gelato*, midway between frozen and liquid. In the 1660s it was still some while before the confectioners began to understand how to prepare and freeze large quantities of those sweet ices in moulds made to imitate all kinds of fruit and indeed almost anything else edible, from a ham to a bunch of asparagus, which could be made in advance, stored in an ice cave and served to a large company of people. Those were the delights of the grand collations of the mid eighteenth century. Meanwhile, for the great summer entertainments of Rome, Naples, Florence, Madrid, Paris, the artificially created ice pyramids and obelisks and fruit bowls for the table were still enough of a novelty to bedazzle the guests and excite the envy of those whose confectioners and butlers were not yet versed in ice-making skills.

The glittering spectacle presented by the profusion of ice *tazze* laden with cherries, green almonds, apricots and tender fennel all begarlanded with summer flowers, jasmine, roses, orange blossom, and the great pyramids of fruit encased in ice would have dazzled Richard Lassels had he been present at the Cardinal's *merenda*. Ice fascinated him. Once, in Venice, he conjured up to himself a vision of 'a hard frost, the streets of Venice all frozen, and people walking up and down upon diamant streets or a crystal pavement'.[42]

It was unfortunate that the princess in whose honour all the festive food and beflowered ice dishes had been prepared failed to arrive in time to see the spectacle. Her galley was delayed by high winds, and it was not until 16 June at the Villa Ambrogiana, on the route from Livorno to Florence, that she had her first experience of Medici ceremonial feasting. But no show of splendour was going to beguile Marguérite-Louise. She had only the previous day set eyes on her nineteen-year-old bridegroom for the first time. The meeting had not been auspicious. The young prince had not even unbent so far as to give his bride a welcoming embrace.[43]

Ice Houses and Sherbets: Tales from Turkey and the Medici Legend

Pierre Belon of Le Mans, the French botanist-naturalist who spent five years, from 1546 to 1551, travelling in Turkey, Greece, Asia Minor, Egypt, the Holy Land and Persia, was gifted with a reporter's eye. No detail of daily life as he observed it was too trivial for him to note down in his journal. So it was that when in 1553 he published his 500–page travel book entitled *Les Observations de Plusieurs Singularitez et Choses Memorables . . . En Grece, Asie . . .*, his countrymen were able to learn that among the singularities to be observed in Turkey were special buildings for the storage of the snow and ice which, all the summer, was sold to cool 'the beverages they call sorbets'. A description of these fruit *cherbets* or sherbets is followed by a little dissertation on the Turkish custom of storing snow in vaults, or what we call ice houses, or alternatively building the snow up into stacks. 'When it has snowed and frozen hard, when the Bora wind, also called the *Bise*, which blows between Greece and the North, and which is the coldest wind known, is in full force,' says Belon, 'the Turks gather the snow, filling certain houses constructed like vaults or else like a hillock of earth . . . and expressly made for the purpose, in the least southerly situation, such as in a low-lying place, behind some high wall, or in the shelter of a hill: the snow must be built up as though to make a wall of masonry, putting ice here and there. This wall will stand two years without melting. This manner is commonly followed throughout the country of Turkey.' Belon now remarks that he thought it certain that 'the same could be done in France: for we have seen it in several regions where the climate is hotter than in France, and it lasts all the summer'.[1]

It was Pierre Belon's description of Turkish ice houses which led the eighteenth-century French social historian Pierre-Jean Baptiste Le Grand d'Aussy to make the assertion in his *Histoire de la Vie Privée des Français*, published in 1782, that when eventually the French did build and stock ice houses, it was according to Turkish methods rather than those of their Spanish and Italian neighbours. Le Grand d'Aussy's deduction was based primarily on the contrast between the chaff-covered ice pits and trenches then in use in Italy and Spain* and some Turkish-style constructions of which Le Grand d'Aussy seems to have had personal knowledge, remarking that the conservation of ice is not as easy as people suppose. Adding that at the time Belon published his travel book his suggestions as to the desirability of ice houses were ignored, Le Grand d'Aussy says that it was not until the end of the sixteenth century that the French learned 'the art of drinking cold'.[2] Until that time, he explains, it had been customary for the French to drink all their beverages warmed, and that at all seasons. If exact, this would provide a simple explanation of the violent hostility to the idea of iced wines and water for a long time expressed by the French, and also of the connection in the minds of so many people between the drinking of iced water and wines with apoplexies, seizures, heart attacks, and sudden deaths, particularly those of eminent people. Poison, it goes almost without saying, also came into the question, it apparently being thought to be more difficult to detect in an ice-cooled beverage than in a warmed one. Thus when in 1536 the Dauphin François, eldest son of François I, on his journey back to Lyon after the defeat of Charles V's troops invading Provence, died suddenly at Tournon on the Rhône, an Italian cup-bearer, Count Sebastiano Montecuculli, was accused of administering poison in a glass of ice-cold water served to his master when the young man was overheated after taking violent exercise. Under torture, Montecuculli confessed – asserting that Antonio de Leyva, Charles V's general, had

---

* These are said by Le Grand d'Aussy to have been described by Jean Liébault in the augmented and much reprinted edition of Charles Estienne's *L'Agriculture et Maison Rustique* which he brought out in 1570. Diligent search in the 1570 and 1572 editions of this work has yielded no reference to ice pits or snow stocks.

instructed him to poison not only the Dauphin but the King himself and all his family – and was duly executed. Henri, Duke of Orléans, married three years previously to Catherine de Medici, now inherited his brother's title and honours, and the anti-Italian French Court, opposed from the first to the marriage of the royal Duke into the upstart *nouveau riche* banking family of Florence, was provided with a splendid excuse for accusing Catherine's relations – the fact that the girl had no surviving close family at all was brushed aside – of plotting the whole affair in order to aggrandise her position and assure her husband's accession to the throne. It was an accusation proved false even at the time by Montecuculli's repeated assertions, under torture, and again at his trial, that it was the Emperor Charles V who had instigated the crime, with what motive being so unclear that later historians decided that Montecuculli's confession was not a credible one, and that the likelihood was that the Dauphin, always of a sickly constitution, had died of drinking too freely of cold water after overheating himself at tennis. So we have the guilty iced water and the guilty Catherine legends securely implanted in French minds.

To return now to Le Grand d'Aussy and his assertions concerning the lack of ice houses in Paris prior to the end of the sixteenth century, it does seem to me that there must have been ice stores of some description in or around the city well before that time, or we should not find the Spanish physician Nicolas Monardes recording, as early as 1571, that 'much ice' was then carried from Flanders to Paris, a distance of sixty leagues, or about 180 miles.[3] I have not discovered corroboration for the Monardes statement, but have no reason to suspect he was inventing, his reporting in this case having very much the air of being based on evidence carefully acquired to support his plea for his own city of Seville to be supplied regularly with snow and ice, as were other comparably important and civilized European cities. Why the Paris ice should have come via Flanders is not immediately apparent, but possibly the Ardennes mountains were the source of supply.

We have, in addition to the Monardes story, that notorious fable, *L'Île des Hermaphrodites*, satirizing the extravagant luxury and effeminate preoccupations of Henri III, third son of Catherine de Medici and Henri II, in which the spectacle of the monarch cooling his wine with both snow and ice at table, and ordering blocks of ice and stacks of snow to be preserved for the summer, are held up to that ridicule invariably meted out to innovations and refinements in all the arts, and most particularly in matters connected with eating and drinking. That Henri III allegedly introduced table forks after his celebrated state visit to Venice in 1575, the year of his accession to the throne of France, and that the ladies and gentlemen of his court used them in order to protect the starched ruffs then in fashion, provided another subject for sarcasm at the expense of the King, admittedly an entirely inestimable young man, assassinated at the age of thirty-eight, whose only useful legacies to his country appear to have been those very innovations – if his indeed they were – at the time regarded as so frivolous and so reprehensible.

Those stories surrounding Henri, his addiction to ice-cooled wine, and his outlandish demands concerning the storage of ice and snow for the summer, pose an interesting question: did nobody, at the time, or in the years immediately following her death in 1589 (only a few months before that of her son), point the finger of scorn at the young King's mother, the powerful and by this time detested Catherine, as having either imported insensate Italian luxuries to France, or at the least brought up her sons in decadent foreign ways? No contemporary accusation that Catherine perverted French taste with the introduction of ice, iced wine, and table forks seems ever to have been made against her, her homosexual third son and his *mignons* being in those respects the sole targets of the satirists. Nor, apparently, did Le Grand d'Aussy, collecting material two centuries later for his social history, produce any evidence whatever connecting Catherine with the introduction of ice, let alone of ices or frozen sherbets, to the French court of the sixteenth century, and no hint or breath of any such connection is to be found in his pages.

How curious, then, that in modern times – meaning from about the mid nineteenth century on – it has come to be believed that Catherine de Medici was accompanied to France by a bevy of Italian confectioners who taught their French colleagues how to make ices and frozen sherbets. Since the story is widely believed in Italy, appears indeed to be central to the credo of the Italian ice-cream trade, and is one I was myself once gullible enough to believe and repeat, it is necessary to say here that although the source of the story remains unidentified, it is plain that its origins are in the nineteenth century, the likelihood being that it arose out of a linguistic confusion such as I have described on p. 61, connected in some way perhaps with the stories of the ice introduced into France during Henri III's reign – or shortly before it – and while Catherine herself was still in a powerful position as Queen Mother and Regent.

I do know that of two people who helped disseminate it in England one was Abraham Hayward, QC, author of *The Art of Dining*, published in 1852. In a footnote to his chapter on Paris restaurants, Hayward remarked that it had been established that Catherine de Medici and her Florentine confectioners had brought the art of making ices to the French capital. He gave no chapter or verse, but his footnote gives the impression that it was something he had recently read, whether in French or in English perhaps we shall one day find out. It would be agreeable to nail the legend to its origin.[4] The second English writer, who did more than Hayward to establish the Medici story, was Mrs Isabella Beeton. Very probably she had read it in *The Art of Dining*. Among many startling statements to be found in her famous *Household Management* of 1861 – 'the Italians with the exception of macaroni, have no specially characteristic article of food' is a fair example – was her suggestion that in the light of Catherine's great innovation in the matter of ice-creams she might be forgiven the massacre of St Bartholomew,[5] a remark which for sheer inconsequence surely carries off a gold cup.

Nor would it be the first time that a legend had arisen around so innocent an assertion as that made by the topographical historian Lefeuve in his *Histoire de Paris Rue par Rue, Maison par Maison*, published in 1875, and according to which a Sicilian named Procopio Coltelli, allegedly grandfather of the founder of the famous café Procope, sold sorbets at a Parish bath establishment constructed on Catherine's instructions. This establishment, situated at the Sign of the Saint Suaire de Turin – the Holy Shroud of Turin – in the rue des Fossés-Saint-Germain, was on the very site taken over by Procopio the grandson when in 1686 he moved his café from its original premises in the rue de Tournon. Given the already built-in confusion of the two Procopios – it is conceivable that the elder one was flourishing a whole century before his grandson, that is, in the 1580s, but surely not, as suggested by Lefeuve, ever since Catherine's marriage in 1533 – plus the linguistic trap of the term *sorbet*, and we have a fine myth in the making.[6]

When Catherine de Medici left Florence to go to France in the sixteenth century, it was reported that she took with her the best of chefs to make sure that she would be supplied with frozen creams and ices every day, runs one version of the Catherine story. A catch there – apart from the little matter of nobody yet knowing how to freeze 'creams and ices' – is that when the fourteen-year-old orphaned Catherine was dispatched to Marseille to marry the Duke of Orléans (he too was only fourteen), her entire household was French, she herself having already been naturalized as a French subject. No doubt these were precautions taken by her uncle, Pope Clement VII, to help disarm French opposition to the marriage, precautions which turned out a good deal less than successful.

The circumstances in which Catherine married Henri would surely have been known to an historian of Lefeuve's standing, so it is curious that he appears to have paid so little attention either to dates, to the events of Catherine's life and reign, or to the unlikelihood of the older Procopio having arrived as a young man in Paris 117 years before the birth of his grandson, an event we know to have occurred in 1650, even if we do not know where it took place (p. 111).

One other point Lefeuve would or should have known was that in sixteenth-century France the term *sorbets*, if used at all (it does not appear in the dictionaries until much later), would have implied simply syrups, pastes, powders, lemonades and other fruit juices, sweetened and diluted with water in the Turkish fashion, and regarded primarily as healthful, sustaining, restorative beverages. When, therefore, Lefeuve alleges that after the bath, taken for health reasons rather than for cleanliness but also, he implies, for the pleasure of dalliance with the young and compliant female bath attendants, the customers at the elder Procopio's establishment were offered a collation to the accompaniment of music played by Italian musicians, and followed by the dispensing of *sorbets*, to us it is now plain what was meant, but did Lefeuve's readers appreciate the point, or did they jump to the conclusion that *sorbets* were the kind of ices to which, in the 1870s, they were themselves accustomed?

The whole story of the Holy Shroud of Turin and Procopio the elder needs more investigation. Not that it is not a reasonably plausible one. Procopio could easily have appeared in Paris, say in the 1570s or 1580s, and have been granted a concession by the Queen Mother to run what sounds, from Lefeuve's evidence, like an early European version of a Turkish bath establishment. If indeed that were the case, the offering of Turkish-style sherbets to the clients would have added novelty to the proceedings and authenticity to the atmosphere. Given the evidence that by the 1570s Paris was supplied with ice and snow, it is even conceivable that in summer the sherbets could have been ice-cooled, or beaten up with ice or snow to make them into the *sorte de breuvage doux appellé Cherbet* described by Pierre Belon when he revealed in his book how in the summer the sherbet-makers of Turkey mixed snow or ice with the drinks they sold, and how in that country it was the normal and accepted custom for such drinks to be diluted with ice or snow. Ice-diluted and ice-cooled sherbets do not, however, equate with frozen sherbets any more than putting a few pieces of ice into a glass of drinking water turns that water into ice, or than the milk half-frozen in the bottle on your doorstep on an icy morning has become ice-cream. It should not be necessary to state truths so crashingly obvious, but it is surprising to discover the ease with which such basic confusions took root, and in the minds of an extraordinary number of people grew into a belief in this or that fairytale, as for example that during the siege of Acre in 1194 Saladin sent frozen sherbets to Richard Cœur de Lion on his sickbed, that Marco Polo learned the secret of making ices at the court of Kubla Khan and brought it back to Venice, or that the use of ice to cool drinks, frozen sherbets and frozen creams all arrived at the French court, as if cloud-borne from some celestial sphere, at the same moment during the sixteenth century. Since Catherine de Medici was for fifty-six years of that century at, or close to, the centre of French court life, for thirty of them as Queen Regent and virtual ruler of France, since into the bargain she was of Italian birth, and since it was from Italy that the most skilled ice-cream experts later came, the innovations were, at a date long after the event, attributed to her influence, to members of her largely mythical Italian household or alternatively to Italian confectioners she had brought with her from Florence as it were in her wedding trousseau, regardless of whether or not such persons were actually ever in her service.

(References to chefs and cooks in this context may be disregarded. The making of ices, when eventually they became a reality, was at first the responsibility of the department called the Pantry or Office, and those of its staff in charge of the service of wines and beverages. Professional confectioners, distillers, and the specialists called *liquoristes* and *limonadiers*, and also independent caterers such as Audiger, whose story is told on pp. 77–110, did later become involved in the business of making and purveying ices, but of the kitchen and cooks proper it was not the province.)

One point at least in all the cloud and fog of uncertainty we may be sure about is that however many Sicilian, Florentine, Venetian, Neapolitan and Roman confectioners, pastrycooks, sugar workers, makers of liqueurs and scented cordials, and distillers of aromatic waters may have been maintained at the French court or operating in the capital in Catherine's time, none of them knew how to make ices and they could not have taught the French how to make them. We do, however, know that it was during the last twenty years of Catherine's life, and most probably during the reign of her son Henri III, that ice-cooled drinks first became fashionable in France (in Italy they had long been so), that experiments in artificial freezing were being made by Giambattista Della Porta in Naples, perhaps by others of his kind elsewhere in Europe, and that it has been reported of Francesco de Medici, Grand Duke of Tuscany, who died in 1587, that he had been addicted to a kind of iced or half-frozen eggnog of his own invention (see p. 11).

In short, it was during the last two decades of the sixteenth century that people began to imagine that syrups and the kind of sherbet drinks they had learned about from the East might be even more attractive if they could be frozen instead of just mixed with snow or ice. 'Some are made of figs, others of plums, and of pears and peaches, others again of apricots and of grapes, yet others of honey,' Pierre Belon had written, 'and the sherbet-maker mixes snow or ice with them, to cool them: for otherwise there would be no pleasure in drinking them: in summer the decoctions could not be made cool enough.'[7] Was it in an effort to make their own versions of these tempting sherbets even colder than the originals, but without actually mixing the ice or snow directly with the beverages, that the first attempts at freezing them were made? It would, at that time, have represented a refinement. 'The Ambassadors of France, Spain, Venice, Ragusa, Florence, Chio, Transylvania and Hungary, who are more particular about their drinks than are the Turks,' Belon affirmed, 'do not wish to mix snow in their wine, so they put the wine in snow-cooled water, and drink cool all summer without putting ice or snow in their stomachs.' Whether that kind of 'drinking cool' was or wasn't cool enough for immediately succeeding generations of French, Spanish, Venetians and Florentines, it was a long time before anyone found out how to make their sherbets more icy without directly stirring them up with snow or ice, and it was over 100 years before Francesco Procopio, allegedly the grandson, more probably it seems to me the great-grandson, of that shadowy Turkish bath operator, made his elegant café, his frozen sherbets, and his hot coffee and chocolate one of the attractions of Louis XIV's capital.

Perpetual Snow

'The peak of the Mulhacen,' observed Fernand Braudel,[1] 'is white with snow, while down below, Granada swelters in the heat.' It was surely the sight of these snow-crowned mountain tops of the Sierra Nevada and a number of others like them in Europe and Asia that originally inspired the Greeks, the Romans, the Persians, the Ottoman rulers of the Turkish Empire and the Moghuls of Northern India with the idea that during their burning summers that same snow could somehow be used to alleviate the terrible heat by providing the means of cooling their water and their wine. The peaks of Mount Olympus, of the Taurus range in Turkey, of the Alpes Maritimes in southern France, of Mont Blanc and the Piedmontese Alps, of the Atlas mountains in North Africa, above all of the majestic Himalayas, all must at one time have provided the dwellers in the cities below with the blessed cooling draughts which helped them to bear the heat, the dust, the thirst of their scorching summers.

'What a marvellous thing it is to see those mountains of Granada covered in perpetual snow,' wrote Nicolas Monardes, a Seville physician, in 1574, 'even throughout the great heat and burning summer, at times when we see that there is none on the Pyrenees, which every winter are covered with snow but which in summer melts away completely.' The King of Granada, Monardes adds, was accustomed to drink his water cooled with snow, and he quotes the historian Alfonso of Palencia's chronicle of the war of Granada as his source of information.

It is from this work of Monardes, entitled *Tratado de la Nieve y del*

Bever Frio,[2] that much insight into the use of snow in sixteenth-century Europe is to be gained. We learn of the various ways in which it was preserved, of the different methods adopted for cooling beverages, of the distances it was sometimes transported, of its use by Arab doctors and the last Moorish kings of Granada. In his own time, Monardes writes, 'snow was in common use at the court of Castille by their Majesties, the Princes and Princesses, and all the great Nobles and Gentlemen and the common people who reside there'. Some of the grandees of the court kept private snow stores in the mountains, and in Castile drank their water icy cold even in the winter.

In Asia, 'in many parts of Africa, in all Europe, in all the lands belonging to the Grand Turk', Monardes recorded that snow was preserved, while for Constantinople the use of snow was so widespread that it was sold publicly all the year round, and the same, says Monardes, 'is done at present in all German states, and in Flanders, Hungary and Bohemia and other parts, where snow is kept in houses or in caves during the winter, and from Flanders much ice is carried to Paris, a distance of sixty leagues'. That last assertion is significant. In 1574, when Monardes published his treatise on snow, the widowed Catherine de Medici was still virtually ruler of France (the St Bartholomew's Day massacre had taken place two years previously), her second son Charles IX reigned in name, and in 1575 her third son was to succeed as Henri III. It has sometimes been claimed that it was that luxury-loving young monarch who first introduced the use of snow or ice at the French court. Monardes proves otherwise. He makes a number of such points. One, of equal interest, is that although snow was taken for granted at the court of Philip II, it was not at the time in use in Seville, and here we find what was perhaps one of the main purposes of Monardes' treatise – a strong plea for the introduction there of snow, backed by numerous examples of the medical benefits to be obtained from its use.

The controversy concerning the use of snow-cooled beverages, their benefits, or contrariwise their disastrous and even fatal effects, which raged among the medical practitioners of the sixteenth and seventeenth centuries, is very clearly brought home to us by Monardes, who opens his treatise with a light-hearted and whimsically poetical address to an influential functionary of the town. In the words of the contemporary English translator of the treatise, John Frampton, Merchant, Monardes writes:

To the excellent Lord The Earle of Barajas, Assistant of the Citie of Seville, etc., the Doctor Monardus your Phisition wisheth health . . .

Most excellent Lord, the faire and white snow doth complaine unto mee, saying that she being so ancient, and of so many ages, celebrated of so many Princes, Kinges, wise and valiant men, and being had in so great estimition, and price, that with great care they seeke after her, and with greater care they do conserve her, for to give health and contentment to all persons: yet for all this, many people with little consideration, and not knowing what they say, dooe persecute her, putting undecent names to her: and that which dooeth most grieve her, is that some Phisitions, either for ignorance or for malice, do speake evil of her, not perceiving what so many learned men have treated and said of the great utility and profit which she doth to many, as experience doth show, and all people doe understand, chiefly when they doe drinke their drink most cold with the benefit which doth remaine to them thereof, they do prayse and extol her. Moreover she saith, that she forceth no person to use her, but if any will use her, she can give such order and manner to make cold the drinke as is convenient for all persons, giving the degrees of coldnesse which everyone would have, and which doth best appertaine to them, and this with al assurance with onely leaving or placing the vessel wherein to drinke is joyned neere to her, the which none of the olde writers nor of the late did speake against, or forbit. And especially let this manner of making could [cold] not be done with stinking water of a well, nor with the most burning saltpeeter, but with pure water being clean and cleare. These complaints and many other the faire lilly white Snow hath uttered unto mee, and in the end shee lastly said to mee, that I should also seeke her some one person, wise and discrete, that with worthiness and greatnes might valiantly succour and defende her from her adversaries. And seeing the greate reason that she hath, and the bondage that I am in for the preservation of her honour, seeing in all this realme who might dooe it I have not founde who hath the partes that the faire Lady Snow desireth, and who with most just title may dooe it so well as your most excellent Lordship . . . And so the faire Ladye Snow is in greate hope and trust that having suche a noble protector, she shal be defended from evil tongues and that she shall bee taken and held in the same estimation that her workes and greatnes do rightly deserve.[3]

Accustomed as we now are to regarding ice as an essential commodity in all seasons and in all countries, it is easy to sympathize with Monardes' impassioned advocacy of snow, and to share his pleasure and joy in its use. His little eulogy on the subject is written in moving terms:

It is a great thing that in the height of Summer when we are all fire with the intense heat of the weather, when thirst is so great that it suffocates, when our bodies burn and sweat, that with a little snow we are enabled to drink so coolly when it suits us, and with safety and healthily; which brings so much pleasure and content that it is beyond any estimable price or intellectual explanation. And let anyone who has drunk snow-cooled beverages be a judge of this my Apologia.

It was of course a costly business to transport snow down from the Sierra Nevada. As Monardes explains, the mountain road was long and arduous (it was known as the *camino de los Neveros*, the road of the snow porters, who brought the snow down in panniers loaded on donkeys), and on the way some of it melted, so it arrived 'much diminished'. For that reason, according to Monardes, it was so dear.

The mountain in the Sierra Nevada from which snow was brought to Granada was, Monardes asserts, six leagues above the city, a league being three miles. An eighteen-mile trudge up the mountain and the same down again with the laden donkeys must certainly have been hard labour for the porters, but it may be doubted that what they earned accounted for the high price of snow in Granada. The middlemen who sold it would have pocketed the major share of the profits. According to Roger Thévenot,[4] the rights to sell snow were later auctioned, at any rate in Madrid. But that was not until 1645. Thévenot also, incidentally, cites a writer called Porras as recording that in Seville supplies of snow were well organized by 1621, as they were also in the cities of Valladolid (the former royal capital), Toledo and Murcia. Less than fifty years, then, after the publication of the Monardes treatise, the trade in snow had become a quite important one.

Curiously, Monardes does not mention Portugal among those countries to which snow was, to his knowledge, supplied. The omission may be another significant point in his treatise. In 1580, the King of Portugal having died leaving no direct heir, the crown was assumed by his son-in-law, Philip of Spain. In October 1584, ten years after Monardes wrote his book on snow, an English merchant called John Sanderson, a passenger in a ship called the *Merchant Royal*, bound for Constantinople, sailed out of the harbour of Motril, half-way between Málaga and Almería. From far out to sea Sanderson beheld one of the peaks of the Sierra Nevada and noted that 'it was continually covered with snow'; and that 'of the same they carry to Lishbourne [Lisbon] to mix with their wine; which citie is esteemed to be 300 miles from thence'.[5] An interesting note, from which it may well be deduced that it was the Spanish who introduced snow to Portugal after the union of the two kingdoms. How was it transported 300 miles? Hardly by donkey. More likely in carts drawn by teams of fast horses. Such transport, combined with a long history of the use of ice, it must have been which was later to make Spain celebrated for the speed with which fish was carried from the coast to all parts of the country, everywhere arriving as fresh as if it had just come out of the sea.

Icemen of the
Seventeenth Century

Table Jewellery

It is some time between the years 1615 and 1620 AD. The scene is an
arbour in the garden of a Mauretanian palace. Juba, governor of the
town, is in conversation with Arsidas, who has landed by accident on
this part of the North African coast. He is anxious to be on his way
to deliver letters to the Queen of the country. Juba, however, cannot
allow the guest to leave until the laws of hospitality have been observed.
It is high summer, a table has been laid in the arbour, and presently a
banquet is served, a banquet implying on this occasion a collation of
fruit and sweetmeats rather than a full-blown feast.

As they sit down to table, Arsidas is startled to see a dish of apples
encased in what appear to be shells of clear shining ice. In disbelief he
touches one and finds it is indeed ice. Bewildered by the trick that is
being played on him, he takes an apple, bites into it, and is amazed to
find it quite fresh, with its natural taste, although his palate is somewhat
numbed by the cold. Juba is delighted at the success of his ice-
encrusted apples, and when Arsidas demands to know by what means
he 'had gotten ice out of Scythia', meaning the frozen North, 'to
keepe his African Apples in', Juba only deepens the mystification by
telling his guest 'when you entred the Garden, these Apples were
hanging on the Tree, and the Water, that now is Ice, came out of the
Spring'.

Enter now an Egyptian boy, bearing sweet wine in a cup made of
solid ice. Arsidas drinks off the wine and returns the cup to the
attendant, who at once dashes it to the ground. Arsidas is dismayed
'that so precious a Cup for summer, though of brittle matter, should

55

be spoyled', but Juba reassures him, explaining that there are plenty more such cups and that it is considered base to use the same one twice.

Arsidas is now so consumed with curiosity that he can eat no more until the mystery is explained. Juba relents. 'It is quite new with us,' he says, 'the trick of calling back winter in midsummer.' He shows Arsidas a number of brass trenchers, drinking bowls, chargers and all manner of banqueting vessels which turn out to be double moulds, the inner one slightly smaller than the outer. Into the narrow space between the two moulds water is poured, as molten lead or pewter is poured into casts, the inner mould being held steady by a flange fitting over the rim of the outer one; the filled moulds are set in great wooden vessels filled with layers of crushed black (i.e. unpurified) salt and snow, of which, Juba explains, there is always a plentiful supply, 'kept in straw the whole yeere long in the bottome of deepe Sellers', or snow wells. The filled wooden vessels are taken down to the wine or oil cellars and left for three hours, when the ice vessels and dishes are frozen and ready to be taken out of the moulds. The ice-encrusted apples are made by dropping the fruit into water poured into the inner moulds, 'and they sticke closed in the ice'.

Juba concludes his discourse by telling Arsidas that 'this kinde of coolnesse' is a welcome refreshment 'in extremity of Summer's heat and something the more pleasing for the novelty of it; being but lately and happily found out by some luxurious palate for satisfying his curiosity'.

The source of this tale is an allegorical romance called *Argenis*. It was written in Latin by John Barclay, a Scot born in the duchy of

An early 20th-century mould for making an ice bowl.

Lorraine and, at the time he was writing, resident in Rome. The book was first published in Paris in 1621, Barclay having died prematurely only three weeks after he completed the manuscript.

It should be explained that the main characters in *Argenis*, although disguised under allegorical names, were intended by Barclay to represent historical figures of the recent past such as Henri III and Henri IV of France, Philip II of Spain, Queen Elizabeth, Pope Clement VIII and so on. The Mauretanian garden is the park or grounds of the Villa Madama, formerly a Medici summer villa on the outskirts of Rome, owned in Barclay's time by the Spanish princes of Naples. Barclay himself had lived for five years in a rented villa near the Vatican, cultivated tulips – rather before the onset of Tulipomania in Europe – and was in his day a much respected writer and poet, one evidently admired by Ben Jonson, who had once announced his intention of translating *Argenis*, an intention which must have been serious since this translation was entered at Stationers Hall in 1623, thirteen years before Kingsmill Long brought out the English version from which I have quoted.[1]

Now, I am well aware of the perils of treating as fact what has been written as fiction. As remarked by Professor J. R. Partington, the great modern historian of chemistry, 'poetry and drama have often been used to prove that all kinds of inventions were known in antiquity . . . we have seen that a recent author has proved to his own satisfaction that gunpowder was invented by Moses, and poets, if they are worthy of their craft, can invent anything'.[2] Agreed – and in view of such a warning, I would think twice about setting down in print my conviction that John Barclay was writing an eye-witness description of the ice goblets and ice-encrusted fruit produced in the heat of midsummer had I not come across corroborative evidence, hitherto unnoticed, that it was indeed in the early 1620s that artificially frozen ice was being used for ornamentation and to create sensational effects on the tables of Italian noblemen and the great princes of the Church.

Italy in the early decades of the seventeenth century was entering a new Ice Age. With their well-stocked snow wells and ice cellars the nobility of Rome, Florence and Naples could enjoy ice-cooled fruit and wines throughout the summer months. From June to September cherries, figs, grapes, peaches, plums, apricots, mulberries, straw-berries, pears, were served either smothered in crushed snow (for storage snow was compacted into massive blocks and lasted even longer than ice) or set over a separate dish containing the snow or ice. Melons were invariably sliced and the snow was always underneath. Peeled peaches in wine were served in the same way. Jellies, junkets, creams, blancmangers of hashed chicken and ground almonds, were all kept in their pristine state by the indirect cooling system, and indications of innovations in the use of ice and snow appear in published records of the feasts of the 1620s. At a dinner in Rome on 2 July 1625, for example, for the first cold service – this was always provided by the butler's pantry and often differed little from the final dessert service, for which again the butler and his aides were responsible – there were not only the usual sliced melons and fresh figs with sugar over and snow under in separate dishes, and the expected junket set over snow and decorated with sugar and ribbons of rosewater-scented butter, but a showy centrepiece consisting of jelly (jellymania was rife in seventeenth-century Italy) in which was enclosed a hollow glass column filled with small pieces of ice, the whole resting on a wooden pedestal and surrounded with obelisks of variously coloured jellies, and pyramids of gilded wood. This remarkable piece of table décor reappears a number of times in the same compendium of records. On one occasion the glass column was filled with flowers, on another with live fish swimming in water. The attendant obelisks and pyramids, both popular shapes for jellies at the time, were soon to be adapted for decorative ice centrepieces, later still for ice-creams. Indeed they survive to this day, little changed in outline.

The man who recorded these details of Roman feasting in the 1620s was Antonio Frugoli, a native of the then independent republic of Lucca, whose book *Pratica e Scalcaria*, a comprehensive volume on the art and practice of stewardship, was published in Rome in 1631. About half the book is taken up with detailed lists of the dishes served at eighty different dinners, suppers and banquets, six or seven for each month in the year, and covering the years 1618 to 1631.

No name-dropper, Frugoli does not reveal the identity of the host or the guests at any of his meals, and at no point tells us who his

employer was – possibly it was that Cardinal Capponi, appointed Archbishop of Ravenna in 1621 and formerly papal legate in Bologna, to whom he dedicated his book – so although he asserts that he personally drew up all the lists of dishes and himself officiated on all but one of the occasions described, we have to be content with the information that this dinner was given in Rome, that one in Madrid, others in Bologna, Perugia, Ferrara. We also get glimpses of the kind of meal served to an important man on his travels through Italy. The dinner we are here chiefly concerned with, however, was a ceremonial one, given in Rome in 1623.

It is 15 August, the feast of the Assumption, then, as now, one of the most important festivals of the Italian year. Regardless of the sweltering heat of a Roman August, the dinner is in every way an exceptional one. There are altogether twenty-four cold dishes supplied by the *Credenza*, the pantry, in two services of twelve dishes each, one at the opening of the meal, one at the end. The pantry will also supply the dessert and the confectionery which conclude the banquet. From the kitchen proper there are twenty-four hot dishes in four services, each separated into two courses. Most unusually, both fish and meat are served, and in great variety, many of the meat and poultry dishes being garnished with small morsels of fish such as fried *calamaretti*, soft-shell crabs boiled in milk, then fried in butter, slices of pickled tunny alternating with the decoratively carved oranges and lemons for which, again, the butler and the pantry staff are responsible.

For a high summer afternoon in Rome the food is oppressively rich, heavy with sweet-sour sauces and syrups, everything strewn with sugar or sugar-coated comfits. Even to the reader it is a relief when the second course of the second hot service is cleared away, the napkins changed, and the dessert brought in. Compared to all that has gone before, this course is very low key. There are sliced truffles with carved oranges, a tart filled with conserve of rennet apples, three lobsters in the shell with a dressing of oil, pepper and clear verjuice (there was nearly always some kind of fish in the dessert course, usually oysters), pears and peaches in syrup strewn with aniseeds, more peaches in wine, Spanish olives, muscatel and early autumn grapes, a box of plum conserve, fresh pears, young sweet fennel, fresh peeled almonds, and six jars of the quince sweetmeat called *cotognata*. Perhaps to make up for the relative modesty of the dessert spread, the pantry has supplied a showy centrepiece: *un monte di diaccio con diversi frutti dentro*, a mountain of ice with divers fruits within, and in the centre a fountain spurting jets of cold orange flower water which lasted, says Frugoli proudly, 'more than half an hour'.

A pleasing sight indeed, that glittering icy Vesuvius, the fruit gleaming within its depths, the jets of perfumed water spouting from its crater, cooling the atmosphere, refreshing the eyes and reviving the flagging spirits of the company at dinner – there are only eight of them – and what a change, too, from the endless sugar paste and marzipan centrepieces or *trionfi* which at the time adorned every important feast. As Frugoli himself observes in his dedicatory epistle to his readers, 'every day we see new inventions', and this particular novelty was really quite a simple affair to create. An advance on Barclay's ice-encrusted fruit, all that was needed was a conical mould with a central tube, and a cover for the base. The mould was set on its narrow end and filled with different kinds of small fruit such as cherries, strawberries, plums and apricots. Water was then poured in, care being taken to leave a space for its expansion during freezing, and the covered mould buried in ice and salt.[3] When released from its mould – a delicate operation – the ice mountain was set on a great dish, the clockwork fountain, devised by some skilled water engineer and not nearly such an innovation as the ice mountain (Leonardo, who died in 1519, had designed one), was placed in the centre, and the sensational novelty was borne to the table to the sound, one surmises, of flutes, viols, and triumphal fanfares.

When the dazzled guests had finished their sweet fennel, their peaches and pears and grapes and conserves, and the fountain had stopped playing, the napkins were once again changed, the top table-cloth was removed, hand water was brought round, and twelve por-celain dishes of confectionery and two chargers of candied sweetmeats were put on the table. At last the dinner had reached the stage of the handing round of toothpicks concealed in nosegays of flowers, arranged on porcelain dishes, one for each person present.

On only one other occasion in all the eighty dinner, supper and banquet lists he gives does Frugoli mention such an item as the *monte di diaccio*, and that was two years later, for a dinner on 18 May 1625 at the royal palace in Madrid, where he appears to have accompanied his master on a number of occasions. This time it was the feast of Pentecost and there were two fountains and two *monti di frutti diversi diacciate*, two mountains of divers iced fruit, by which it is difficult to tell if Frugoli meant fruit set in ice, or preserved and sugar-frosted fruit in pyramids, or simply fresh fruit with snow or crushed ice. Here indeed is a fair example of the kind of linguistic trap which has been respon-sible for many improbable legends concerning the early history of ices. It has been all too easy, to later generations, to interpret sixteenth-

and seventeenth-century Italian and French allusions to plain ice, iced drinks, glazed creams, and sugar icing and frosting as meaning ices and ice-creams. In this instance, I think it likely from Frugoli's phrasing that he did mean the same kind of ice and fruit pyramids as had appeared at the Rome feast of 1623. The Spanish royal palaces were always plentifully supplied with ice, and as for the necessary moulds and table fountains, Frugoli, as was usual at the time, would have travelled with them in his luggage, along with a quantity of plate, serving dishes, and other such impedimenta.

If the ice pyramids were so new in the 1620s that Frugoli mentions them only twice, by the 1660s they seem to have become obligatory decoration at summer banquets. For the marriage celebrations in Florence in 1661 of Prince Cosimo de Medici and Princess Marguérite-Louise of Orléans, fluted silver moulds over a foot high were used for the freezing of the fruit and ice, and by the 1690s in Spanish Naples no summer wedding celebration, reception, banquet or outdoor party appears to have been complete without its quota of ice and fruit pyramids, about which one question remains unanswered. Was the fruit frozen into the ice regarded purely as decoration? Or did the company wait until the ice started to melt and then set about demolishing the pyramid and crunching the ice and fruit between their teeth?

The ice bowls and dishes described by John Barclay, although not mentioned by Antonio Frugoli, had also become fashionable showpieces for banquets. They seem to have been used mainly for the service of those graceful arrangements of fresh fruit intertwined with fronds, leaves, flowers and vine tendrils so familiar from the still-life paintings of the period. Together with the pyramids, the ice dishes are mentioned over and over again by the two stewards, Venantio Mattei and Antonio Latini, who published their books, *Teatro Nobilissimo di Scalcheria* and *Lo Scalco Alla Moderno*, in 1669 and 1692 respectively. It was Mattei who recorded the Medici feasts in Florence in 1661,[4] and Latini, steward to the Prime Minister of Naples, who described, blow by blow, some of the very grand receptions held in the seaside villas and country estates of the Spanish rulers of Naples. From Latini's accounts of these receptions it is evident that the obelisks and pyramids of fruit encased in ice and the *vasi di ghiaccio*, the ice vessels, were made regularly and in quantity, from April to September.

Much has been written, and a good deal invented, about the origin of ices and the birth of the ice-cream industry. The subject is indeed one of some interest, in particular to the social historian. To my mind, however, once given the successful breakthrough in the technique of creating ice, no part of the early saga is more striking than the dazzlingly simple idea of the man, whoever he was, who thought of applying the technique of metal-casting to the production of ice bowls, drinking goblets, and fruit dishes. Because the fashion for such ornaments died out long ago and was superseded by more ambitious devices and centrepieces hand-carved out of great blocks of ice, at first natural, later man-made, little attention has been paid to the initial and most ingenious invention of ice-casting, as it may fairly be termed. Yet the same technique was used to make ice dishes and bowls nearly three centuries after John Barclay described them.

Moulds for them were still current up to the time of the 1914 war, and were illustrated in trade catalogues and in the advertisement pages of books such as those of the famous Mrs Agnes Marshall, whose cookery school in Mortimer Street, London, flourished in the 1890s and 1900s. For grand dinners and special occasions sumptuous and ingenious elaborations were evolved. One that would have impressed John Barclay and his contemporaries was an ice bowl resembling cut crystal, with a silver rim frozen on to it, recorded in July 1898 at the Savoy Hotel in London. The occasion was a dinner offered by the Savoy's head chef, M. Joseph, to Coquelin, the famous French actor. The ice bowl contained *pêches à la cardinal*, and beneath it was a silver spirit lamp to keep the peaches from freezing.[5] Full marks for showmanship, not to say refinement of a marvellously perverse kind.

As for the early moulded centrepieces, they too had a long life. Antonio Frugoli's *monte di diaccio* of 1623 was only slightly modified and updated in its twentieth-century version – a tall clear ice cone, with a circle of small ice-cream bricks arranged around its base and in its hollow centre not a fountain but one of those drawing-room

Ciocca's mould to make
an ice cone with a hollow
centre.

firework devices to which a match was put as the *gelato luminoso* was
carried to table, sparks flying from its summit. A *sensation*, says Signor
Ciocca, author of the 1913 manual[6] in which he described and illustrated his ice volcano.

Mark Twain likened ice to jewellery which once only the rich could
wear but was now available to everybody. In the United States the ice
table-jewellery of seventeenth-century European invention under-

The *gelato
luminoso.*

went, as was to be expected, a change massive in more than one respect. Blocks of factory-made ice, according to Mark Twain, 'a foot square and two feet long, hard, solid, crystal clear', within their icy depths big bouquets of fresh, brilliant tropical flowers, were 'set on end in a platter, in the centre of dinner tables, to cool the tropical air; and also to be ornamental, for the flowers imprisoned in them could be seen as though through plate-glass'. Twain's description of the ice factory at Natchez near New Orleans in which these ice blocks were produced dates from 1883,[7] when the output was thirty tons a day, and manufactured ice was fast replacing natural ice in the towns inland from New Orleans. Factory ice was cheap, and even what he called 'the humbler dwelling-house quantities' retailed at only six or seven dollars a ton. So that rather formidable block of ice gradually melting on your dinner table was no insensate luxury. Neither can it have been very convenient, or very efficient in cooling the tropical air. But air-conditioning was still, in the 1880s, in its infancy. Like man-made ice, as distinct from nature's own product, artificial cooling of the air was for long regarded with great suspicion and its development in the United States was hampered by puritan prejudice and even religious opposition.

A Trifling Invention

'Ice,' declared Thoreau, in a majestic passage in *Walden*, 'is a fit subject for contemplation.' He was of course referring to natural ice, and its harvesting from the lake near his woodland retreat, but when in 1624 Francis Bacon wrote that 'the Producing of Cold is a thing very worthy of the Inquisition' he meant the production of cold or ice by artificial means. Before he died in 1626, victim of a chill brought on, tradition has it, as a result of collecting snow with which to observe its preservative effects on a chicken, Bacon knew that scientific 'inquisitions' into the production of ice by artificial means had been successful, although he himself had not actually performed the experiment. In *De Augmentis Scientarum*, completed in June 1622 and published the following year, he alluded to 'the late experiment of artificial freezing' and to how 'salt is discovered to have great powers of condensation'. Again, in his last work, *Sylva Sylvarum*, posthumously published in 1627, he mentions 'Salt put to Ice as in the producing of the Artificial Ice'.[8]

The 'late experiment' alluded to by Bacon was probably one demonstrated in 1620 by Cornelius Drebbel, the Dutch-born inventor who was given rooms in Eltham Palace, financially subsidized by James I, and in return entertained his royal master with all manner of ingenious inventions and demonstrations, some of them being held at the time to pertain rather more to the black arts than was respectable or acceptable.

Self-regulating ovens, thermometers, a submarine boat, a thunder and lightning machine, an instrument of perpetual motion, and a camera obscura were just a few of the inventions, by no means all of them original, but always expertly adapted, which Drebbel constructed and demonstrated. The one Bacon was referring to seems to have been an early attempt at an air-conditioning device, and quite a successful one. The King, who had requested the demonstration, chose a hot summer day, and attended the show in the Great Hall at Westminster. Drebbel's device reduced the temperature in the Hall to such a degree that James and his attendants fled, shivering.[9]

What salt or combination of salts Drebbel was using in his cooling machine is far from clear, and Bacon himself is unspecific, but in a passage in *Novum Organum*, published in 1620, the year of Drebbel's demonstration, he observed that 'Nitre (or rather its spirit) is very cold, and hence nitre or salt when added to snow or ice intensifies the cold of the latter, the nitre by adding to its own cold, but the salt by supplying activity to the cold of the snow.'[10] So it would appear that by this time the scientists and chemists had perceived, after long decades of experiment with nitre only, that common salt was just as effective in liquefying the ice or snow and in doing so reducing its temperature to below freezing point, so that when the mixture was packed round and over a vessel of water, that water would eventually turn to ice. (The freezing phenomenon, only imperfectly understood at the time, and for a long while after, is explained in easily comprehensible terms by O.E. Anderson, Jr, in his *Refrigeration in America*:[11] 'In changing from a solid to a liquid, ice absorbs heat which is known as its latent heat of fusion. The heat is absorbed from surrounding substances.')

The efforts to produce man-made ice had begun in the final decades of the sixteenth century, when the use of saltpetre or nitre as a refrigerant, introduced to Europe early in the century, most probably from India, had become commonly known in Spain, Italy, Germany and Holland. The medical profession had been referring to the effects of nitre as a cooling agent since 1530, when Dr Zimara of Padua University mentioned the new discovery in his *Problemata*, a treatise on the works of Aristotle. By 1550 Blas Villafranca, a Spanish doctor practising in Rome, was instructing readers of his *Methodus Refrigerandi ex vocato salnitro vinum acquamque*, published that year in Rome, on the correct way to cool their wine and water by the new method, at the same time declaring that all the nobility and gentry of Rome now used the method. A decade later a Dutch physician known as Levinus Lemnius, whose entertaining hotchpotch of a book, *Occulta Naturae Miracula* or *The Secret Miracles of Nature*, first appeared in Antwerp in 1559, explained that in summer, wine in cask could be prevented from souring by transferring it into pots, putting these into a vessel filled with cold water 'and then put in Saltpetre, and it will so cool the wine that your teeth can hardly endure it'. Seeking to explain this phenomenon, Lemnius further informed his readers that it was 'the quality of this, which makes such a noise in Guns; for take this out, and the powder will make no noise, nor will it drive the bullet so far',[12] an explanation which can hardly have done much to either enlighten or reassure people already suspicious of the connection between gunpowder and the new method of cooling imported from the Indies. To opposing factions of the medical profession, those in particular of Spain and Italy, who thought it already bad enough that a revival of the decadent Roman custom of storing snow for the summer and using it to chill fruit and wine was now gathering momentum in both countries, the use of nitre for cooling drinks was yet one more perilous and pernicious practice to be stamped upon. If putting ice and snow directly in your wine and water was to invite colics, convulsions, paralysis, blindness, madness and sudden death, to drink water or wine chilled by immersion in a tub of saltpetre-cooled water was little better or safer. Nitrous particles, it was believed, penetrated metal and even glass flagons and accordingly burned up your intestines, a theory which persisted for nearly two centuries.

Medical opposition in no way deterred the chemists and natural philosophers, as scientists were then called, in their researches into the possibility of creating ice by means other than nature's own, and not all physicians were reactionary about such experiments. Many were interested in the use of ice in medicine. In 1584 Dr Baldassare Pisanelli of the Bologna Medical Faculty reported, in his influential treatise on the nature of foods and beverages, that cold drinks were often beneficial and that the introduction of snow storage and distribution into Sicily some twenty years previously had done much to alleviate the malignant fevers which every summer killed off hundreds of people. In Messina alone, so Pisanelli claimed, there had been 1,000 fewer such victims every year, and it had become common for even the poorest artisan to regard snow as a necessity of life equal to bread and wine.[13] Naples also was at this time supplied with snow stored for the summer either in ice pits or in the natural caves of the foothills of Monte Somma and Monte Mauro, the new craze for snow-cooled wine and fruit no doubt yielding a respectable revenue in snow and ice taxes to the Spanish rulers of the kingdom. There, in the capital, then regarded as the most beautiful in all Italy, a notable figure called Giambattista Della Porta was working on an experiment which would take the science of refrigeration a faltering, but important, step on its way.

Della Porta, the 'Neapolitane', as he was called by his English translator, was a younger son of one of the ancient, noble families of Salerno. He had been well known in Naples since the age of fifteen, when he had published in 1559, a book called *Magia Naturalis* or *Natural Magic*. The title covered all manner of natural phenomena and a fair amount of occult absurdities and medieval mumbo-jumbo. This early work was translated into several languages, including, Della Porta himself asserted, Arabic. Thirty years later, still in his prime, and renowned throughout most of Europe for his learning as a natural

Giambattista
della Porta

philosopher and mathematician, and for important work in the field of optics and lenses which pointed the way to the invention of the telescope, Della Porta prepared a new and greatly enlarged version of his first book. Published in 1589 under its original title, the work now contained twenty 'books' or sections, instead of the original three. Each one was devoted to a different subject, the whole adding up to a fairly astonishing ragbag of alchemy, the counterfeiting of gold and gems, distillation, the art of invisible writing, the concoction of cosmetics, and long-familiar preoccupations such as the transmutation of metals and the spontaneous generation of animals. Somewhat unexpectedly, there were also 'books' on preserving – translated into English as 'increasing Household-Stuff' – on gardening, on fishing, fowling and hunting, and on cookery. A final book of miscellaneous experiments and information was very properly entitled 'The Chaos'. It was in this last section that there appeared an item which is referred to by Professor Partington as being a notably early mention of the use of a freezing mixture of snow and saltpetre.[14] The experiment in question was one which involved the transformation of air into water by means of condensation. A brass basin filled with the snow and saltpetre mixture was to be set over a second vessel, and in this receptacle the drops formed on the outside of the basin would be collected. An exercise not destined to have a brilliant future, but interesting for Della Porta's description of the 'mighty cold' created when his bowl of saltpetre and snow was shaken about. Apparently overlooked, however, by Partington and by all historians of the science of refrigeration whose works I have consulted, a more relevant and practical experiment in artificial freezing is contained in Della Porta's section on cookery. From this it becomes clear that he had been experimenting, with all that care for which he was known, with his two primary cold substances, snow and nitre. The former, as we know, was readily available in Naples, and the latter, it can be assumed, was obtainable from some local refinery where it was prepared for use in the manufacture of gunpowder. The idea of amalgamating the two known refrigerating substances to produce one perhaps twice as cold, if not Della Porta's own, was certainly new at this time. Thermometers to measure the precise degree of cold obtained by the mixture were still a long way in the future. The only way of testing the strength of the cold was by observation of its effect on a third substance. Would a liquid, say water, milk, or wine, placed in a bottle and plunged into the mixture change consistency? Would it coagulate, congeal, freeze, as opposed to becoming merely very cold as when immersed and rotated in one only of the refrigerating elements, snow or saltpetre alone?

Sir Lewis Namier wrote that most secrets are in print if you know where to look for them. Now I do not think it likely that for nearly 400 years Della Porta's description of 'how wine may freeze in glasses' has been in print and that nobody, no trained scholar or professional researcher into the history of cold or the origin of ices, has noticed the relevance of the celebrated Neapolitan's freezing formula and directions, but it does appear as though this particular piece of chemical history, at one time probably well known, became obscured by time, perhaps dismissed by generations educated in more modern freezing techniques and unaware of the contemporary significance of the then novel secret. At any rate I have come across no reference to it in any relevant source, and it was, it must be said, presented by Della Porta himself in a curiously casual way, and with a declared aim no more serious than the gratification of the currently fashionable whim, 'the chief thing desired at Feasts', so he wrote, being 'that wine cold as ice may be drunk, especially in Summer'. His discovery, according to his own testimony, would make wine freeze so 'that you cannot drink it but by sucking and drawing in of your breath'.[15] This uncomfortable pleasure was to be achieved by rotating a flask of wine diluted with water in a tub of snow and powdered saltpetre or, he added, *salazzo*, the name used in Naples to designate the residue left after crude nitre had been cleansed of all impurities. These impurities included a considerable proportion of common salt, the smallest part of which inhibited its effectiveness in gunpowder. The fact that Della Porta emphasized, in both experiments involving artificial freezing, that

A long necked, bulbous flask being rotated in a tub of snow and saltpetre from *Methodus Refrigerandi ex Vocato Salenitio Vinum, Aquamque* by Blas Villafranca, 1550 (see p. 67).

CLACIÈRE ARTIFICIELLE PORTATIVE

approuvé par l'académie de Médecine.

1600   1601

POUR

GLACER

SANS

GLACE

au moyen de

SELS & ACIDES

Système

FUMET

Bᵀᴱ S.G.D.G

SORBETIÈRE POUR GLACÉS & SORBETS   CYLINDRE POUR GLACE BRUTE

De toutes les glacières factices qui ont paru jusqu'à ce jour il n'en est pas une qui offre au Consommateur autant d'avantages que les glacières artificielles portatives.

De ces deux appareils distincts, l'un est destiné à faire des glaces et sorbets et l'autre à faire de la glace brute ou à frapper soit une carafe d'eau soit une boisson pharmaceutique.

Ces appareils d'une grande simplicité sont appréciés pour la facilité de la manutention, la promptitude et l'infaillibilité des résultats.

APPAREIL N°1		APPAREIL N° I	
Moyennant une dépense de 1ᶠ50 produit glaces et sorbets pour 12 personnes.	16ᶠ.	Pour faire un pain de glace brute du poids de 1 Kilog	12ᶠ.
APPAREIL N°2		APPAREIL N°2	
Moyennant une dépense de 3ᶠ. produit glaces et sorbets pour 25 personnes	20ᶠ.	Pour faire un pain de glace brute du poids de 2 Kilog	16ᶠ.
		Mesure	1,50
		Roulette	1,75

Avec chaque appareil il est livré une notice qui donne la manière de s'en servir

Je me charge de la vente des SELS et ACIDES de 1ᵉʳ Qualité au prix de   25ᶠ. les % Kilos

On ne livre pas moins de 25 K°ˢ de Sels et 45 K°ˢ d'Acide.

LETANG FILS, 108, RUE VIEILLE-DU-TEMPLE, PARIS

A page from the 1912 catalogue of Letang, famous Paris mould manufacturers. The cylinder on the right would make a cyclinder of ice 'by means of salts and acids' and came in 1- and 2-kg sizes; the sorbetère on the right would make ices and sorbets, it also came in two sizes to serve 12 or 25.

salazzo would be just as effective as saltpetre proper, may not have had great significance to him other than in its cheapness, for nobody was then aware that it was precisely the common salt content of the nitre rather than the nitre itself which brought about that lowering of the temperature explained on pp. 56 and 75, but it does reveal that his experiments had been original and numerous, and that his contribution to the science of cold was rather more worthwhile than has appeared from the rigmarole involving the collection of drops of water from the outside of an ice-filled bowl, Della Porta's own comment on that experiment being, understandably, to the effect that having showed the way, he leaves others to get on with it.[16]

However sceptical we may be today about Della Porta's freezing technique if and when put into practice on the extensive scale presupposed by those 'Summer Feasts' in Naples, I see no reason to doubt that his laboratory experiments did produce the near-frozen wine he described. Anyone who has experimented with the freezing of wine will know that even diluted it makes thin grainy ice, which melts fast, and that was presumably what Della Porta was aiming at. At any rate he did the correct things to achieve it, diluting his wine – he doesn't say by how much but it was in any case normal in his time for Italians to drink wine diluted (only barbarians like Germans drank it neat) – and keeping it on the move in the freezing mixture. Everyone had been taught to do this to hasten the cooling process when chilling wine or drinking water in saltpetre-water. The technique had been learned from India and is still familiar from the token gesture of the wine waiter turning the bottle in an ice-pail, although he may not have much, or indeed any, idea of the reason for doing it.

Two further points of interest about Della Porta's directions for freezing wine are first that, for the benefit of doubters, he added an aside to the effect that 'some keep snow all the summer' – a reference to those who had ice houses – and that he included the recipe in the section of his book devoted to cookery, following immediately after one for the spiced wine called Hippocras. Thus it may have been brought to the attention of the persons to whom it would have been most useful, in other words stewards and wine butlers responsible for the wines and all beverages served at banquets and in great private households. If their masters were clamouring for ever colder and icier wine, as claimed by Della Porta, here was the way to achieve it.

Although Della Porta's frozen wine could have been the ancestor of the modern frozen sherbet, I don't think it was. Sherbets came to Europe, from Turkey, Persia and India, as sweet, syrupy, fruit- and flower-scented essences, pastes and powders. Some were freshly prepared from fruit juice, sugar and spices, some were made for storage in boxes and jars, and were exported. They were drunk diluted with cold water and frequently also with ice or snow, or were chilled by indirect contact, but as countless travellers from the thirteenth century onwards have testified, they were not ever – and indeed still are not – frozen. Nor were Italian *sorbetti*, French *sorbets* or English sherbets at first frozen or even necessarily iced, the term sherbet and its European equivalents being another of those linguistic traps into which unwary nineteenth- and twentieth-century gastronomic historians have tumbled, assuming that right from the first a sherbet or *sorbet* was the part-frozen, grainy refreshment, neither quite solid nor quite liquid, which it eventually became and which until as recently as the 1950s it remained. Except, that is, in the United States, where the term sherbet has for so long implied a frozen milk-based or fruit juice confection that I have been very conscious during my researches that unless some explanation such as I have now supplied were forthcoming, American readers would be baffled by allusions to sherbets as differentiated from frozen sherbets. That nobody need go further than Webster to discover that 'a water ice to which milk, egg-white or gelatin is added before freezing' is not the primary but only the third meaning of sherbet is less to the point than the prevailing American belief that a sherbet is a frozen dessert, not an iced drink. When I questioned James Beard on the subject, he was quite emphatic that in the United States a sherbet indicates some kind of ice-cream or frozen confection.

All this said, I think it can be accepted that it is eminently possible that Della Porta's frozen wine could have been the ancestor of the half-frozen sherbets which the Italians called *neve* or snows, the French *neiges*, and the Spanish *garapiñas*. There are, it goes without saying, other contenders for the position, contenders whose claims, though vague, might prove valid if hunted to earth. The beginnings of ices therefore are still surmise and conjecture. But through the haze of rumours and reports and citings of freezing mixtures, frozen milk confections, and all the rest, one fact shines clear. It is that in the 1580s, at about the time that Della Porta was preparing his second version of *Magia Naturalis*, artificial freezing was an idea which was in the air, or, to put it more portentously, one which had entered the European consciousness and was soon to become a reality. It was, to be sure, a few decades before the successful freezing of sherbets, with all the problems posed by their heavily sweetened content, could be achieved, but in the production of solid ice by the recently evolved artificial means progress was more promising.

In Naples – the recurrence of Naples in this story may well be more than just coincidence – by 1607, a physician known as Latinus Tancredo, who must at least have been acquainted with Della Porta, had established that saltpetre would intensify the cold of snow to a degree when, so he claimed, a glass of water – by a glass he meant a flask or carafe – quickly moved around in the mixture would become solid ice. This discovery, although probably by that time no longer very new, he published in his book *De Fame et Siti*. Like Della Porta, Dr Tancredo was unaware that it was the common salt content of the crude nitre he used[17] which was the important factor in the lowering of the temperature of the snow to below freezing point, but at some time between 1607 and 1620, when Francis Bacon wrote of common salt supplying 'activity to the cold of the snow' and referred to the making of artificial ice as a known phenomenon,[18] someone had worked out that saltpetre wasn't necessary to the success of the operation, and although its use in freezing mixtures persisted for four centuries – Escoffier was still using it in 1934[19] – it was coarse, unrefined sea or rock salt which was the more usual alternative in the making of artificial ice and the freezing of sherbets and ices of all kinds. Later, about forty-five years after the publication of John Barclay's startling description in *Argenis* of the ice goblets and how they were made, the celebrated English scientist Robert Boyle, and after him many who had the benefit of accurate thermometers to measure the degree of cold, found that other salts, notably sal ammoniac, activated the ice and effected freezing a great deal faster than common sea salt[20] (too fast in fact for the successful production of ices, *neiges* and *sorbetti*, which were best when gradually rather than abruptly frozen). By the time all those things had been worked out, the science of refrigeration had moved another step or two on its protracted progress.

It was not yet, nor for a long time, with any intention of replacing natural ice, but rather in the cause of pure science and the investigation of natural phenomena that the experiments were being made. Once the aim had been achieved, the art of producing ice by artificial means was of no particular use other than as an entertainment, a spectacle, almost a conjuring trick. As can be deduced from the circumstance that when James I died in 1625 'Cornelius Dreble the engineer' walked in the funeral procession alongside the King's favourite ballet dancer and just ahead of the Court comedians,[21] inventors at that time were habitually regarded as entertainers maintained to divert royalty and other eminent persons with ingenious demonstrations, tricks and mystifications. Thus it was that often an innovation which to posterity proved to be of great significance was in its own time treated as of little account. From the eighteenth-century German scholar Johannes Beckmann we learn that when Fugger's bills of exchange first appeared they were shrugged off as being of use only to gamblers, and that the sinister invention of gunpowder was treated as trifling. It is in his valuable paper on the history and origin of artificial ice and cooling liquors[22] that Beckmann remarks on these facts, so although he was writing at a time long prior to the period when the commercial exploitation of man-made ice had become a possibility, we may reasonably infer that he classed its invention as an important and undervalued discovery, as indeed it was. For the time being, however, the growing international trade in natural ice – Frederick Tudor sent the first overseas cargo of American ice from Boston to Martinique in 1806 – provided for what were then the world's limited requirements, and man-made ice was of interest only to those scientists and physicians who were clearsighted enough to see its potential both as a preservative in the storage and conservation of food and for its uses in medicine. Even to the confectioners who were making and dispensing ices in cafés and in wealthy private households, man-made ice was of very secondary importance.

Ices for the Sun King

Audiger's Tale

Most people interested in the history of food know the popular legend which attributes the introduction of ices to the French court to Florentine confectioners brought to Paris by Catherine de Medici when in 1533 she married the young Duke of Orléans, the future Henri II. This legend originated in the mid nineteenth century (see p. 45). A second myth concerning the popularizing of ices in Paris, only slightly less widespread than the Catherine story and with a shade more foundation, is that which attributes the innovation to Francesco Procopio and his café in the rue des Fossés-Saint-Germain, established in 1686 and subsequently famous as the café Procope. The origins and the pros and cons of the Procopio story are bound up with the foundation of the Guild of Limonadiers in 1676 and are discussed on pp. 111–128. A third theory, less known but believed by some historians of French court life and manners in the great days of Louis XIV to be the most likely one, credits a professional confectioner and distiller of liqueurs and aromatic waters named L. Audiger with having made the first ices in France for the young King and his courtiers during the 1660s or thereabouts.

For Audiger's part in this story we have only his word to go on. His brief account of his life is of great interest but has many gaps and is both confused and confusing. It is concerned mainly with the frustrations of an ambitious and hard-working young man in search of the patronage and privilege which will enable him to earn an independent living in his chosen profession. With its glimpses of backstairs palace intrigue, of the treachery and cupidity of minor officers of the crown and of the whims and caprices of powerful men and women who can ruin an officer of their household by instant and unexplained dismissal, or by abrupt withdrawal of patronage from a tradesman, and by promises of assistance betrayed, Audiger's tale is most illuminating. He has his successes and triumphs, good fortune as well as ill, and all of it condensed into twenty pages of narrative simply entitled *Avant-propos* to Part IV of his book *La Maison Réglée*, published in Paris in 1692. Evidently written more than thirty years after the initial events described in this memoir of his life, it was in part due to a faulty memory for dates, but in part also I think to the omission of passages which either he himself or his publisher may have cut from his narrative, that even at the time the story was confused, and today needs much untangling. Readers unfamiliar with chronicles of French court life of the decades 1660 to 1690 will like identification of the persons involved, and some minor details of Louis XIV's military campaigns during the same period must be established before the story begins to hang together. That is why my interpretation of his tale, which follows, is longer than Audiger's own version of it. Reading between the lines, it seems to me quite a wonder that the story was published while so many of the people concerned were still alive.

It must first be explained that Audiger's work was a French version, of which there were very few, of all those very numerous stewards' handbooks published in Italy between 1560 and 1700. The main parts of *La Maison Réglée* set out, in a good deal of detail, the duties, responsibilities and precise place in the hierarchy of the various officers and domestic servants employed in the running of the households of the contemporary nobility and gentry. Audiger also touched on the duties and responsibilities of masters towards their servants, a subject on which he had some cause to feel strongly. If masters and mistresses wish to have good servants they must themselves be good, and treat servants rather as adopted children than as slaves. They should provide written memoirs, signed in duplicate, of all the work and every duty which that servant is expected to perform, and in this way there can be no argument between the parties and no possibility of mistakes, and if on the one hand the employers can then demand nothing further, the employees cannot fail to account for everything with which they have been entrusted. Invoking the example of the late Monsieur le Prince de Condé (the King's first cousin), a man for whom Audiger at all times expresses boundless esteem, he suggests that faithful servants, when retired, should be given pensions, or else some light employment on the estate, where they might peacefully end their days.[1] Those of Audiger's former employers still alive when his book appeared and whose treatment of him had left a good deal to be desired would no doubt have dismissed his words, if they troubled to read them, as an impertinence. But Audiger had at most times had influential protectors and was clearly not unduly afraid of retribution on that particular score.

As related by himself Audiger's personal story opens in Rome. The year, according to him, was 1660, but was actually, as we soon discover, 1661. From the tenderest age he had wished to learn the arts of confectionery and distillery, had been trained by the best officers in France, and having thus had the opportunity to travel throughout the kingdom and even to accompany various persons of quality to Spain, Holland and Germany, he had at last decided to go to Italy, there to perfect his knowledge of the making of all kinds of waters, both of flowers and fruits, both frozen and not frozen, *sorbec* (sherbet) creams, *orgeat* (at the time a paste of melon seeds and almonds with sugar, milk and orange flower water diluted with plain water), pistachio, pine-kernel, coriander, anis, fennel and other seed waters of all kinds. Although Audiger does not at any time refer to the event, the pub-lication in April 1659 of a book entitled *Le Maistre d'Hostel* in which was included a chapter on syrups, Italian fruit, flower, and spiced waters, and another on what were then called *Breuvages Délicieux*, meaning both alcoholic liqueurs and refreshing fruit juices such as lemonade and orangeades, may well have fired his ambition to go to Italy to learn about them at first hand. At any rate, while there he learned also to distill all kinds of flowers, fruits and seeds, both by the hot and cold methods, and to prepare chocolate, tea and coffee. Given the numerous coffee houses established in Paris by the 1690s, and the quantity of books on the subject which by that time had appeared in the French language, it was odd that Audiger should then remark that 'few people in France know how to prepare these beverages'. However, he seems on sure ground when he says, 'I was one of the three who made them fashionable. The first was one named More, who was sent from Italy to Cardinal Mazarin through the offices of his *maître d'hôtel*, Signor Pronty. The second was André Salvator, who was sent to the Maréchal de Gramont, who was very particular in such matters and was willing to go to the necessary expense, which was considerable.'[*] From Audiger's account it would appear that in Italy he had worked closely with these two men, that they preceded him to France, and that eventually, having spent fourteen months altogether in Italy, he left Rome by the *diligence*, or post carriage, 'at the beginning of January 1660'.

There now follows the story, which is often related, of how Audiger obtained early peas from a field near Genoa, of how he had them packed, and of how he conveyed them to Paris. How he contrived to stop the *diligence*, a high-speed mail coach drawn by six horses in long, non-stop stages, Audiger does not relate, but having already spotted a field of peas between Florence and Genoa, an unusual sight anywhere in January, he sees, further on, nearer to Genoa, some more, incomparably finer. He descends from the coach, finds the peasants to whom they belong, and negotiates a deal with them. They bring him two basketsful, adorned with a quantity of the rosebuds bordering the field. Remarking that the roses were no less unusual for the season than the peas, Audiger narrates how he had a special case made, how the peas and the roses were packed in it together and how he then rejoined the post carriage for Paris. The post drivers had evidently obligingly waited while these transactions were carried out, and Audiger arrived in Paris on 16 January, about a fortnight after leaving Rome. According to contemporary accounts that was approximately the normal time taken for the journey by fast *diligence*.

Two days after his arrival in Paris, on Thursday, 18 January, Audiger

---

[*] We know of More and André Salvator only through Audiger, but we have no cause to doubt his word. Pronty was certainly Cardinal Mazarin's *maître d'hôtel* at the time. The Maréchal de Grammont or Gramont was Antoine, Lieutenant-General and Marshal of France since 1641.

is taken to the Louvre by Monsieur Bontemps, the King's First Valet, who gains him an audience with the young monarch. His Majesty, says Audiger, was accompanied by Monsieur (his brother, soon to become Duke of Orléans), Monsieur le Comte de Soissons (a prince of the House of Savoy, son of Charles Victor Emmanuel II of Savoy-Carignan, who ranked as a prince of the blood), Monsieur le Duc de Créquy (First Gentleman of the Bedchamber), Monsieur Le Maréchal de Gramont, the Comte de Noailles, the Marquis de Vardes (Head of the Swiss Guard, subsequently disgraced, imprisoned and exiled from court following the discovery of a series of disreputable intrigues and odious betrayals involving the Queen, Madame, Duchess of Orléans, Louise de la Vallière, the King's mistress, and the King himself), the Comte de Moret, and several other great nobles of the court. When Audiger presents his case of early peas to the King in person, the courtiers exclaim, with one voice, that nothing could be more beautiful, more of a novelty, that never in France had anything of the kind been seen at this season. The Comte de Soissons even takes a handful of the peas and shells them in the presence of his Majesty, and they are found to be as fresh as if they had just been gathered. His Majesty, having graciously expressed his satisfaction, orders Audiger to take the peas to Sieur Baudoin, Controller of the Mouth, and to instruct him to apportion them out for a little dish to be made for the Queen Mother, one for the Queen, one for the Lord Cardinal, and the rest to be kept for himself, for a dish which he will ask Monsieur to share with him.

It is here that it becomes clear that while Audiger's memory of the events he describes may well be perfectly accurate, his dating of them is a year out, and that it was in January 1661, not 1660, that they occurred. In January 1660 the King was not yet married and was not even in Paris, but in Aix-en-Provence, having spent Christmas 1659 in Toulouse while Cardinal Mazarin was endlessly negotiating with the Spanish foreign minister, Don Luiz de Haro, for the terms of the marriage settlement of the young King to the Infanta Maria Teresa. On 27 January 1660 Louis had received his rebel cousin, the Prince de Condé, at Aix and there, in the presence of the Cardinal, the Prince made his personal peace with the youthful King following his involvement in the recent insurrections of the Fronde against the Cardinal, the Queen Mother, Anne of Austria, and the King himself. A week later, on 2 February 1660, the King's uncle, Gaston d'Orléans, died at Blois. Court mourning having once more delayed arrangements for the King's marriage, it was not until 5 June 1660 that it was solemnized at St Jean de Luz on the Spanish frontier. Six weeks later, on 26 August 1660, Louis and his bride made their triumphal entry into Paris.

Reading 1661 rather than 1660, then, we may return to Audiger's account of his presentation to Louis XIV of the early Italian peas. His Majesty had ordered Bontemps to reward Audiger with a present of money, a present the latter had declined, asking instead if he might present a petition to the King regarding the privilege – that is, the licence – and permission to make and have made for sale and retail, all kinds of liqueurs★ in the Italian manner, both at the court and to His Majesty's suite, and in all other cities of the realm, with prohibition to all others to sell or retail them 'in hurt of myself'. Monsieur Bontemps tells Audiger that his request is in order and he does not think it will be refused.

So far, so good. By the combination of his sharp eye, his opportune purchase of the early peas, and his imaginative idea of presenting them to the King, together with his good fortune in finding Bontemps, the influential First Valet, and through him obtaining an audience with the young monarch, Audiger has, so he believes, achieved his ambition of establishing a monopoly in the manufacture and sale of cordials and liqueurs not only to the court but throughout France.

In the March following the presentation of the peas, Audiger goes to Vincennes, where the King is in residence, to present his official petition. The King returns it to him, telling him to take it to M. Le Tellier and to ask him if the proposition is feasible. Michel Le Tellier was at the time Minister of State for War, having previously served in many legal and administrative offices. It would presumably have been

★ The term liqueur, although it embraced some alcoholic cordials such as Rossolis and Populo, also covered lemonades and other fruit beverages, and all those compositions made especially for freezing.

in a legal capacity that his advice was required by the King on this occasion. Since Cardinal Mazarin, although ailing, was still virtually ruler of France, the King no doubt felt it necessary to conform with the existing laws of the country. In later years he was to disregard them when so minded. In obedience to the King's command, Audiger goes off to find M. Le Tellier, conveniently encounters him at the foot of the staircase, presents his petition and explains that the King has ordered him to do so and to wait for a reply. Le Tellier laughs, says there is nothing to prevent His Majesty granting the petition and supposes it will not be opposed, *given that there is no one in France who knows the composition of these Liqueurs or who does a business in them*, and that he will do his best to be of service in the matter. Thereupon Le Tellier and Audiger betake themselves back into the presence of the King – the apparent ease with which Audiger gets in and out of the royal Audience Chamber strikes the modern reader as a trifle unusual, but throughout his reign Louis XIV reiterated his belief that a King of France should be approachable by his subjects – and as soon as he perceived the two men together the King again asks Le Tellier if he can grant the privilege or licence which Audiger is petitioning for. M. Le Tellier having replied in the affirmative, His Majesty orders Audiger to dispatch the Letters Patent.

Shortly after the audience, on 9 March 1661, the death of Cardinal Mazarin occurred. The court moved, first to Compiègne, then to Fontainebleau, where on 1 November the Queen gave birth to the Dauphin, to be known throughout his life as Monseigneur. Audiger, still in pursuit of his patent, once more seeks out M. Le Tellier, who himself hands over the papers, at the same time asking Audiger if he will teach something of the making of cordial waters to his, Le Tellier's, butler. Audiger agrees to do so. As instructed by Le Tellier he takes his patent to M. Herval,* principal Clerk to the Council, so that Herval may put it before the Council and be good enough to give it his support. This is apparently accomplished according to plan. The next step is for Audiger to retrieve his patent from Herval and deliver

---

* Barthélémy Hervart, known as Herval, had been since 1657 one of the controllers-general of finances.

it to the Chancellor Séguier. That dignitary tells him he must wait to see that nobody raises an objection.

Things now begin to go wrong, although owing less to the interminable workings of French seventeenth-century administration than to a private squabble on the part of Chancellor Séguier and his grandson-in-law, the Comte de Guiche. The Count, Armand de Gramont, son of the Marshal and a famously handsome and wild young man whose indiscreet conduct at court was to arouse the King's displeasure on numerous occasions and to cause more than one major scandal, had promised to sponsor Audiger's petition. No doubt Audiger owed his introduction to the Comte de Guiche to his former colleague from Rome, André Salvator. As will be remembered, it was Salvator who had been engaged by the Maréchal de Gramont as an *officier* expert in making liqueurs and cordial waters. For Audiger the association of his petition with the Comte de Guiche was unfortunate. Guiche was notoriously neglecting his wife, Séguier's granddaughter, and openly paying court to Madame Henriette, the recently married bride of Monsieur. Madame, gossips said, reciprocated Guiche's infatuation. Since the King himself had also been indulging in a quite serious flirtation with his sister-in-law, Audiger's involvement with Guiche was becoming increasingly inauspicious. Without actually referring in so many words to the current court scandals, and merely saying that the Comte de Guiche '*n'était pas bien*' with his wife, Audiger decided to withdraw his Letters Patent. Without having obtained the necessary seals from Chancellor Séguier he locked the documents away in a coffer to await more favourable circumstances.

At this point the story makes sad reading. Audiger, in spite of his setbacks, pursues his cause, presenting several petitions to the King, informing him of Chancellor Séguier's refusal to seal his Letters Patent and saying that he has wasted much time and spent all his money. Whether he meant to imply that that money had been spent in bribes Audiger does not say, but he does recount how one day he gets another chance to speak to the King. The King, who appears to have been uncommonly patient with Audiger and his importunities, replies that he is vexed about the affair, but that he can do nothing more to help, and if Audiger will ask some other favour it will be accorded him.

Audiger, however, can think of nothing to ask of the King. Uncharacteristically, he abandons his project.

Some months later – we must now be in the spring or summer of 1662 – we find Audiger in the service of the Comtesse de Soissons, as her *faiseur de liqueurs*. Perhaps the appointment had been made on the suggestion of the Comtesse's husband, who had been present on the occasion of Audiger's presentation of the Italian peas to the King, but the idea could equally well have originated with the monarch himself, who was a frequent visitor in the Soissons household and was indeed, according to contemporary chronicles, seeing the Countess every day. Formerly Olympe Mancini, one of Cardinal Mazarin's numerous and notorious Italian nieces, the Countess had in 1658 been hurriedly married off by the Cardinal to the Comte de Soissons when it was realized that the young King had fallen for her.★ Louis meanwhile had transferred his attentions, and more seriously, to Olympe's sister Marie. That affair too had been cut short by Mazarin's insistence on the King's marriage to the Spanish Infanta, while Marie was bundled off to Italy as the bride of Prince Colonna. Once the Cardinal was dead, the King resumed his affectionate, if not actually amorous, relations with Olympe de Soissons. She was a woman of high spirits and ready wit which compensated, contemporaries agreed, for a quarrelsome temperament and a boundless capacity for troublemaking. As for the King, throughout her turbulent career, and however scandalous her conduct, he appears to have retained a certain regard and even affection for Olympe.

It was not long before the Countess showed off her new acquisition in the form of an Italian-trained *liqueuriste* and confectioner to the most exalted company in the land. The King, Monsieur and 'several noble lords and ladies of the court' were entertained by Olympe to 'a kind of collation' at which his Majesty and Monsieur ate and drank Audiger's confections – he does not say what was in the solid part of the collation – and pronounced them very good. The Countess thus

★ The date of the Soissons marriage given by Voltaire in his *Age of Louis XIV* as 1663 is erroneous. That was the year of the birth of Prince Eugène, the Soissons' second son.

perceived that Audiger was thoroughly well versed in his business, and she was highly satisfied with him. Before long, however, the ever-active and ambitious Audiger began to find he was under-employed and – reading between the lines – underpaid. He showed the Countess a letter from the Queen of Poland, the former Princess Marie (Louise-Marie de Gonzague, Duchesse de Nevers, 1611–67, who had married successively two brothers, Wladislav IV of Poland and his successor Jean Casimir), inviting him to join her household as head butler, confectioner, and *liqueuriste*, at a salary of 800 francs, with permission to take on apprentices. The Countess quickly perceived that if she wanted to keep Audiger she would have to devise more lucrative work for him. Telling him that she could make his fortune for him just as well as the Queen of Poland, she decided to consult M. Le Normand, Controller of her Household, as to how to contrive better terms and greater prestige for Audiger. Le Normand suggested that the distribution of the bread and wine, the laying of the table, and the care of the linen and plate be handed over to Audiger. These duties and perquisites were traditionally among those of the *sommelier* or wine butler, and since the Countess had realized that Audiger was fully trained in these duties, we can only assume that she now dismissed her existing *sommelier* in order to give his job to Audiger.

As combined wine butler and *liqueuriste*, a newly created office, Audiger stayed three years in the Soissons household and on a number of occasions served the King and the Princes, meaning Condé, his son the Duc d'Enghien, known at court as M. le Duc, Condé's brother, the Prince de Conti, and their wives, as well as Monsieur and Madame, who was Henrietta Anne of England, sister of Charles II and younger daughter of Charles I and his French widow, Queen Henrietta Maria, still living at Saint-Germain where she had established her little court during the years of exile from England. The Princesse de Carignan, the Comtesse de Soissons's mother-in-law, also ranked as a princess of the blood. Audiger had been much praised and his efforts had been appreciated by his employers. They seemed pleased with him and he with them.

At this stage the King's military activities began to impinge on the domestic life of the Soissons household. When in 1663 the Count went on the campaign which culminated in the siege of Marsal, a stronghold in the then independent duchy of Lorraine, Audiger attended him. Subsequently, the Count, in his capacity as Governor of Champagne, went on a tour of the province, again attended by Audiger. On their return to Paris the Count informed everyone that Audiger had performed his duties to perfection and let it be known that his services had been much appreciated. Evidently the Count overdid his praises. Growing jealous of Audiger, his fellow officers in the Soissons household determined on his downfall. Eventually the unhappy Audiger was dismissed, whether by the Count or the Countess he does not reveal, but at any rate without being given a reason. No doubt his colleagues in the household could have found it easy enough to prove that Audiger had been in some way making more than he was entitled to out of his office, but there are hints that there was something more than petty jealousy and domestic strife to account for his dismissal. When he says that at the time he had much *chagrin*, which caused him *quelques affaires*, some troubles, he might possibly have been referring, in an oblique way, to the court affair of late 1664 and early 1665 in which the Comtesse de Soissons, together with the Marquis de Vardes, with whom she was carrying on an affair, and the Comte de Guiche, were implicated in the forging and planting of the famous Spanish letter, revealing to the Queen the extent of the King's infatuation with Louise de la Vallière. The letter, intercepted by the Queen's Spanish lady-in-waiting and delivered directly to the King, had occasioned an outburst of rage terrifying to all who witnessed it, and resulted in the eventual imprisonment of Vardes and the banishment from court of Guiche. With Olympe de Soissons the King at last lost patience. She too was banished from court, together with her husband. Although the couple were back in Paris by October 1666, it seems probable that Audiger's summary dismissal from their household coincided with the King's command that they remove themselves from the capital. If that indeed had been the case, Audiger would certainly have considered it impolitic to say so when he published his story a quarter of a century later.

Audiger, having been dismissed from the Soissons household, did not immediately seek similar employment elsewhere, but instead joined a cavalry regiment, left Paris and took part in several military campaigns. He may have found it wise to distance himself from the capital, the court, and the dangerous intrigues of high society, or perhaps he had become temporarily attracted to the idea of a military career. At the time a vigorous recruiting drive was in progress. By December 1665 the King, having levied his infantry troops for the spring campaign of the following year, had turned his attention to the raising of cavalry. 'Everybody at court is seeking employment in the King's troops,' reported the Duc d'Enghien in a letter written to his mother-in-law, the Queen of Poland, on 26 November 1666. On 4 December the Duke's father, the Prince de Condé, wrote to the same lady that 'they are now working on the cavalry'.[2]

According to Audiger's own testimony, he eventually transferred from the cavalry to the infantry and was granted a lieutenancy in the Regiment of Lorraine.* After what he calls the Campaign of L'Isle he had had enough of the military life, resigned his commission in favour of a relative and returned to Paris. By L'Isle it would appear that Audiger meant Lille, then one of the Flemish frontier towns held by the Spanish. The siege and surrender of Lille, at which the King was present, took place in the summer of 1667. It would probably have been in the winter of 1667–8 that Audiger relinquished his commission and resumed his career as a confectioner and distiller. Entering the service of the Président de Maisons (René de Longueil, later Marquis de Maisons) at the magnificent Château de Maisons,† Audiger was soon once more serving the royal family.

This time it was the Queen and the Dauphin, now seven years old, the age at which the royal princes traditionally emerged from the nursery and were transferred into the care of a male tutor, who were being entertained at the Château de Maisons. It was the Dauphin's first collation outside the royal palaces, and the King's Household officers had agreed in a friendly way that Audiger should do the service on this occasion. He was even invited to Versailles to lend a hand with

---

* Commanded by the Chevalier de Lorraine, favourite of the homosexual Monsieur.
† Built by Mansart between 1642 and 1646.

the preparation and service during the summer fêtes and divert-issements planned for the entertainment of the court and which were to last a fortnight. These prolonged festivities, with theatrical presentations, ballets, fireworks, tremendous collations and court balls, were a great feature of life at Versailles during the 1660s and 1670s. The first of the famous great fêtes of Louis's reign had been that of 1664, at the height of his affair with Louise de la Vallière, the second in 1668 when Madame de Montespan had at last triumphed over the King's former love.

Monsieur de Maisons had graciously granted Audiger permission to assist M. de Lazur, the King's head butler, at the Versailles fêtes, but on his return to Maisons, all was not well. Audiger and his employer fell out and parted company. Without apparent delay Audiger was then taken on by Colbert, the King's Chief Minister. This meant that he was once more getting close to the royal circle. Was he still hoping for that Patent? At Sceaux, Colbert's country château, the King, the Queen, the Dauphin, Monsieur and Madame were all entertained to dinner, and were served by Audiger.* Afterwards the Colberts presented him with the crystal glasses, dishes and carafes in which the royal refreshments had been served. A singular honour. The happy relationship with the Colberts appears to have lasted for two years when Madame Colbert, who was *fort changeante*, highly unpredictable, suddenly decided to make a clean sweep and on flimsy pretexts sacked Audiger, together with all the other household officers. Colbert himself, however, perhaps embarrassed by his wife's caprice, obtained employment for Audiger in Holland as *officier* to his son-in-law, the Comte de Saint-Aignan, later Duc de Beauvillier, and off he went.

According to Saint-Simon, who knew Saint-Aignan well after he became Duc de Beauvillier, Audiger's new employer was a man of singular good nature and punctilious habits, who treated his servants with meticulous politeness. In all probability then, things went well

---

* A famous royal visit to Sceaux took place in 1677, when Racine's *Phèdre* was performed in the Orangery. The occasion described by Audiger was evidently an earlier one.

for Audiger, and neither employee nor employer found cause for complaint. Nevertheless, quite abruptly, without saying how long he stayed with Saint-Aignan, and in the same sentence in which he related his departure for Holland, he recorded his return to Paris, merely adding, 'I established myself as Limonadier in a shop in the Place du Palais Royal.' What happened, I believe, was that in 1670 the Comte de Saint-Aignan left with the army on the victorious campaign against Holland, taking Audiger in his suite, and on his return presumably no longer had need of Audiger's services.

The reader of Audiger's chronicle is relieved to come to the end of the tales of petty jealousies, unjust dismissals, summary removals from one household to another. They are common to the annals of domestic service, on however high a social level, but now that at last Audiger was established in his own business he was apparently contented. Recording that for twelve years he furnished the King's Household with all manner of liqueurs, and also on special occasions those of all the great noblemen, he mentions that he was called in to assist at all the great feasts and celebrations given when the King decreed that the court should entertain the Prince Bishop of Strasbourg. This must have been in 1674, when the Prince Bishop, François Egon, Prince Furstenberg, Bishop of Strasbourg since 1663, visited Paris. The feasting of the Prince Bishop was a political move intended to further Louis XIV's designs on the then free German city of Strasbourg.* His Majesty, we learn from Audiger, had set the example, and everyone followed suit. The Prince de Condé and the Duc d'Enghien delegated Gourville, the family's man of business and confidential adviser, to present the Bishop with Rhine wines, preserves and some *rossolis*,[3] the Italian liqueur so sought after at the time. In turn Monseigneur de Strasbourg entertained the Dauphin and the nobles; Audiger was once more called in to supply all the necessary preserves and liqueurs, and until his death in 1682 the Prince Bishop was regularly supplied with these delicacies by Audiger.

The chronicle of Audiger's triumphs as an independent confectioner

---

* Eventually seized by French troops in 1681 and in 1684 ceded to Louis XIV by treaty.

and *limonadier* continues happily for a while, with yet more royal collations, desserts and garden entertainments. One such occasion was provided by a certain M. Rossignol, described by Madame de Sévigné as M. le Président Rossignol,[4] at the Château de Juvisy. The court was travelling from Fontainebleau to Paris, the Princesse de Carignan's *officier*, one Rolland, was organizing the dessert and the liqueurs, while Audiger himself served the King, Monsieur and Madame.* The collation was stage-managed in the garden by Audiger in such a manner that in every walk and alley along which the royal party passed there were refreshments, an ingenious entertainment which aroused many comments to the effect that the garden was everywhere growing collations. Royal jokes don't change much through the centuries.

Going back a year or more in his chronologically confusing story, Audiger all of a sudden remarks that the King has left on yet another Flanders campaign, that known as Les Brouettes, the Wheelbarrow Campaign. This was the campaign of preparation for the invasion of Holland and the hasty fortifying of Dunkirk, the port ceded to Great Britain in 1658 and sold to Louis XIV in 1662 by Charles II for 5 million livres. The Brouettes or Dunkirk Campaign took place in the summer of 1671, immediately following the famous three-day fête given by the Condés at Chantilly from 23 to 25 April, when the entire royal family and court were present, together with hundreds of lesser guests and a swarm of uninvited ones. Four tables for royalty and fifty-six for the lesser personages were set out of doors on a carpet of thousands of jonquils. In charge of the food supplies was Vatel, the Prince de Condé's High Steward. It was on the second day of the fête, following minor shortages at dinner on the first afternoon, when some of the guests at the lesser tables had had to go without roast meat, that the unhappy Vatel, sleepless and frantic with anxiety because it was a fish day and supplies again appeared to be failing, committed suicide. Reading the story as related in detail by Madame de Sévigné in a letter written to her daughter on 26 April 1671 – the account was given to her by Moreuil, First Gentleman of the Condé household at

---

* The second Madame, Elisabeth Charlotte of Bavaria, Princess Palatine.

Chantilly – and appreciating the confusion attendant upon a fête given on so massive a scale, one can only marvel that there had not been other serious casualties. The King's comments on the Vatel affair remained unreported, but he reproved Condé for the extravagance and excesses of the three-day fête. Ordering his cousin to confine himself in future to two principal tables only for royalty, the monarch left Chantilly for Dunkirk, where he arrived on 3 May.

Asserting that during the period of the summer campaign of 1671 the Duc d'Enghien took him to Chantilly, Audiger describes how he stayed there a week helping the Condés to entertain a large party of important guests, among whom were the Princesse de Conti and Madame Colbert. As usual, Audiger reports in his account that he received many kind compliments on his cordials and liqueurs and was even asked by the Prince to instruct his own *officiers* in the art of making these delicacies. Because Condé's *officiers* were all his friends, Audiger agreed to do so.

Once again Audiger was confusing his dates, or perhaps again he had made a cut in his narrative and had failed to correct the resulting discrepancy. It was at any rate not until 16 January 1680 that Marie Anne de Bourbon, Mademoiselle de Blois, twelve-year-old daughter of the King by Louise de la Vallière, was married to Condé's young nephew, the Prince de Conti, and was left at Chantilly under the chaperonage of Madame Colbert, whose husband had been appointed her official guardian. In a paragraph immediately following his description of the Prince's house-party, Audiger in fact confirms that he was referring to 1680, not 1671. 'The following winter,' he writes, 'the same Prince gave a great ball for Monseigneur the Dauphin and Madame la Dauphine, all the Princes and Princesses, and lords and ladies of the court.' It was in the spring of 1680 that the Dauphin and the Princesse Marie Anne de Bavière had been married. For the Condé ball for the young royal couple Audiger prepared 'quantities of Liqueurs, *d'Eaux glacées* and *Eaux à boire*'. *Eaux glacées* or water-ices were still something of a royal luxury, and in spite of what *limonadiers* and café owners such as Dubuisson wrote a century later about ices being made only in the summer until about 1750, in French royal circles of the 1680s it was clearly not at all unusual to have them served, and in abundance, in midwinter. As part of the dessert at the wedding banquet of the young Contis that January, for example, there had been a quantity of saucer-dishes filled with *eaux glacées*, and liqueurs were in silver goblets.[5] At Chantilly Audiger had evidently inaugurated a tradition, and on numerous subsequent occasions we find ices associated with the Condé fêtes. After the ball given for the Dauphin and Dauphine, the ageing Prince (who was eventually succeeded by his son in 1686) expressed his great satisfaction to Audiger, and, making him a handsome present, told him that everything he had provided had been admirable.

Audiger was now in the full flood of his popularity with the royal family. Every time Monsieur entertained his brother at Saint-Cloud he sent for Audiger, who also supplied him when he went on campaign. When the King and Monsieur went on campaign, it should be explained, they were followed by large retinues, including the royal ladies in their court finery. Provisions were luxurious, although the time was yet to come when the Duc de Saint-Simon started complaining that in the trenches the confectionery and desserts provided for the army commanders looked like ballroom suppers and even included ices and a profusion of liqueurs.[6] For the time being Monsieur appears to have been content to have cordials and liqueurs made by Audiger for his summer campaigns, in the winter ordering red and white Hippocras★ from him, and when in residence in his apartments in the Palais Royal without his household officers, sending for Audiger to provide his collations.

Things were going well for Audiger – to supply the royal households and attend so many fêtes and functions he must have had quite a flourishing business and numerous assistants – when out of the blue came disaster. M. de Livry, the King's High Steward, attempted to foist an unacceptable associate upon him, 'a little difference' ensued, and as a result Audiger found himself deprived of Monsieur's custom and patronage. It is difficult not to suspect that Monsieur had tried, through Livry, to get employment in Audiger's business for one of his notoriously homosexual protégés and that in one of his customary fits of fury at being thwarted he attempted to ruin Audiger.

★ The heavily spiced wine which was a survival from medieval days.

Obliged to look elsewhere for a source of income, Audiger began to think about his still unratified licence. Taking his papers to an acquaintance who happened to be Secretary to Monsieur de Riantz, King's Procurator at the Châtelet, he was advised to show them directly to that functionary, who was a good friend of Chancellor d'Aligre. From this piece of information we see that Audiger has once more skipped back in time, probably to late 1675 or early 1676, for Aligre died in October of that year, and was succeeded in his office by Audiger's old friend Le Tellier, now aged seventy-four.

Leaving his papers in the hands of de Riantz was a sad mistake on Audiger's part. De Riantz was obviously a thoroughly shifty official who, instead of speaking up for Audiger, himself proceeded to establish a Guild such as Audiger claimed he had envisaged, in order that he, de Riantz, would have the benefit of selling the Masterships.

Audiger was now enraged. He did indeed have more than one genuine grievance. First, a Chevalier de Châtillon, a member of the King's Bodyguard, appears to have asked the King for the licence accorded to Audiger, and received the reply that Audiger already had it, that it was impossible to grant it to two people, and that if he, Châtillon, considered it worthwhile he must arrange matters with Audiger. Somewhat oddly, Châtillon brought his mother along to see Audiger and to offer him a thousand *pistoles*★ for the rights accorded him so long ago by the King.

Hurrying off to retrieve what he realized were now very valuable papers from de Riantz, Audiger received the reply that they could not be found, but that a search would be made for them. At last Audiger discovered that he had been duped and that not only was de Riantz selling Masterships in a newly-formed Guild of Liqueur-makers, but that he, Audiger, was about to be asked to buy one. He now turned to his old master, Colbert, explaining to him that the new Guild could only have been based on the privilege accorded him by the King. Colbert, predictably, behaved perfectly properly, giving Audiger a note for M. Desmarets, his brother-in-law and a Treasurer, asking him to send Audiger on to see a functionary called the Partisan, Master of the

★ A *pistole* was the equivalent of about 10 *livres* in cash.

City of Paris. This man wrote ordering the treacherous de Riantz to receive Audiger, and to give him his papers as a Master Limonadier, for he had already paid. This, as Audiger interpolates, was incorrect, for he had paid nobody anything. The Partisan's intervention had, however, ensured that he received his Mastership without having to pay. That, concluded Audiger, was all he had to show for the privilege he had been accorded in 1661.

Audiger was still boiling with indignation. A Guild of 200 ignorant men, gathered from the dregs of the populace, each of whom had paid fifty *écus* for his Mastership, had come into being. Had he known what was happening, things would have been very different. He would have created one of the finest Guilds in Paris, one which would have been loved and respected by honest men. He would have joined it with the trade of confectioner rather than with that of *eau-de-vie* vendor, and would have named it the Guild of *marchands de liqueurs et de confitures*, and this would have attracted only honest persons, whereas among the *eau-de-vie* vendors there was nothing but scum. Furthermore, 100 established Masters would have yielded 100,000 francs to the King for Paris alone, without counting the fees from other cities of the realm. The ignorant, heartless and irresolute men who made up the Guild created by de Riantz yielded a much reduced revenue to the King, and they allowed their bread to be snatched from under their noses by Armenians. The last observation was an allusion to the coffee-sellers of Paris, who had originally been Levantine shopkeepers, hence the Turkish style of dress which became traditional to the waiters in coffee shops. The dress was adopted by Francesco Procopio when he opened his first café in the rue de Tournon in 1675. Audiger, in fact, may well have been directing his remarks at Procopio, who from being a street vendor and then a waiter had become a licensed *marchand de liqueurs* and *limonadier* by buying a Mastership without being required to undergo the tests which subsequently became obligatory in the profession. By the time Audiger came to write his story he could hardly have been unaware of the success of the new Paris cafés. Relatively few as they then were, they were already in 1692 becoming fashionable, and Procopio's establishment opposite the new Comédie Française in the rue des Fossés-Saint-Germain had been a success since the day the new theatre opened in 1687.

What is curious in Audiger's narrative, which, confused and involved though it is, does have the ring of truth, is his claim that it had been his intention to set up a Guild of *marchands de liqueurs et de confitures* when in reality what he had been asking for was a personal monopoly in the manufacture and sale of those commodities made in the Italian fashion. There was in fact already a Guild of Confectioners, as Audiger must have been aware, so the Italian part of it all was clearly the key distinction in his mind. Italian liqueurs and cordials were at that time considered to be, and no doubt were, in every way more refined, elegant and desirable than the rough and fiery products of the French *eau-de-vie* distillers, whose trade had already been incorporated in 1674. Those distillers, whether or not beknown to Audiger, had regarded the newly-formed Guild of *limonadiers* as dangerously competitive. Granted the rights to distil, manufacture and sell liqueur wines, aromatic essences, syrups, fruits in *eau-de-vie*, and tea, chocolate and coffee, the *limonadiers* were considerably less subject to harassment from excise men, assayers, and police authorities than were the *marchands d'eau-de-vie*. It was therefore the *eau-de-vie* distillers who had applied to the *limonadiers* to join them in the formation of one sole Guild or corporation. This, then, was the association of 250 master distillers and *limonadiers* registered in 1676, the news of whose existence had come as such a shock to Audiger and the formation of which he criticized so bitterly.

Audiger now returns to his personal tale, which ends on a more cheerful note. He describes one glorious occasion upon which he served the King and his entourage, one which would have been remembered by many readers when Audiger's book was published in 1692. It had occurred only five years previously, in January 1687. In December 1686 the King had been painfully but successfully operated on for an anal fistula. A month later, fully recovered, he attended a service of thanksgiving to God and Our Lady at Notre Dame. A *Te Deum* was composed for the occasion by Lully and afterwards the City Fathers gave a great banquet at the Hôtel de Ville attended by the King, all his family and the court. For this celebrated day in the history of Louis XIV's reign, Audiger was invited to serve in the capacity of *maître d'hôtel* at the table of thirty covers reserved for the princes of the blood. Once more it was the Condés, their ladies and their children who were attended by Audiger, but the Grand Condé had died of smallpox only a few weeks previously, and it was now the former Duc d'Enghien who was M. le Prince.

The young Prince de Conti, husband of Louis XIV's illegitimate daughter Marie Anne, had also (in 1685) died of smallpox and had been succeeded in the title by his younger brother, formerly Prince de Roche-sur-Yon. As well as serving the Princes, Audiger had made all the liqueurs for the King's table – his brush with de Livry had evidently been forgotten – as well as for the entire gathering. After dinner the King departed for Versailles, leaving the Dauphin and the Dauphine, Monsieur and Madame, and a number of Princes, Princesses, Lords and Ladies to see the firework display. There was then a magnificent ball which lasted until two in the morning. To Audiger fell the honour of serving the 'portable collation of all manner of fruit, and waters, both liquid and frozen'. Once again, then, we find the French royals enjoying water-ices in the middle of winter. Everyone, it goes without saying, was pleased. A few days later the Gentlemen of the City thanked Audiger, with the greatest courtesy. Ending his tale, Audiger was unable to refrain from boasting of his attendance upon the King at Achères on several occasions when he was reviewing his troops and when he was entertained by M. de Noailles,★ occasions on which he served the King's drinks with his own hands. He then apologized if to some readers his preamble had seemed fatiguing and even pointless, but expressed his conviction that there would be those who would view it favourably. In that speculation he was correct. His tale has provided posterity with valuable historical testimony of the efforts, setbacks, and successes of a man struggling to make his way in his chosen profession, as well as an insight into the strangely haphazard manner in which that profession appears to have developed in France.[7]

★ Created Marshal of France in 1693.

The incorporation of the Guild of Limonadiers and Distillers in May 1676 appears to have been, as Audiger complained, a haphazard affair. Much of his criticism of it was justified. Each of the 250 Masters of the new corporation had been required to pay 120 *livres* over and above the sum already contributed to the purchase of the right to establish themselves as a corporate body. Some part of that money had no doubt gone into the pocket of the crafty de Riantz, the official who had stolen Audiger's privilege document. The fact that none of the new Masters in the Guild had been required to pass any of the professional tests usual when an artisan or tradesman – as for example a baker, a pastrycook, a carpenter, a tailor – having served his apprenticeship and spent two years as a journeyman, applied to join his Guild as Master of his trade and gain the privilege of himself taking on apprentices, particularly aroused Audiger's scorn. He had himself received what he regarded as a correct training, on his own initiative he had travelled to Italy and had spent fourteen months there perfecting his knowledge, and excluding his two- or three-year military interlude had been actively practising his trade in Paris, or wherever his employers had required him, for a period of fifteen years. His talk of riff-raff who had simply bought their way into the trade was understandable, even if among the new Masters of the Guild there were a few genuine and experienced practitioners like himself, as surely there must have been.

What Audiger did not say, and of course did not dare to, was that at the time of which he was writing it was the King himself who was raising money by the sale of offices throughout the country. By means of the imposition of extortionate levies, existing Guilds were being progressively crippled. By the sale of Masterships in Guilds newly formed much in the manner described by Audiger, the whole system was being brought into disrepute. By 1691, the year prior to the publication of Audiger's book, and a matter on which he kept silent, the King had exacted further payments from a score or more of Paris Guilds amounting to almost 600,000 *livres*. Of this the *limonadiers* had contributed 24,000, the pastrycooks 20,000, the vinegar makers 10,000, the wine merchants 120,000, the mercers the immense sum of 300,000 *livres*, the grocers 120,000. In 1694 the King was to find an excuse for further levies, of 25,000 livres from the *limonadiers*, 16,000 from the pastrycooks, 198,000 from the mercers, and the extortion was to continue until the end of his reign and far beyond.★ Together with the catastrophic consequences of the revocation in 1686 of the Edict of Nantes, after which thousands of protestants, regarded as among the finest and most hard-working artisans and merchants of France, fled the country to escape religious persecution or compulsory conversion, Louis XIV's levies succeeded, in the words of the social historian Franklin, in definitively ruining all the Guilds, and all but wiping out the commerce of France.[8]

How much Audiger knew of, or suspected, what was going on, we cannot of course tell, but the King must certainly have played, to say the least of it, a somewhat devious part in the affair of the promised privilege. A strong sense that something is missing from the end of Audiger's story is very naturally accounted for by his need to obtain the royal licence to publish his book. He had learned the wisdom of discretion in the matter of how much he revealed or complained.

Snow or Concrete?

Between the prefatory matter and the text proper of Audiger's *La Maison Réglée* the publisher, or perhaps the author himself, inserted four pieces of doggerel verse written by a M. Duchesnay. Addressing Audiger in one of these so-called sonnets Duchesnay, using the exaggerated language customary in such laudatory epistles, assures his author that 'Your useful and learned Treatise/ Is a work worthy of admiration/ And one which must lead you/ To the glorious temple of immortality.' The statutory prophecies of everlasting renown thus honoured, Duchesnay passes on to what he had readily perceived was

---

★ The entire Guild system was abolished by the Assemblée Nationale in 1793.

Audiger's own proudest claim to fame. But, says the versifier, 'You attach far more glory/ To the honour of having so many times/ Prepared and served the food and the drinks/ Of the most puissant of all Kings.' Referring to Audiger's recipes for the various delicacies, liquid and solid, which he had had the honour of serving the most puissant of all Kings, Duchesnay called the reader's attention to 'a thousand fine secrets' for the preparation of 'Chocolate & Coffee/ Red and White Rataphia, Orangeade and Tea/ Compote and Jelly', but in doing so quite overlooked the famous ices which his author is credited with having introduced to the French court in the 1660s. That is not really surprising. It had never been Audiger's boast that *eaux glacées* were an innovation for which he had been responsible, and he made no claim that his recipes for preparing them or his directions for freezing them were novelties. It is indeed self-evident from his statement, made at the opening of his little narrative, to the effect that one of his aims in going to Italy was to perfect his knowledge of the confection of 'all manner of flower and fruit Waters, frozen and liquid', that he did not regard them as anything new. Putting his water-ice recipes and freezing methods into print was, however, a new departure, whether or not he realized the fact.

At the time of the publication of Audiger's book in 1692, there had already appeared, it is true, those directions for freezing pyramids of flowers or fruit encrusted in ice which had figured in the antiquated book of secrets called *Recueil de Curiosités Rares et Nouvelles* (see p. 39) published in 1674 under the name of a Sieur d'Emery (in 1685 translated into English, and entirely erroneously attributed to the much respected Nicolas Lémery, apothecary to Louis XIV). It is possible that Audiger had used those directions and adapted them when he prepared the book for publication, but his wording is very different from that of the Sieur d'Emery, and his instructions a great deal more practical. It seems to me more likely that it was in Italy that Audiger had acquired his proficiency in the creation and presentation of his ice pyramids. We know, after all, that such decorative centrepieces were being made at the time he was in Rome, and during the summer of 1661, when Audiger was employed by the Comtesse de

This plate from the 1734 edition of Massialot's work shows the service of a dessert for 12 to 14 covers. In the foreground 'a large dish of ice with a pyramid in the centre'. The eight small dishes around the edge of the table contained pâtisserie, fruit or *fromages glacés*.

Soissons, word can hardly have failed to come from Florence about the banquets given by the Medici for the marriage of their Hereditary Prince and the French Princess Marguérite-Louise. Stories of the ice goblets, the sparkling ice fruit dishes, the sensational 2-foot-high ice pyramids which had adorned the Medici banqueting tables, would have been noted by men like Audiger and his friends André Salvator and More. It was perhaps Audiger's own idea to present his ice pyramids as centrepieces round which little goblets of *eaux glacées* proper would all be arranged on handsome saucer-shaped dishes. The correct shape of the dishes was of course vital to the presentation, and thanks to illustrations included in later editions (from 1715 onwards) of Massialot's *Nouvelle Instruction pour les Confitures, les Liqueurs et les*

Fruits, we know just what Audiger intended when he wrote the directions later taken up by Massialot and his illustrator.[9]

As for the recipes for those *eaux glacées*, none – with the exception of the La Varenne formula for a *neige de fleurs d'orange*, published in 1682,[10] and another for a coriander *neige* – had appeared in print in France prior to 1692, the year in which, by coincidence or otherwise we cannot know, both *La Maison Réglée* and Massialot's *Nouvelle Instruction pour les Confitures* were published for the first time, both books offering, also for the first time, a variety of *eaux glacées*. In Audiger's case, there was also the odd *cresme glacée* and in Massialot's a chocolate water-ice and a custard ice.

As examples of the extreme, not to say crude, simplicity of early French ices, a few of Audiger's and Massialot's are worth quoting. The methods of freezing given by the two men differ somewhat and are also interesting to note. First Audiger's *cresme glacée*, his version of ice-cream:

Pour faire de la Cresme glacée. To make iced cream. Take a *chopine* [16 oz] of milk, a half *septier* [8 oz] of good sweet cream, or else three *poissons*★ [12 oz], with six or seven ounces of sugar & a half spoonful of Orange flower water, then put it in a tin or earthenware or other vessel to freeze it.

This *cresme glacée* is the only ice of its kind for which Audiger gave a recipe. All his others were for water-ices made from fruit juices, aromatic mixtures, or infusions of various herbs, seeds, and spices. As the recipes stand they were intended by Audiger merely as refreshing beverages, but when the beverages were to be frozen, then you had to double both the proportions of the main flavouring ingredient and the sugar. The extra strong sweetening and flavouring, plus an imperceptible quantity of musk and amber, turned your simple aromatic waters into *sorbec du Levant*, Audiger explained. Such *sorbets* were very different then from that odd one called *sorbec d'Alexandrie* which in varying versions had been appearing in print in France since 1659, and which involved the concentrated extract of a boiled round of veal and a syrup made with two pounds of sugar.[11]

★ The more usual spelling of this measure was *posson*, a quarter of the *chopine*.

In the following recipes the double allowances of sugar and flavouring ingredients specified by Audiger for frozen waters are already incorporated. The musk and amber I leave to the reader's imagination, as did Audiger:

Cinnamon water for freezing.
Take a [32 oz] pint of water which you put in a vessel and boil in front of the fire. When it has boiled you draw it away from the fire and put into it about one ounce of cinnamon sticks with four to six cloves. Stop the vessel securely and leave the water to cool. Then extract eight ounces of this water and add to it two [32 oz] pints of fresh water, with eight ounces of sugar or thereabouts, and you cool it and freeze it.

Strawberry water for freezing.
For a [32 oz] pint of water crush one [16 oz] pound of strawberries in the said water, add eight to ten ounces of sugar, and then the juice of a lemon. If the lemon is a strong one, it will suffice for two pints. When the sugar has melted, and all is well incorporated, filter the mixture through a sieve [chausse], and cool it.

To make green Fennel or Burnet or Chervil Water for freezing.
[As can be seen from this formula, the parsley, tarragon, basil, and chervil sorbets regarded as rather daring novelties in the early 1980s are not as new as might be supposed.]
    You must take two handfulls of one or other of the green herbs and infuse them in a [32 oz] pint of cold water for an hour to an hour and a half, then you add six to eight ounces of sugar, and you filter the mixture before freezing it.
    To all the above Waters you may add prepared Musk and Amber, but so little that it is all but imperceptible.

How to freeze all the above Waters.
    The manner of freezing each of the above Waters is to put three, four, or six containers [boîtes] or other vessels according to their size in a tub, at one finger's distance each from the other, then you take the ice, which you pound well, and salt it when it is pounded, and promptly put it in the tub all round your boxes, until the tub is full and the boxes covered. For a tub of this kind, in which there are to be five or six boxes, and to freeze them rapidly, and

well, two *litrons*,★ or about twenty-four ounces of salt are needed. When all is thus arranged you leave it for half an hour, or three quarters, taking care that the boxes do not get submerged as the ice melts, and that no water gets into your boxes, and to prevent this you make a hole at the bottom of the tub in which you insert a tap by which from time to time you draw off the water. Then you move the ice covering your boxes and stir the liquor with a spoon so that it freezes into a snow, and if it has frozen solid you break it up with the said spoon that it dissolve, for otherwise it will have no taste, and when you have done the same with each of your boxes of liquor, and observed great care that no salty ice has got into them, you re-cover them with ice and salt as before, and if you are in a hurry to freeze them faster, you must increase the quantity of salt, and you will not need to stir them again until you come to serve them, and do not dress them [i.e. in goblets or glasses] until you are ready to do so. In general this is how all *eaux glacées* are made.[12]

On the whole Audiger's freezing instructions make good enough sense, although 24 oz of salt to a tub of ice large enough to contain and cover six boxes of liquor to be frozen seems a rather scanty proportion. That would depend, of course, on what size of container Audiger meant when he specified 'boxes', a term which at the period could have meant almost any kind of vessel (one calls to mind the pewter 'basons' used by Hannah Glasse), but was probably one with a capacity of one Paris or 32 oz pint, since that was the quantity in which he made up the majority of his waters for freezing. Audiger did not anywhere use the term *sorbetière* or *sarbotière* to denote his freezing boxes or pots.

How optimistic, one may wonder, was Audiger's reminder that stirring the partly frozen liquor would subsequently cause it to freeze into snow? At any rate, his readers were warned of the danger of the whole container or boxful of liquor freezing into a solid mass and ending up as one large piece of all but tasteless ice.

In contrast to Audiger's recipes for waters for freezing, those of his contemporary, the anonymous author of *Nouvelle Instruction pour les*

★ A dry measure used by retailers of pulses, millet, salt, etc. According to La Varenne a *litron* of flour was 12 oz.

Confitures, usually nowadays assumed to have been Massialot, are seldom specific as to proportions and, when they are, have so little sugar that they would inevitably have frozen into a solid block of ice. Massialot's freezing instructions are equally imprecise and unsatisfactory. However, owing to the widespread influence on European cooking – English, Italian, Spanish, German – exercised by translations of Massialot's two works, *Le Cuisinier Roial et Bourgeois* and *La Nouvelle Instruction pour les Confitures*, his recipes are part of our gastronomic history, and a selection of the relevant ones should be seen alongside those of Audiger, whose work, although at least twice reprinted in the original,* was not, so far as I know, translated into any other language.

It was, incidentally, through the 1702 English translation of the Massialot works, published in London in one volume as *The Court and Country Cook*, that English confectioners and pastrycooks evidently learned about the making of ices. The work was widely plagiarized and adapted by professionals writing under their own names, and although ices had come to England long before 1702, and 'iced creame' had been appearing there at least since 1671 (made and frozen, I think, more in the manner of La Varenne's *neige de fleurs d'orange* – see p. 387 – than in that of Massialot), no really new directions for preparing and freezing them were to appear in print in the English language until Hannah Glasse's 1751 edition of *The Art of Cookery Made Plain and Easy* came out with her now well-known recipe for a raspberry cream ice.

First, then, Massialot's method of freezing:

To freeze all sorts of Waters and Liquors.

You must have a *cave* which is a kind of case of whatever size you wish, which is furnished within with pewter moulds in which you place your Waters. You set these moulds or other vessels in the *cave*, you cover them with their own covers. All the empty spaces you fill with broken ice, with handfuls of salt everywhere, and on the top of your moulds, for this is what

---

* In 1697 (in Amsterdam) and 1700, in Paris. Possibly there were other as yet unrecorded editions.

makes the Waters freeze. The *cave* should be pierced with a hole about half way up the side, in order to allow the water to drain off, for fear it might submerge your moulds. From time to time you break the ice which has formed on the surface [of the liquid in the moulds], and you replace the salt all round your moulds, to freeze the rest; & when you wish to serve your Waters, you take these little pieces of ice (*glaçons*) with which you fill your little basins (*chiques*) or other porcelain cups.

It will be found that this is expensive because of the salt, but the water which drains off from the *cave* may be retrieved, and by boiling and reducing it in a cauldron or a marmite, the salt dissolved in it may be separated; it may thus be utilised several times.[13]

Shaky though he appears to have been on the techniques of freezing, Massialot did have one or two original things to say on the subject of ices in general. He was of the opinion that only the red fruits, particularly strawberries and raspberries, were really to be re-commended for ices from the point of view of colour and scent, but allowed that apricots and peaches had some merit for the purpose. Flower waters included jasmine, violet, tuberose, orange blossom and jonquil; a white milk water called *eau virginale* was composed of milk, water, lemon juice and a quarter pound of sugar to the 32 oz pint of liquid, a chocolate water was made with an unspecified proportion of grated chocolate to the 32 oz pint of water and again a quarter pound of sugar; like orange and lemon waters this was good for diversifying the colours of the ices, particularly in winter, when flowers and soft fruits were wanting. The presentation of ices of contrasting colours was already an important point for the confectioner, and Massialot's suggestion for 'a simple dessert for four people' as described in his 1705 edition comprised, in addition to the obligatory symmetrically placed pyramids of fresh and candied fruit and sweetmeats to be arranged on a square platter, a dish of *Gobelets d'eaux glacées* to be placed in each of the four empty corners. Undoubtedly, Massialot knew how to dress his desserts with elegance, and always in the latest of taste.★ On the whole,

★ For special occasion desserts for great tables, Massialot recommended hiring what he called *machines*, in other words, made-up centrepieces comprising sets of dishes,

though, and in spite of one apparently innovative recipe for a custard ice-cream which he called *Fromage à l'Angloise* and which appeared among a group of creams, junkets, and fresh cream cheeses rather than in his chapter on *eaux glacées*, Massialot's ices give us even less cause than do Audiger's to disagree with the confectioner Emy, who wrote in his *Glaces d'Office* (1768) that the early ices were composed mostly of water with a little fruit and powdered sugar, and that they were nothing more than pieces of ice as hard as concrete. But the reader may judge for himself.

Eau d'Abricots

You must take well-ripened apricots, peel them & discard the stones. Weigh one pound of them and cut them in pieces & put them in a [32 oz] pint of water previously boiled; add a quarter pound or five ounces of sugar for the pint of water, & when your fruit has infused some time you finish it as the other waters, by beating it and pouring it several times from one vessel to another, and before putting it to freeze or to chill you filter it.

Eau de Chocolat

This Water may serve in Winter, in times when flowers and fruit are wanting. It is made by grating chocolate only, in water according to how much you need; you add a good quarter of sugar to the [32 oz] pint; and the whole having infused some time, you freeze it or chill it.

Eau de Violettes

Take a sufficient quantity of violets, for example two good handfuls for two [32 oz] pints of mixture. Pick off the petals & put them in the water, with a quarter or eight ounces of sugar; and having infused from the morning

---

baskets and platters, in various shapes and sizes, hexagonal, round, oval and so on. The name of the dealer he recommended as being the most knowledgeable on the arrangements of desserts, and the best supplied with everything necessary was, and is, striking. It was 'the Sieur de la Varenne, at the sign of the Renommée du Griffon d'Ozier, second on the right after the entrance to the Faubourg Saint-Antoine'. According to Bertrand Guégan in his Introduction to *Le Cuisinier Français*, 1924 (p. xlv), the La Varenne we know as author of *Le Cuisinier François* and *le Patissier François*, who had been *Ecuyer de Cuisine* to the Marquis d'Uxelles in the 1650s, had died at Dijon in 1678, aged over sixty, but he could well have had a son or other close relative flourishing in just such an appropriate enterprise.[14]

to the evening, or during five or six hours, you filter your liquor through a cloth, or just a tammy, and put it to freeze as directed for all the similar Waters.

Fromage à l'Angloise

Take a *chopine* [16 oz] of sweet Cream and the same of milk, half a pound of powdered Sugar, stir in three egg yolks and boil until it becomes a thin pap [*petite bouillie*]; take it from the fire and pour it in to your ice mould, and put it in the ice for three hours; and when it is firm, withdraw the mould, and warm it a little, in order more easily to turn out your Cheese, or else dip your mould for a moment in hot water, then serve it in a compôtier.[15]

Such were the ices known to Louis XIV, his family and his court. It seems to me that by making a sugar and water mixture in the proportions specified by Audiger or Massialot and scenting it with a few drops of flower essence, say violet, rose, orange blossom, or alternatively of oil of cinnamon, or of some other spice extract, and freezing the resulting water, one might easily obtain much the same sweetened and faintly scented ice as was enjoyed by, let us say, the young Duchesse de Bourgogne, much-loved wife of the King's eldest grandson, when the court celebrated the birth of her first son, the Duc de Bretagne. It was August 1704 and Madame reported that in spite of the war there were magnificent fêtes. At Marly, on the 14th of the month, she attended a sumptuous entertainment arranged to show off the splendours of the King's favourite country retreat to the English Court at Saint-Germain. (James II had died in exile there in 1701 and his widow, Mary Beatrice of Modena, with their son, the Pretender, and a daughter born at Saint-Germain in 1692, lived there until her death in 1718. James's second daughter, Anne, by his first wife, was now Queen of England.) The royal collation was served in a grassy clearing, *une véritable salle verte*, and the great marble horseshoe table at which the royal party sat was covered with a fine tablecloth drawn so tight that until one touched it, it too appeared to be marble. Set on tiered banks of greenery, ices in all sorts of colours were arranged in pyramids, making a fine effect in their crystal dishes of various sizes. After the collation there was a breathtaking firework display, lasting for a good half-hour, followed by another meal. After the meal the King took Queen Mary Beatrice through all the pretty bosquets to the sixth pavilion. When the English royals returned to Saint-Germain, Madame retired to her rooms, and the King and his family to his private closet.[16]

The ices had obviously been one of the high points of the day. Presented as they were against a backdrop of greenery, pale pink, yellow, green, and milky white pyramids of ice set in crystal containers sparkling in the leafy shade, they must have dazzled the youthful princes and princesses of France. From all we read of the ices of the period it becomes clear that it was the sheer magic of their appearance, the fact that they could be produced at the height of summer, or at any other time that the confectioners were asked for them – only the previous week the King had included a whole collection of fruit, sweetmeats, ices and liqueurs dispatched by a symbolic Pomona and brought by a Goddess of Love, among the presents he had showered on the Duchess of Burgundy immediately after her son's birth[17] – which constituted their potent appeal. Whether or not they had any particular taste, or whether they were really just crunchy lumps of coloured and faintly scented ice rather than snowy, melting fruit juices were irrelevant matters.

As for Audiger's omission of any references to the novelty of ices, he had, according to his own testimony, been practising his profession for thirty-five years. That takes us back to the late 1650s. I think we can assume that at that time Audiger knew about ices even if he had not yet mastered the techniques of making them. There was also an already long-established tradition of desserts, creams, blancmangers, jellies, chilled by contact with ice or snow. The transition from chilled to frozen had no doubt appeared to Audiger and his contemporaries to have been a logical step. Matters hadn't of course been so simple, and as we now know, the step in question had been an extraordinarily significant one. But Audiger and his colleagues did not appreciate that point. They did not know of the long years of painstaking research and experiment carried out by scientists in their efforts to find an artificial method of creating freezing conditions. Sometimes, indeed, I wonder how many of these scientists, or natural philosophers, shut in their laboratories, experimenting in the abstract, and with nothing so frivolous as frozen sherbets and creams in mind, were aware of the concurrent activities of those confectioners, *limonadiers* and other such specialists, who had made ices and decorative pyramids of frozen fruit and flowers and cast-ice goblets and bowls expected features of the festive tables of seventeenth-century Europe. It was because nobody marked the particular moment when frozen fruit, spice, and flower waters such as were described by Audiger and Massialot first appeared on those festive tables that, later, legends were invented concerning their origin.

The Limonadiers of Paris
and the Café Procope

The story of Francesco Procopio and his café is not really central to
the story of ices. I tell it here for two reasons, first to dispel some of
the myth which credits Procopio with the introduction of ices to
Paris, secondly because the café he founded was a true innovation,
and as one of those institutions which much later came to be known
as *café-glaciers*, probably did play its part in popularizing iced drinks
and frozen sherbets and creams in the French capital.

Although the precise place of Procopio's birth is unknown, we do
know from a document concerning his naturalization in 1684 that his
original nationality was Sicilian. We know also that the date of his
birth was 1650. This has been learned from the record of his marriage
at the church of Saint-Sulpice on 26 February 1675, at which time he
was aged twenty-five. He was then living with his mother, Domenica
Sémarque, widow of Onofrio Couteau or Coltelli, in the house of a
Sieur Petit, *maître pâtissier* in the rue de Tournon. The bride, Marguérite Crouïn, daughter of Louis Crouïn and Marguérite Feray,
dwelling *chez* M. Picard in the rue de Condé, was aged twenty.[1]

At the time of his marriage, Procopio was renting three shops or
stalls, with private rooms above, on the outskirts of the enormous
Foire Saint-Germain. Here, every year from 3 February until two
weeks before Easter, the duration of the annual Fair, Procopio pur-
veyed hot coffee, chocolate, tisanes, lemonades, and perhaps also
alcoholic beverages in the form of those fancy liqueurs and cordials so
popular in Paris at the period. That he also at this time sold ices, as
has been claimed, is highly unlikely, although the sweet syrups and

lemonades he provided may well have been glamorized with the name of sherbets or *sorbets*. It is unlikely that these would have been frozen in the winter months of February and March, and although he might have been able to obtain ice – by this time the public sale of ice was well established in Paris (see p. 43) – to cool the drinks he sold in his cramped little boutiques amid the frenetic hurly-burly of the Fair, it is improbable that he would have done so. If in many parts of Italy it was customary, as reported from time to time by travellers, to drink iced wine and lemonade all the year round,[2] such was not yet the case in France, where chilled and frozen fruit and waters were still a novelty at Court (see p. 92).

The date of Procopio's marriage, the fact that he was recorded in the Saint-Sulpice register as being a *marchand* or established merchant, and that shortly after the closing of that year's Foire Saint-Germain he opened a café in new premises in the rue de Tournon are significant landmarks in his story. In those days, to attain the status of a *marchand* – in Procopio's case a *marchand distillateur* and *limonadier* – indicated that the man concerned had been granted a Mastership in his professional Guild and was fully qualified to set up in trade on his own account. The Mastership implied that a practitioner had served his apprenticeship, that he had learned his trade from an established professional, that he had satisfied the examiners that he was properly conversant with and skilled in all aspects of his chosen business and that he might in his turn take on apprentices. In Procopio's case, however, things were rather different. He had started his working life as a street vendor of coffee and had drifted into service as a waiter at a stall or tent situated near the Porte Syndicale, leading to the Foire Saint-Germain, owned by an Armenian named Pascal who sold hot coffee, tea and chocolate. Pascal required Procopio and Grégoire, his fellow waiter, to dress in the Turkish fashion (at the time it was called Armenian) and to entertain the customers with songs and fairground patter. When the Fair was over for the year, Pascal took his waiters with him to the Quai de l'École (later the Quai du Louvre), where he opened a humble café. It was presumably during his period in Pascal's employment that Procopio learned something of the arts of distillation and the confection of syrups and aromatic waters, knowledge of which eventually qualified him, at any rate in his own eyes, to describe himself as, initially, a *marchand*, subsequently as a distiller, *limonadier* and *marchand de licoers*. As things turned out, it was not long before Procopio's Armenian employer decided to pack up his failing business and go off to try his fortune in London, leaving his waiters to fend for themselves. Grégoire moved to a café in the rue de Bussy and eventually acquired it, but Procopio, going into partnership with a man called Logerot, put his savings into the three stalls at the corner of the rue Mercière at the Foire Saint-Germain in which we find him operating at the time of his marriage in 1675.[3]

Francesco Procopio dei Coltelli had entered, therefore, with only minimal training and without undergoing tests, what was in effect a newly recognized profession, that of *limonadier* and *liquoriste*, before long to be officially incorporated and eventually amalgamated with another recently established or rather re-established Guild, that of the Distillers. It is clear that Procopio had taken advantage of that sale of Masterships in the Guild then in process of formation which had so infuriated Audiger (see pp. 77–99) and which had marked the beginning of that scandalous practice which was to become ever more widespread and more ruinous to France's industries as Louis XIV's reign progressed and as his military campaigns and wars, his building, his mistresses, and his court diversions grew ever more expensive to maintain.

How the young Procopio had obtained the finance to buy his Mastership and to open his new little café in the rue de Tournon we do not know. Possibly he had received a legacy, possibly his bride had helped with a dowry, possibly even his own savings from the business in the rue Mercière had been more substantial than one would expect from such a small-scale enterprise. However the money had been raised, Procopio had invested it wisely. Evidently he had a good business head, was hard-working, and as his later career was to prove, was gifted with flair and vision, plus that capacity for being in the right place at the right time which is so often the hallmark of the successful innovator.

If the young Procopio had had the foresight to buy his Mastership as a *marchand limonadier* well in advance of the incorporation of the Guild and thus anticipate the change for the better in the status of his elected profession that that incorporation would bring about, he did not have long to wait for it to become a reality. In March 1676, just a year after his marriage – Marguérite was about to give birth to their first child – the Guild of *limonadiers* and *marchands d'eau-de-vie* was formally constituted. Two months later, in May 1676, the new Guild was joined by another body, that of the Distillers. The whole Guild at the time consisted of 250 men who had bought their Masterships on the understanding that in future no practitioner would be accepted as master until he had served his three-year apprenticeship. By this means the right to take on apprentices, which was one of the main financial attractions of a Mastership, preserved its validity.

For the next twenty-eight years the Guild of *limonadiers*, distillers and *marchands d'eau-de-vie* seems to have flourished, in spite of frequent complaints of harassment by the inevitable assize officers and tax gatherers, and disputes with rival Guilds such as those of the Apothecaries and the Confectioners. The list of commodities the members of the Guild were permitted to make and/or retail makes interesting reading. Alfred Franklin, head administrator of the Bibliothèque Mazarine in the early years of this century, quoted the following in his *Dictionnaire Historique des Arts, Métiers et Professions exercées dans Paris depuis le treizième siècle* (1905) under the heading *Limonadiers*: Spanish wines, Muscat wines, wines of Saint Laurens. (The wine of Saint-Laurent-du-Var in Provence was celebrated at this period. Madame de Sévigné alludes to it frequently, and in the most glowing of terms. A couple of decades after the granting of the *limonadiers'* charter the famous English physician Martin Lister, visiting Paris in 1698, thought that 'the Red St Lauran was the most delicious Wine I ever tasted in my life'.[4] The Saint-Laurent wines were made with half sun-dried grapes, like the Roman *Vinum passum*, Lister said, but the grapes were dried in bunches on the vines, not after picking as with ordinary raisins.) Wines of La Ciotat in Provence, made in the same way as those of Saint-Laurent, were also on the list, as were wines of Malmsey, presumably wines made from the malmsey or malvasia grape, at the time grown in Greece, Italy, Spain, Crete and also by the Portuguese in Madeira, rather than the daunting concoction of honey and *eau-de-vie*, hops and dregs of beer called Malvoisie by Olivier de Serres and

described in detail in his *Théâtre d'Agriculture* (1600).[5] Liqueur wines –
very sweet new wines still uncleared from the must – *rossoli* and *populo*
(two much prized Italian compound liqueurs; in the 1660s the finest
were made at Turin, capital of the duchy of Savoy), spirits of wine,
lemonades ambered and perfumed, and *eaux de gelées*, could all be
made and/or sold by the *limonadiers*. Those *eaux de gelées* were not, I
think, as some have believed, some kind of frozen confection, but
syrup-like jelly conserves made from the water in which fruit had
been cooked for solid marmalades and pastes, strained off and boiled
with sugar. The whole process is described by Massialot in *Le Cuisinier
Roial et Bourgeois* (1698 edition). These jellies, which can have had
very little flavour of the fruit, may well have been used to mix with
sherbet-style drinks, possibly even in preparations for frozen *neiges*,
but that is conjecture. Next come *glaces de fruits et de fleurs*, taken by
Franklin and others to be fruit and flower ices, although in the context
glaces could equally well have meant sugar-iced or glazed fruit and
flowers. But let us give the ices the benefit of the doubt, at the same
time bearing in mind that in Richelet's *Dictionnaire François* of 1680
there is as yet no entry for *glaces* in the sense of confectionery ices,
which appear only under *nege* (Richelet's spelling), while *eau glacée*
under *glace adj.* could mean just that, frozen water, or just possibly a
frozen sweet water such as *eau de coriandre* and the *limonade* described
by Audiger in *La Maison Réglée* of 1692 as being specially made for
freezing with a double allowance of fruit juice, flower or spice essence,
and sugar. When frozen these were called collectively *eaux glacées*, and
were among the delicacies Audiger claimed he had several times served
at fêtes and collations given both for and by the royal family during
the 1660s, 1670s, and 1680s (see pp. 85–97).

The definition of *glace*, or rather the only one of its many meanings
which concerns us here, is one which leaves little room for confusion.
It is, Richelet says, 'a confectioners' term for cooked or powdered
sugar mixed with a little egg white to put on fruit', thus *une belle glace
de confitures, une glace de confitures, une glace de cerises*, in other words an
icing or frosting which gave its name to the fruit or preserve so frosted.
(*Confitures* did not mean jams in the modern sense, but all those fruits,
flowers, roots, and so on which were preserved in syrup and eaten as

liquid conserves but also often later made into dry conserves by extracting the fruit from the syrup, the fruit being dried slowly in an *étuve* or drying stove. John Evelyn's rendering of *confitures* was 'suggar plums', to which he likened the ice formations he saw in the natural cave called La Goutière in France in June 1644.)[6]

Here I should add that although Richelet did not list a further culinary complication, the term *glace* was also commonly used by the pastrycooks (as distinct from the confectioners) of the late seventeenth century to denote an icing or glaze for cakes and pastries much as it is still used today. Massialot's recipe for *sultanes*, sugar biscuits or wafers powdered with sugar and baked on papers, with heat above and below, provides a good example of pastrycooks' usage of the term *glace*. When baked and well glazed, the wafers are rolled into cornets, the glazed surface outwards: *que la glace reste en dehors* is Massialot's direction.[7] That *glace* could not, in the context, mean ice-cream is elementary enough, yet I have seen it rendered as such.

In later times *une glace* also came to mean, as it still does, the glaze formed by the reduction of a fruit syrup to coating consistency, but in that sense the term does not seem to have been seventeenth-century usage, and we have, heaven knows, enough potential traps without it. Certainly enough to make one give pause before jumping to conclusions about the *limonadiers' glaces de fruits et de fleurs*.

After the *glaces*, whatever they may or may not have been, come *sorbecs*, meaning sherbet drinks. The word *sorbet*, alternatively *sorbec*, attained dictionary status in 1680, in Richelet, as *une sorte de boisson qui nous vient du Levant*, a kind of beverage which comes from the Levant. Audiger says that his extra-sweet aromatic waters when scented with musk and/or amber become *Sorbec de Levant* (see p. 102),[8] but Antoine Furetière in his *Dictionnaire Universel*, 1727 edition (first published 1690), talks of a solid and much-esteemed *sorbet* from Egypt, and cites *une boîte de sorbet* and *un pot de sorbet* as examples.

After the sherbets on the list of commodities the *limonadiers* were permitted to trade in came coffee, followed by cherries, walnuts and other *fruits confits à l'eau-de-vie*. Sugared almonds, coriander seeds, aniseeds, and all the sugar-coated comfits known collectively as *dragées* could be sold in retail quantity only. The right to make them belonged to the confectioners. While those considered to have medicinal properties could also be made by the apothecaries, the *limonadiers* were not permitted to poach on rival trades, although they and the distillers were often enough accused of doing so. Thus, with time, concessions by the disputing parties, and the frequent modification of the statutes governing the overlapping Guilds, the commodities and products each were permitted to make and/or sell became less sharply defined.

Francesco Procopio and his wife, who in the twelve years from 1676 to 1688 bore eight children, remained at the rue de Tournon premises for ten years, moving only in 1686 to that site in the rue des Fossés-Saint-Germain with which his name was henceforward to be associated. It is this move to the rue des Fossés-Saint-Germain which links Francesco so closely to that earlier Procopio whose activities as manager or owner of a bath establishment on this very site a century earlier I have touched on on p. 45. It would indeed be too extravagant a coincidence if the younger Procopio's move to those premises had been a chance one, and I think that we must suppose that he had inherited or otherwise come by the lease of the premises (later he bought them) from a relation who had all along been running some business there, a point which adds some support to the theory that Francesco himself, so far from having arrived in Paris from Palermo or Messina to seek his fortune, had very possibly been brought there at an early age and educated in France. An interesting crumb of evidence testifying to the likelihood of a French education is produced by Auguste Jal, compiler of a *Dictionnaire Critique de Biographie et d'Histoire* (1867), who asserts that he had seen no fewer than nine examples of Procopio's signature, that his handwriting was undoubtedly French, and that if not born in France, he had at any rate spent his boyhood there. The point is not one very important to his story, but does seem to indicate that Procopio's family were already firmly established Parisians by the time he married and settled into the rue de Tournon premises. Jean Moura and Paul Louvet, authors of *Le Café Procope*, published in the Bibliothèque d'Histoire Parisienne series by Perrin et Cie in 1929, are of the opinion that a member of the Coltelli family was still running the ancestral bath establishment in the rue des Fossés-Saint-Germain and, perhaps foreseeing the imminent demolition of the neighbouring Jeu de Paume, from which he derived the customers who were now the mainstay of his business, made overtures to his relation the coffee merchant of the rue de Tournon and eventually passed on the lease of the establishment in the rue des Fossés-Saint-Germain on terms advantageous to Francesco. The premises were large. Out of three houses Procopio kept two, emptied them of the old bath apparatus and trappings, redecorated and refurnished them, and, reserving a part of them as living quarters for his now large family, reopened the former Holy Shroud of Turin as a café.

In those early days, when Paris was a good deal behind London in the number and popularity of such establishments, the cafés of the French capital were still dark, cramped, cavernous little boutiques, more like crowded apothecary shops in which it so happened that you could get a dish of hot coffee or chocolate or a tisane as well as buying drugs and simples, sugar and spices than those centres for gossip and exchange of news in reasonably spacious surroundings into which the London coffee houses had developed. (But in London many of the old coffee houses had been destroyed in the Great Fire of 1666 and new ones had sprung up.) Procopio was to change the Paris café out of all recognition. According, at any rate, to tradition – and the story at this stage does seem to me to owe more to tradition than to hard fact – it was Procopio's revolutionary idea to decorate the walls of his renovated establishment with fine large mirrors, to hang crystal chandeliers from the ceiling, to provide marble tables at which customers could sit in relative comfort to enjoy their coffee and chocolate, their sweetmeats, their sticky, scented fruit syrups, and in the summer, those famous frozen sherbets and *neiges*.

At this point in the story, the authors – or that one responsible for the actual writing and the padding, as opposed to the hard research, contained mainly in the footnotes of *Le Café Procope* – digress into fantasy, some of it on the overheated side. We are to envisage Procopio at work in a kind of alchemist's laboratory, surrounded by bubbling alembics and rumbling furnaces, shelves of stoneware jars, bottles of essences and cordials, marble mortars and pestles. He is measuring this, adding a drop or two of that, stirring up a fruit syrup, tasting a medicinal mixture and – here things begin to look decidedly fishy –

checking his thermometer, an historical anomaly which reveals the whole vision as having been conjured up from a source much post-Procopio and relevant only to a quite different aspect of his story. To be specific, that source turns out to be a work by a certain master-distiller named Dubuisson whose *L'Art du Distillateur* was published in 1779, nearly a century after the opening of the café Procope, an event which in turn had taken place some forty years prior to Réaumur's successful establishment of this spirit thermometer in 1724. It was an aid which would have solved many of the problems confronting Procopio and his contemporary fellow distillers and *limonadiers*, but one which quite certainly they did not possess. It is true that thermometers were not, in Procopio's day, unknown to scientists. As early as 1597 Galileo had made an attempt at producing one. Robert Boyle and Robert Hook of the Royal Society had both made their own in the 1660s. Ferdinand II, Grand Duke of Tuscany, who died in 1670, had all manner of experimental thermometers and barometers; the gentlemen of the Accademia del Cimento in Florence also used one at the same period, and members of the French Académie Royale des Sciences were much preoccupied with thermometers early in the eighteenth century, but it was not until 1714 that a German scientist called Daniel Fahrenheit was able to produce an accurate, mercury-based version, to be followed ten years later by Réaumur with his spirit variation. At the earliest, then, it could not have been before the end of the 1720s and was probably considerably later that thermometers would have been available to distillers, brewers, *limonadiers*, and other such operators. Dubuisson in his book specifically refers to his Réaumur thermometer.[9] To suggest that Procopio also used one was the kind of anomaly on which legends take root and flourish.

Before returning to the story of the café Procope, or at least to what are the known facts in its early history, it seems relevant to note that wherever he was born and brought up, Procopio must surely have been well esteemed and well established among the Italian community of Paris some while before he became known as proprietor of the café which was to bear his name. Some of the factual information given in footnotes in *Le Café Procope* reveals that at the baptisms of at least three of his children, Elisabeth in 1676, Marie Marguérite in 1678, and –

after the move from the rue de Tournon – in 1688, Marie Anne, the chief godparents were Italians of some social standing. In Elisabeth's case Angelo Maria Riva, described as an Italian gentleman, held the infant at the font, Don Jean Baptiste Romano, gentleman of Messina, stood sponsor to Marie Marguérite, and Marie Anne was held by Don Cristoforo Papi, Duke of Pratoamene.[10] Procopio had certainly maintained happy relations with his Italian compatriots. That some time after 1702, when his café was still known as 'the boutique at the sign of the Holy Shroud of Turin',[11] he abbreviated and naturalized his name, dropping the Coltelli suffix (his children retained it) and calling himself simply François Procope and his now successful *boutique* the café Procope, seems to indicate that he had also to a great extent made himself at home in the life and the business world of the capital. He had already in a sense entered its history.

In 1689 the company of actors known as the King's Comedians and of which Molière had been the guiding light, chief dramatist and star attraction (he had died in 1673) had been homeless and theatreless for two years. Religious harassment and hostility had driven them first from their premises in the rue Mazarine and subsequently from some half-dozen others in which they had attempted to settle, at each attempt frustrated by the veto of local parish priests. At last, early in 1689, the company came to roost in what was now the rue Neuve-des-Fossés-Saint-Germain-des-Prés. Buying the old Jeu de Paume, that very place which had once been so useful a source of customers for the Holy Shroud of Turin, plus an adjoining private dwelling house, the King's Comedians demolished the two and commissioned a fine new theatre. Designed by François d'Orbay, the theatre opened its doors on 18 April 1689 to a packed and expectant house. (Here the authors of *Le Café Procope* launch into a couple of pages of eye-witness-style commentary as they describe the scene. Carriages clatter up to the doors of the theatre, beplumed hats are doffed, jewels glitter, candles flicker, the crowds jostle and so on. I will try to confine myself to a few bare facts.) The opening plays were, as was customary, a tragedy, *Phèdre*, and a comedy, *Le Médecin Malgré Lui*. The star was

Marie Desmares, formerly Racine's mistress and famous under her stage name of La Champmeslé.

Procopio's move to Saint-Germain-des-Prés and the new furnishings of his café were paying off in a way even the boldest of entrepreneurs could hardly have foreseen. Across the street in the new theatre he rented space for a *loge de la limonade*, a refreshment stall, and in it installed a young woman happily known as *la distributrice de douces liqueurs*, a sort of French Nell Gwynne selling sweet drinks instead of oranges. In summer the theatre refreshments included cherry, red-currant, and strawberry waters, in winter spirituous liqueurs and those sweet wines which were part of the stock-in-trade of all the *limonadiers*. Procopio's café, now busy from morning until late into the night, came to be regarded as an extension of the foyer of the theatre. Poets and dramatists, actors and writers, rubbed shoulders with clergy, lawyers and men of business, military officers and government officials. It all sounds very picturesque. Ladies of quality would arrive in their carriages, drink their hot chocolate or coffee from silver or porcelain drinking bowls filled by Procopio's serving boys – dressed in the Turkish-style costumes still statutory in French cafés – and drive off without actually setting foot inside the premises.[12] The future of Procopio, his family, and his café was assured. The café as an institution had entered Parisian literary, political, and social life. Imitators and rivals proliferated. Grégoire, Procopio's one-time fellow waiter, having acquired a café near the old theatre in the rue Mazarine, now followed it to Saint-Germain-des-Prés and opened in the same street as Procopio.

In 1696, only seven years after the triumphant opening night of the new theatre, Marguérite Procopio, alas, died, whether in giving birth to yet another infant history does not relate. But Procopio, decidedly not afflicted with the impotence or at any rate sterility held at that time to be the scourge of coffee drinkers, married again within the year, and four more children were born of his second marriage, to Anne-Françoise Garnier, daughter of a Sieur de Vaulier. The youngest of those children was Claude, born in 1704.

It remains to record a few dates in the Procopio story, dates which have their small importance in the dispelling of the confusion created, as will presently emerge, by that same Dubuisson whose activities as a distiller were erroneously ascribed to Procopio by the authors of *Le Café Procope*. In 1716, then, after running his café for thirty years, Francesco Procopio handed over the business to his second son, Alexandre, born in 1686. (The elder son, Michel, a hunchback, at first destined for the church, made himself a distinguished career as a physician and surgeon.) Francesco, however, appears to have kept for his retirement a secondary business in the shape of a café within the annual Foire Saint-Germain. This he had apparently created by making three stalls into one large room – had he perhaps never relinquished his interest in those early boutiques he had rented? – redecorating and furnishing it in an elegant contemporary style. Procopio's second café was also successful and had become a haunt of fashionable visitors to the Fair, or so it was reported by the *Bulletin de la Société Historique du VI arrondissement* for July 1901, and certainly the King, accompanied by the Prince de Condé or his son the Duc d'Enghien, made a point of visiting the Fair at least once every year,[13] so a smart café there would certainly have made business sense to a man of Procopio's initiative. By this time coffee and cafés had become enormously popular in Paris. Already in 1698 Dr Martin Lister, staying in Paris for six months, had reported of the Fair that there were 'Many shops of Confections where the ladies are commodiously treated, and also coffee-shops, where that and all sorts of strong Liquors are to be sold' and among the permanent institutions of the city he noted 'very many publick coffee-houses, where Tea also and Chocolate may be had, and all the Strongwaters and Wine above mentioned'.[14] The Strongwaters and Wines included 'ratafias which is a sort of Cherry Brandy made with Peach and Apricock Stones, highly piquant, and of a most agreeable flavour' and a muscat wine distilled with orange peel and orange flowers which, Lister says, was made in Provence and called *Vatée*, a name I have failed to identify with any recorded liqueur (it is also mentioned by Le Grand d'Aussy, in the work referred to on p. 42). A fennel-flavoured water called *Fenouillet*, made on the Île de Ré, was another of the popular tipples – it was like our aniseed water, Lister says. All this drinking of 'Strongwaters' and sweet strong wines from Italy and Spain as well as products native to France was a new thing in Paris, at any rate according to Lister. They had been made fashionable, he said, by 'the gentry and nobility who had taken to them in an effort to relieve the tedium and the fatigue of the endless military campaigns of the present decades, and on their return home had introduced the habit into daily life', a point which helps to explain the tremendous popularity of the cafés where such drinks could be bought. Lister also complained that by drinking so much the French, particularly the women, had become 'fat and corpulent'. He was of the opinion that 'the daily drinking of coffee, tea and chocolate with sugar, as much in use in private houses in Paris as in London', was 'another cause of corpulence', in which he was surely much ahead of his time.

Altogether Procopio had been on to a fine thing when he bought his Mastership and set up as a *limonadier* in his first café. With the growing popularity of the strong wines and liqueurs noted by Lister, plus the rapid increase of coffee drinking and the extraordinary grip on Paris social life which the café as an institution so quickly exercised – by 1716 there were 300 in the capital, or so it is claimed – he had created a valuable business to hand on to his son. Alexandre appears to have made the most of it, adding the trade of *marchand d'épices*, spice seller or grocer, to his assets. To be in a position to buy spices for his liqueurs, aromatic waters and medicinal beverages would have been of some importance financially to Alexandre. As a *marchand d'épices* he was also permitted to sell sugar and a number of those commodities such as olive, walnut, and almond oils, sugars, soaps, Bayonne and Westphalia hams, which we should now expect to find at a good grocery store. One begins to wonder where all these goods were stocked and sold. The Procopios must have taken on extra premises.

By the 1720s literary figures of the stature of La Fontaine and Fontenelle were beginning to frequent the Procope. Later came Diderot d'Alembert, and that unrepentant coffee addict, Voltaire, although whether they were habitués to the extent later claimed – Voltaire's table was for generations preserved and exhibited on the premises almost as a holy relic – is to be doubted. What cannot be doubted is that the café Procope did frequently figure in the memoirs, the letters, the satires, the journals, of the eighteenth century. That it became a favourite meeting place of the revolutionaries of the 1790s is also well established. But did Robespierre really sit in the café devouring pyramids of oranges in the hope of improving his complexion, did General Bonaparte lurk there in threadbare overcoat and ill-fitting boots, struck off the active service list and looking for influential personages to buttonhole? The café Procope, at any rate as seen through the eyes of its historians, should surely be used as the background of a movie epic.

In those turbulent days of the 1790s the Procope was under the aegis of a man named Zoppi, the establishment itself often being referred to as *chez Zoppi*, or *le café Zoppi*. (Was Zoppi of Venetian origin? The name, from *zoppicante* or *zoppo*, a limping man, was also that of a nineteenth-century dynasty of hotel and tavern keepers still operating in Venice in the 1960s.) The Procope was now far removed from its origins. Alexandre had died in 1753 and was not followed by his son into the business, which passed into the hands of the distiller Dubuisson, who ran it until the 1770s, when he turned it over to a M. Cusin but himself retained the ownership of the premises, passing it on to his heirs, in whose hands it appears to have remained for a couple more generations.

It is now with Dubuisson himself and his book rather than with the fortunes of the café Procope that we are concerned. Published in 1779, *L'Art du Distillateur et marchand de liqueurs, considerées comme aliments médicamentaux* deals mainly with the subject announced in its self-explanatory title with special emphasis on the medicinal value of his various brews, but Dubuisson did also include useful material on the making and freezing of sherbets, ices, and creams, on the apparatus and implements required for the work, on the distinctions to be made between the different categories of *congélation*, on the making of coffee and chocolate, in short on all the skills necessary to a *limonadier* and distiller. In setting down his directions for the benefit of future aspirants to the trade Dubuisson was very naturally recording his own methods and recipes, not without some boasting as to the modern improvements he had himself evolved. If later generations of readers misused his work, thoughtlessly attributing it to a much earlier period to which it did not apply, it was scarcely his fault. But by the cavalier transposition of descriptions of techniques which were Dubuisson's own and which therefore belonged to the second half of the eighteenth century, to its very beginning and even further back, it was made by the authors of Le Café Procope to appear as though in Francesco Procopio's day the arts of distilling, liqueur-making and of the confection and freezing of ices were considerably more developed than was in fact the case. Misleading though that transposition may have been, and is, to anyone attempting to unravel the Procopio story, a statement actually made by Dubuisson himself has been the cause of even greater confusion. 'It is believed,' he wrote, 'that it was about the years 1655 or 1660 that M. Procope Couteaux, native of Florence, introduced the custom of eating ices in the capital of France. All that we can be sure of is that this artiste was the most celebrated distiller and liqueur merchant in the Paris of his time, and that it is principally to him that we owe the enrichment at that time of the repertoire of refreshing liqueurs.'[15]

It is surely rather curious that Dubuisson, flourishing as he did so close in time to Francesco Procopio, having bought the café from his son, or that son's heirs, and knowing, as he can scarcely have failed to know, at least one member, if no more, of the Procopio family, did not inquire of any of them – some were certainly living at the time he wrote his book – at what date the café's founder had first operated as a professional limonadier and café owner. That date, as also the date of Procopio's marriage and hence that also of his birth, was obviously lost to subsequent generations (Lefeuve, the historian of Paris streets and houses, claims that the family was wiped out in the Terror[16]), but that Dubuisson should simply hazard two dates between which Procopio is supposed to have introduced ices to the French capital is to say the least unfortunate. That Procopio was a bright and enterprising young man we have seen. That he was running a business and selling ices at the age of five or at most ten years old is asking us to believe rather too much. We, of course, have the benefit of information and of indisputable dates, revealed by diligent nineteenth-century research in the Saint-Sulpice archives, which Dubuisson did not have, but it is Dubuisson's dates, coming as they did from a source so close to

Procopio's own time, which, through repetition by Le Grand d'Aussy and on his authority by countless others, have been and still are commonly believed. Granted, the dates are only a matter of some twenty-five years out, and twenty-five years is a short time compared with the 150 plus to be allowed in the case of the Catherine de Medici myth. Perhaps instead of complaining about Dubuisson's inaccuracy we should accept his vagueness as a point indicating that by the 1770s Procopio had already entered the realm of Parisian legend, that that mysterious process which fuses fiction and actuality and crystallizes the mixture into what we call tradition was already at work on the origins of the French ice-cream trade and Procopio's involvement in it.

Knowing, as we now know, that Dubuisson's assertion that Procopio was a native of Florence was quite without foundation in fact, I do still wonder if he did not just possibly get his dates right, but attach the wrong events to them. In view of the historian Auguste Jal's opinion, quoted on p. 117, that Procopio's French handwriting presupposed an education in France, it is after all possible that it was in 1655, at the age of five, that the boy was brought to France, that Dubuisson had been told this, and after running the café for a quarter of a century had understandably got dates and events blurred and muddled in his head and did not trouble to check the accuracy of his account. It would be agreeable to give Dubuisson the benefit of the doubt, because so far as I can see the story crediting Procopio with the introduction of ices to the paying public of Paris came into being following the publication of his book in 1779 and still rests solely upon his testimony, repeated only three years later by Le Grand d'Aussy in his *Histoire de la Vie Privée des Français*[17] (1782) and subsequently in varying forms, some of them on the fanciful side, by numerous historians of Paris and Parisian life, of French modes and manners, of Paris cafés, of French literary life during the eighteenth century, of gastronomy through the ages, of the ice-cream trade, of the Comédie Française. In the course of two centuries since the appearance of Dubuisson's book the stories have grown ever more remote from the original and been ever more fantasized. One way and another it seemed time to re-examine the story as it was first known and again in the light of research carried out long after Dubuisson's book was published. That I have been able, in a limited degree, to sort out the fantasy from the known facts is largely due to the authors of *Le Café Procope*, the work many times cited in this chapter. With its two authors so plainly at variance with each other, one doing the sober research and inserting footnotes quite often in open correction or contradiction of his collaborator, the latter busily stirring up the narrative and dishing out the popular *ragoût*, the dividing line between fiction and fact has never been more clearly demonstrated.

To conclude the story of the café Procope, very briefly, there is still a café with the same name, on the same site in the same street, now called rue de l'Ancienne-Comédie. A plaque on the wall informs the passer-by that here Procopio dei Coltelli founded in 1686 the oldest café in the world and the most celebrated centre of literary and philosophical life in the eighteenth and nineteenth centuries. It was frequented, so the plaque proclaims, 'by La Fontaine, Voltaire, the Encyclopédistes, Benjamin Franklin, Danton, Marat, Robespierre, Napoléon Bonaparte, Balzac, Victor Hugo, Gambetta, Verlaine et Anatole France'.

The impression conveyed by that plaque, of a café with an existence unbroken since 1686, is a trifle misleading. The original café did indeed remain open for 186 years, in itself a respectable enough record, but in 1872, soon after the collapse of the Second Empire, the old Procope closed its doors as a public café. The property was acquired by a lady called Baronne Thénard, who appears to have been enlightened enough to have leased it at a nominal rate on condition that the lessee, Théo Bellefonds, undertook to preserve the original character of the café. Complying with his landlady's conditions, Bellefonds trans-formed the café into an artists' club, and founded a journal entitled *Le Procope* which appeared spasmodically and ran into all of nine issues. Literary and artistic societies held their dinners and gave enter-tainments on the premises (it was during this period that Verlaine, befriended by Théo Bellefonds, was from time to time sighted in the former café), and students of the École des Arts Décoratifs held their first fancy-dress ball there, ending it in traditional student style with a memorably wild and drunken carouse.

For a brief period following the demise of the Procope as a private literary and artistic club, the premises became a modest restaurant, frequented by the students and white-collar workers of the quarter, and in the 1920s once more a café. For a time the newly re-opened café was called Au Grand Soleil, an indignity remedied when eventually a new proprietor, more alive than his predecessor to the publicity value of the cafe's legendary associations, restored its founder's name.

Neiges, Sorbets,
Glaces, Fromages

We have seen how Dubuisson confused the dates of Francesco Procopio's activities in Paris and started two centuries of mythologizing
about the café Procope and its owner's innovations. But for Le Grand
d'Aussy's *Histoire de la Vie Privée des Français* of 1782, and a century
after him through Alfred Franklin and his series of works of almost
identical title,* Dubuisson's *L'Art du Distillateur* would scarcely now
be known even by name. It is all the same a useful study for anyone
delving into the history of French ices and of their composition and
nomenclature in the eighteenth century. Dubuisson, after all, ran the
café Procope for a quarter of a century or more, and his son ran
another café, the Caveau in the Palais Royal, so from his work there
is much of interest to be learned about Parisian ices and what they
were like in the period between, say, 1750 and 1780.

Dubuisson's book, it has to be said, makes uneasy reading. His style
is labyrinthine, his mind a jumble of contradictions and obsessions. In
the first of its two volumes well over 100 pages are devoted to criticism,
refutation and demolition of the work of a contemporary referred to
throughout as M. Machy, with no hint as to the title of the offending
work. This author turns out to be Jacques François Demachy or De
Machy, a master apothecary, whose *L'Art du Distillateur Liquoriste*
appeared in 1775, four years before Dubuisson's own book. Details of
Dubuisson's demolition attempt are endlessly tedious, and only a
minor part of it is concerned with the preparation and freezing of ices.

---

* The series title is *La Vie Privée d'Autrefois*.

On that subject his main points of contention are the proportions of sugar to fruit juices, and the method of administering the sugar. Demachy directed that it should be first cooked to a syrup, while Dubuisson held that this was a needless complication. (Demachy's practice was perfectly sound. It is still today considered the more advisable one.) As for the rights and wrongs of the proportions and the methods, they seem to me to be so involved as to defy analysis. The true crux of the matter was that Demachy had trespassed on Dubuisson's professional territory, and in the course of exposing him to ridicule the latter worked himself into a rage verging on paranoia.

Criticizing the composition of a lemonade destined by Demachy for freezing, Dubuisson remarks that if only the former had not been ignorant of the fact that *liqueurs* – meaning those preparations made especially for freezing, and not to be confused with spirituous *liqueurs* – had always been called *sorbets*, the nomenclature would perhaps have aroused his curiosity, and he would have discovered not only the etymology of the word, but that the composition of those *sorbets* is quite different from that of ordinary refreshing beverages, or, to use the then professional term, *liqueurs rafraîchissantes*. Now, while accepting the distinction to be made between a rather thin lemonade and a thick syrupy sherbet and the difference in the quality of the ices the two would make when frozen, it cannot for one moment be accepted that the preparations intended for making ices had 'always' been called *sorbets*. In fairness, however, to Dubuisson's intention, it must be said that his phrasing is constructed in so confusing a manner that his statement may not have been quite so preposterous as it appeared. I think what he was attempting to explain, in his muddled way, was that ever since ices had been known the basic preparations for them had been called *sorbets*. Elsewhere he tries again to say that when *sorbets* are frozen they become *glaces*, and this makes a little more sense. Even so, the statement is still incorrect. It was not that the term was unknown. Spelt *sorbec*, it had been appearing in French travel chronicles at least since the mid sixteenth century when Pierre Belon published his celebrated *Les Observations de Plusieurs Singularitez* ... in 1553.

By the 1660s it had reached French dictionaries. There was that curious recipe for *sorbec d'Alexandrie* which had appeared in *Le Maistre d'Hotel* of 1661, imports of *sorbec* in paste or powder form were arriving from the Levant, and in 1723 Jacques Savary des Bruslons recorded in the first volume of his *Dictionnaire Universel de Commerce* that the duty charged at that time was as much as 20 francs per pound (see pp. 153–158). Among confectioners and *glaciers*, however, the word was not in ordinary usage, or at least not as applied to any preparation used as a basis for ices.

Dubuisson's study of those works of his contemporaries and predecessors relevant to his subject appears to have been remarkably sketchy, at any rate as far as the preparation and freezing of ices was concerned. For a start he made no mention in his treatise of three important works of relatively recent date and, although not written by professional *limonadiers*, of the highest relevance to his own dissertations on the art of the *glacier*. First of these was *La Science du Maître d'Hôtel Confiseur*, published anonymously in 1750 but known to have been the work of Menon, author of the enormously successful *La*

Cherubs confecting ice cream in the frontispiece of Emy's *L'Art de Bien Faire les Glaces*, 1768.

Cuisinière Bourgeoise and written as a sequel to his *La Science du Maître d'Hôtel Cuisinier* of 1749. The second was Gilliers's *Le Cannaméliste*, published in 1751 and reprinted in 1768, and the third Emy's *L'Art de Bien Faire les Glaces d'Office*, which appeared in that same year. From even a superficial study of those three very professional works Dubuisson could have discovered that the term *sorbet* was simply not at the time common usage among professionals and denoted neither ices nor the preparations used for them. To Menon, whose *Maître d'Hôtel Confiseur* had, incidentally, been reprinted in 1760, 1768, and 1777, water-ices were *glaces* or *liqueurs glacées*, or, if frozen in the individual fruit moulds so fashionable at the time, *fruits glacés*. Simple cream ices were either *glacés à la crème* or *mousses à la crème*, the latter being frozen in individual silver or glass goblets in compartmented ice *caves* or chests fitting inside a second case packed with ice and salt. A deeply recessed cover was filled with the same mixture. Then there were *fromages glacés à la crème*, custard ices frozen in moulds fashioned to resemble different cheeses, round, log-shaped, in wedges like pieces of Parmesan, and at this period, more fanciful shapes such as stars, hearts and fluted pyramids. A further category were the ices called *glaces en beurre*. These were enormously rich and thick custards made with 18 to 20 eggyolks to the (32 oz) pint of cream and $\frac{1}{2}$ lb of sugar. They could be frozen in *fromage* moulds or spooned straight from the freezing pot on to plates 'in the same fashion as fresh butter, with some iced water'.

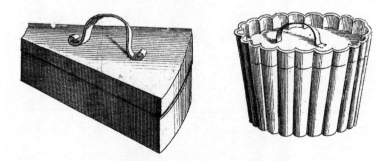

Two moulds for ices from *Le Cannameliste français*, 1751, by Gilliers.

Yet another variety at this time was the *biscuit de glace,* composed of cream thickened with sponge cake crumbs dried in the *étuve* or drying stove. Frozen in the usual way, the composition was transferred either to the paper cases in which the cakes had been baked, or into rectangular tin cake moulds. They were maintained in the frozen state on shelves fitted in a chest or a drum-shaped container with ice above and below. Menon was enthusiastic about his biscuit ices. They were agreeable in presentation, he said, and made excellent eating.

Turning to Gilliers, who was confectioner to ex-King Stanislas of Poland, Duke of Bar and Lorraine, and father-in-law of Louis XV, the reigning King of France, we again search in vain for any occurrence of the term *sorbet.* In his sumptuous and very comprehensive alphabetically arranged work, devoted entirely to the art of the confectioner, Gilliers gives many recipes for frozen fruit syrups, designated as *neiges* when they are scooped straight from the freezing pot into goblets, and as *fruits glacés* when transferred to the hinged lead moulds of the period. Like Menon, Gilliers refers to his preparations for water-ices as *liqueurs.* He is very definite on this point. 'Liqueur is the name given to all liquid compositions made for ices' is his terse entry under that term. As with Menon, his custard ices are *fromages glacés,* composed generally

Freezing tub from Gilliers'
Le Cannameliste français, 1751.

of 6 egg-yolks to the (32 oz) pint of cream, with sugar to taste. They are first frozen in the ordinary freezing pot then transferred to the appropriate moulds and returned to the freezing tub for an hour. Gilliers's definition of a mousse is 'a sweet cream whipped to a froth, flavoured to taste, and frozen'. The goblets in which they were frozen and served were appropriate to a royal household, of a generous size, and made of fine crystal or glass.

The third and, in Dubuisson's time, most recent publication relevant to his own work, was Emy's specialized and exceptionally well-documented little book on ices. Once again, there is no mention of a *sorbet*. Fruit ices are *glaces*, made on a basis of previously prepared syrups. Emy calls these *liquides, liqueurs rafraîchissantes* and *liqueurs fraîches*, as distinct from *liqueurs spiritueuses*. A *glace moulée* is the same thing as a *fruit glacé*. If a frozen fruit composition is refrozen in a *fromage* mould it becomes a *fromage de fraises, d'ananas, d'oranges* and so on. Cream ices are *glaces de crème, aux pistaches, aux amandes*, with cinnamon, with cloves, with vanilla, with walnuts. He has a rye bread cream ice and even a truffle cream ice. These are all made on a basis of 1 (32 oz) pint of cream to 4 egg-yolks and $\frac{1}{4}$ lb of sugar – an unusually low proportion for the time. When refrozen in *fromage*, tablet, *biscuit*, or *cannelon*

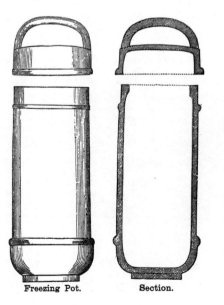

Freezing Pot.   Section.

Freezing pot and section from Biertumpfel's *How to Make Ices, c.* 1890. He advises that they should be made of the very best pewter. Although he describes the method of freezing using such pots as primitive, compared with the newly invented machines, such devices remained in common use until the beginning of this century.

moulds the compositions become, once again, *fromages glacés*. A *fromage aux épingles*, a self-explanatory nomenclature, is known alternatively as *à l'anglaise*. It is an uncooked cream or fruit composition, made not too sweet, frozen directly in a *fromage* mould and left in the ice and salt mixture for 3 to 4 hours without being worked at all. It is therefore full of little ice splinters or *épingles*, the term in use by the *glaciers* of the period.

Now an interesting point about the total exclusion of the nomenclature *sorbet* from all three of the works briefly summarized above is that, equally, the three authors all use the word *sarbotière*, nearly always at that time spelt with an *a*, and sometimes, as by Menon, written *salbotière*, to denote the vessel in which the prepared liquids, *liqueurs fraîches*, creams and so on were set to freeze. So for a long time the *sorbetière*, or sherbet-container, and the *sorbet* or sherbet, appear to have lived, as it were, separate linguistic lives. It was Dubuisson's uncalled for sarcasm at Demachy's expense which brought home to me the curious anomaly in the French usage of the day. Possibly the term *sorbet* as applied to the preparations made especially for freezing was the professional *limonadier's* usage, unfamiliar to the confectioners and *glaciers* in private service and royal households, and the 1770s must have been the time when it was replacing the former *neige, eau glacée* and the rest. But such changes of usage don't occur overnight, *neige* was still a common term, and the scorn heaped on Demachy by Dubuisson seems to have been a trivial criticism which he attempted to turn into a major issue.[1] That he may have had a good reason to regard the term *sorbet* as one consecrated by the tradition of his trade will be touched on later in this chapter. As far as the etymology of the word is concerned, I don't think that Dubuisson can have made much of an investigation into it. He never refers to the matter again.

To turn to a positive aspect of Dubuisson's work, one of his more informative chapters deals with the composition of ices, and is headed *Des Différends Sorbets de Crème et des Fromages Glacés*. The author divides these into egg-thickened creams and fruit juice *sorbets*. The latter are still very much on the sweet side, but the creams are almost modern in composition, most of them made in the proportion of 6 egg-yolks to 2 (32 oz) pints of double cream plus flavourings and only

10 oz of sugar – much the same as that given by Emy. This unusually low sugar content is in contrast with a lemon *sorbet* in which $1\frac{1}{2}$ lb of sugar are diluted with only 1 (32 oz) pint of water plus the juice of 9 large or 11 average-sized Italian lemons.[2] Such a high proportion of sugar would make for great difficulty in the freezing, and at best his water-ices would have been very cloying, but that may have been the taste of the customers who frequented his café. Menon, whose proportions of sugar were much more restrained, made the point that those basic compositions destined to be frozen, rather than simply iced and served in liquid form, required extra sugar and fruit juice because the freezing so greatly diminished the strength of both.[3]

A claim of some interest made by Dubuisson is his assertion that he initiated the preparation and freezing of ices all the year round, asserting that until 1750 they had been made only in the summer. According to his own testimony, the reason Dubuisson started making them every day was that doctors had been prescribing ices for various maladies. This meant that in winter ices had to be made specially to order. Two incidences of the efficacy of ices as a medical cure back up Dubuisson's story. An old gentleman whose digestive functions were much weakened was ordered by his doctor to eat absolutely nothing after dinner with the exception of two cups of cream ices, and these were to constitute his supper. The diet restored the patient's digestive functions and he lived to a very advanced age. A celebrated doctor prescribed lemon ices as a remedy for a patient suffering from a violent quinsy, and having been informed that the treatment was successful, Dubuisson decided to keep those two kinds of ices always ready in his laboratory, no matter what the weather.[4] Times had changed dramatically since the days when the majority of doctors were condemning ice and iced drinks as a well-nigh deadly danger. Dubuisson even goes so far as to assert that all the cream ices and sorbets he gives in his book are medically beneficial, and that he has deliberately omitted any which are mere luxuries or showy novelties. Presumably he counted strawberry, raspberry, redcurrant, rose-hip and cherry *sorbets* among the unnecessary luxuries, since he gives no formal recipes for them, contenting himself with a comparison of his own and Demachy's methods of preparing them, plus a note to the effect that in order to preserve the brilliant colour of all those red fruit *sorbets* which are turned violet in colour by lengthy contact with pewter, they must be frozen in a silver *sorbetière*.[5]

As a matter of interest, the ices Dubuisson chose as having medicinal properties are – apart from the basic cream ice flavoured with orange blossoms preserved in syrup which was one of his two basic winter ices – a caramel cream ice which he calls *crème brulée* (Emy also had one), a pistachio cream ice, chocolate, vanilla, almond, cherry kernel, tea, and coffee cream ices. His *sorbets* are lemon, orange, *bigarade* orange, muscat grape, black coffee, rose, carnation, preserved orange blossom, peach, apricot and greengage. What determined his choice Dubuisson does not reveal, but evidently he did not go so far as the Italian doctor he mentions, Mazarini by name, who regarded cold beverages and frozen *sorbets* as being so necessary to the life and health of the Italian people that in years when there was a snow famine the incidence of contagious illnesses greatly increased. I don't think that Dubuisson can have known of another Italian physician at that time, Filippo Baldini, who wrote a whole treatise on *sorbetti*, published in Naples in 1775,[6] examining the medicinal properties of all the different varieties from cinnamon (one of the most beneficial, Baldini thought) to pineapple and strawberry, and including of course chocolate, coffee, and ices made from various different milks (see p. 161).

As more fully explained on p. 142, it is an interesting and curious point that it appears to have been only in Naples and southern Italy that at that time ices were commonly known as *sorbetti*, and the circumstance is so striking that it is tempting to speculate whether Dubuisson had not originally learned his trade from a Neapolitan, a Sicilian, or at least a master *limonadier*-distiller with Neapolitan and Sicilian traditions. Possibly he had been apprenticed to Alexandre Procope, Francesco's son, and hence had taken the *sorbet* nomenclature for granted.

One point that emerges clearly from Dubuisson's recipes, as also from those given by Menon, Gilliers, Emy and other authors of the mid eighteenth century, is that whatever their nomenclature the French sherbets of the time, sometimes frozen, sometimes merely iced, had grown far away from those Levantine and oriental beverages described by the travellers of the fifteenth and sixteenth centuries. By 1779 Dubuisson could remark with pride that only thirty years previously, taking his readers back to about 1740, 'ices were still in the cradle'. Rashly, he went on to say that in his opinion ices had now, in 1779, reached a peak of perfection which he did not think could be surpassed. But Dubuisson did not, so far as I can see, have anything very new to reveal either in the way of technique or in the composition of his ices other than decreeing, for cream ices, the addition of 3 egg-yolks to every (32 oz) pint of cream instead of only one as had hitherto been customary. To him this was an innovation, eliminating the old distinction between the relatively rich *fromages glacés* and plain *glaces*, but ten years previously Emy was advocating 4 yolks to every (32 oz) pint of cream for all his cream and custard ices. Dubuisson had also deluded himself into the belief that the formula he had established was an immutable one. He couldn't know that within the course of the next century those modest 3 egg-yolks to the (32 oz) pint were to be increased to 12 and even more,[7] only to be once again in our own day drastically cut down.

At one moment in Dubuisson's wandering narrative he promises some interesting information on the three contemporary principal Parisian artists in ice-making, and also a new style of ice box or cupboard for the conservation of large quantities of moulded ices. Alas, he is so overcome with scorn for Demachy's omission to consult those three artists – presumably Dubuisson himself was one of them – or to inspect their new ice *caves* or cupboards that he forgets to name the artists in question and fails to describe the new *caves*.[8] Thus it was that what might have been useful documentary evidence was over and over again submerged in Dubuisson's outbursts of rage, and when it did get through was to a large extent invalidated by unreliable evidence and unsubstantiated claims.

From the title page of the book we do, however, at least learn that it was sold *chez* M. Cusin at the café Dubuisson opposite the old Comédie Francaise (in other words the original café Procope), *chez* Dubuisson *fils* at the Caveau in the Palais Royal and at the author's house opposite the Imprimerie du Parlement in the rue Mignon. Perhaps we have there our three principal artists in the making of ices? Certainly the younger Dubuisson's café du Caveau was busy, fashionable and at that time one of the best known of five or six cafés in the Palais Royal. According to Le Grand d'Aussy's story it was at the Caveau, where the Duc de Chartres (elder son of the Duc d'Orléans) went now and again to eat an ice, that he was one day presented with a great novelty, a cream ice moulded to represent his coat of arms. The ice had a specially firm composition, with the consistency, flavour and colour of butter. Hence these new ices were known as *glaces au beurre.* They became fashionable, Le Grand d'Aussy says, about 1774, but he had not read Menon's *La Science du Maître d'Hôtel Confiseur* or he would have known they were current at least as early as 1750. Dubuisson *fils* is also credited by Le Grand d'Aussy with the introduction to Paris in 1779 of liqueur-flavoured ices.[9] But that again is a dubious claim. They may have been popularized by the café du Caveau, but Emy had published several such formulas in 1768, and it would be surprising indeed if they were novelties even at that time. As Le Grand d'Aussy says himself, no sooner had one *glacier* launched a new ice or *sorbet* than it was copied by everyone else in the capital, and every *limonadier* and all the confectioners in private service were vying with each other to invent new flavours and combinations of flavours. The *Encyclopédie Méthodique des Arts et Métiers* of 1781 lists eighty different varieties. The inventiveness of the *glaciers* of the late eighteenth century foreshadowed that of twentieth-century American firms such as Baskin Robbins, Dayville and Häagen Dazs.

In 1786, only seven years after the publication of the elder Du-buisson's book, the younger one sold his café du Caveau for the handsome sum of 90,000 *livres* (it continued to flourish for many years), while the oldest and most famous of the Palais Royal cafés, the Foy, changed hands eighteen years – and another world – later for 100,000 francs.[10] The Foy had an exceptional privilege, permission to serve refreshments in the gardens of the Palace, although not to set tables. Everything had to be balanced on chairs. Its good coffee, lemonades and ices were well known, and Foi or Foy, the café's founder, had been a contemporary of Francesco Procopio's, or so Dubuisson says, and one of only two other of the original *limonadiers* to serve ices. The third was called Lefèvre. Those three men, Dubuisson claims, had the monopoly of the sale of ices '*pendant un très-long espace de temps*'.[11] He had evidently never heard of Audiger, who had been obliged to establish his mastership as a *limonadier*-distiller when the guild was constituted in 1676, and who had set himself up in premises in the Palais Royal in 1680 or thereabouts. That Dubuisson was ignorant of Audiger's activities was only to be expected, but that early Gunter-figure, catering to the nobility and the royal family, must not be forgotten. His career as an independent *limonadier*-distiller was for at least twelve years concurrent with that of Francesco Procopio and with the activities of Foy and Lefèvre. Audiger operated on a quite considerable scale, and without doubt there were other such freelance professionals. Technically, of course, Audiger's ices and sherbets were made for service at private functions, fêtes, collations, alfresco entertainments in the gardens and parks of royal palaces, embassies, grand town houses, and at official civic banquets and balls, and could not strictly be described as being offered for sale to the general public. All the same, I don't think that Dubuisson's claim about there having been for a long time only three men serving ices in Paris will stand up to examination.

Ices Under the Volcano

Cinnamon Bricks and Candied Eggs

In Naples, it was reported by the eighteenth-century Burgundian advocate Charles de Brosses, the nobility lived in Spanish rather than in the Italian style. He came to the conclusion that this circumstance explained their lavish hospitality, a notable contrast with the lack of it in other Italian states. The Duke of Monte-Leone, a prince of the house of Pignatelli, 'receives visitors very affably. However, he keeps no table, but every evening holds the most magnificent assembly in the whole city. This costs him, it is said, over fifty thousand francs in candles, ices and refreshments etc.'[1] Lady Morgan, Irish wife of Sir Charles Morgan, whose writings on post-Napoleonic France included a celebrated panegyric of Antonin Carême and his cooking, and who was in Rome and Naples in 1820, described an aspect of Neapolitan life rather different from that of the extravagant entertaining of the Spanish-orientated nobility, but one just as relevant to the spirit of the city. 'Everywhere,' said Lady Morgan,

are spread the fantastic stalls of the fruiterer, and the *aquajolo*, the iced-water vendor, all flowers and foliage, supported by cupids and angels, surmounted with a Madonna in heaven or sinners in purgatory, and streaming with flags of gilt paper and red stuff. Half-naked beggars stop to *ber fresco*, drink cold, or eat an ice, confidently trusted to them with a silver spoon, by the merchants they habitually deal with . . . the pavement is strewn with mounds of oranges, and the air resounds with that acute Babel-like noise which belongs exclusively to Naples.[2]

A scene even now recognizably Neapolitan.

When Lady Morgan stayed in Naples it was a century and a quarter since an Italian from the Marche named Antonio Latini, steward to Don Stefano Carillo y Salcedo, Spanish Prime Minister of Naples and the Two Sicilies, had written that 'in the city of Naples a great quantity of *sorbette* is consumed, they are the consistency of sugar and snow, and every Neapolitan, it would appear, is born knowing how they are made'.[3] That the term *sorbetto* did not appear in either the 1686 or 1691 editions of the *Vocabolario* of the Accademia della Crusca in Florence was relevant only to the Tuscan language. Naples had its own vocabulary.

Latini's book *Lo Scalco alla Moderna* (*The Modern Steward*) was pub-lished in two bulky parts, the first in 1692, the second in 1694. Together the two volumes made up the last and most comprehensive of the extraordinary series of works produced by Italian stewards, carvers, major-domos and master cooks which had begun with the publication in 1549 of Messisbugo's *Banchetti*, closely followed in 1560 by Domenico Romoli's *La Singolare Dottrina*, and ten years later by

Antonio Latini

Bartolomeo Scappi's magisterial *Opera* with its famous plates of the Vatican kitchens, its banquet lists, its astonishing range of recipes. There had been many others, among them Vincenzo Cervio's *Il Trinciante (The Carver)* in 1581, Giovanni Battista Rossetti's *Dello Scalco* in 1583, Antonio Frugoli's *Pratica e Scalcaria* in 1631, Francesco Liberati's *Il Perfetto Mastro di Casa* in 1658, Venantio Mattei's *Teatro Nobilissimo di Scalcheria* in 1669. Of them all Latini's work was possibly the most ambitious in scope, covering in Part 1 alone the duties of the steward, the carver and the other upper functionaries of a great household, the methods of cooking every comestible animal and bird, domestic and wild, the making of soups and broths, the boiling, roasting and frying of meat, the making of sauces (a tomato sauce in the Spanish fashion is, I think, the first published Italian recipe for what was to become the scourge first of Neapolitan cooking, later that of all Italy), the confection of vinegars and conserves, the preservation of fruit, the cooking of composite dishes, the use of condiments and spices, the making of fritters, pastries and pies, the service of banquets and their accompanying *trionfi*, which included the pyramids of fruit in ice and the ice vessels which were by Latini's time almost obligatory for grand occasions at the courts of the rulers of Italy and of its lords temporal and spiritual. In Latini's second volume his scope was equally wide. Every conceivable comestible to be served on non-meat days was dealt with in detail. As well as fish cookery in all its aspects, this 1694 volume covered recipes for dairy and egg dishes, macaroni, gnocchi, lasagne, salads, fish jellies, cold dishes, invalid food. There were separate chapters on *zabaglione* and on *sorbetti*, the last a departure quite new in the works of Italian stewards. As far as can be judged from the sketchy recipes provided by Latini, the *sorbetti* of Naples at this time were semi-frozen sherbets very different from the hard and glassy water-ices of contemporary Paris.

The opulence of the rulers of Spanish Naples in the late seventeenth century is reflected in Latini's notes on the banquets and fêtes which he had stage-managed or at which he had assisted in his capacity as the Prime Minister's steward. Many of those grand dinners had been held at the seaside villas and palaces of the Spanish nobility and were often followed by an alfresco reception. After one April banquet at

Torre del Greco there was a second entertainment following the dinner proper at which iced chocolate, pyramids of fruit in ice, water-ices and other cold refreshments were served, not only to the officially invited guests but to all their servants and followers, 'even of the lowliest condition, and up to the number of three hundred'. Winter and summer the Spanish and Italian nobility of Naples had all their fruit served smothered in snow. '*Ogni cosa con Neve*', as Latini reported of the chargers of muscatel and Catalonia grapes which made up part of the dessert at a September dinner at Miradoja. A December wedding breakfast at Castel San Franco, served to twenty-four people, was followed by a sumptuous concert after which hot and iced chocolate, abundant ices and small biscuits of every sort were circulated among the guests. One June, a banquet was given in Naples itself by the general of the Neapolitan navy to twenty of his senior commanders. Massive quantities of fruit appeared among the ten cold dishes of the first service. There were white and red melons sliced and set on branches of bay, with snow under and over, peeled figs with bay branches under and snow over, Damascene plums and Perdrigon plums also with bay leaves under and snow over 'according to the custom of Spanish gentlemen in Spain'. Some of the food those Spanish gentle-men enjoyed was overpoweringly sweet. A muscatel pear tart had a cover of marzipan iced with sugar and studded with pieces of candied orange peel, a ham cooked in wine with the 'customary spices' was encased in a pastry crust decorated with pastry arabesques stuck with candied cinnamon and long comfits, the whole iced with sugar icing in two colours. Such elaborately presented hams were fashionable at the tables of the Spanish grandees. Sometimes the fat of a ham would be studded with whole cloves as well as pieces of cinnamon, and all round the dish there would be pastry barquettes containing sailors fashioned out of almond paste, 'their oars in their hands', and any empty spaces filled in with candied fruit, the rind of the ham lifted to form a sail. It was at about this period, or a few years earlier, 1681 to be precise, that the French Comtesse d'Aulnoy, spending several months in Spain proper, complained that the food was so spiced, scented, saffroned, and sweetened that she could eat only jellies and 'white meats', meaning creams, cream cheeses, junkets and similar dairy foods. She had found some of the Spanish hams much superior to those of Bayonne and even of Westphalia, but spoiled by sugar comfits melting in the fat. Most decidedly Madame d'Aulnoy would not have cared for the ceremonial food of contemporary Naples.

Rather oddly, the same lady, whose stay in Spain lasted several months, and who described in detail the receptions she attended and the food and drinks served, and who referred many times to the use of snow and snow-cooled beverages as necessities of Spanish life, made no mention of having eaten ices or of seeing anything like the ice ornaments which according to Latini were such features on the tables of the grandees of Spanish Naples. On numerous occasions he listed, among the *trionfi* variously fashioned in sugar, paste, pleated napkins, moulded butter, also some fashioned in ice. 'Obelisks of ice, *altissime*, very high, filled with fruit of every sort', an '*altissimo* pyramid made of ice', and 'great ice vases filled with fruit' are entries quite usual in his banquet notes.[4] It was obligatory to accompany each service from the kitchen with a different set of *trionfi*, cold dishes, statues, inventions, with fruit, confectionery and 'candied delicacies in royal dishes', Latini said. He explained that these last were so named not because they were used specifically for kings and monarchs but because they were of regal capacity and suitable for display and embellishment, thus reaffirming the status of the guests. Much inventiveness was required by the men responsible for the ornamentation of banquets. Latini mentions, among many fantasies, an obelisk of jelly with little coloured fishes inside and a sugar coronet, flecked with gold leaf, around it; a lion fighting a bull, and a hunter with dogs on a leash, all made out of butter; an open pie of marzipan paste filled with various fruit, four lions made of ice frosted with snow, and various sugar fruit all around it – a compliment perhaps to a visiting Medici prince or envoy from Florence, where the making of snow lions was such a popular winter pastime. Baskets filled with flower heads and a variety of fruit frosted with snow were other banquet adornments, and once Latini lists a *ghiaccio* of strawberries, sugared and first rinsed in good wine, by which I think he meant that the berries were embedded in some ornamental piece of ice other than a pyramid or an obelisk. Creams or clotted creams were *aghiacciate*, frozen, served with sugar over, and were either what the French at that period called *fromages glacés* and the Italians *stracchini gelati*, or possibly nothing more complicated than dishes of ordinary creams, iced rather than frozen, *aghiacciate* in that context being open to interpretation as iced or frozen. A familiar ambiguity.

Fortunately, no such linguistic uncertainty attaches to Latini's *sorbetti*, their confection, their freezing, their service. Giving their alternative nomenclature, *acque aggiacciate* – the inconsistencies of spelling are his own – the Italian equivalent of Audiger's *eaux glacées*, he provides just enough information for posterity to judge what the ices of Spanish Naples in the 1690s were like, at the same time giving away no technical secrets and making no revelations which might have annoyed the professional confectioners who were his colleagues. He was careful also to write without trespassing on the territory of the *ripostieri*, shopkeepers. As recipes, then, Latini's formulae for *sorbetti* were far too sketchy to be of practical use to the uninitiated, but since they appear to be the first formally printed ones in the Italian language, a summary of their content is useful as a comparison of Neapolitan taste in ices with that of the French at the same period, the 1690s.

As was usual for at least the whole of the century to come, in Neapolitan ice parlance, Latini's units of measurement were *giare*, the two-handled goblets in which at that time water-ices were piled up in pyramid form for service. For the preparation of the waters to be frozen Latini's starting point therefore was always so many *giare* of water, usually 10. From other available evidence it emerges that 10 goblets amounted to approximately the equivalent of 2 Paris (32 oz) pints. To make a cinnamon ice on this basis, 12 oz of pine-nuts and 48 oz of sugar were required. Latini gave no further instructions, except to say that freezing ingredients were 12 lb of ice to 3 lb of salt, proportions which were fairly constant unless the ice was to be frozen in *tavolette*, tablets or bricks, in which case 1 lb of salt to every 2 lb of ice was needed. Neapolitan bricks must have been quite a luxury at the time. Could such a very sweet mixture actually freeze into bricks? It seems doubtful.

Two of Latini's ices made on a different basis of measurement were, first, a milk, water, sugar and candied fruit mixture composed of $1\frac{1}{2}$ carafes of milk, $\frac{1}{2}$ carafe of water, 3 (12 oz) lb of sugar and 6 oz of candied citron or pumpkin, with the usual 3 lb of salt to 12 lb of ice for the freezing, and, second, a frozen chocolate *scomigilia* or mousse, rather unusual for its time and no doubt evolved by the chocolate-addicted Spaniards. Two (12 oz) lb each of chocolate – unsweetened presumably – and sugar were whipped up in the usual 10 goblets of water and worked or stirred, it would seem from Latini's hazy instructions, during the whole of the freezing process. The mousse was to be served as soon as it was frozen. In France such frozen mousses were supposedly not introduced until 1720, when Francesco Procopio's son Alexandre initiated a craze for them when he made the ices for one of the great Condé fêtes at Chantilly, so it is interesting to find them already a part of the Spanish–Neapolitan tradition in the 1690s.

A curiosity among Latini's ices is one consisting entirely of *robba candita*, candied things, and sugar, frozen in *una piramide ordinario*. 'A common pyramid' must have been a very large mould, since it required 6 [12 oz] lb of sugar. How much water was then added to this surprising mixture Latini omitted to mention. To him and his contemporary readers, the capacity of a common pyramid mould was obviously as well known as that of a common ice or sherbet goblet, but he does specify that the freezing ingredients were 48 lb of ice and 10 lb of salt, enough to fill a pretty large freezing tub. One must suppose that Latini, in his capacity as major-domo and overall organizer of so many fêtes and entertainments, had frequently seen the confectioners at work on their ices and ice ornaments and was probably even responsible for accounting for their cost in snow, salt, spices, sugar and so on. He was not therefore romancing when he wrote down what seem to us most unlikely proportions of ingredients, particularly of sugar to fruit. For 12 goblets of lemon *sorbetta*, for example, he specified 3 lemons to 3 [12 oz] lb of sugar, and for 24 goblets of strawberry ice 5 lb of fruit to 3 lb of sugar. For 24 goblets of ordinary chocolate ice proportions were as for the *mousse*, 2 lb each of chocolate and sugar, and if to be frozen in bricks the mixture required 24 lb of snow and 6 lb of salt, a much lower proportion of salt to snow than was needed for cinnamon bricks.

In Latini's world of Spanish grandees, high-ranking naval officers, important government administrators, Neapolitan noblemen and their families, ices were invariably prepared for early evening collations and were made in quantity. Many times he noted that after the midday dinner all the guests retired to their rooms to rest, and that for the second part of the entertainment quantities of drinking chocolate, both hot and iced, and all kinds of frozen sherbets were prepared. In the shade of the lemon and orange groves, among the scented roses for which the gardens of Naples were then renowned, the fine ladies and gentlemen and their children would stroll and talk and play, the sea shimmering below in the evening sunlight, the islands of Ischia and Capri barely discernible in the hazy distance, in the foreground the plume of smoke rising from Vesuvius to remind them of the ever-present menace of the volcano.

A level of Neapolitan society rather less exalted than that of the haughty-faced Palatine count Antonio Latini and his Spanish masters was catered for by a now obscure little booklet consisting of twelve pages, 5 inches by 4, devoted entirely to the making and freezing of *sorbetti*. Published in Naples, crudely printed and scruffy, the booklet evidently appeared at about the same time as the two voluminous parts of *Lo Scalco alla Moderna*, but possibly a few years later. It is unknown to the bibliographers and apparently unrecorded in Italian national collections, was anonymously printed, undated, and entitled *Brieve e Nuovo Modo da farsi ogni sorte di Sorbette* con faciltà*. The only mention of its provenance was the announcement on the title page that it was sold by 'Cristofaro Migliaccio alla strada della Librari, accosto la Chiesa di S. Liguoro'. That street of booksellers next to the Church of San Liguoro is not much of a clue, but fortunately in the recipes there is abundant internal evidence that the publication was a Neapolitan one. Neapolitan words, coinage, measurements, and typical ingredients combine to proclaim the origin of the recipes and their author. The type in which they are set is characteristic of the late seventeenth century, and although it could still have been in use until many years later, turns of phrase such as '*che tutte sara bene*' and '*sara piu perfetta*', that all may be well, it will be more perfect, and cooking instructions like 'let it boil an Ave Maria while' indicate that the author was a man of the seventeenth century.

---

* The spelling is that of the booklet's author.

Although so small and so humble, this little *Sorbette* booklet, intended perhaps as a sales boost for the necessary equipment such as freezing pots and small moulds, and certainly directed at professional practitioners, was remarkably informative and instructive. Into its twelve small pages are crammed twenty-four recipes, of which twenty-three are for ices, the odd one out a portmanteau formula for making *acquavita* syrups in various flavours such as cinnamon, anis, bitter almond or apricot kernel, juniper, the implication being that the confection of such things was all part of the sherbet-maker's business.

As we learn from Latini, ices in brick or tablet form were already current in the Naples of the 1690s. The unknown author of the *Sorbette* booklet advocated what he called *pezzi* – in later parlance more usually *pezzi duri*, hard pieces, meaning those ices made in the shape of a variety of fruit such as peaches, apricots, pomegranates, oranges and so on, although I think that at the time this little booklet was written, the term was more of a collective one, applied to individually moulded ices generally. The author makes specific reference also to pyramids and *ricotelle*, individual log-shaped fluted moulds, in France called *canelons* or tubes, and he presents a good variety of flavours. Some of the mixtures are quite complex compared to those given by Latini, and his recipes make attractive reading. Even his basic lemon sherbet is scented with orange flower water and enriched with a couple of ounces of minced candied citron. Another lemon preparation, intended specifically for freezing in *pezzi*, calls for a large proportion of the juice of fresh muscatel grapes pressed through a wet napkin and scented with 1 grain of musk, or 2 of ambergris. A Portugal or sweet orange ice has halved orange segments embedded in it; strawberry ice is similarly studded with fresh whole strawberries and given body with a small proportion of a typically Neapolitan syrup known as *alacca*, made from the must of sweet black grapes grown in the Campania and more correctly called *aglianico*. The cinnamon ice so beloved in Southern Italy and Sicily is here provided with special interest in the form of 3 oz of whole pine-nuts to every 10 goblets of the basic preparation. A variation on the cinnamon theme is an ice made on a basis of pounded melon seeds, whole pine-kernel comfits and *cannella bianca lattaginoso*, a cinnamon water thickened with syrup of cinnamon, the kind of syrupy drink we would call cream of cinnamon.

Evidence that in seventeenth-century Naples there was no lack of fresh cow's milk and cream is forthcoming from Latini's two volumes and from the author of the little *Sorbette* booklet, who gives several milk-based ices. One is made from reduced milk scented with orange flower water and cream of cinnamon, thickened with cream and butter and further enhanced with the minced candied pumpkin sweetmeat known as *cocuzata* – this author spells it *cocozzata* – another, called *Imperiale ammantecato*, with 10 egg yolks to 2 *carafas* of milk (a Naples *carafa* was the equivalent, approximately, of today's litre) to make a custard sweetened with 16 oz of sugar, scented with cream of cinnamon, and with minced candied pumpkin stirred into the ice when it was already about three-quarters frozen. Jasmine flowers, apricots, muscatel grapes, strawberries, bitter cherries, muscat pears, pistachios, chestnuts, and the inevitable chocolate all figure as main ingredients in these exotically perfumed ices. An unexpected one, given the period, is vanilla, which evidently came early to Naples via its Spanish overlords and their colony of Peru. A vanilla ice in those days was not custard-based but simply an infusion of 1 large bean pulverized with sugar and immersed in 10 goblets of boiling water. Crushed melon seeds were added, then the infusion was wrung through a napkin, the customary 16 oz of sugar stirred in and the mixture set in the snow to freeze. This ice could be made green with spinach juice, or *alacca* syrup could be added, but in that case no further perfume or spirit should be used. A *torrone* sherbet was another ice which required exacting preparation. Naples pine-kernels and almonds were steeped in cold water for a day, then pulverized, wrung through a cloth, the resulting milk diluted with 10 goblets of water and sweetened with 24 oz of sugar. Ambergris was added for scent, or alternatively crushed coriander – to please the ladies by its appearance the latter was advised – and when the freezing was nearly completed almonds split in quarters or pine-kernel comfits were stirred in.

Picturesque names for ices were already coming into fashion in Naples. One, made with milk and heavily flavoured with pulverized cinnamon bark as well as cream of cinnamon, not thickened with eggs, but with the favourite minced candied pumpkin embedded in it, was called *sorbetta d'Aurora*, sunrise sherbet. A *candito d'ova a tavolette*, egg candy in bricks, was something between the Florentine Count Lorenzo Magalotti's *candiero* or *zabaglione* ice and the favourite Spanish sweetmeat called *ouva miscide* or *ova filate*, in Spanish *huevos mesidos*, egg-yolks beaten in clarified sugar then syringed into vermicelli or lasagne. For the *candito* 12 well-beaten egg-yolks were cooked in 16 oz of sugar previously clarified in 10 goblets of water (2 litres) with $\frac{1}{2}$ egg white and strained. The egg-yolk and sugar confection was stirred until it was cold, and was then half frozen before orange flower water and crushed sweet orange peel in syrup were stirred in. Alternatively this ice, which must have been something like frozen *advocaat*, could be scented with musk, ambergris or $\frac{1}{2}$ oz of cream of cinnamon; then, the author asserts, all will be well.

What then was the *nuovo modo*, the new method of making *sorbetti* promised in the title of the little Neapolitan treatise? It was simply, I think, a technique which involved two distinct stages of freezing. First the basic sherbet was set in the snow and salt and frozen until it was *desemolata*, literally degrained or degritted. In other words, when the first layers of ice had formed they were broken up, the half-frozen sherbet beaten until smooth, and the solid ingredients such as minced candied pumpkin, orange segments, split almonds, whole strawberries, pine-kernel comfits and so on were then stirred into the mixture in the freezing pot. A second session in the snow and salt brought the ice to the correct stage for service. It was an obvious enough method of ensuring that the heavy or solid embellishments added to the ice remained in suspension instead of sinking to the bottom of the *sorbettiera*. Since making a preliminary syrup was not yet at the time part of the routine of the ice-maker, the second stage of freezing would also have enabled the operator to check that the sugar had properly dissolved and was evenly distributed throughout the mixture. When strong perfumes and heavy essences such as musk, ambergris, or cinnamon extracts were called for in a recipe, they too were added only when the freezing process was half completed.

Directions in the little booklet are on the whole clear and easy to follow. Proportions are fairly constant. Ten goblets of water or milk (2 litres, near enough) and a $\frac{1}{2}$ *rotolo* or 16 oz of sugar are the basis for all the sherbets frozen to be served in goblets, but for *pezzi*, small pyramid moulds and *ricotelle* an extra 8 oz or $\frac{1}{4}$ *rotolo* was to be allowed. This, the author explained, was to give more body to the mixture. Reckoned in modern English measurements, these proportions would work out at 1 lb 8 oz of sugar to $3\frac{1}{2}$ pints of liquid, or 24 oz to 68 oz, and in US terms 3 cups of sugar to $8\frac{1}{4}$ of liquid. That seems a rather over-heavy proportion of sugar for successful freezing in a mould, and certainly too sweet for most modern tastes, 3 to 4 oz per English (20 oz) pint being the allowance for most of today's home-made ices, but the Neapolitans were notorious for the amount of sugar they consumed. Indeed all Italian ices are still by a long way too sweet for my own taste.

For the freezing of all the *sorbetti* given by the author of the Neapolitan booklet, proportions of snow and salt were calculated in an unusual way. For every *rotolo* or 32 oz of sherbet in small moulds or *pezzi* he allowed 5 of snow and 1 of salt, but for freezing loose, as he called it, $\frac{3}{4}$ *rotolo* of salt was sufficient. Few writers of recipes for ices and frozen sherbets were as specific as to quantities and proportions as this one, and we must assume that he was perfectly conversant with the business of the ice-maker, which Antonio Latini was not, frankly admitting his lack of specialist knowledge. Insistence on the very small doses of expensive perfumes needed for ices was one of the special points of interest of the *Sorbette* booklet author. He gave the precise cost of musk and ambergris, $2\frac{1}{2}$ *grana* per grain for the first, 4 *grana* per grain for the second. Cream of cinnamon was 5 *grana* the ounce. The Neapolitan *grana*, *graino* or *grano* was the smallest coin in the currency, worth about the equivalent of an English halfpenny. Those prices sound negligible, but in the values of the time they did add appreciably to the cost of Neapolitan ices, as also no doubt to their charm and glamour.

For an interesting comparison with Latini's frozen chocolate mousse, here is the chocolate ice recipe given in the *Sorbette* booklet:

To make ten goblets of chocolate, in little time, take ten ounces of the same, one pound [12 oz] of sugar, put in six or seven scant goblets of water, not more, a quarter of an hour's fast boiling will suffice, but it must first be beaten very thoroughly in a vessel and then passed through a hair sieve. After the quarter hour's boiling it is put to cool, beating it meanwhile with the chocolate mill. And to make it more creamy, soft and smooth, when it is cold take two or three egg-yolks and put them to the prepared chocolate, mixing and beating well and it will be more perfect.

A later note on chocolate ice tells the reader that when the chocolate is cooked, 'for each pound two *chicchere* [small chocolate or coffee bowls] of water should be boiled and put to the vessel [containing the chocolate], this is set in the snow and the chocolate stirred well, and then it is frozen, and it will be found perfect'. Given that at the time when this recipe was written chocolate was a very different substance from the smooth, machine-produced blocks or tablets we know today and that the author of the recipe was probably using very hard and roughly made unsweetened chocolate, requiring a great deal of working and frothing with a chocolate mill, his directions seem perfectly reasonable.

Sherbet Trade with the Levant

The prodigious consumption of snow in Naples and the Neapolitan addiction to iced drinks were frequently remarked on by visitors from cooler climates. Only some half-dozen years after Antonio Latini had written that knowledge of the making of ices seemed to be a Neapolitan birthright, the English essayist Joseph Addison spent some weeks in Naples and, in the published account of his Italian travels in the years 1701, 1702, and 1703, described how snow was a necessity of life there, revealing that already at that time it had become the subject of what later came to be known as a protection racket, operated by *banditti*, the Camorra of the day. Indicative of the extent to which he had been struck by the Neapolitan snow trade was Addison's

reference to it as 'among the Natural Curiosities of Naples'. He had
been told that 'snow cools or congeals any Liquor sooner than ice',
and attributed the great annual consumption of it to the Neapolitan
custom of drinking 'very few Liquors, not so much as Water, that have
not lain in Fresco, and every Body, from the highest to the lowest,
makes use of it'.[5]

As we know from the experiments carried out by the Neapolitan
Giambattista Della Porta and published by him in 1589, Naples was
probably the home of artificial freezing. The art had been brought
into being by the early Neapolitan fondness for drinking half-frozen
wine and had been made possible by the ready supply of snow in the
city and the accessibility of cheap residue from the saltpetre refineries
supplying the naval arsenal and the Spanish garrison. Subsequently it
had been discovered that in the freezing process common unrefined
sea salt was just as efficacious as saltpetre. Just when that had happened
we do not know. Johannes Beckmann thought that it might have been
Santorio Santorio (1561–1638), a professor at the universities of Padua
and Venice, who invented an air thermometer, a pulse meter and other
instruments much ahead of his time, who established the efficacy of
common salt in conjunction with snow for the production of artificial
cold. In his Commentary on the works of Avicenna, published in
1626, Santorio related that in the presence of many spectators he had
converted wine into ice by means of snow and common salt, and this
was certainly known by 1620.

It was in 1620 that John Barclay wrote his *Argenis* (see p. 55) and
described how ice goblets and dishes could be created in the heat of a
Mediterranean summer. (Before his death in 1626 Francis Bacon also
knew about the use of ice and common salt for freezing purposes
although he had not himself made the experiment.) If not common
knowledge in Italy, it was at least known to the butlers employed by
the Roman nobility and the cardinals that a combination of common
salt and snow packed round moulds filled with water would bring
about the desired result. It was still a long time, however, before the
Neapolitans, the Spanish, the Florentines, the Sicilians, the Romans,
the Parisians, started eating water-ices or drinking half-frozen sherbets.

That eventually Neapolitan ices, as also those of Sicily, were based on oriental sherbets can hardly be doubted. By implication, the assumption would be that sherbets came to Sicily and Naples by way of the Arabs and the Spanish. But did they? And if so, when? Remembering that in the 1580s the Florentine Grand Duke Francesco, whose mother was the Spanish Eleanora of Toledo, daughter of the Viceroy of Naples, and whose ties with Spain were strong, did not know how sherbets were made and was writing in person to the Venetian Mafeo Veniero asking him for recipes for those 'Turkish beverages', the questions are hardly easy to answer. Had such beverages then been known in Naples, Francesco and his family, his stewards, butlers, confectioners, would also have known about them and how they were made. Equally, it might have been expected that a man such as Della Porta would have found a place, in that wondrous collection of secrets and recipes which was the 1589 edition of his *Magia Naturalis* or *Natural Magick* (see p. 68), for a few formulae for those exotically spiced, perfumed and sugared drinks which were so very much more complex than the aromatic and scented waters then known in the various Italian states. Had he known about them he would surely have recorded a method of making them, however speculative, but he offered no such information.

Further evidence that in Naples sherbets were still unknown in the early decades of the seventeenth century is provided by the Roman marquess Pietro Della Valle. Writing in 1615 from Constantinople to his Neapolitan friend Mario Schipani, Della Valle explained that

unlike ourselves they [the Turks] do not use water boiled with citron or coriander, but mix ordinary clean water with *scerbet*, a certain composition which they make sometimes liquid, sometimes solid, if they wish to preserve it for a long time and carry it with them, without it running. They make it of sugar, lemon juice, seasonings of fruit and flowers and other ingredients, something like the conserves and marmalades of Naples; when they want to drink, they put some of this composition in a jug of water, leaving it time enough to dissolve if it is hard and the water takes its colour, savour and aroma entirely.

Elsewhere in the same letter, written on 14 March 1615, Della Valle mentioned roses, violets, musk and ambergris among the ingredients with which sherbets were scented, and told Schipani that he would 'try to learn their composition, in order to be able to make them in Italy'. It would be wrong to take Della Valle's evidence as conclusive, but reflecting on the frequency with which the European travellers of the time reported back to their countrymen with descriptions of the charms of the perfumed sherbets of the Turkish dominions, as also those of Persia and Moghul India, it is difficult not to come to the conclusion that had they already been so familiar in any European city as much visited as the Naples of the period, we should have heard about them there long before the 1690s when Latini made his remark about the Neapolitan knowledge of *sorbetti* making. Was he having a dig at the exuberance and boastfulness of the Neapolitans? Or was he perhaps making one of those generalizations of the 'all Englishmen are milords' or 'every Frenchman knows how to make a sauce' kind?

Without going into tedious detail or inconclusive conjecture as to the probability of the odd Turkish, Persian, Armenian or Arab sherbet-maker having been brought to Naples by some Spanish grandee or foreign ambassador, or of the likelihood of an apothecary of one of those nationalities having set up shop selling sherbets there, I can safely say that I think it more likely that those beverages, in their solid or powdered forms, perhaps both, had become articles of trade between the Turkish Empire and the major markets of Western Europe. At least thirty years before Latini wrote about the *sorbetti* makers of Naples, 'sherbets made in Turkie of Lemons, Roses, and Violets perfumed' were among the beverages sold at a London coffee house, Morat's in Exchange Alley, and were advertised by the owner in a London journal, the *Mercurius Publicus*, for 12–19 March 1662. Two years previously Charles II's Restoration government had put a heavy and absurdly impractical tax on all drinks made from imported sherbets, chocolate, tea and coffee sold in the coffee houses. At '8d the gallon made and sold' the tax was supposed to be collected on the spot by excise officers appointed to call at the coffee houses twice a day to assess the duty owed. Hardly a workable proposition, but for nearly thirty years the dogged British Treasury persevered in the attempt to collect its dues on coffee house beverages. By the time the tax was superseded in 1689 by direct import duties per hundredweight of coffee and cocoa beans and a prohibitive 5s. per pound of tea brought into the country, plus a separate duty, again of 5s. per pound, on chocolate ready made, sherbets from Turkey no longer figure in the Excise list of coffee house beverages. In the interval it had no doubt been discovered that acceptable substitutes for the imported solid sherbets could be made at home. Certainly sherbets soon fell out of fashion in London coffee houses.

In Naples, sherbets perfumed with essence of roses, violets and jasmine which would 'keep for whole years together in faïence jars because they are not in liquid form',[6] as reported by the French traveller Poullet in his *Relations du Levant* (1667–8), seem to have been the kind imported. 'Sherbet is as hard as our *cassonade*,* and one dissolves a spoonful or two in a large cup of water,' Poullet explained, and among the hundred and one globe trotters of the early decades of the century, Henry Blount, author of *A Voyage into the Levant* (1634), had described sherbets as being 'dried together into a consistence reasonable hard, and portable for their use in warre, or elsewhere, mingling about a spoonfull with a quart of water'.[7] Ambergris is usually remarked upon by Europeans as one of the characteristic perfumes used in lemon sherbets, and as the Frenchman Baudier added in his *History of the Imperial Estate of the Grand Seigneur* (1635), 'the ice refreshing it in Summer makes it more delightfull'.[8]

There at any rate, embodied in those newsletters from the Levant, we have the basic ingredients of many a Neapolitan *sorbetto*, and when the unknown author of our *Sorbette* booklet calls for $1\frac{1}{2}$ oz of the *sorbetta di Levante*, which he uses in three of his fruit ices, those made with apricots, muscat pear and muscatel grapes, we know approximately what he meant, and we know that almost certainly it was imported from Alexandria, that port being the source of the most highly esteemed sherbet in the whole of the Turkish empire.[9] Sir John Chardin tells us that the Alexandria sherbet was kept in pots and in boxes, and it was in powder, like crushed sugar, and that a spoonful in

* Cotgrave's dictionary (1611) translates *cassonade* as 'powder sugar, especially such as comes from Brasile'.

a large glass of water made 'an excellent liqueur' which needed no beating as did the French syrups he was accustomed to.[10]

We can now see that the first true Neapolitan ices of the time were those described in that curious little booklet, and that with the exception of his chocolate ice, Antonio Latini's recipes were so shaky as to be virtually useless. What he did tell posterity about the ices of Naples was not only the way they were served, but that all classes there enjoyed them and were accustomed to them, so it is yet another oddity that in 1700 Joseph Addison was silent about the consumption of ices in Naples. He had been in no doubt as to the importance of the snow supply to the Neapolitans but made no mention of what must have been its second most important use after the cooling of wine and water, the freezing of ices. He even surmised, when he came to publish his account of his Italian travels, that 'a Scarcity of snow would cause a Mutiny at Naples, as much as a dearth of Corn or Provisions in another Country'. It is no surprise to find him expressing the opinion. At the time he was in Naples, shortly after Philip of Anjou, Louis XIV's grandson, had inherited the throne of Spain, it was customary for the Spanish government to farm out snow monopolies to merchants who in return for the privilege were under obligation to retail it all year round at an agreed price per pound. Addison had discovered that the snow stores were situated 'in a high mountain at about eighteen miles from the town, which had several pits dug into it'. He was referring, I think, to Monte Gauro or Garro, the Mons Gaurus of classical Rome, now called Monte Barbaro. (There were ice stores also on the slopes of Monte Somma.) The filling of the snow pits was accomplished much as it was in Sicily. During the cold season 'they employ many poor people to roll vast balls of Snow which they ram together, and cover from the Sunshine. Out of these Reservoirs they cut several Lumps as they have occasion for them, and send them on Asses to the Sea-side, where they are carried in Boats and distributed to several Shops at a settled Price, that from time to time supply the whole City of Naples'. Effective means of terrorizing the snow merchants had been devised by the *banditti*. 'While they continued their Disorders in this Kingdom they often put the Snow Merchants under Contribution and threaten'd them, if they appear'd tardy in their Payments, to destroy their Magazines, which they say might easily have been effected by the Infusion of some Barrels of Oil.'[11]

Addison's experience of the year-round use of snow in Italy – he had encountered it also in Florence, where he discovered that the snow merchants paid as much as £1,000 a year into the Grand Duke's treasury for the privilege of a snow monopoly – did not stop him, a few years later, writing a sardonic description of an elaborate continental-style dessert composed of crystallized and candied fruits, jellies and ices. For foreigners the use of snow for cooling wine and water seems to have been acceptable to Addison, for his compatriots to be eating ices quite another. In the *Tatler* in March 1709 he published an attack on French cookery as represented by a dinner given by a friend who, on the contrary, much admired the style. With its emphasis on made-up dishes and kickshaws, a larded turkey and the like, while a noble roast sirloin of beef was relegated to the side table, the dinner had displeased Addison from the start. He had nonetheless managed to help himself twice to the roast beef, and was even quite impressed when the dessert was brought on. With its pyramids of frosted fruits and candied sweetmeats, its dishes of cream beaten to snow, its 'little plates of sugar plumbs like so many heaps of hailstones, its multitude of Congelations in Jellies of Various Colours' it looked like a 'very beautiful Winter-Piece'. Addison, however, was quick to find further cause for displeasure. His fellow guests were so insensitive as to dismantle the beautiful frosty landscapes and to help themselves to the sugar-plums, the ices, creams and jellies. Commenting acidly that he had taken his leave 'as soon as the Show was over' and had returned to finish his dinner at home, he later told his *Tatler* readers that he could not but smile to watch his fellow guests 'cooling their Mouths with Lumps of Ice which they had just before been burning with Salts and Peppers'.[12] His friend's dinner made good journalistic copy as well as comment on Addison's own less than endearing social manners. More usefully, with his jibe at people cooling their mouths with lumps of ice he left us, unknowingly, quite clear testimony as to the then status of ices in England as part of a grand Frenchified dessert. At the same time Addison revealed, once again unconsciously, that the London confectioners had not yet developed ices into anything much beyond mere lumps of ice. In fact the whole dessert described in Addison's *Tatler* article might have been, and probably was, made and presented just as instructed and depicted in *The Court and Country Cook*, the 1702 combined translation of Massialot's two works, *Le Cuisinier Roial et Bourgeois* and *Nouvelle Instruction Pour les Confitures*. Massialot's recipes for ices, whether in the original French or in English translation, still prevailed in London as in Paris. It was to be a while yet before the Neapolitan style of confectioner's ices penetrated the capitals of Europe.

In Sickness and in Health

Remembering the dire warnings of the medical professions of Europe concerning the catastrophic effects of drinking iced water, iced wine and any other artificially chilled beverage whatsoever, and most particularly when the person concerned was in any way overheated in body, it is startling to read, in a volume of letters written by an Englishwoman from Italy in the 1770s, that part of the treatment given in the vapour baths of Naples was the eating of ices midway through each session. But Lady [Anne] Miller, often a useful source of information on social customs in the Italy of the time, goes into detail about this practice. Of the famous baths at Pozzuoli, she wrote that at the end of one particular passage about 130 yards in length there was a spring of water so extremely hot that the boatmen who rowed her and her husband could scarcely bear the heat of the steam from the springs and returned from thence as soon as possible, although not without performing what must have been an age-old tourist guide's trick – a demonstration of the cooking in the steam of a couple of eggs brought for the purpose in a pail, the eggs being quite done when the men emerged from the passage. Her husband, having accompanied the boatmen to the boiling source, returned from thence in a violent heat and perspiration. Contiguous are caverns, or rather small cells in the rock, where are broad seats cut out of stone on which sick people extend themselves, and take the vapour bath as they call it here; these recesses being filled with as thick, and a much hotter steam than that in the slips of the baths at Bath in Somersetshire. When the patients have been so sweated on these stone sophas, as that their strength is almost exhausted, they take ices, which enable them to continue their operation much longer than their strength would otherwise admit of; nor has this practice ever been known to produce other than the most salutary effects. These baths are esteemed most efficacious in virulent scrophulous distempers, the evil not excepted.

A few days later the Millers, nothing if not assiduous sightseers, inspected the famous Grotto del Cane, the Grotto of the Dogs, near the Stufa di S. Germano, another set of vapour baths.

A very hot vapour from the ground fills four chambers round which are placed stone seats, on these the patients are laid, rolled up in blankets; when they come out of the baths, they go into bed, and in order to produce a second perspiration, eat ices, which never fail to produce the desired effects. The disorders commonly cured by these baths are rheumatisms, scurvies and other scrophulous humours.[13]

Perhaps after all there was something in that tale of the Turkish-style baths in the Paris of the late sixteenth century and the iced drinks offered to customers there after the bath. At any rate in the Naples of the 1770s, medical approval of ices had gone so far as to be made the subject of a whole treatise written by a Neapolitan physician, Dr Filippo Baldini, devoted, without recipes, to notes on the historical uses of snow, and ice and iced drinks in classical times, followed by an involved and wordy dissertation on the benefits of *sorbetti*. First published in 1775, the treatise was reprinted in 1784 with a new chapter on the fashionable pineapple.

This new edition was dedicated to Donna Marianna Branciforti, born Pignatelli of the house of Monte-Leone – daughter or sister of that duke of Monteleone whose lavish evening receptions had so impressed Charles de Brosses – and lady-in-waiting of '*nostra Clemen-*

tissima Sovrana', in other words Queen Maria Carolina of Naples, daughter of the Empress Maria Teresa and sister of Marie Antoinette. In the main body of the work Baldini examined the medicinal virtues and properties of various categories of those *bevande ghiacciate*, frozen drinks, *detto presso di noi Sorbetti o Gelati*, by us called sherbets or ices. First came an explanation of their basic composition, in which he included the snow and the salt used for freezing. Preferably sea salt should be used but rock salt would do. One part of salt to every two parts of snow conserved in the grottoes was the proper proportion. As an economy soda might be used instead of salt. Baldini believed, as had many medical men before him, that in melding with the snow and bringing about the freezing of the liquor, minute salt particles penetrated the walls of the pewter cylinder in which it was contained; this was a desirable and beneficial thing, the salt stimulating the intestines, maintaining and promoting the regular circulation of the blood, preventing inflammations, operating as a mild refrigerant especially in the heat of fevers. As for the sugar which constituted the major component of all ices, its benefits were boundless. From headaches to stomach ulcers there were few ills it would not soothe and ameliorate. The Turks used it to heal wounds, after having first cleansed them with wine. A certain Duke of Beaufort had lived to a great age because for forty years he had swallowed 1 lb or more of sugar daily. When his body was opened after his death his intestines were discovered to be entirely sound. A celebrated character called Malory lived hale and hearty to 100 years old because every day he had consumed large quantities of sugar with his meat, vegetables and fruit. It followed that *sorbetti*, with their sugar and salt content and their intensified cold, conferred infinitely good effects on our bodies. After six or seven pages of discussion centred on the question of contemporary over-eating, particularly of heavily spiced and sauced foods and of the drinking of wines and liqueurs brought from the remoter regions to the detriment and neglect of those produced by nature in 'our own climate', Baldini came to the conclusion that *sorbetti* alleviated overheated stomachs and counteracted the effects of excess alcohol. Here perhaps we have the germs of the mid-meal sorbet of the nineteenth century.

The benefits of ices were not merely negative and preventative. They promoted regular and gentle evacuation, toned up the nervous system, contributed marvellously to vital natural and animal forces and helped to maintain the human body safe and sound. In short, if in these particular passages of Baldini's work one were to substitute the words natural fibre or wholemeal bread for *sorbetti* one could almost believe one were reading the latest issue of a health magazine.

Progressing from the general to the particular, Baldini examines each category of ice, starting with those made from subacid fruits, including lemons, oranges, strawberries and pineapple. To these he added bitter cherry, verjuice grapes and peaches as fruits suitable for ices. Rather oddly, he omitted any mention of apricots, pomegranates or raspberries.

The second category of ices were those called the *aromatici*, containing a salt, an oil, and an essence both stimulant and bitter. Such ingredients included chocolate, coffee, cinnamon, pistachios and pine-nuts. The ices made with them were all water-based. Cinnamon ices were among the most highly esteemed. They were valuable in the arrestation of diarrhoea and dysentery, they were mildly anodyne and narcotic, consequently a solace to the invalid. However, they should not be taken to excess. Coffee ice was a good digestive, and all the useful attributes of the coffee bean extended to ices made from it, as also the bad ones which caused palpitations and prevention of sleep. Again, consumption of them must not be taken to excess. Pistachio, owing to the essential oil contained in the nuts, was among the restorative medicaments, and was an aid to digestion, but Dr Baldini had little to say about the benefits of ices in which it was the key ingredient. A *sorbetto* based on the milk of pine-nuts also contained an essential oil and was valuable for consumptives and anyone with lung trouble or a persistent cough. Anyone suffering pain when urinating should go for pine-nut milk ices.

The third category of ices to be considered by Baldini were those based on all types of animal milk. Starting with asses' milk ices, good as blood purifiers, he went through those based on goat's milk, valuable in cases of diarrhoea, dysentery, haemorrhages, and in the prevention and cure of many other atrocious maladies. Cow's milk sorbets were efficacious in the treatment of many severe illnesses, among them paralysis and scurvy. Everyday experience had taught the doctor that the continued use of cow's milk reduced in *sorbetti* had never failed to produce beneficial effects or to alleviate 'violent symptoms'. Finally, sheep's milk ices were particularly beneficial in cases of emaciation, diarrhoea, dysentery, haemorrhage and scurvy. Bringing his treatise to a close, Dr Baldini remarked that although the use of *sorbetti* for pleasure and as a luxury had become common, he had no doubt that from now on it would continue also as something medically beneficial.

At the very least, the doctor's patients must surely have found ices a pleasanter remedy than most of those current in the eighteenth century. It was curious, though, that Baldini, so ready with classical quotations, nowhere made the slightest allusion to more recent developments in the history of iced beverages or to the origin of the word *sorbetto*. No hint of any knowledge he might have possessed concerning the composition of the oriental beverages on which the ices of Naples had been based appeared in his book. Had the introduction of ices been so soon forgotten? Was the learned doctor quite unaware of the existence of *sorbetti* other than those he knew in Naples? Evidently. One point, however, that in his capacity as a medical expert he did make clear was that he had little regard for the currently fashionable vapour baths, the *stufe* described by Lady Miller. He even went so far as to say that if instead of those baths people would take aromatic ices they would avoid many maladies.[14] There is nothing like a medical man or a scientist on a runaway hobby-horse, but it was odd that Baldini had not heard that people were currently making the best of both options, sandwiching their ices between two sessions in the steam baths.

A contemporary of Dr Baldini, and at the time already well known in Naples, was Vincenzo Corrado, a Benedictine monk in the Celestine monastery of S. Pier a Majella. Born in 1738* at Oria near Lecce in Apulia, Corrado was the author of several works on agriculture, gardening, fruit trees, silkworms, bees, and a general one on the

---

* Faccioli, in vol. 2 of his *Arte della Cucina*, gives the date as 1734 and the date of his death as 1836.

products of the Kingdom of Naples. Food and cookery were also among Corrado's special studies. His first cookery book, *Il Cuoco Galante*, was published in 1773, and eventually ran into seven editions. The fifth, which appeared in 1801, was augmented with a chapter of potato recipes and a dissertation on the use of potatoes in breadmaking. These unusual features had evidently been inspired by Parmentier, whose works had been translated into Italian. Another interesting novelty in *Il Cuoco Galante* was a chapter entirely devoted to tomato recipes. As noted on p. 143, Latini's 1692 volume had included at least a couple, and by Corrado's time, it is clear, the tomato was well established in Neapolitan kitchens. In his book on confectionery entitled *Il Credenziere de Buon Gusto*, published in 1778, Corrado even offered a recipe for candied tomatoes. It is with this work, dealing with the business of the butler and confectioner rather than with that of the kitchen proper, that we are concerned here, for he included an eleven-page chapter on *sorbetti* which in a sense complements the medical dissertations provided by Dr Baldini.

From Corrado's recipes we discover that ingredients of Neapolitan ices in the 1780s were very similar, although more widely varied, to those specified in the early Naples *Sorbette* booklet. Lemon, citron, strawberry, bitter cherry, sweet orange, muscat pears, muscatel grapes, chestnuts, pistachios, *orgiato*, candied eggs, Imperial (a rich custard), jasmine, cinnamon, chocolate, milk, *torrone*, are all familiar Neapolitan ices. Corrado offered in addition violets, pomegranates, melon, water-melon, peaches, fresh fennel seeds, called in Naples *caroselle*, milk with coffee, a mixture called *sorbetto butirato*, a custard with butter as well as with milk and eggs, a *sorbetto alla Veneziana*, which was yet another variation on the cinnamon theme, and an early version of *tutti frutti* which Corrado called *sorbetto di varie Frutta*. The last included apricots, pears, jasmine syrup, fresh fennel seeds, candied citron, orange and pumpkin peel, bitter cherries, pistachios, all added to an already half-frozen lemon or other citrus-based water ice, which was then refrozen.

The familiar Neapolitan *giare* reappear in Corrado's recipes, although he does not invariably use them as units of measurement. What had changed very noticeably since the days of Latini and the *Sorbette* booklet were the techniques of preparing the sherbets and of freezing them. It had for some time now been regular practice to prepare a preliminary sugar syrup, and in the freezing process to revolve the cylinder in the snow and salt mixture until a finger-thick coating of ice had formed on the inside, when it was broken down, mixed with the still liquid parts, and the process continued in the same way until freezing was completed and the *sorbetti* had become white and soft or *mantecato*. This consistency achieved, the sherbets were served in *giare*.

Corrado called *sorbetti* noble beverages, *bevande nobili*, but left his readers in no doubt that they were frozen beverages. They were *ghiacciate, congelate*. He was commendably careful to make his meaning plain. However, his freezing mixture was far from a strong one. His proportions, in English terms, were 3 lb of salt to 16 of snow, less than one to five. His sugar allowances, on the other hand, were on the high side, although he varied them according to the basic ingredients. Ices based on the subacid fruits, for instance, needed more sugar than those made with milk products. Sugar syrups for ices were of two kinds, thin and more condensed. They were made with pound for pound (still the 12 oz pound) of clarified sugar and water cooked only to the *manuscristo* height, an old sugar boiling term long fallen into disuse but preserved perhaps in the kitchens and confectioneries of the religious houses, and meaning what we call the thread. When a thicker syrup was needed, he boiled it to the blow stage. Custard ices to be frozen in *stracchini* or cheese-shaped moulds, which might be rectangular, log-shaped, or triangular, were made a little sweeter in

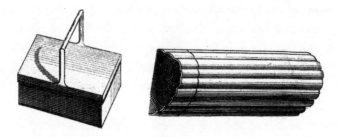

Moulds for ices from Gilliers' *Le Cannameliste français*, 1751.

proportion than those fruit ices destined to be transferred, after a preliminary freezing, to *pezzi*, the hinged fruit moulds popular at the period. For custards Corrado made no prepared syrup but added the sugar directly into the egg, milk and cream mix, as we make them today, except that in Corrado's time they were much richer. A *sorbetto di latte all' Inglese*, for example, called for 36 oz of cow's milk, 12 oz of cream, 12 oz of butter, 12 egg-yolks and 24 oz of sugar, with a little flavouring of oil of cinnamon. The musk and ambergris of the earlier ices have gone, and cinnamon in one form or another is the commonest aromatic to go into Corrado's ices. For comparison with earlier recipes, here are three from the *Credenziere*:

For a chocolate ice, 2 (12 oz) lb of chocolate, $1\frac{1}{2}$ (12 oz) lb of powdered sugar are to be boiled in 36 oz of water. When the chocolate and sugar have dissolved, press the mixture through a fine sieve and return it to the saucepan to cook until the chocolate adheres to the spoon. Turn it into a vessel and beat it until cold, then put it into the snow and freeze it. Note that there is no aromatic flavouring, and probably something such as cinnamon or vanilla was already in the chocolate.

For a *candito d'uova* or egg candy ice, 30 egg-yolks diluted with 36 oz of thin sugar syrup are to be put into a saucepan over the fire and stirred until thickened. Pass the mixture through a sieve straight into the vessel in which the ice is to freeze, and with a copper spoon beat it until cold, and put it into the snow. It may be seasoned with cinnamon water or oil of cinnamon. It will be seen that the candied egg ice is growing more and more to resemble the *bomba* of the nineteenth century.

For a *torrone* ice, dilute 12 egg-yolks with 2 *carafe* (about a litre or a little more) of cow's milk and cook this very slowly with 12 oz of sugar, then press it through a sieve. When it is cold and set in the snow add 12 oz of almonds, blanched, toasted and crushed fine with $\frac{1}{2}$ oz of coriander, and moistened with 2 oz of cinnamon water; it is once more sieved and beaten until light, then frozen.

Some of Corrado's ices were calculated for production on quite a large scale. For 100 *giare* of milk-based *sorbetti*, for example, he allowed 16 (12 oz) lb of sugar, and for 100 of lemon or other subacid fruit *sorbetti* an extra 6 lb were required. For the freezing mixture for this quantity he allowed 200 (16 oz) lb of snow and 40 of salt. The proportions, one part of salt to five of snow, were the same as those required for smaller quantities. Corrado disclaimed specialist knowledge of *sorbetti* making, remarking that although he could have prolonged his chapter on the subject, he preferred to leave further ideas to the professional *Credenzieri*, who knew very well that at the present time there was no vegetable which could not be made into a *sorbetto*, or at any rate take its name.

In his preface to the *Credenziere* book the author referred to the erudite Dr Filippo Baldini and his medico-physical essay on *sorbetti*, and noted how originally people had been content to cool their beverages by putting the vessels in wells, but subsequently

began to use snow and ice, even, as Pliny had said, in winter, and then came Alexander the Great who was the first to invent snow pits, during his Macedonian campaign, covering them over with oak branches, so that he would always have snow ready when he needed it. Thus little by little the use of ices was introduced, and then was invented the preparation of *sorbetti*, so much to the taste of everyone who tried them, that it could be said today *sorbetti* are the delight of the entire human race.

That the 'little by little' had lasted from the days of Alexander the Great to the seventeenth century AD was a matter that Corrado did not go into. Highly literate though he was in his fields of research, of which cookery and the art of the confectioner were only two, gastronomic history was not Father Vincenzo Corrado's strong point. Neither, for that matter, was botanical history. He firmly believed, for example, that potatoes were indigenous to Italy, and had been transplanted thence to America, rather than the other way round.

For today's readers, Corrado's virtues are those of a lively cookery writer with an inventive gift for rather light and elegant recipes, particularly those for vegetables and sauces. Presumably his cooking skills and knowledge of confectionery techniques and distilling were acquired first-hand in monastery kitchens and stillrooms, those rich sources of traditional lore and learning relating to the allied arts of cookery, medicine, gardening and baking – sources of which we ourselves were so summarily deprived by Henry VIII. When in 1789 the second edition of *Il Credenziere* was published, the printer Michele Migliaccio (was he a descendant of that Cristofaro Migliaccio who had published the Neapolitan *Sorbette* booklet of so long before?) wrote a brief foreword to the book. In this equivalent of a publisher's blurb, Migliaccio referred to his author as the 'famous Oritano'. Corrado, he claimed, was 'possessed of an ingenious vivacity, clarity of ideas, felicity of expression ... and immense love of every kind of knowledge'. In spite of lapses such as the one concerning potatoes and his beliefs about the history of ices, the gifts attributed to Corrado by Migliaccio were not so greatly exaggerated.

When only twenty years old, Corrado had had the good fortune, and the talents, to be chosen to accompany the Father-General of his Order on a three-year peregrination round Italy, visiting other Celestine houses. On such a mission the young man would naturally have been entertained with his Superior to the best the religious houses had to offer in the way of hospitality. Judging by the experiences of Père Labat in Sicily (see p. 186), Rome, and Civita Vecchia earlier in the century, Italian monastic cooking was very often refined and inventive. On feast days hospitality was lavish. Many religious houses were known for their confectionery and sweetmeats, candied fruit and marmalades, and for the quality of the fruit and vegetables cultivated in their gardens. Experienced travellers knew that in Italy they would fare better with the monks or nuns than at the inns, where the cooking was often atrocious. After a visit to the Priory of St Luke near Bologna, Père Labat had been regaled with a collation of chocolate, ices and pastries by the Mother Superior but had declined an invitation to stay for dinner because he had already sent his servant ahead to order his meal at an inn. Presently he had cause to regret having turned down the Mother Superior's proffered hospitality. Arriving at the inn, he discovered that a capon and four pigeons which he had himself supplied from Bologna were boiling in a cauldron in a bucketful of water. The preliminary treatment completed, the birds were to be spitted and roasted to rags.[15] It was typical of the cooking of Italian innkeepers at the time.

In December 1770, Sir Charles and Lady Miller, planning their journey over the Apennines from Bologna to Florence, took the precaution of obtaining a letter from the Cardinal Legate to the Superior of a convent of White Benedictines in the mountains. It was situated not far from the 'wretched inn' where they would have been obliged to stay had it not been for the Cardinal's introduction. Arriving unannounced at ten o'clock in the evening, and at a convent where ordinarily women were not permitted to cross the threshold, the Millers and their servants were nevertheless received with the greatest courtesy. They were entertained to a charming dinner served on fine china plates, 'an admirable gravy soup in a beautiful terreen of the same china', a braised *poularde*, as good as you ever saw from Bresse, a fry *très recherchée* after the Italian ecclesiastical fashion, and a stuffed pigeon garnished with small cakes made of a kind of paste (chestnut flour, perhaps?) 'quite agreeable with the pigeon'. The dessert was preserved grapes, roasted chestnuts, beurré pears and Parmesan cheese. With the main part of the meal there had been white and red wines in crystal carafes, with the dessert a bottle of very fine old Cyprus. The tablecloth was of 'fine damask, callendered and pinched, forming a Mosaic pattern. The napkins were curiously folded', the cutlery and saltcellars were shining silver 'so clean that they appeared quite new'. As Lady Miller commented to her correspondent, 'you know the church in all countries inclines to good fare'.[16] She and her husband had enjoyed, and fully appreciated, the kind of carefully prepared, refined food which Corrado knew and wrote about.

One Naples convent which in Corrado's day was known for the excellence of its cooking was San Gregorio Armeno, an establishment to which only the daughters of the nobility were admitted. Dr John Moore, a resident of Naples in the 1780s, recorded a remarkable collation offered by the noble nuns of San Gregorio to King Ferdinand IV, his wife Queen Maria Carolina and her sister the Princess of Saxe-Teschen. Dr Moore was present on the occasion of the royal visit. His report deserves to be quoted in full.

The company were surprised, on being led into a large parlour, to find a table covered, and every appearance of a most plentiful cold repast, consisting of several joints of meat, hams, fowl, fish, and various other dishes. It seemed rather ill-judged to have prepared a feast of such a solid nature immediately after dinner; for these royal visits were made in the afternoon. The Lady Abbess, however, earnestly pressed their Majesties to sit down; with which they complied ... the nuns stood behind, to serve their royal guests. The Queen chose a slice of cold turkey, which on being cut up, turned out to be a large piece of lemon ice, of the shape and appearance of a roasted turkey. All the other dishes were ices of various kinds, disguised under the forms of joints of meat, fish and fowl, as above mentioned. The gaiety and good humour of the King, the affable and engaging behaviour of the royal Sisters and the satisfaction which beamed from the plump countenance of the Lady Abbess, threw an air of cheerfulness on this scene.[17]

The prowess of the sisters at San Gregorio in the very specialized field of creating ices in the guise of roasted birds, joints of meat, hams and so on, of tinting the de-moulded ices in the appropriate colours and of conserving them in ice-cupboards or conservators – in Italian these were called *armadii frigoriferi* – until the moment came to spread them out in the form of a cold collation was clearly prodigious. The pewterers who cast the elaborate hinged moulds, actually out of lead rather than pewter, also played an important part in the success of entertainments such as the one which comes down to us thanks to Dr John Moore. His description of it reminds me of nothing so much as a page, or rather a folding plate, in the great French confectionery book of the eighteenth century, Gilliers's *Le Cannaméliste*, made actuality. The plate shows some dozen of the hinged moulds used for the creation of these pretend ices. A ham, a jole of salmon, a salmon trout, a freshwater crayfish, a pear, a gourd, a gherkin, a boar's head, a pomegranate, a melon, a very large egg with a separate round mould for the yolk, chestnuts, truffles, an asparagus, a tongue, even sponge fingers. Given a clever mould maker there was no fruit, vegetable, or article of food which an experienced confectioner could not imitate in a cream, custard, or water-ice. The spread put before the King and Queen of Naples was a show of skill in the same vein as those sugar feasts of the sixteenth century at which everything on the table, including the cloth and the napkins, the drinking cups, the plates, the fruit, the decorations, had been made of sugar in one form or another. Ferdinand and Maria Carolina of Naples may not have felt unmitigated delight at having to munch their way through those hard, sugary, painted ices, but they seem to have carried out their royal duties gamely enough.

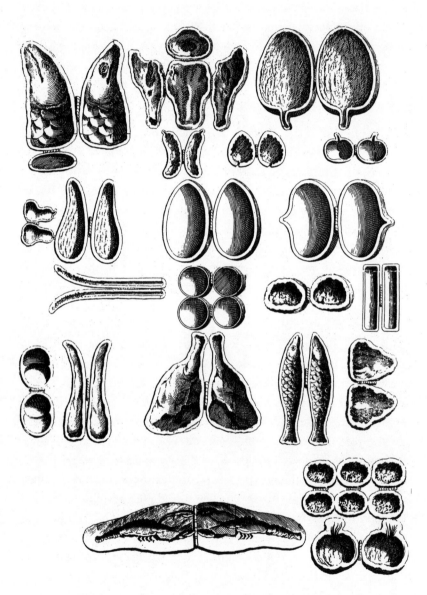

Moulds for ices from Gilliers' *Le Cannameliste français*, 1751.

The Queen's Ice Pail Maker

William Fuller, author of *A Manual Containing Numerous Original Recipes for Preparing Neapolitan Ices*, was the inventor of a freezing tub, or as he called it 'a freezing machine for making ices in a few minutes of matchless smoothness, at less expense than is incurred by any method now in use'. His little manual was published and sold 'by William Fuller only' at 60 Jermyn Street, St James's Street, London. The design for his machine had been granted provisional protection by the Patent Office in 1853, and in 1856 he patented his improved version of 'that description of pail in which ice-creams or water-ices are made',[18] so although no date appeared on the title page of his sales manual it may be assumed that it was in the latter year he produced it. Included in the manual were a description and drawing of his freezing tub, instructions for using it, seventy-four sketchy recipes for ices and ice puddings, plus a light sweet sauce for puddings and instructions for preserving fruits for the making of winter ices.

Fuller had been producing and selling ice-cream pails at the Jermyn Street premises at least since 1842, when his name appeared in the

Fuller's ice cream freezing machine.

London *Post Office Trades Directory* as an 'ice pail maker' – a description which has sometimes misled lexicographers into concluding that such tradesmen were makers of pails for the chilling of wine rather than for the freezing of ices. Fuller was the only member of his particular profession to be listed in London that year, so although ices had already been with us for about 150 years and although without question there were others operating in the same or a similar market, the trade as a recognized entity must have been of fairly recent establishment. By 1853 Fuller was listed as ice pail maker to the Queen, so was certainly on friendly terms with the royal confectioners.

Among Fuller's competitors was Thomas Masters, who was demonstrating his ice and ice-cream freezing apparatus (Master's ice-making and ice-cream freezing apparatus, for which he took out a patent in 1843, is discussed on p. 341) at several London establishments, including the Royal Polytechnic Institution, Regent Street, the Zoological Gardens, Regent's Park, and Sweetenings Fish and Oyster Establishment, Cheapside. Compared to the Masters apparatus, Fuller's ice pail was very simple, used ice and salt in the conventional way, and still required the continuous use of both hands during the freezing operation. With one hand the operator turned a central handle which rotated the bowl-shaped vessel containing the preparation to be frozen, with the other, using a spaddle, he scraped down the ice crystals as they formed. The turning and scraping continued throughout the freezing process. Fuller maintained that his apparatus was cheap, durable, expeditious, easy to work, economical in its use of ice, clean in operation, and in short was for general use. Further, it could be kept in working order without trouble or the additional expense incurred by frequent repairs. Those objects, said Fuller, were well known to be 'not always attainable' in the more expensive and complicated ice machines, the last remark undoubtedly a dig aimed at Masters, who had gained himself enviable publicity during the Great Exhibition of 1851, where he had demonstrated his ice-cream freezing apparatus, attracting the particular attention of the Queen and Prince Albert on the occasion of their visit on 8 June that year.[19] (If the criticism of the Masters machines published by Dr Riddell in his *Indian*

Domestic Economy of 1850 is anything to go by (see p. 265), and they were made quite impartially, Fuller's remarks were justified.)

Judging by Fuller's businesslike description of his apparatus, his own chief market would have been that of the professional confectioners, owners of shops and catering businesses, and also those in charge of the confectionery and pastry kitchens of the great town houses of neighbouring St James's Square, Piccadilly, Arlington Street, Bond Street and Berkeley Square. There were numerous hotels in the neighbourhood, such as the Clarendon in Bond Street, the York at the corner of Stafford Street and Albemarle Street, and Grillons, also in Albemarle Street. Among his fellow tradesmen in Jermyn Street was Richard Wall, a successful pork butcher purveying meat pies and sausages to the gentry of St James's and ancestor of those Wall brothers who in 1922 had the idea of selling wrapped ice-cream bricks from a tricycle. Among his other customers there would also have been picturesque characters such as the contemporary Duke of Beaufort's Neapolitan confectioner, who is famously supposed to have aroused His Grace from sleep one night in order to inform him that having been to the opera earlier in the evening to hear a work by Donizetti, he had that instant invented a new *sorbet* which he had decided to name after that divine composer, and 'I hastened to inform Your Grace.' No doubt there were others who sat up at nights experimenting with new combinations of ingredients and thinking up new shapes for the presentation of their *bombes* and *parfaits*. Abraham Hayward, who recounted the Beaufort anecdote in his *Art of Dining*, published in 1852, made a point of listing the names of the chefs then employed by English noblemen, and also of some of the pastry cooks and confectioners in private service in the capital or in great country mansions. Three of his confectioners Hayward considered in the front rank were named Perusini, Raffaelle and Vincent, while among the finest pastry cooks at that time working in England was Alphonse Gouffé, brother of Jules, chef of the immensely prestigious Paris Jockey Club. Alphonse eventually became Queen Victoria's chief *pâtissier* and translator of his brother's books.

The Fuller ice pails, then, were well known in the royal pastry and confectionery kitchens. Those palace pails would have been the ones referred to in Fuller's Patent specification of 1856, which he described as being of large size, with a spindle rotated by means of bevel gearing and a winch handle. The manual he sold with his apparatus 'could not', Fuller considered, 'fail to be agreeable to everyone who wished to excel in the production of ices, those indispensable luxuries on the table.'

A more commercially minded man than many inventors, Fuller was well aware that novices and apprentices as well as men of experience would be operating his ice-making apparatus and took the precaution of warning the inexperienced that if any mixture failed to freeze in the machine it would be because there was too much syrup in it. The remedy would be to thin it down with plain unsweetened fruit juice or other liquid, according to the kind of ice being made. If, on the other hand, the ice became clotted in freezing, it had insufficient syrup, and more must be added. Fuller made no mention of saccharometers. If he knew of their existence – and if he had seen the 1844 revised edition of Jarrin's *Italian Confectioner* he would have learned of that author's high opinion of the efficacity of the new instrument, which he himself was selling – he would also have known that few of his customers would have possessed or bothered to buy this innovatory syrup gauge. It was not until about 1865, when William Jeanes, confectioner at Gunter's, published a new and revised edition of his 1861 *Gunter's Modern Confectioner*, that the professionals followed Jarrin's lead and began advising readers to invest in saccharometers to test the precise density of their syrups.

Where Fuller obtained his Neapolitan ice recipes he does not reveal, but there is no doubt that they have a common ancestry in Vincenzo Corrado's *sorbetti* and those of the early Naples booklet. Here in Fuller's crammed little pages we find once more the familiar sweet fennel seed, cinnamon, chocolate, *torrone*, chestnut, lemon, orange, almond, and *orgeat* ices typical of Naples. The candied eggs, the pistachios, the milk custards, the coffee, the flower essences – lily, hyacinth, jasmine, orange and lemon blossom – are the ingredients of William Fuller's Neapolitan ices just as they had been in the days of Dr Baldini, Vincenzo Corrado and their common predecessor, the unknown author of the booklet. Among the newcomers introduced in the late eighteenth century were a tea cream – the result perhaps of a craze for tea in post-revolutionary Paris – a champagne water-ice and a plum pudding ice. The last, less fearful than it sounds, was no more than a heavily vanilla-flavoured cream custard into which currants were stirred before the cooled cream was turned into an appropriate mould for freezing. When turned out, more currants were strewn over the pudding. Chinese ice was another fancifully named confection. Composed of 30 egg-yolks, 24 oz of powdered sugar, 4 oz of pistachio paste and $1\frac{1}{2}$ pints of water simmered until the consistency of cream (you'd have to be mighty careful to prevent the eggs scrambling), coloured and flavoured according to the operator's taste, strained, frozen with the addition of a small amount of any preserved fruit – Chinese ice was just another version of candied eggs, or the *bomba* of the 1820s and 1830s. I suspect that the nomenclature may have originated in a second floor café in Paris where Turkish-style tents and Chinese kiosks were for a time the height of fashion. It was this café, originally owned by a man called Joliet, which was taken over by Velloni, immediate predecessor of Tortoni and well known for his Neapolitan ices. A clue perhaps to the origins of Fuller's recipes.

Among his other rich confections Fuller offered Portugal ice-cream, a composition of 12 oz of almond paste, $3\frac{1}{2}$ pints of cream, 4 oz of fine chocolate powder, 24 oz of sugar, and flavourings of powdered vanilla and cinnamon. After freezing, sliced almonds, pistachios, or preserved fruits were added. Take away the chocolate and this notable invention was approximately the one which came to be known as *plombières*, nobody knows why, unless it was considered to be related to one of the several varieties of rich fruit cakes known at that time as *gâteaux de plomb*.

Should the ice-cream specialists of the day ever have been daunted by the surplus egg-whites left on their hands after churning a few gallons of Portugal or Chinese ices according to Fuller's directions, he did at least provide them with one formula, called Sicilian ice-cream, calling for whites only, 16 of them to $3\frac{1}{2}$ pints of cream and 15 oz of powdered sugar, all whipped up together for ten minutes, simmered until thickened, strained, flavoured, frozen. Sicilian ice was certainly light compared to the Portugal and so-called Chinese confections.

The use of whipped egg-white in the ices of this period is of some interest. As an addition to cream- and egg-enriched ices, meringue was a recent development in the technique of the professional confectioner. Did it come about as an experiment in the use of leftover egg-whites? William Fuller appears to have been a great advocate of the practice, directing that meringue should be put into 'all ices except liquid ices, to make them smooth and light'. Earlier confectioners such as Joseph Bell, Frederic Nutt and their contemporaries had not used meringue at all. Thomas Masters, whose recipes, published in *The Ice Book*, predate those of Fuller by twelve years, included meringue only in his Roman Punch and Victoria Punch ices. Basically these consisted of a hard-frozen lemon water-ice diluted with rum, champagne, brandy, orange juice. Three or 4 whisked egg-whites were gently mixed with sugar and stirred into the lemon ice, now softened by the wine and spirits.

Masters gave no directions for re-freezing the punches, so they were evidently served more as alcoholic lemon sherbets than as ices proper. The punch of the British East Indies – punch or panch meaning five or a mixture of five elements – had probably been introduced to fashionable Italian society by a British ambassador or some dandy on his Grand Tour. Lord Byron recorded ices served with stiff rum punch instead of lemonade at the *conversaziones* he attended in Venice in 1816. Writing to Tom Moore on Christmas Eve of that year, Byron remarked that the Venetians thought this custom English and he 'would not disabuse them of so agreeable an error, no, not for Venice'.[20] From Italy punch came back to England enhanced with the addition of a lemon ice and true Italian meringue, which is to say the whisked egg-whites were mixed with boiling sugar syrup, not just plain sugar as directed by Masters and Fuller, neither of whom properly understood the process of making it. Nor, according to Jarrin, was it proper to put brandy, rum and other inferior spirits into true *punch à la romaine*. Kirschwasser, maraschino and sparkling champagne were the only liquors he considered allowable in 'this delicious drink', which had been spoiled, he asserted, by economy or ignorance. If a pint each of Kirschwasser and champagne plus 2 glasses of maraschino made an insufficiently strong punch, then the remedy was to add more Kirschwasser.

In the light of Jarrin's strictures and Fuller's disregard or ignorance of the uses of the saccharometer and of the correct method of adding sweetened meringue to ices, it can be assumed that the latter's freezing pails were superior to his ices. It remains only to add, as far as Fuller is concerned, that he makes an early mention, in English, of the Italian *spongati*, light ices which like the punches also demanded the addition of meringue. A simple chocolate water-ice, for example, could be changed into a chocolate *spongati* by the addition of meringue, and you could make the ice white by using milk instead of water for the chocolate infusion. There were also typical Neapolitan water-ices such as a white cinnamon one, an infusion of crushed cinnamon in boiling water, to which sugar syrup was added prior to freezing, and meringue paste and slices of candied fruits were stirred in towards the end of the process. Another infusion called for 6 oz of sweet fennel seeds in 30 oz of sugar syrup diluted with 1 pint of water and the juice of 3 or 4 lemons. The infusion was left to stand for two or three hours, when it was strained and ready to freeze. When frozen it was enriched with slices of all sorts of candied fruit. Fuller called this Neapolitan water-ice, and indeed the formula went right back to the earliest Naples ices.

If I have lingered over William Fuller, his freezing apparatus and his ice, it is because it appears to me that he was probably responsible for the introduction to London confectioners of the descriptive term 'Neapolitan', at first employed as a prefix denoting certain types of ices, and later commonly used to denote a certain excellence and quality rather than any special method of making an ice or any specific ingredients. Thus in time confectioners all over the country would claim to be purveying Neapolitan ices as an indication of prestige, just as in a later period a restaurant advertising 'French cooking' would be assumed to be offering something a cut above ordinary English fare. It was not until late in the nineteenth century or even early in the twentieth that in England the term Neapolitan as applied to ices came to denote one particular ice, the three-coloured pink, white and green brick so familiar in the 1930s in Lyons Corner Houses and in thousands of teashops frequented by schoolchildren on a day's outing. Those bricks had indeed originated in Naples, or, at least, the shape had been in use there since the end of the seventeenth century, even if the tricolour combination had not evolved until much later, at the time of the adoption of the national red, white and green flag of united Italy.

Days of Snow and Ice

'No human mind can have any idea of the immensity of the disaster,' wrote Cavaliere Alexander Hamilton, pioneer ice manufacturer of the city of Messina, on 23 January 1909. 'Messina is in ruins. After twenty-six years of hard work I now find myself penniless . . . I am wandering about looking to find friends, passing over the ruins of their houses, but I cannot feel to go away, the scene is dreadful.' It had been three weeks earlier, on the morning of 28 December 1908, that Messina was virtually annihilated by the most catastrophic earthquake ever to be recorded in the island of Sicily. Some 84,000 people had perished. Fires had burned for a fortnight. Lesser shocks had occurred almost daily and were to continue for nearly two months. On 27 January 1909 'this morning about 8 a.m. we had rather a heavy shock, lasting over ten seconds. The ground is still moving,' Hamilton recorded.

Cavaliere Hamilton, a British subject who had evidently been brought up and educated in Sicily, had married a Sicilian girl and had made his career in the ice-manufacturing business. He was addressing his piteous letters to the editor of the American journal *Ice and Refrigeration*. They were in part pleas for assistance in restoring his ice factory to working order, in part expressions of gratitude for generous American aid to the stricken city and for personal kindnesses received from the officers of an American naval vessel recently arrived in the port. Among personal losses, Hamilton revealed, were the deaths of his twenty-two-year-old only daughter, Mary, and her recently married husband, both killed by falling masonry when the great 120-foot chimney stack of the ice factory had crashed on to the adjacent family residence. All but one of his ice-making machines had been wrecked.[21]

For Messina, the earthquake which had left the city in ruins and shocked the entire world was the culmination of a series of major disasters going back over 200 years. In 1743, 30,000 people out of a population of 60,000 had been wiped out by plague. Forty years later the earthquake of 1783 had wrecked the city. Cholera epidemics in 1854 and 1887 and the earthquake of 1894 were still comparatively recent memories to the citizens of Messina. Their numbers had all the same, astonishingly, increased to about 120,000. By 1908 their city had been once again flourishing when disaster struck on that terrible morning three days after the Christmas celebrations of 1908.

As always, the earthquake had been followed by attendant disasters, among them the subsidence of the shore by over two feet, resulting in a great tidal wave which lashed the shores of mainland Calabria and eventually reached the coast of Malta. Altogether the number of victims, never ascertained with any accuracy, was estimated to have reached a total approaching 100,000. (In 1943, when aerial bombardment by the Allies again brought disaster to the city, the casualties were believed to have been 5,000.)

To pursue the story of just one man among the thousands in Messina whose lives and livelihoods were shattered by the earthquake of 1908, Cavaliere Hamilton appears to have been more fortunate than most. Of his four ice-making machines, the one least damaged in the wreckage of his factory had been his newest and best. By May of the year following the disaster, in time for the onset of the hot weather, his factory was once again in limited production. Between the end of May and the end of November, he informed *Ice and Refrigeration*, he had sold 800 tons of manufactured ice and what he called artificial snow. He was agreeably surprised that his factory had done so well.

Amid the confusion and the disruption, the cessation of normal services, and the inevitable illnesses and epidemics following all disasters of comparable magnitude, it is not difficult to see that the restoration of the Hamilton enterprise was bound to succeed. The beleaguered citizens of Messina were surely desperate for what comforts they could obtain. Among such comforts ice and snow would certainly have been high on the list. Hamilton wrote that during the cholera epidemic of 1887 he had himself provided Messina with free ice. In 1909 he could not of course afford to make gestures of such a nature, but by July 1910 his business appears to have been once again in full operation. Messina's resilience was phenomenal.

Among the traditional attractions of Sicily were the ice-creams and the snowy fruit juice ices which since the eighteenth century had been popular with all classes of the island's society. The ice-cream men of Messina, evidently as dauntless as the rest of their fellow citizens, were soon back in operation. For their benefit Hamilton had devised a special machine to pulverize his factory-made ice into snow indistinguishable from the natural snow of Etna. Crushed ice, the confectioners complained, was not at all the same thing. Their freezing pots were made of lightweight tin, not pewter, and were easily damaged and cut by small, sharp ice particles. A machine which beat the pulverized snow into layers which formed bales each weighing about 50 or 60 kilos was next devised by Hamilton and his engineers. These bales he could either sell at once to waiting buyers or keep in storage until needed.[22] Beaten-down snow compacted in this manner would have been very little different from the ice-like blocks which had traditionally been rolled half-way down Mount Etna for storage in those natural caverns which the Cavaliere's namesake, the Hon. William Hamilton, George III's ambassador to Naples, had described to the Royal Society. Many such caverns were known in different parts of Etna, he wrote in October 1769, 'some of them made use of as magazines for snow, the whole island of Sicily and Malta being supplied with this essential article from Mount Etna'.[23] Patrick Brydone, who inspected some of the same subterranean caverns the following year, reported to his friend William Beckford that they made the finest ice-houses in the world.[24] They were used by the peasants, he remarked. No doubt it was the peasants who, until the introduction of factory-made ice, had been the traditional suppliers of snow to the confectioners, the cafés, and the street sellers of Sicily.

Given the long history in Sicily of the use of natural snow from Mount Etna, the plentiful supplies, the low price, its widespread consumption in the island – a circumstance frequently remarked upon by travellers ever since the sixteenth century – the success of Cavaliere Hamilton's pioneering ice business, founded in Palermo in 1876, is almost as surprising as the rapid revival of his fortunes after the calamity. The snows of Etna had after all supplied the island for hundreds of years, and had in addition yielded sufficient for the dispatch once a fortnight of four or five hundred tons to Malta via the private brigantine maintained by the Knights solely for that purpose. 'The Knights, burning for the love of God and of their neighbours' and marooned in their dry and arid island, wrote the French Père Labat, a caustic but acute observer, who visited Sicily in 1709, 'are obliged to drink much and often'.[25] Were it not for the succour of Etna's snows, added Père Labat, the Knights would find themselves in a sorry plight. Further, the Sicilian populace had long been accustomed to an allowance of cheap natural snow as part of their birthright. As early as the 1580s Dr Pisanelli of Bologna was writing that every Sicilian peasant considered that after bread and wine, the third essential of existence was snow.[26] The English traveller George Sandys, spending a few days in Messina about 1612, remarked on the excellent wines there and on the supplies of snow in summer at 'a contemptible rate'.[27] The authorities, both civil and religious, likewise took it for granted that revenues and taxes from the sale of snow annually enriched their coffers by many hundreds of pounds. In the eighteenth century the Bishop of Catania's income had been largely dependent upon the £1,000 a year derived from the small patch of mountain reserved for snow for the Knights of Malta.[28]

How then was it that overcoming tradition, superstition, prejudice, the Cavaliere Hamilton's new-fangled ice and snow were successful? Did the clue lie with the massive Sicilian emigration of the time, the resulting labour shortages and increased wages? Or was it due to an ever-increasing consumption of natural snow for refrigeration and preservation purposes? For the freezing of ices alone the confectioners and café proprietors must have needed very considerable supplies. The Sicilians, like the Neapolitans, had from the early days shown an extraordinary aptitude for the confection of ices. The people of the island as a whole had very quickly taken to eating ices in great profusion and wonderful variety. Along with sugar confectionery of all kinds, candied and fresh fruit, cakes and sweetmeats, the Sicilians devoured ices on every festive occasion. They drank iced water, iced chocolate, iced wines. During his brief reign as King of Sicily (1713–20), Victor

Amadeus of Savoy had made fun of the Palermo government as 'the ice-cream parliament'. Eating ice-cream, he said, 'seemed to be the members' most noticeable occupation during sessions'.[29] Half a century later, Patrick Brydone was recording that 'even the peasants regale themselves with ices during the summer heats ... and there is no entertainment given by the nobility of which these do not always make a principal part'. At one of the numerous feasts recorded by Brydone, a dinner given by the nobility of Agrigentum to their Bishop, the great variety of fruits in the dessert was exceeded by that of the ices, all of them presented in the manner then so popular in Italy, 'disguised in the shapes of peaches, figs, oranges, nuts, etc ... a person unaccustomed might easily have been taken in'. One way and another, Brydone commented, 'a famine of snow, they themselves say, would be more grievous than a famine of either corn or wine'.[30]

The widespread use of snow for icing drinks and freezing ice-cream had already, as Brydone noted in 1770, been much intensified by the demands made by physicians who advocated quantities of ice-water in the treatment of fevers, and even sometimes went so far as to smother the patient's breast and belly with snow or ice. Aggravation of any natural shortages of snow were undoubtedly engineered by operators of protection rackets such as Addison (see p. 153) had described in Naples in 1700, although Denis Mack Smith, modern historian of Sicily, who refers to the export of Sicilian snow being subject to piracy, and to the derivation of an important percentage of Palermo's municipal income from snow, also records that in the 1820s, during the occupation of the island by Austrian troops, artificial shortages and prices raised by contractors were drastically dealt with. Soldiers sent up Mount Etna with orders to seize what snow they could find were invested with powers of life and death.[31] Such measures underline the vital importance of snow to the Sicilians, who themselves frequently remarked that without the snows of Etna their island 'could not be inhabited, so essential has this article of luxury become to them'.[32]

Now, by 1910, the use of natural ice and snow was everywhere in Europe being abandoned in favour of the factory-produced article. The uncertain nature of the ice harvests, the equally unpredictable summers of

western Europe, the costs of ice transport and storage, the sheer convenience to large-scale consumers of the rival product, were all factors
which combined to make natural ice unprofitable for the merchants.
Factory ice could be so quickly and cheaply produced, so rapidly delivered when needed, that enterprises such as the Norway ice trade to
France and England were fast becoming commercially impractical. How
the merchants engaged in the trade still made any kind of profit is something of a mystery. Their prices had been cut to a minimum to compete
with the output of the ice factories. In France, by 1910, the Norway
trade was almost finished, a few cities on or near the North Sea coast
being the only ones still supplied by Norway, 150,000 tons out of the total
200,000 at that time consumed annually in France being manufactured
ice.[33] Even in Damascus, a city whose inhabitants had since time out of
mind relied upon the snows of Lebanon for the chilling of their water,
their sherbets and their wine and fruit, there was now, unbelievably, an
ice factory.[34] Did the deities of the mountain look down and smile when
in 1911 a scorching European summer brought an ice famine to the
continent's capitals? In no time, and factories notwithstanding, the ice
purveyors were off once more to the Swiss glaciers, with their ropes and
pulleys and axes, there to hack out blocks of real ice for the parched city
dwellers of Italy, France and Germany.[35]

'There be rose leaves, sugar crystals, And hyacinths clogged with spice,
There be vermicelli saffroned, and cinnamon-flavoured ice' were lines
which might seem to have been written with Sicily in mind, and
although in fact Oscar Ashe wrote them for *Chu Chin Chow*,[36] they
describe pretty closely the desserts and sweetmeats of the island as
over and over again chronicled by travellers in the seventeenth and
eighteenth centuries. Even the saffroned vermicelli was not unknown
in Sicily, where saffron was very commonly used in cooking. Here is
Père Labat in 1709 reporting five or six different kinds of fish cooked
with saffron, a dish of white onions stuffed with minced meat, pine
kernels, raisins from Corinth, coriander, and candied lemon peel,
served with a saffron sauce. With their outer layers of onion serving
as a kind of crust, Père Labat found these confections like delicious
little patties. At the same Sunday meal there was also a minestrone

with vermicelli covered with beaten cinnamon, and to drink, strong red wine cooled in snow and poured from copper-bound wooden pitchers. At the Dominican Priory in Palermo where he stayed, Père Labat inferred that such dishes were nothing out of the ordinary, although as guests he and his companions were given an extra piece of roast veal large enough 'for four men with good appetites'. Excellent fruit and melons, coffee and chocolate appeared in due course and Père Labat, a *fin gourmet* if ever there was one, was highly delighted with his entertainment.[37] (He was not the man to suffer bad cooking or inadequate hospitality without recording such lapses for posterity.)

As for the cinnamon ices of Sicily – also much loved in Naples and highly recommended for their many medicinal properties by the eighteenth-century Neapolitan physician Filippo Baldini (see p. 163) – they are seldom mentioned nowadays. But undoubtedly, just as the stuffed onion confection which had so delighted Père Labat was of pure Arab descent, so the cinnamon water-ices were descendants of the cinnamon sherbets so often recorded by travellers to Persia and Turkey, where those highly spiced and sugary drinks were regarded as valuable stimulants. By the time the Sicilian and Neapolitan confectioners had transformed them into popular ices they had become treats for children. The Prince of Lampedusa, author of *The Leopard*, remembered 'pinkish' cinnamon ices when he wrote of his Sicilian childhood in his enchanting and enchanted memoir, *Places of My Infancy*.[38] His description of the buffet supper at a grand Palermo ball in 1862, with its display of 'monotonous opulence', waxy chaud-froids, 'rosy foie gras encased in gelatine armour, dawn-tinted galantine, coralline lobsters boiled alive, boned woodcocks reclining on amber toasts decorated with their own chopped guts ... a dozen other cruel, coloured delights' is an exercise in delicate irony. Having conveyed the displeasing vulgarity of the spectacle, the Prince moves on to the sweetmeats and the ices. They are more to his taste. As a true Sicilian he cannot but write a little hymn to their charms.

Scorning the table of drinks, glittering with crystal and silver on the right, he moved left towards that of the sweet-meats. Huge sorrel* babas, *Mont*

---

* Presumably the translator meant sorrel in colour.

Blancs snowy with whipped cream, cakes speckled with white almonds and green pistachio nuts, hillocks of chocolate-covered pastry, brown and rich as the top soil of the Catanian plain from which, in fact, through many a twist and turn they had come, pink ices, champagne ices, coffee ices, all *parfaits* and falling apart with a squelch at a knife cleft...[39]

Leaving the Prince of Lampedusa in contemplation of the alluring array of chocolate and coffee *parfaits* and champagne *sorbets* in the supper room at a Palermo ball in the 1860s, we may now return from that fabled land of saffroned vermicelli and cinnamon ices to the reality of Messina in 1910. Here we find our ageing, white-bearded Cavaliere Hamilton still struggling to retrieve his ice trade from the ruins. Miraculously, he has managed not only to re-establish his business but he has also contrived to introduce his fellow citizens to a charming novelty achieved by a long-forgotten little piece of technology. This was nothing less than a mechanically produced version of that old Italian table luxury, the cone of ice encasing a carefully arranged edifice of fresh fruit, a fantasy which had originated in the seventeenth century and had so often adorned the banquet tables of the later Medici in Florence, of the cardinals and princes of Rome, of the Spanish viceroys and ministers of Naples, of the princes of the blood at the Versailles court in the days of Louis XIV.

Hamilton's great speciality, it should be explained, and one of his main selling points, was the fact that his ice was made from distilled water and was therefore not only exceptionally pure but also crystal clear, assets which could not of course be claimed for the compacted snow of Etna. The Hamilton ice was produced in blocks or cones of either 14 or 25 kilos each, and these blocks were clear right up to a pencil-size white core in the centre. An ingenious mechanism had been devised by Hamilton and his engineers by which the white core was drawn off and was replaced by fresh distilled water, reboiled and therefore air-free, so that when frozen the core too was perfectly clear. Next, Hamilton hit upon the idea of arresting the freezing process half-way, drawing off the unfrozen water still in the centre of the ice-can, and thus achieving something like an outsize tubed ice-cream mould made of ice, the hollow centre of which was to be filled with grapes, apricots, peaches and so on. The preparation of these fruit-filled blocks was timed so that they were ready about the dinner hour. 'A ready sale and a good price is obtained for this ice-and-fruit,' wrote the Cavaliere, 'as the ice-dealer sells the ice at so much a kilo and the buyer pays [only] the price of fruit for this ice.'[40]

The profits to Hamilton of his ice-and-fruit must have been very small, but given the Sicilian love of fresh fruit combined with ice, the idea was a brilliant one from the publicity point of view. If the bouquets of brightly coloured flowers embedded in ice described by Mark Twain had delighted the inhabitants of the Mississippi towns of the 1880s, how much more of a joy must have been the blocks of sparkling and fruit-bejewelled ice to the shattered citizens of Messina. As they conveyed their icy burdens home to cool their rooms and deck the tables of their temporary homes they must surely have marvelled at the skill of the ice-magician of Sicily, whose factory was once more on the way to prosperity but who was himself homeless and lodged all alone in one of a row of little wooden cottages put up by the American Red Cross and known as the *Villagio Americano*.

So many inventions of the ice factory era, among them the amiable practice of embedding flowers and fruit and even, I remember reading somewhere, such unlikely objects as Parisian dolls and models of animals filled with sweets, and that other interesting piece of technology, the moulding of ice into drinking goblets to be produced at the rate of 100 per hour, were swept away by the ravages of 1914 that they now seem as remote as Atlantis – and just about as legendary. There were now new techniques to supersede the old ice factories, and more important interests than those of the ice-cream men of Sicily and their fragile tin freezing pots. On 20 August 1914 the British journal *Cold Storage* carried an announcement that Messina now had its first cold store. Italy, still a neutral power, was all the same preparing for the worst. The new cold store was to be stocked with food for Sicilian troops. Its owner was a Sicilian, but its machinery had been installed by a German firm.

A Persian Tale[1]

Ice for Isfahan

Among the many marvels of Isfahan in the days of Shah Abbas of Persia, the Marquis Pietro Della Valle, an Italian traveller who had already spent sixteen months in Turkey, and in Baghdad had married an Assyrian girl, singled out two buildings as particularly worthy of notice. One was the palace or castle in which were housed the 'King's treasures, arms, papers and other things of importance'. The second most interesting curiosity in Isfahan – at any rate to the Roman nobleman – were the ice houses outside the city. They were called *buzchane*,* he wrote in June 1620 to his friend Mario Schipani, a Neapolitan physician. He was anxious to convey the information that these were no ordinary conservatories for snow such as everyone knew in Italy, but areas where ice was not only conserved but made, and in great quantity, for use in the city during the summer months. By the citizens of Isfahan it was used to cool beverages and fruit and was considered essential for the table and, Della Valle explained, was preferred by them to the snow more commonly used elsewhere in Persia.†

As Della Valle told his friend, there was no lack of snow in Persia, and in many places it was conserved as in Italy (although in rather different repositories), but in Isfahan people were more particular, and preferred ice, not, it was to be understood by Della Valle's

---

* He was using the Turkish word for ice house because at the time the court language of Persia was Turkish. The Persian word is *yakjal*.

† Sir John Chardin maintained that snow was always preferred for cooling sherbets (see p. 198).

Pietro della Valle

correspondent, natural ice from 'waters frequently dirty and corrupt' and consequently injurious to health, but ice 'made by artifice from the purest and clearest waters to be found'. Della Valle now tells his friend how this ice is produced and conserved.

Outside the town on a great plain exposed to the north wind – that notorious north wind of Persia, which as Della Valle says 'freely blows' – they raised a straight wall running east to west, ordinarily of about 120 to 150 feet long, of sufficient thickness, and of a height to keep out the sun, and cast shade on the ground even when that planet is at its zenith, at the highest point of its meridian and in the height of summer. This meant that the wall had to be about eight perches★ in height or even a little more. Della Valle now goes into some detail about the construction of the wall. Without having seen one of these walls, or without at least pictures or photographs of the remains of

★ Della Valle used the Italian measure *canna*, which was our rod, pole or perch. At the time this unit varied, but probably he was using the 9 palm *canna*, or about 2 metres, so these shade walls would have been about 50 feet high.

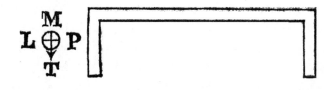

Della Valle's diagram of a shade wall. The Italian orientations L (*levante*) and
P (*ponente*) indicate the rising and setting of the sun (east and west), M
(*mezzogiorno*) and T (*tramontana*) indicate south and north respectively.

some examples, it is not easy to envisage the construction or even to
grasp the precise object of it, but Della Valle's detail is valuable and is
best quoted as he recorded it. 'Of this wall thus running from east to
west,' he says, 'there are as it were two arms, or two other wings of
wall, raised at right angles, from south to north, in a straight line.'
These wings are 'of the same height and thickness as those of the great
wall and of a proportionate length', which is to say they are about a
fifth as long as the main one. If the east–west wall is, say, 60 feet long,
the two arms running north at its extremities will be no more than 12
feet at the most. Here Della Valle gives the simple diagram reproduced
above. The purpose of the two arms, Della Valle explains, is to shade
the enclosed space and to prevent the sun reaching it in the morning
when it rises and in the evening as it sets. Thus the sun at no time
penetrates the enclosure and the whole day long there is perpetual
shade over an area of several yards; and the north wind freely blowing
there has no let or hindrance on that side which encloses or commands
the entrance.

Within this cool and shaded enclosure they dig a trench ordinarily of twenty
to thirty palms* [15 to 24 ft] and this occupies the entire space of the great
wall enclosure. And the winter being come, they dig in the plain which is
exposed to the North beyond the trench and the walls, a number of small
furrows which then fill the enclosure with as many small channels of no more
than four fingers in depth.† In the evening they conduct, very deftly, by

* The palm was approximately 9 inches.
† See, further on, the differing but complementary accounts given by Jean de
Thévenot and Sir John Chardin, both written some forty years later.

certain of the small channels, whether lined or otherwise I know not [they were in fact lined with tiles], clean and carefully selected running water which irrigates the plain in such a manner that all the small channels between the furrows receive as much water as they can hold and no more. This water, being shallow and in small volume, easily freezes during the ensuing night, and the next day at dawn, that is before sunrise, they throw the ice from the channels into the trench.

It being impossible, as Della Valle explains, to pack the ice evenly in the trench, they pour a little more of the same water – in other words it had to be clean and clear – into the trench, and this in turn also freezes, rendering the whole smooth and uniform. 'Thus all the pieces garnered meld into one solid mass reaching from end to end of the trench and of more or less thickness according to the quantity taken from the channels.'

The following evening the process of flooding the channels and of collecting the ice next morning is repeated, and this second batch of ice forms another layer which in turn fuses with the first, and by the same means, i.e. by the addition of extra water, so that the two form one solid block. The operation is continued daily for a month or more until the trench is full from one end to the other and the ice packed up to ground level. In order the better to conserve the ice until it is needed – the heat being not yet excessive – they cover it with straw to protect it from spoiling by the sun. 'They have little to fear from rain,' Della Valle says, 'for in these parts it falls rarely.'*

When summer comes the ice is broken up with pickaxes and carried into the city on horses or mules, each beast laden with two or three blocks. Some is bought by wholesalers for retail in their shops, since there is no house which does not use it and lay in a provision, and some is sold in the streets. 'They break it in pieces with axes and hammers, and put some in their wine' – as travellers invariably testify, the Persians notoriously drank wine in private, very often to excess – 'some in their water, and some again in vessels containing their drinks, and also in the cups from which they drink. They also put some in

---

* The climate of Isfahan, as all travellers remarked, was extraordinarily dry and the air very clear. Rust, for example, was unknown there.

large lumps on their fruit and on other foods, in the dishes served at table.' Della Valle is much beguiled by the way ice is used 'with such nicety that nothing more beautiful could be seen. It is as refreshing, and even more so, than snow; and besides being refreshing it is most rejoicing to the eye with its translucent whiteness.'

Della Valle ends his dissertation on 'these ice-manufacturies' by telling his Neapolitan friend that there is a great number of them in Isfahan, for there is 'a great annual consumption of ice in this city'. He makes a great point of his lengthy description because he thinks it is something 'which merits being made known to our countrymen and used by them'. Just as five years earlier, during his sojourn in Turkey, he had written to Schipani about the charms of coffee and the coffee houses of Constantinople, saying that it would be an excellent idea to introduce the beverage to the Italians, and promising also that he would return home with recipes for the delicious Turkish sherbets which were so different from the aromatic waters of Italy, Della Valle proceeds to weigh up the possibilities of adapting the Persian ice system to conditions at home. 'I have no doubt that were the secrets known in Italy, where the waters are marvellously good, similar constructions could be built, and would not fail to work in the same way; unless the great humidity of our climate might be injurious to the ice, which keeps easily in Isfahan where the soil is extremely dry, and therefore well adapted to its conservation.' Not everybody at that time appreciated the importance of dry soil in the construction of underground ice stores, but Della Valle's powers of observation and his attention to detail made him unusually valuable as a commentator on all that he encountered during his years of travel. Remarking that in Isfahan the ice stores were left uncovered – by which he meant that they were not roofed over, although, as we have already learned from him, the ice was protected by straw – he thought that in Italy they should be roofed and the trenches lined all round with straw. In fact all the precautions customarily observed in the maintenance of Italian snow wells should be taken, and after all, he conceded, 'ours are successful enough'.[2]

Now it is very clear from Della Valle's description that at Isfahan the ice-making and ice-storing operations required none of the great conical mud-built domes which in some parts of Persia were built over the ice storage pits and which may be seen in Elisabeth Beazley's photographs (pp. 207 and 208). To those immense and remarkable buildings I shall return later, and at present follow up Della Valle's account with those of two other travellers, both French, who were in Isfahan some forty years after the Roman marquess. The accounts of these two men, Jean de Thévenot and Jean Chardin, who was shortly to become a naturalized Englishman, confirm that at Isfahan the processes of ice induction and ice storage were somewhat different from those practised in other regions of the Persian empire. Given the widely diverse territories and climatic conditions covered by that empire in the seventeenth century such differences were only to be expected.

Jean de Thévenot was a very experienced traveller. He had left Paris on his first voyage, an extended European tour, on 28 December 1652, when he was only nineteen. Thereafter he made two lengthy voyages to Egypt, Syria, Turkey, Persia and India, and was on his return journey to France when he died at Miana, in Persia, on 25 November 1667, only thirty-four years old. He was a most meticulous observer and left valuable accounts of many unfamiliar customs and activities which he encountered on his travels, among them the detailed description of sherbet-making at Rosetta near Alexandria quoted on p. 391. There can be no question that, whether or not Thévenot had had the opportunity of reading Della Valle's travel letters, first published in 1658 – and he does sometimes appear to be filling in detail which Della Valle omits – his account of the ice-making at Isfahan was written from personal observation.

The Isfahan ice installation described by Thévenot was south of the city, and the walls were only 3 or 4 perches,* or 18 to 22 feet high: the ice pit or trench was 20 feet deep by 20 feet wide and it ran the whole length of the north wall. Running north again from this trench were what Thévenot described as parterres, 6 or 7 perches long and 1 perch broad, i.e. approximately 40 to 45 feet long and 6 feet 6 inches broad, each of these channels separated from the next 'by small furrows

---

* Thévenot expressed his measure in the French *toise*, roughly the equivalent of the English perch or fathom, which varied from 6 feet to 6 feet 6 inches.

of earth, as in a saltings'. That little piece of description makes matters clear. Thévenot then explains that some of the channels are 2 to 3 feet in depth, some 1 foot only.

When it gets very cold they divert river water into these parterres, it freezes rapidly, and when it is set hard they break the ice in the deep channels in large pieces, which they carry to the trench, where they pack them very close: then they break the ice in the shallow channels, and having carried it to the trench, they break it up very small with heavy blows from the back of a spade, and with it fill in all the spaces between the larger blocks already packed; in the evening they throw over it all a quantity of water pouring it from gourds cut in half and attached to the end of poles: the water freezes during the night and bonds all the ice into one mass ...

– acting rather as if it were cement.

Continuing his account, Thévenot says that having refilled all the channels with water, and duly lifted the ice and packed it as before, on top of the first blocks, they continue the process until the ice in the trench has reached a height of one perch and a half or about nine to ten feet.

They then cover it with straw and reeds to the height of two or three feet, and when they want to take it for use they uncover it in one place only. This invention works easily at Isfahan where the air is very dry, and where there is very little damp weather. It would seem that a few of these ice installations would suffice for the whole of a large city; nevertheless a great many are made, close to the City in divers places.[3]

In Thévenot's account it is the detail concerning the two different depths of the ice channels which is particularly illuminating. It is reminiscent of Pierre Belon's description, written some 100 years before Thévenot's, of the Turkish method of packing ice and snow together rather as a masonry wall is built, the snow cementing the blocks of ice together (see p. 41). Again, from Thévenot we get the familiar comment that the ice-packing invention works well at Isfahan because of the extraordinarily dry air – 'than the aire of Spahawn no part of Persia is more healthy ... aire so sure and quick that I very well remember we found it much warmer than in more Northern Cities which had greater latitude,' said Sir Thomas Herbert, who had been in Persia in the 1620s and 1630s. He too remembered 'the Treasure, Arms and Ice stored within the large Castle moated about . . . towards the outside of the City'.[4]

Like all the seventeenth-century European travellers in Persia, Thévenot had remarked that the Persians use a great deal of ice even in winter, but he also rather surprisingly asserted that the Persians never used snow, in which he was much mistaken, as is confirmed by the frequent references to its use and sale made by Della Valle, Sir John Chardin, Dr John Fryer and other travellers, both earlier than and contemporary with Thévenot.

Sir John Chardin was a French gem merchant who became a great oriental traveller but ultimately found that his Huguenot religion made it impossible for him to live unharassed in France, and so made his home in England. There in 1680 he was invited by John Evelyn, Sir John Hoskins and Sir Christopher Wren to become a Fellow of the Royal Society. In the following year he was naturalized, appointed court jeweller to Charles II, and promptly knighted by the monarch. He had spent altogether about eleven years in Turkey, Persia and India, and his complete *Voyages en Perse*, published in 1711, the year before his death, provide full, clear, rich accounts of the customs, manners, laws, religions, social life, products, food, drink, cooking and eating habits of the Persians in the 1670s.

To the accounts of the ice-making operations at Isfahan Chardin contributes some picturesque detail as well as some variations on the way they were organized. Given the number of those installations in the vicinity of Isfahan, there were inevitably differences in construction, as also in the way they were run, the basic principles remaining within the local tradition. 'As I have remarked, much ice is used in Persia,' Chardin tells us, and no longer to our surprise, adds that

in the Summer especially, everyone drinks with ice; but what is remarkable is that at Ispahan, and even at Tabriz, which is more northerly, the cold is dry and penetrating, more than anywhere in France or in England, the majority drink with ice in Winter as in Summer. The ice is sold on the outskirts of the town in open places; and this is what they do: they dig a deep trench, vat-shaped at the base [Chardin is the only observer to give us this detail], with a northerly exposure; and in front of it they dig squares sixteen to twenty inches deep, like so many small basins. When the frost sets in they fill the basins in the evening and in the morning when it is quite frozen, they break the ice and hammer it to pieces with mallets and pack them into the trench, where they break them up again as much as they can, for the smaller the ice is broken the better it seizes up, and in the evening, having refilled the basins as before, they go and pour water from handled calabashes over the broken ice in the trench so that the pieces congeal together better. Then when night comes, they summon the people of the quarter who, with great cries of joy, with fires alight around the edge of the trench, and with music to enliven them, go down into the trench, drag one on top of another these masses of ice, which they call *codrouc*, meaning base, or foundation, and throw water between them so that they meld together. Thus in six weeks, an ice pit of 6 feet or more in depth, long and wide as they choose, is filled with ice right to the top.

Falling snow, Chardin recorded, was a great hindrance to the work, and had to be quickly swept away. As all ice harvesters soon discovered, melting snow also melted the ice. When the ice pit was filled it was covered with water reeds called *bizour*, found in Persia on the shores of 'waters', by which I think Chardin meant lagoons, marshes and lakes. In the summer, when the ice pit was opened, it was another fête for the quarter.

The ice was sold by the donkey load, eighteen *sols* the load, which is made up of two quarters of ice, each weighing 60 lb. This came to about two *deniers* a pound. 'The Chippings and offcuts' were the perquisites of the local people who had helped in the work, 'and each goes to collect his provision in the morning'. Like Della Valle, Chardin was particularly struck by the beauty and cleanliness of the ice. Not the smallest impurity or cloudiness was to be seen. 'Spring water was not clearer or more transparent.' This is an interesting statement. Coming from two such reliable witnesses as Della Valle and Sir John Chardin we must believe it. Presumably, since the river waters of Persia were rarely noted for their purity and clarity, the streams feeding the underground conduits which in turn fed the ice basins of Isfahan were either conducted from a spring or else passed at some stage through some kind of filter. But with all that, we now get a remarkably contradictory statement from Chardin. 'Snow is also stored in places where it is convenient,' he says, 'although there is an abundance of ice. This is done out of nicety; for they find their beverages more agreeable with snow than with ice, and especially with Sherbet.'[5]

Why, one wonders, go to so much trouble to make ice if what people really preferred was snow brought down from the mountains and stored, as Chardin said, 'in places where it was convenient'? The answer is, I think, that some people preferred ice, others snow, that both, as recorded by Della Valle, were easily available in the great bazaar of Isfahan, and that in certain sherbets, beaten snow would make a more pleasing effect than ice. If we remember that in Italy and France the early attempts at ices were called *neve* and *neiges*, all becomes clear. At first the European confectioners were probably aiming at simple imitations of the Persian sherbets with their snowy appearance, and only later started applying the new ice-and-salt freezing techniques to these sweet drinks. Chardin, in any case, is usually careful to distinguish between ice and snow as used for cooling purposes. Further on, I shall describe how, when he was lying dangerously ill at the town of Laar, it was snow brought down from the mountains and sent to him as a gift from the local Khan which brought him relief in his fever. But when he attended a banquet given by the five Sarhat brothers of Isfahan, the richest Armenian merchants of Persia, a feast which Chardin describes in detail as opulent and exotic as the setting and the wondrous succession of dishes served, he notes that on the buffet with the gold plate and porcelain, the wine flagons and crystal jugs, there are two great basins filled with broken ice, 'clear and clean as drops of water'. In Persia, Chardin explains, a piece of ice is put into the glass, it is presented, and the wine is poured over it.[6]

The common domestic use of ice in Persia was no recent development. The tradition dated back at least to the fifth century AD, and probably long before. Sir Percy Sykes, in his *History of Persia* (1921), explains that in the middle of that century the reigning member of the Toba Wei dynasty, rulers of Northern China from AD 386 to 584, dispatched an envoy to Po-sz (Persia), and between AD 455 and 513 ten missions passed between Persia and the Toba Wei dynasty. A member of one of the Chinese embassies recorded a fine description of the country and its products:

Po-sz has its capital at Suh-Li [Ctesiphon]★ . . . with over 100,000 households. The land is fairly level and produces gold, silver, coral, amber, very fine pearls, vitreous ware and glass; crystals, diamonds, iron, copper, cinnabar, mercury; damask; embroidery, cotton, carpeting and tapestry . . . the Climate is very hot, and families keep ice in their houses. The land is stony sand for the great part, and for irrigation purposes water has to be conducted.[7]

Robin Lane Fox, in his *Alexander the Great*, gives an even earlier instance of the use of ice in the ancient Persian empire, again recorded by a Chinese, and in that same part of it, once called Babylonia, now Iraq. 'The Persian conquerors,' Mr Lane Fox considers, 'could scarcely have found Babylon congenial, for the heat was appalling, and five hundred years later a Chinese visitor would still find their successors living in underground houses cooled by ice.'[8]

Was the ice reported by those two Chinese witnesses, in the second and fifth centuries respectively, already being made by the induction system dependent upon the network of khanats – already of ancient origin† – or was it ice brought down from the mountains and stored for the summer, as it is supposed to have been stored by Alexander 700 years before (see p. 168)? That point will in all likelihood remain one of speculation. The evolution of such pieces of technology is often difficult, if not impossible, to pin down to a precise period. Very possibly Sir John Chardin had made similar inquiries and had been met with blank looks. He certainly commented in a slightly exasperated tone that 'one would not believe how little curiosity they have in the East about these kind of observations. Nobody among their scholars records discoveries made in the arts and sciences.'[9] To the age of scientific inquiry in Europe, to this future Fellow of the Royal Society, the attitude of indifference concerning such things was incom-

★ Ctesiphon was on the Tigris, close to the modern city of Baghdad.
† Jacquetta Hawkes, in *The Atlas of Early Man*, puts the development of irrigation systems in Mesopotamia and Persia at somewhere between 8000 and 5000 BC.

prehensible. Today, faced with modern scientific research and archae-ological discovery, it is perhaps easier for us to appreciate the Persian lack of interest in precise dates. When your country's culture, indeed its very existence, depends on developments such as those which created effective systems of irrigation and which had occurred already several thousand years ago, the significance of a century or so is small. Could Chardin's detail concerning the popular fêtes when the Isfahan ice stores were opened indicate a venerable origin? It is reminiscent of that Chinese poem describing the celebration of the ice house opening as long ago as 1100 BC which I have quoted on p. 228.

Luxuries for the Road

European travellers in Persia were much struck by the way the Persians on the road provided themselves with so many comforts. Pietro Della Valle remarked that this was due to the fact that the Persians, not only the army but the court, the merchants, the artists, were forever on the move, and as a consequence had elevated the art of travelling comfort-ably to a high degree of refinement. Della Valle, who himself travelled with his young Assyrian wife accompanied by a varying assortment of her relations, plus maidservants and menservants, a cook, an outrider, a camel driver and so on, marvelled how the Persians provided them-selves while on the road with every luxury which they enjoyed in the cities. They had portable baths, portable heaters for the bath water, portable kitchens, and by that he meant not only the usual campaign ovens and cooking equipment essential for travellers, but *foconi*, braziers which were carried on camel back and used for cooking food while actually on the march. Della Valle attributes the inventive genius of the Persians in the matter of amenities for the road to sheer necessity. As he said, they were more often on their journeyings than in their fixed abodes, but their natural love of luxury, a national characteristic, also played a large part in their industrious search for comfort.[10]

One piece of travelling equipment not mentioned by Pietro Della Valle, but described in detail by Sir John Chardin, was the travelling provision chest called a *yakdan* or *yactan*, literally an ice-container, *yak* meaning ice and *dan* or *tan* any object intended to contain another. Chardin's *yactans* are of two kinds. They are either rectangular wooden boxes, 18 inches wide and 20 to 22 inches deep, lined with felt, or else cloth cases lined with leather. Both were carried on horseback, like packs, on the croup, and attached to the saddle without inconveniencing the rider. In one side of the box the table linen and other necessaries for the table were packed, together with food for the day's journey. On the other side were stowed coffee, sherbets, liquors and ice, together with anything else one might need on the way. Chardin travelled in some style. He had a servant whose special task it was to take charge of the *yactan* and look after the goatskin filled with drinking water which was hung under the horse's belly. Water carried in this way, Chardin reported, could be drawn very cool, especially during the night and early morning.[11] (In the summer, travel was of course by night, rest during the heat of the day.)

Chardin, as so often, provides the best and fullest detail in the matter of his provision chests but his contemporary, the English physician John Fryer, has left us what is without question the most picturesque prose and the most lively account of the manner in which the Persians travelled and the equipment they carried with them. Dr Fryer, whose travels in East India and Persia lasted from 1672 to 1681 and whose account was published in 1698, was much fascinated by the Persian love of entertainment and feasting, by their prolonged hunting excursions, their gardens, their cooking, their wine, their prodigious appetite for sweetmeats, their coffee houses, *hammams*, wind-towers, in short by every aspect of their material life. The lavish use of snow and ice in Persia was more of a surprise to this Englishman of the 1670s than to the Frenchman of the same period, while to the Italian of fifty years earlier the fact that ice was commonly used had been no novelty, and it was rather the way the Persians had perfected the art of inducing its production which impressed him. That aspect did not strike Dr Fryer at all. In England the storage of ice in ice houses and the drinking of wine and water chilled with ice were fashions new since the restoration of Charles II in 1660, and Persia provided Dr Fryer with what was probably his first experience of this luxury. He did not invariably approve of the custom of drinking iced wine and snow-cooled sherbets, but in the great heat of the Persian summer found such indulgences irresistible.

When he arrives from India on his second visit to Persia in March 1676 Fryer reports that on the Persian Gulf coast the heat is already 'parching'. The local Khan, an acquaintance from Fryer's first visit, is staying at his cool retreat in the hills, but sends a welcoming gift to Fryer and his party. It takes the form of 'Apples candied in Snow' and ice brought by a messenger travelling overnight. 'By Break of Day we drank a Glass of Wine quenched with a Lump of Snow and Ice, to the Caun's Health'.[12] Those apples 'candied in snow' seem to me curiously reminiscent of the ice-encrusted apples conjured up so long ago by John Barclay in his *Argenis*. They must have been stored all through the winter, perhaps actually immersed in snow in the ancient manner so that they really did look as if they were candied (see p. 202). At least we know, thanks to Chardin, that the apples and the ice had probably been packed for the journey down to the coast in a *yactan*.

When he arrives in Shiraz, the first important city on the journey, Fryer notices 'Repositories for Snow and Ice' which are 'fine Buildings', and says they 'preserve it to cool their Wine with, and sell it constantly in the Market for such uses'. He makes it plain that he himself draws little distinction between the two, and finds that at Shiraz 'Ice dissolved in their liquors is as prevalent even among the Vulgar as Drinking Tobacco' – he meant smoking the hookah.

When he reaches Isfahan he sees the 'Fruiterers shops placed at the Entry', just as Della Valle had seen them fifty years earlier, 'and in the wide open Places under the Chief Cupoloes of their *Buzzars* [Fryer's spelling is as engaging as his turn of phrase] vending, beside Fruit, Sherbets of Pomegranates, Prunelloes, Limes and Oranges, with Ice and Snow to cool them', and here he finds that 'Ice dissolved in their liquors is as prevalent as at Siras, so that the Poor, have they but a Penny in the World, the one half will go for Bread, and dried Grapes, or Butter-milk, and the other for Snow and Tobacco'. He notes this Persian taste for iced drinks on many occasions: 'They mightily covet cool things to the Palat, wherefore they mix Snow, or dissolve Ice in their Water, Wine, or Sherbets', but as a physician he regards the habit as harmful. 'Nor can I excuse that destructive Custom of drinking Ice with their Liquors ... Cold things, such as Snow and Ice are Enemies to the Stomach and Lungs; and so on.' He also expresses a very Western distrust of fresh fruit. 'But the most pernicious of all is the cramming themselves with much Fruit, which is a temptation hardly to be denied, where such Plenty and so Excellent are offered; however they fill the body with crude and rebellious Humours.'[13]

It is interesting to speculate whether, in the years to come, Dr Fryer and Sir John Chardin, whose peregrinations in Persia and India were contemporary and who were both to become Fellows of the Royal Society, ever discussed or compared their experiences in Persia. If they did so Fryer may have been surprised to learn of the successful ice cure which Chardin had undergone after he fell ill of a dangerous fever contracted in the unhealthy environment of the port of Bandar-Abassi on the Persian Gulf coast (p. 217).

Like Della Valle, John Fryer was impressed with Persian travelling equipment, particularly so with the gorgeous gold and silver drinking vessels and flagons they carried on their hunting expeditions.

When they go out on this sport they return not in a Day's time, as we do, but remove from place to place, where Game is to be had; take with them their Wives and Family, and Travel in State with full prepared Tables, and act the Bacchinals like Alexander; for which purpose they have their Tents and close Carriages, their Gogolans for Provisions; they carry also Bulger-Hides, which they form into Tanks to Bathe themselves, and Women, in their Progresse; for drinking cups they have both gold and silver ones, as also large Flasks of that Metal; besides Earthen Jars for Water, and Puckeries, which are porous Vessels to keep their Liquor cool.

Gogolans, it should be explained, were porous earthenware jars, in India called gurgulets or guglets (a word derived from the Portuguese) which were packed in specially fitted cases. Underneath the water jar the shallow gold or silver drinking bowls 'which we call *Toss*,★ and is

★ I assume he meant *tasse* or *tazza*.

made like a wooden Dish, purposely so shap'd for convenient carriage', took up the minimum space. The cases which Fryer sometimes called Coosdans were 'made neatly of Rattans or Canes, covered with a Coverlet of Scarlet, Bordered with Silk for Shew as Well as to keep the Dust off'.[14] In other words a luxuriously fitted valise such as was carried by the French royal servants when their masters went stag-hunting.*

Those travellers who managed without carrying ice for the road could usually find it at the main stopping places along the great mercantile caravan routes where the big caravanserais and ice installations or *yakjals* were established, or on occasion would be offered some by a friendly fellow traveller. Jean-Baptiste Tavernier, like Chardin a jewel merchant, and yet another of those French travellers of the period to whom Persia came to be more familiar than their native France, noted on a journey from Kerman to Isfahan, twenty-five days march distant, 'the first day I set out, at my Stay in the Evening I met with a rich Moullah who seeing I had Wine, civilly offer'd me some of his Ice to cool it. In retaliation I gave him some of my Bottle.' On another journey, in 1664, his last in Persia, Tavernier arrives at Erivan in Armenia on 14 September and encamps in a beautiful grassy spot between the fort and the old town. He and his party stay in their tents because he has learned that there are sick people at the caravanserai. When he goes to pay his respects to the Khan of Erivan, he finds him in his cool underground chambers under one of the arches of the fine stone bridge over the river. With the Khan are his Captains and other officers, who have bottles of wine cooling in ice, and 'all kinds of melons in great dishes, underneath each of which was another filled with ice'.[16] It was the fashion which had some time since become familiar at the banquets of the Medici in Florence and at the feasts of the noblemen and cardinals of Rome, but to Tavernier it was evidently a novelty.

As for the great Shah Abbas, who had made his capital at Isfahan a

---

* In the time of Louis XV a cold collation packed in a red cloth valise embroidered with the arms of France was carried by the King's wine courier. In it were silver flagons of wine and water, napkins, bread, biscuits, fruit and preserves.[15]

byword for magnificence and beauty, when he progresses from his capital, first to Casvin and thence to his summer camp at Sultaniah where his army is on exercises, a vast gold treasure accompanies him. Even Pietro Della Valle, a man little given to excitable description, is awestruck when he sees the Shah's pavilion and the gold plate laid out, not for a special banquet but just for a few specially favoured visitors who have been invited to converse, drink wine (as was common knowledge at the court, Shah Abbas was a great wine drinker) and partake of informal food such as salted pistachios, sweetmeats, pickled cucumbers, fruit, and all manner of such trifles laid out on gold and silver platters, uncovered, each platter containing one layer only of food, but very closely packed. The platters are all set on rich brocade cloths laid on two long tables close to the ground. On the side on which the guests are to be seated, on the finest carpets, are a quantity of covered vessels, one for every two places, which were special receptacles for the shells of nuts, skins, fruit stones and other debris. A third table serves the purpose of a *credenza*, or buffet, and is laden with gold drinking vessels, dishes, basins, ewers, platters, flagons, candlesticks, in such profusion and so closely packed together that not an inch of brocade cloth is to be seen. These, Della Valle explains, are not taken into camp just for show, they are for use when the occasion arises. He also sees immense gold basins filled with drinking cups of all sorts and shapes. Some of the basins hold at least a dozen of these drinking cups, some more than twenty.

Having seen a great deal of snow being prepared and many covered dishes of food waiting in a little courtyard of the King's palace at Escref, Della Valle observes that at the meal in the Divan Khane to which he is invited, the guests are served wine from gold carafes, but the Shah's personal carafes are always of crystal. Laid on the monarch's carpet are four or five dishes, one filled with snow, the rest with food, and his gold cup filled with red wine is constantly in front of him. The Shah tells Della Valle that the wine is very light and pours some for him, putting snow into the drinking cup. He scrapes snow with his knife, rinses his empty cup, refills it and puts in the freshly scraped snow.

In spite of the overpowering display of wealth, Della Valle is not much impressed by the rather rough and plain design of many of the vessels and wonders whether the Persian goldsmiths are not very skilful or whether the Shah doesn't like paying them. However, he now describes something which he considers really notable. It is a wine cooler, a *rinfrescatoio* filled with snow, and with gold wine flasks standing in it. The cooler is rectangular like a *cassetta*, a chest, or a *cuna*, a cradle, of better workmanship and design than most of the Shah's treasure, and with balusters and other fine ornamentation. It is solid gold, and 'so large that two men I believe could only with difficulty have lifted it. This piece alone, without the flagons which were in it, Father Giovanni and I myself estimated at a weight of twenty thousand sequins, more or less.'[17] At a mere 365 oz troy or 25 lb avoirdupois the pair, the famous and massive Marlborough gold ice pails now in the British Museum begin to seem rather humble trifles in comparison with the Shah's wine-cooling cistern.

Snow upon the Desert's Dusty Face[18]

'December locks up all in Ice and Snow, and constipates the Pores of the Earth that it cannot be tilled; the Tops of Mountains are all capped, and the Sharp Winds and Serene Air make it less tolerable than in Great Britain, it being ready to cut you through.'[19] John Fryer's description of the short sharp winters of Isfahan as he experienced them in the 1670s conveys a vivid picture of the climatic conditions in which the people of that great city developed their ice-making system, and over the centuries evolved local variations and traditions. In other areas of the vast and varied territory which during the passage of millennia has constituted the Persian empire, other techniques and different styles of ice house were adapted, dictated by prevailing weather conditions and to some extent also by local building traditions.

Those high walls which at Isfahan protected only the underground ice-storage trenches from the sun were elsewhere built as shields from the prevailing night winds of the district as well as to provide daytime shade. In these cases the ice pool or reservoir, in form like a long narrow and shallow swimming bath, was dug in the shelter of the main wall, along its entire length, with the two short arms, only one fifth as long, protecting the extremities. The pit for the storage of the ice would then be dug on the other side of the wall and was usually covered over with a huge conical mud-brick dome, stepped like a Babylonian ziggurat, the steps giving easy access for maintenance of the dome walls and the summit of the building. Other types of ice store were long trenches covered with a series of small, low domes running along the base of the main wall on its south side, the north being commonly used for the ice pool. For the workers carrying the ice, access to the domed ice houses was across a ramp leading from the pool via an opening in the wall. On the far side of the great dome was a porch and small doorway through which the ice was eventually taken out, the entrance being sealed until the warm weather came.[20]

From the accounts given by Della Valle, Thévenot, and Chardin we know that at Isfahan the ice storage trenches were not covered with

An ice house near Sabsavar, in use in 1970. Photograph: Elisabeth Beazley.

207

An ice house with a curved shade wall near Sirjan (1975).
Photograph: Elisabeth Beazley.

any kind of dome, but only with thick layers of dried water reeds, while the pools and channels for the ice-making operations were dug in the open plain and left unprotected by walls. This is confirmed by Maxime Siroux, a French architect who was in Persia in the 1940s and whose work on the caravanserais and roadside buildings of Iran was published by the French Institute of Oriental Archaeology in Cairo in 1949. Siroux does not specifically mention Isfahan in the context – his ice house chapter is very brief – but is definite that in areas where the winter cold was short and sharp the ice pools were out in the open, and spread over very large areas covering 'several hectares',[21] an observation which gives an idea of the extent and importance of the ice-making operation. (One hectare is 10,000 square metres, the equivalent of 12,100 square yards or nearly $2\frac{1}{2}$ acres.) Given the quantities of ice used by the Persians and the constant reminders to be found in travellers' records that it was obtainable at almost give-away prices, that in the streets of the great cities iced water was free, iced sherbets commonly drunk all the year round, and fresh fruit almost invariably iced, the magnitude of the ice-making installations comes as no surprise. The Isfahan system is one I have gone into at some length because it has struck me as significant in its points of resemblance to the ice-making activities of Bengal in the eighteenth century. Two of those points were the vast extent of the area covered by the channels and furrows – the installation at Allahabad spread over 4 acres – and the way in which both Thévenot in the seventeenth century and Fanny Parks in the nineteenth likened the appearance of the plains when prepared for ice-making to a saltings or salterns.

At Shiraz the ice-making system differed quite substantially from the one practised at Isfahan, and a point very relevant to it is made clear by Elisabeth Beazley in her most illuminating ice house chapter in *Living with the Desert* (the whole book is of the greatest fascination). Here I cannot hope to do better than quote from Miss Beazley, whose knowledge of Persia is first-hand and whose researches and observations are those of a professional architect. Discussing the provision of protecting walls, in certain areas, for the ice pools as well as for the ice stores, Miss Beazley stresses the adverse effect of wind on the formation of ice: hence

the second function of the wall is to protect the pool from the wind. Moving water, even if only ruffled by a breeze, freezes more slowly than still water, and temperatures will only fall markedly when the air is still. Then each layer of cooled air near the surface stays where it is, because it is more dense, and so takes another turn of cooling, giving very low temperatures near the ground, perhaps several degrees lower than that of the air only a metre or so above it.[22]

Maxime Siroux, in this context, considered that protection from wind was the sole function of the walls, and Miss Beazley quotes James Morier, author of the celebrated *Adventures of Haji Baba of Isfahan* and also of a detailed journal kept when he accompanied Sir Harford Jones on an embassy to the Shah of Persia in 1808 and 1809, describing the ice-making installation he saw outside Shiraz. It was early January, so ice-making would have been in full operation: 'A wall is built the whole length of the reservoir to screen the ice from the south wind which is the hottest.'[23] As Miss Beazley comments, Morier made no mention of shade from the sun. Maxime Siroux, on the subject of wind protection and the high walls, says that during extreme cold they also permit the production of ice in the daytime. It seems curious to me that he makes no mention of the winter sunshine, but both Morier and a later writer, Dr C. J. Wills, confirm the daytime ice-making at Shiraz. 'The ice pool or trench is about fifty paces in length and fifteen in breadth; other dikes are cut transversally, which as they fill with water are emptied into the reservoir. When the first layer is congealed, another draught is made from the dikes, and thus the ice is accumulated.' Fifty years later, Dr Wills, medical officer to HM Telegraph Department at Shiraz during the 1860s and 1870s, and author of *The Land of the Lion and the Sun* (1881), gave a good description of the ice-making. Six miles from the city, he explained, the delicious stream called Ab-i-Rookhni, or Stream of Rooknabad, was diverted from its course during the first cold night of the season. In the pool, which was 30 feet by 300 feet long and 2 feet deep, a few inches of water was collected. The water was frozen by the morning and the ice left intact. More water was then admitted into the pool and another inch or two of ice made. When 3 to 6 inches thick, the ice was broken and collected for storage in a deep well on the spot; and so day by day the process goes on during the short winter until the storehouses are full.[24]

Realization that the ice in the pool was left undisturbed, another layer made during the day, and the process continued until the ice was thick enough to make it worth lifting, brings home the necessity of the protecting walls. Like Morier, Dr Wills describes these as being 300 feet long, the same length as the pool, and gives their height as 30 feet. The walls were to protect 'the open pond from the hottest rays of the sun'. Although it would surely have been necessary to exclude as much as possible both sun and wind if the ice-making was to proceed satisfactorily, Dr Wills makes no reference to protection from the wind. On the subject of the walls, Miss Beazley tells us that the line taken by them varies considerably. 'The straight ones are typical, but others are curved; perhaps the most fascinating seen consisted of two curved walls and two ice pits, like some strange winged creature.'[25] These are, or were in 1975, at Sirjan, and were perhaps the ones rather bafflingly described to me by a Persian lady of my acquaintance as having bent walls, which before seeing the photographs in *Living with the Desert* I took to mean leaning, like the tower of Pisa. The same lady also told me that during the massacres following the Ayatollah Khomeini's revolution and the downfall of the Shah, ice houses were sometimes used as hiding places by refugees fleeing from the fanatical police of that bloodthirsty period.

The accounts left by James Morier and Dr Wills definitely establish the Shiraz ice-making system as distinct from the one in use in Isfahan. Both were clearly adapted to suit local climatic conditions, and both seem to have worked well enough. We have seen how frequently travellers remarked upon the quantities of ice consumed in Isfahan, and at Shiraz the story is much the same. Morier, attending an entertainment given by the Shah's minister in Shiraz in honour of Sir Harford Jones and the members of his Embassy, noted that 'they are very fond of ice, which they eat constantly, and in great quantities'. At dinner the Minister kept a bowl of common ice in front of him and went on eating it throughout the feast, even after all the dishes were taken away. It was then January, and very cold, but Morier thought the reason for the eating of so much ice was the need 'to qualify the sweetmeats which they devour so profusely'.[26] Indeed, the prodigious consumption by the Persians of sweetmeats which were little more than solid sugar was notorious, and given that their sherbets also were highly sweetened and perfumed, Morier's diagnosis was well justified.

To Dr Wills, as a resident of Shiraz, the plentiful supplies of ice, its low price, and the regularity with which it was delivered by the ice-seller all through the warm weather, were impressive. 'A huge block is thrown down in one's doorway each morning,' he reported. Even so a shortage did sometimes occur, and when that happened, Wills revealed that blocks of snow were brought down from the mountains, 'but as these are some distance, and as snow melts faster than ice the weights being equal, the price rises'. In Wills's day, when the ice was running short an order was issued putting every household on half allowance, and he considered that a wise measure, as it made the cooks careful and ensured that everybody got their share. In normal times, though, so common was the use of ice that 'the poorest are enabled to have it, a big bit being sold for a farthing, and even the bowls of water for gratuitous drinking at the shop doors are cooled by it'.[27] Free ice for cooling the drinking water dispensed in the streets was an old tradition in Persia. Jean-Baptiste Tavernier, who returned from his last voyage to Persia in 1670, recorded that in Isfahan there were workers who went through the streets 'with a goatskin filled with water, a cup on one hand, and ice in a bag, who provide water for drinking to those who ask for it. They take no money from anyone, and are paid from a fund provided by legacies,'[28] and at a June festival at Isfahan Chardin noted that rich people paid for vessels of iced water to be placed outside their doors so that everyone could drink.[29]

A curious point about the many accounts of Persian travel quoted in this chapter and plenty more which it would be repetitious to cite is that while their authors often go into the most minute detail of almost every aspect of life in Persia and seldom omit to give an account – or at the least a mention – of every notable building and public edifice they see, not one of them – if we except John Fryer's casual reference to the ice repositories of Shiraz as 'fine buildings' – so much as acknowledges the existence of any of the gigantic conical structures which in many places concealed and protected the ice stores so vital to daily life in Persia. It seems scarcely possible that such conspicuous and strange buildings – strange that is, to European eyes – could have gone unnoticed by men so avid for information and with such eager eyes for the curiosities of a world outside their own as were Della Valle, Thévenot, Sir Thomas Herbert, Tavernier – whose travels covered a period of forty years – and Sir John Chardin. It is, I suppose, possible that travellers failed to distinguish the great ice houses from other domed desert buildings such as water cisterns and ziggurat-stepped buildings of the kind described and illustrated in *Living with the Desert*. Della Valle, curiously enough, does mention that on their way from Isfahan to Cascian he and his party stopped for a night at a place called Buz-abad, 'which if I am not in error means the ice-colony', but although it was the last week of January, and only five leagues – about fifteen miles – from Cascian, he makes no reference to any ice-making activities or ice houses.[30]

Whatever the explanation for the uncharacteristic silence on the part of travellers, until the appearance of Elisabeth Beazley's work all I knew of these most arresting buildings was just one photograph and one sole written account. It so happens that neither appears or is mentioned in *Living with the Desert*. The account, which is of much interest, and which was written by Edmond O'Donovan, a Victorian journalist, is here quoted in full, and the photograph, from a Russian source, is reproduced on p. 215.

O'Donovan was special correspondent of the *London Daily News* in the 1870s, and in 1879 undertook a journey to the oasis of Merv in Turkmenistan, south of the Oxus river, at a time when Russian inroads on the Turkoman and Kurdish territories of Central Asia, and their known designs on Merv, were considered to be a threat to Afghanistan and to the North West frontier of British India. In 1880, on his long ride from Askabad toward the Merv oasis, O'Donovan makes a detour from Luftabad to visit the abandoned city of Khivabad, built about 1740 by Nadir Shah, the Conqueror. Nadir had invaded Northern India, pillaged the treasures of Delhi (they included the famous Peacock throne) and on his homeward march had subdued Bokhara and Khiva, forcibly removing thousands of the inhabitants of those two cities in order to resettle them in the new town of Khivabad. A few years later, however, when that 'bloodthirsty monster', as O'Donovan calls him, was assassinated, the citizens of Khivabad felt safe to return to their former homes, leaving their fine new city entirely uninhabited. When O'Donovan saw this ghostly place the buildings were still in a good state of preservation, and near the walls were 'two very large conical structures of baked brick, plastered outside with loam. They are sixty to seventy feet high and their floors are excavated to a depth of ten or twelve feet. These are ice houses, in which the snow and ice from the hills were packed in immense quantities and preserved for use during the summer months.'[31]

Judging by O'Donovan's description, the Khivabad ice houses were much like the disused one at Yazd or Yezd in central Iran which Elisabeth Beazley says is typical of the monumental scale and size of Persian ice houses, the diameter being about 30 feet. O'Donovan's estimate of 10 to 12 feet for the underground depth of the ice pits was probably on the low side. In the darkness of a disused ice house it would be easy to misjudge the depth of the pit, and, significantly, he does not mention any remains of shade walls or evidence of ice reservoirs or channels. Had he seen any it is likely he would have remarked on them, for he already knew something about the ice-making in Persia, and some while previously, on his journey from Teheran to Kuchan, he had travelled with a pilgrim caravan and had halted for some days at Sabsavar, the green city. The place hardly lived up to its name, but here he had at least found plenty of ice for sale, and at a very reasonable price, a contrast to his frequent notes complaining of the over-pricing of provisions available to travellers. He had been told how the ice was made, and subsequently wrote that 'during the winter the cold is severe, and the inhabitants pour water, during the frosts, into large shallow tanks, afterwards removing the ice and storing it in deep cellars for summer use'. This system of ice-making struck O'Donovan as 'entirely out of keeping with the usual character of the Persians, but the luxury of ice in such a climate can only be appreciated by one who has felt its excessive summer heat'.[32] He had not, of course, seen the ice-making process in operation at Sabsavar and does not mention having seen a domed ice house in the vicinity, although there surely was one. A magnificent Babylonian ziggurat ice house dome near Sabsavar, intact and in use in 1970 (see p. 207) may have been one that was there in O'Donovan's day, but since he remained in the town during his brief stay there he would not necessarily have seen it. Aware, in any case, of Persian ice-making techniques well before he came upon the Khivabad ice houses, he still specifically says that there the ice and snow were brought down from the hills. That seems perfectly feasible. The Allah Akbar mountains, the highest peak of which range is about 6,000 feet, were within practical reach of Khivabad and blocks of snow could certainly have been carried down for storage in the ice houses O'Donovan described.

As for the huge Merv ice house, that is another matter. It is said to date from the fifteenth century. No other information concerning the gigantic ruin, which must have been at least as high as the ice houses at Khivabad, has come to light. The Merv oasis was annexed by the Russians in the late 1880s, but when O'Donovan went there in 1882 it was still occupied by Turkomans and Tekké tribesmen; and to

The ruin of the 15th-century ice house at Merv in the Republic of
Turkmenistan.

Europeans the place was unknown, the old cities of the oasis legendary.
Remarkably, O'Donovan even succeeded in visiting the ruins of
Bairam Ali, last of the three ancient cities of Merv, sacked in 1784
after Bairam Ali Khan was killed there when the town was attacked
by Emir Masum, ruler of Bokhara. O'Donovan did not describe the
older cities in much detail, and he did not mention seeing any ice
house, ruined or otherwise, but what he did see on another occasion –
he spent altogether five months in the oasis among the Tekké, who
were none too willing to let him go, mistakenly suspecting him of
Russian sympathies – and from half-way between himself and the
ruins was 'a large shallow sheet of water, where unused irrigation
trenches expended their supplies upon an uncultivated plain'. I should
guess that this was once an ice-making installation fallen into disuse
since the destruction by the Emir of Bokhara of the great dam on the
Murghab which filled the channels and fertilized the whole area.

For the ancient cities of Merv, snow from the mountains would not have been a practical proposition, and ice-making systems would have been considered essential. In the words of James Fraser, another Persian traveller who made a journey into Khorasan in 1821 and 1822, although without actually reaching Merv,

the oasis is about 240 miles distant from the principal cities, viz, Khiva, Bockhara, Balkk, Herat, and Meshed, from each of which place the road to it lies through a perfect desert. It is difficult to conceive how a situation so unfavourable could have tempted a mighty sovereign to fix his residence there; yet the Seljook princes made it their residence, and in the time of the Caliphs it was one of their eastern capitals ... the river Moorghaub fertilizes a small track of land along its banks; but except for this insulated and very limited spot there is no place fit for the habitation of man to be found within a great distance around.[33]

In such unpromising and inhospitable terrain did the successive conquerors of Asia build royal cities (in this oasis Alexander is supposed to have ordered the foundation of one of his many Alexandrias), and so resourceful and ingenious were they in coming to terms with the hostile conditions surrounding them that for centuries Merv was so populous and prosperous a centre that the city became renowned as Queen of the World.

Reduced, by the time of O'Donovan's visit, to a series of crumbling walls, ruined bastions and ramparts, remains of palaces and citadels, dried-out cisterns and water courses, traces of baths and storehouses, Merv's ancient cities were a melancholy spectacle, the sole building used for any human purpose a caravanserai serving the caravans travelling from Meshed via Merv to Bokhara. As the last caravanserai before 200 miles of waterless waste, the Merv oasis was an essential halting place, and still a large and important establishment. Two colossal brazen pots, each nearly 5 feet in diameter, often simultaneously in use for the preparation of food, were evidence of the size of the merchant caravans still passing through Merv. On his journey to Sabsavar O'Donovan himself had been attached to a caravan of 600 pilgrims, so had first-hand knowledge of the needs of these armies of men and camels and horses on their long and gruelling journeys. To me it seems surprising that in such an important stopping place as the

Merv caravanserai there was no ice available to travellers. It was May when O'Donovan was there, and the heat was already blazing, yet none was on offer.* His thoughts must have been on the subject, for he noted that there were deep vaulted chambers in which to take shelter from the glare of the sun and that to enter them was 'like entering so many icehouses'.[35] That he did not see or mention the real ice house or what remained of it at that time is not exactly surprising. Amid the dereliction of the older cities and the miles of ruins it was difficult to identify buildings and his escort of Tekké tribesmen hampered his investigations. They were anxious to be gone from these abandoned places, the habitations of djinns and bad spirits, the trysting place of raiders and robbers.

Snow for a Fever

As an example of the sharply contrasting attitudes of the medical professions in Europe and in tropical countries such as Persia to the administration of iced water and other cooling beverages in the treatment of fevers, the story related by Sir John Chardin of his own cure in the case of a malignant fever could scarcely be more apt.

Having left the port of Bander-Abassi on the Persian Gulf on 20 May 1674, Chardin is on his return journey to Isfahan when he falls ill with a delirious fever. A French surgeon looks after him as best he can, but his servants are all ill and men from the neighbouring villages are called in to carry him in an improvised litter as far as the town of Laar, three days' march distant. Here he sends for the Governor's physician. Chardin himself and the French surgeon both believe him to be dying but the

---

* Elisabeth Beazley quotes R.B.M. Binning[34] as reporting that on a journey from Tehran to Kashan in May 1851 the luxury of ice was to be had at nearly every stage; the ice receptacle having been opened at the approach of warm weather, for a single *shahee* one could procure as much of this as required.

Persian physician diagnoses his complaint as the malady of Bander-Abassi (presumably what we now know as malaria) and tells him he will recover quickly. Having written out three separate papers of pre-scriptions and instructions for the apothecary, the physician leaves, telling his patient that he will very soon feel cool and refreshed.

The treatment prescribed by the physician involves the drinking of a very large quantity of different medicines, 4 pints of willow water* and a jugful of tisane.† The apothecary, who remains by Chardin's bedside throughout his illness, tells him that he is going to have a terrible thirst and wishes he could procure snow-cooled water for him, but no snow is to be had by anyone save the Governor. Chardin suggests bribing the official who keeps it and the apothecary replies that this would be useless because there is so little that seals have been put on the place where it is stored. (Chardin learns subsequently that the snow for Laar is all brought down from the mountains after a nine-day journey, and that only the eighth part of what is sent arrives in town, the rest having melted en route.)

In his fever, Chardin becomes desperate for snow to cool his drinking water and finally sends personally to beg some from the Governor, who responds with a supply. The apothecary fills a bowl with barley water and willow water, putting in a good lump of snow. When the snow is half-melted, the apothecary tells his patient to drink as much as he likes, and Chardin finds the beverage delicious and all the more agreeable in that he is drinking it on doctor's orders.

His fever continuing, Chardin is moved by the apothecary from his bed to a mat on the floor, with nothing but his own shirt for covering, not even a sheet, and two pillows under his head. Two men are brought to fan him. His room is washed with cool water every hour, and finally he is seated on a chair, drenched in cold water, and then washed with rosewater. Chardin blesses his Persian physician whose treatment is so voluptuous, but the French surgeon, who has not left his bedside,

* The *sherbet-i-beed-mishk*, made from willow flowers distilled with water, highly regarded as a soothing draught in fevers. Fryer says it was made from 'taylets of willows', by which I think he meant not catkins but pussy-willow buds. As a 'compound of Cool-Water' he found it 'very sweet-smelling and refreshing'.
† At that time most probably some form of barley water.

cannot refrain from expressing his indignation at this outrageous cure. All that cold water, a cold bath at the height of a fever, those pints of medicine, those iced drinks; 'Believe me,' warns the surgeon, 'instead of being quickly cured, you will soon be dead.'

Chardin, however, now declines to believe that his last hour has come, and before long begins to feel that his fever is abating. This is confirmed when the apothecary takes his pulse. In the evening the physician comes back. Chardin regards him as a Prophet or an Aesculapius. The doctor orders him a pottage of rice cooked in water, with cinnamon and dried pomegranate rind★ pounded together. It is the first nourishment he has taken for five days. Next morning the doctor orders him an emulsion of cold seeds, some more of his medicine, some raw cucumbers. All day he drinks barley and willow water with snow, eats watermelons and cucumbers and sucks pears. They put verjuice with his midday and evening pottage, and this improves its flavour.

After a day of violent purging, Chardin is finally rid of his fever, and by the 31st of the month, the doctor tells him he is to eat nothing but rice and chicken for ten days, and on 3 June allows him to resume his journey, but on condition that he continues his medicine for thirty-five days. This medicine is a confection of *gemme* and mithridate† and has warming effects, which counteract those of the excessive cooling remedies which had rid him of his fever. The French surgeon, who is still travelling with Chardin, persuades him to abandon the Persian physician's cure on the grounds that it is overheating. The surgeon is clearly intent on proving the Persian in the wrong. Chardin subsequently realizes that it was his French companion who was wrong, and he regrets having taken his advice. He suffers after-effects of his illness for the next four years, but is in the end completely cured when he goes to India. The hot weather there finally does the trick, he claims.[36]

★ O'Donovan mentions a decoction of wild pomegranate bark, i.e. tannin, as being efficacious in the treatment of delirious fever brought on by the sting of the dangerous insect called *arga persica* or *mouche de Miane*.[35]

† *Gemme* means pitch or resin. Mithridate was a complex confection used as a poison antidote. One of its ingredients was the herb *thlaspi arvense* or pennycress, known also as mithridate mustard.

Between conflicting advice from his Persian physician and his French surgeon, Chardin was probably fortunate to recover from his virulent fever. He was obviously blessed with a robust constitution, much cheerful common-sense and a will to survive. To read that the climate of India actually cured anyone of recurring malarial fever is noteworthy, to say the least.

It is interesting to learn that nearly two centuries after Chardin's day, Lady Shiel, wife of Sir Justin Shiel, Envoy Extraordinary to the Shah of Persia 1844–52, found that all maladies there were still divided into cold and hot (the Galen doctrine)★ and were to be attacked by compounding opposite medicines. 'Thus a hot disease is to be combated by a cold remedy. The classification of these last are somewhat fanciful,' Lady Shiel recorded in 1851. 'Pepper, I know is "cold" and ice, I think is "hot", for it is applied to the stomach in large pieces during cholera.'[37] That pepper was 'cold' was a tenet long held by some schools of medicine, although according to John Gerard of *Herbal* fame, more usually by Indian physicians than by Arabs and Persians. Given that pepper could be held to be cold, why should not ice be hot? As everybody knows, ice burns bare flesh. As for the use of ice or snow in fevers, it had been common practice in the Levant and Persia at least since the days of Galen. The Spanish doctor Nicolas Monardes of Seville, whose *Boke Which Treateth of the Snow* was written in 1574 and translated into very picturesque English in 1577, quotes Galen as reproving two predecessors, Erastrato and Thessalis, for forbidding the use of cold water to patients ill with fever, saying that he himself 'hath healed many sicke persons that had the griefe of the stomacke, with most cold water, and made cold with snowe. And in the 8, 9, 10 and eleventh of the same *Methodo*, hee healeth the Fevers and other diseases with water that is most cold.' Amato Lucitano 'in the 7th century speaketh of one that had a hot burning fever and for the great heat and inflammation he had in the throte could not swallow down anything, and with a peece of frost, chewing it continually, not only it tooke away the difficulties of the swallowing down, and the

---

★ The doctrine propagated by the Greek physician Galen, who flourished in the second century AD.

inflammation in his throate, but did also ease him much of his fever'. From the celebrated Avicenna, who was born in Bokhara in AD 980 and became physician to several successive sultans of Persia, Monardes collects many instances of advice on the use of snow and ice – provided that both are clean and free from impurities – to chill water for patients suffering from 'griefs of the stomach', 'hot griefs of the liver' and the acute pain concomitant to that disease, 'trembling of the heart' and even, most strangely, toothache. But Avicenna perfectly sensibly advised that in serious maladies snow and water mixed should be taken in very small doses, not drunk off in one draught. With the mixture of snow and sugar to be taken as a health preservative every morning in summer prescribed by Rasis, another tenth-century Arab physician, we are getting close to the *sherbet-i-kand*, which was simply water in which candy sugar was dissolved and was really the basic sherbet of Persia, India and Turkey as described by so many travellers, from Ibn Battutah onwards. Remembering also the story that peaches, pears and snow were sent by Saladin to Richard Cœur de Lion when in 1192 the latter was lying ill of a fever during the Third Crusade, we are reminded that in Arab countries the use of snow as an aid to the cure of many maladies and most especially of malignant fevers was generally accepted and that there was nothing novel about the treatment prescribed by Chardin's Persian physician in his illness. It is only surprising that the two Frenchmen, both Chardin himself and his companion the unnamed surgeon, had never before come across similar cases of treatment and were not even conversant with the tenets of Galen or the writings of Avicenna, Rasis, and other Arab physicians whose works were available in Latin translations.

Ices in Porcelain Basins

And now, what is Persian sherbet? Dr C.J. Wills, in a discussion of sherbet glasses, sherbet spoons, sherbet decanters and the customs surround the serving and drinking of sherbets, answers the question for his readers. We have met Dr Wills before, giving his description of the ice-making installations at Shiraz and commending the plentiful supply and moderate cost of household ice in that city. In a later volume of Persian reminiscences, *Persia As It Is* (1887), the author explains that the English drink called Royal Persian Sherbet, made from 'a white effervescing powder, flavoured with essence of lemons, which in the summer-time was sold to us children' exists only in the imagination of the English confectioner, and that in Persia a sherbet is a draught of sweetened water flavoured to the taste of the drinker.

The varieties of sherbet may be divided into those made from the fresh juice of fruit, which are mixed with water and sweetened to the taste; and those made from syrup, in which the juice of fruit has been boiled ... But there is one all-important point that the English would do well to imitate: Persian sherbet is served very cool, or iced. Blocks of snow or lumps of ice are always dissolved in the sherbet drunk in Persia, unless the water has been previously artificially cooled. Fresh sherbets are usually lemon, orange, or pomegranate; and the first two are particularly delicious. The fresh juice is expressed in the room in the presence of the guest, passed through a small silver strainer, to remove the pips, portions of pulp, etc: lumps of sugar are then placed in the *istakhan;*★ water is poured in till the vessel is two-thirds full, and it is then filled to the brim with blocks of ice or snow.

The preserved sherbets are generally contained in small decanters of coloured Bohemian glass similar to the *istakhans* in style. They are in the form of clear and concentrated syrup. This syrup is poured into the bowl or *istakhan*, as the case may be; water is added; the whole is stirred, and the requisite quantity of ice or snow completes the sherbet ... The varieties of the preserved syrups are numerous: orange, lemon, quince, cranberry – the raspberry is unknown in Persia – cherry, pomegranate, apricot, plum, and grape juice; while various combinations of a very grateful nature are made by mixing two or even three of the above.[38]

I have quoted Wills's description at length, although by no means *in toto*, in order to stress the point that Persian sherbets, described by

---

★ The glass tankards or tumblers, often elaborately gilded and painted in colours, in which sherbets were served.

so many travellers, and in such rich detail, were in the late nineteenth century (as still today) the sweet or sweet-sour fruit drinks of tradition, heavily iced, but not frozen. When ices came to Persia, probably in the eighteenth century, they did not merge with sherbets nor did they at any time supersede them, as so largely happened in Europe and America (although less so in England, where sherbet somehow turned into that regrettable schoolboy fizz described by Wills), but became an additional feature of the sweetmeat course at collations and banquets. The popular belief that ices were known in the great days of the Persian Empire and at the court of the Caliphs of Baghdad was based purely on a romantic fantasy, backed up by ignorance of the history of freezing techniques involved in the making of ices, and supported by the now all too familiar linguistic confusions. It is difficult to see how anyone who had actually read the travel accounts of Pierre Belon, Pietro Della Valle, Chardin, Thévenot, Tavernier, Dr John Fryer, and dozens more could confuse the sherbets of Persia and Turkey with the ices of Europe, but possibly the initial misunderstanding arose via Spanish Naples, where ices were from the first known as *sorbetti* or sherbets, rather than as the *neve* of the rest of Italy, the *neiges* of France and the *garapiñas* of Spain. By the middle of the eighteenth century, when the terms *sorbetti* and *sorbets* had been disseminated by Neapolitan *gelatiere* throughout Italy, France, and the rest of Europe, whence they soon reached America, the linguistic confusions were readily to hand for the myth-makers of the nineteenth and twentieth centuries.

As to the first appearance of ices in Persia, they were quite certainly not yet known there in the late seventeenth century when so many European travellers were writing their accounts for posterity, or we should have heard about them from one or other, if not all, of those assiduous observers. Chardin, always the most alert of travellers when it comes to food and drink, does refer to the Persian *paloudeh*, a kind of syrupy fruit sherbet thickened with a cooked starch and sugar mixture pressed through a perforated ladle or colander to form small, soft and well-separated teardrops which were carefully stirred into the bowl of sherbet, together with rosewater and plenty of ice. This was eaten at the morning meal and made a refreshing hot weather breakfast, 'exceedingly pleasant and grateful to the stomach', as was remarked by the author of a recipe for *paloudeh* which under the title 'Curious Persian Cold Soup' found its way into *The Family Receipt Book* of 1853. *Paloudeh* could not have been confused with the ices of Europe, and I have described it here mainly as an instance of the thoroughness with which Chardin noted, down to the last detail, even what the Persians ate for breakfast. Appropriately enough, it is from Chardin's nineteenth-century French editor, J. Langlès, professor of Persian at the Paris school of oriental languages, that an early reference to European-style ices in Persia is forthcoming. Langlès's ten-volume annotated edition of Chardin's *Voyages* was published in Paris in 1811, and it was in a footnote to the latter's observation that the Persians prefer snow to ice with their beverages, especially with sherbet,[39] that Langlès remarks, 'They also know sweet ice preparations similar, more or less, to those which we take, and they call them *berf, neige.*'

It was now exactly a century since the original publication of Chardin's complete *Voyages*, and a further thirty-four years since his own Persian and Indian travels had come to an end. According to his own testimony, Chardin left Persia for the last time in 1677; consequently the up-to-date evidence concerning Persian sweet ices supplied by Langlès in 1811 is particularly useful. How long such ices had then been known in Persia he does not of course tell us, and had he inquired it is highly unlikely that anyone would have been able to enlighten him, even though they were still a comparative novelty.

Curiously, James Morier, the diplomat who accompanied Sir Harford Jones to Teheran in 1808 and 1809, mentions no ices at any of the ceremonial banquets he attended in Persia in company with the other members of the diplomatic mission, but had probably experienced them there on his later journey through Persia between 1810 and 1816. At any rate, when in 1824 he came to write *The Adventures of Haji Baba of Ispahan*, admittedly a fictional tale, but one in which the background is based on Morier's own knowledge of Persia, he describes preparations for a banquet to be held in the house of a physician who is to receive a visit from the Shah, an honour which appears likely to ruin him. A detachment from the Shah's own army of cooks has already spread itself far beyond the limits of the kitchen quarters. 'Besides the cooks a body of confectioners established themselves in one of the apartments, where the sweetmeats, the sherbets, the ices, and the fruit were prepared; and they called for so many ingredients that the doctor had nearly expired when the list was presented to him.'

James Morier does not, unfortunately, elaborate on the nature of the ices to be prepared by the royal confectioners, nor, visiting the Shah's mother in 1851, does Lady Shiel: 'Tea, coffee and pipes were brought in repeatedly and after some time a nice collation of fruit, various kinds of sherbets, ices, and cakes were spread on the table, and on the ground.' We have to wait until 1883 and Dr Wills's *In the Land of the Lion and the Sun* before we find a full description of the ices of Persia. Very delicious they sound too: 'The Persians well understand the art of making water-ices and ice-creams, and various ices unknown to us are made by them; as tamarind juice, pomegranate and cherry water ices; iced *mast* or curdled milk,★ and various ices of pounded fruits, as apricots and cherries which are very good.' The size and shape of the moulds used for Persian ices in those days are details which Dr Wills duly notes, thereby giving us an unforgettable picture of a Persian grandee and his European guests attacking their outsize ices, and at the same time providing us with the precious evidence linking the ices of Persia with those of eighteenth-century India:

Ices are served with them on a more lavish scale, and a larger quantity eaten, than with us. When I accompanied Captain St J – in a call he made upon the Muschir [the local potentate], four conical ices, the size and shape of an *ordinary* sugar-loaf, were placed in handsome Chinese porcelain basins before each of us. In fact the cheapness of provisions generally causes among the well-to-do a lavishness and profusion (not to call it waste) unknown in Europe.

I am not sure how large an 'ordinary' sugar-loaf would have been in Persia in those days, but certainly not less than 2 lb, which would mean that the ices were made in 2 pint conical moulds, like those described by Fanny Parks at Allahabad in the 1830s and General Sir Robert Barker in the 1770s, at the same East India Company station.

★ *Mast* is more accurately translated as yogurt.

But Sir Robert Barker's silver moulds were comparatively modest in size, holding just 1 pint, whereas Fanny Parks describes 2 pint pewter moulds and calls them by their proper Indian name of *kulfi*. An interesting and significant connection. Is there also a connection between these outsize ices and the huge ice pyramids of the Roman and Florentine banquets of the seventeenth century? Certainly that sugar-loaf shape, which in the course of time became our *bombe* and is still, although modified in size, closely akin to the Indian *kulfi* mould, has been the recurring theme throughout the 300-year-old history of ices and ice decorations. It was natural, no doubt, that the sugar-loaf shape should provide the prototype. Chardin described how the sister of the late Shah Abbas of Persia used to send him wonderful sherbets made like *sucre en plume*, which seem to have a distinct relation to modern candy floss and were so light that, although they were the size of 8 lb sugar-loaves, they weighed only 12 oz.

To what extent, to the sugar-addicted Persians, the semblance of a sugar loaf in spun sugar and later in towering snowy fruit ices was symbolic of something precious and ceremonial and how far it was simply the most practical shape for the freezing and turning out of these confections, it would be hard to say. In Europe there had plainly been another reason – quite apart from the prevailing pyramid and obelisk mania of the period – for the popularity of the cone as a shape for the decorative ice centrepieces of the seventeenth century; the expansion of the water during freezing, it had been established, caused many other shapes of mould to crack or shatter, whereas the cone, provided its cover was not too close-fitting, was not subject to such accidents. It will be remembered also that the cone-shaped silver vessel used in the freezing experiments carried out by the learned gentlemen of the Florentine scientific academy in the 1670s was described by Count Lorenzo Magalotti, secretary of the Academy and author of the frozen sherbet recipe in verse form quoted on p. 26, as being 'such as we used to cool our sherbet and other Drinks in Summer'. For the making of ice on a domestic scale the cone-shaped mould persisted long after the factories were churning out hundreds of tons of ice per day, and was certainly in use until the 1914 war.

Cathay to Caledonia

Anyone who believes that Marco Polo saw frozen milk on sale in the streets of Peking and that he returned to Italy with a recipe for Chinese ice-cream should try finding the tale in the account of his travels. At no point did he mention anything in China, or anywhere else, which even the most credulous could possibly construe as being frozen milk, nor anything in any way resembling ice-cream even at its most primitive. Indeed the only point in the whole of his narrative at which he makes more than a passing reference to milk of any kind is when he describes the dried milk and the *kumiss*, or fermented mare's milk, of Mongolia. That at some time somebody imagined that *kumiss* somehow equated with ice-cream is, I suppose, just conceivable. How otherwise to account for the persistent legend seems to me well nigh impossible, unless perhaps the tale was invented in fun and was later believed even by quite serious people. If only Marco had just once mentioned the Chinese use of ice, in his time already ancient, referred to the Imperial ice stores, or recorded the eating of ice-cooled melons or the restaurants specializing exclusively in iced foods, the assumption that he had also experienced some sort of icy milk delicacy would have been an easy step. But nowhere does he give so much as a passing hint of such usages. And that in itself is quite odd.[1]

When the Polos arrived in China in the second half of the thirteenth century, Chinese methods of refrigeration already went back about 2,500 years, perhaps longer. The harvesting and storage of ice are recorded in a poem of circa 1100 BC in the *Shih Ching*, the famous collection of Food Canons, and there is mention of a festival held when the ice houses were opened for summer use: 'In the days of the second month, they hew out the ice … in the third month they convey it to the ice houses which they open in those of the fourth, early in the morning, having offered in sacrifice a lamb with scallions.'[2]

Coming – in Chinese terms – to comparatively modern times, the T'ang rulers of 618–907 AD and their court used ice to cool their houses in summer as well as for preserving perishable foodstuffs.[3] Cooling delicacies such as smooth mixtures of crystalline rice, cow's milk, camphor, and mysterious ingredients called dragon brain fragments and dragon eye ball powder were enclosed in metal tubes which were then lowered into an 'ice-pool' and thoroughly chilled. Professor Edward Schafer, of Berkeley University, California, describing this T'ang Imperial treat in his entrancing book *The Golden Peaches of Samarkand*, explains that camphor was probably chosen on account of its resemblance, when flaked, to ice and snow, and its consequent cooling effect. The idea of things looking cool making you feel cool must be even older than the most ancient of Chinese cultures, as old no doubt as mankind itself. As for camphor, it was prized in China for medicinal purposes as well as for its pretty, icy appearance. To me, it equates with the smell of mothballs. Note, by the way, that Professor Schafer is careful to emphasize that this 'clear wind rice' was 'thoroughly chilled'. It was not frozen. Nor was any attempt made to freeze it. The distinction is one to be borne in mind before anyone jumps to the conclusion that in 'clear wind rice' we have evidence of some ancient form of ice-cream.

As things turned out, the ice technology of China did in time come to exercise an important influence on our own, but that was not until late in the eighteenth century and had at first nothing much to do with the development of the ice-cream trade, then barely in its infancy. Primarily, it was the expansion of our fishing industry which we owed to Chinese expertise in the matter of transport and preservation of fresh fish by means of natural ice. The result was a dramatic increase in the demand for that commodity and the consequences were to be far-reaching.

The story is an interesting one, more prosaic perhaps than the fairytales of ice-cream mythology – Billingsgate-bound cargoes of fish packed in ice are not as romantic as argosies of sherbets and sugar, snow and fruit, carried on camel-back through the Holy Land to crusading warriors, or seaborne with attendant confectioners in papal galleons across the Mediterranean to attend a royal wedding in Marseille – but in its way the China to Scotland story, although fully substantiated, is every bit as unlikely.

In 1785 a Scottish gentleman named Alexander Dalrymple, an official of the British East India Company, who for the previous six years had been hydrographer to the Company (later he was to fill the same office for the Admiralty), was on a visit to London. One day, calling at East India House, Dalrymple chanced to meet Mr George Dempster, an eminent fellow Scot, Member of Parliament for the Perthshire burghs of Perth, St Andrews, Dundee, Forfar and Cupar (Fife) and a former director of the East India Company. The two men fell into conversation. In the course of their talk Dalrymple, who had spent several years on voyages of observation in the islands of the South Pacific and had also made himself familiar with the Chinese coastal trade and the Company's trading post in Canton, told Mr Dempster how the Chinese fishermen were in the habit of carrying ice on their boats in order to preserve their catches at sea.

What Alexander Dalrymple explained to George Dempster during their chance meeting at East India House was that the fishermen of the China coast drew their supplies of snow and ice from storehouses situated along the coastal areas and estuaries. Evidently the China coast in those days had ice houses and snow stores rather like the plains of La Mancha had windmills. All the employees and officers of the East India Company stationed at Canton during the eighteenth century could not but have been familiar with the sight of those little stores and with the use of ice by the Chinese fishermen. The Company's officers were themselves only too glad to have access to ice for cooling the wines of which they consumed such prodigious quantities. 'Claret, madeira and hock, all excellent and all made as cold as ice,' recorded William Hickey, describing a sumptuous dinner for thirty people held at the Company's establishment at Whampoa, the Canton anchorage for foreign trading vessels, during a prolonged visit there in the summer of 1769.[4] How, in the stifling heat of a Canton summer, the wines had all been iced, Hickey did not reveal, although he could certainly have explained that the Chinese coastal ice stores were rather small above ground buildings, in outline not unlike English haystacks, very different from the cavernous underground ice houses already common in his day in English public and private parks and gardens, and essential to the caterers and confectioners of the capital. These unfamiliar little Chinese coastal stores were filled with ice harvested from low-lying surrounding fields deliberately flooded in winter and in summer given over to rice cultivation, an ingenious and economical way of obtaining ice for storage. Although it might have been supposed that summer storage of ice in above-ground buildings was not very practical, the opposite proved the case. Their insulation was so effective that the ice could be kept for as long as two years. If in a mild winter the ice crop was insufficient to fill the stores, there would still be plenty of the previous year's supply to fall back on.

The fish merchants likewise, Dalrymple revealed, used ice and snow to maintain their fish in a state of perfect preservation during transit over long distances inland. The information, although new to George Dempster, would not have been so to anyone who had read a similar first-hand story which had appeared in 1763 in *Travels from St Petersburg in Russia to Diverse Parts of Asia* by John Bell of Antermony, a compatriot of Dalrymple's. The book, which had attracted a good deal of favourable attention at the time of its publication, included a detailed account of a journey made by Bell, a doctor in the service of Czar Peter the Great of Russia, in his capacity as physician to an embassy from Russia to the Emperor of China. Arriving in Peking in November 1720 after an overland journey across Siberia lasting sixteen months, Dr Bell recorded that at Christmas a Jesuit priest, Father Paranim, 'sent us a present of a large sturgeon and some other fresh fish, brought from the river Amoor [nearly 1,000 miles north of Peking, on the border of what is now Manchuria]. These can only be carried to such a distance in the coldest season, when they are preserved by being kept frozen among the snow.' John Bell had perfectly understood the principle of preserving fish by rapid freezing: 'provided the fish is immediately exposed to the frost after being caught,' he wrote, 'it may be carried, in snow, for many miles, almost as fresh as when taken out of the water.' Bell would also, of course, have been familiar with the sight of frozen fish and entire frozen animal carcasses piled up in St Petersburg's winter market, hence his additional observation that 'the method of preservation by freezing is practised with success in northern countries'.[5] His story had been written purely for the record, and apparently nobody who read it thought of attempting to apply the Chinese system of exposing fish to natural freezing for safe carriage from Scotland to the markets of London and Southern England. That was understandable. Climatic conditions in Scotland are not really such as to permit the development of natural freezing on a regular basis. The potential benefits of using ice as a temporary preservation for fish in transport were also unappreciated. The inauguration of a completely new method of carriage of perishable foodstuffs such as fish was still to come, awaiting a man, or men, with vision, initiative and the means of putting ideas to the practical test.

As things turned out, it was not until twenty years after the publication of John Bell's account of his stay in Peking that chance circumstances brought together a Scottish Member of Parliament and a Scottish official of the East India Company, and that this meeting, followed by prompt action on the part of a Scottish fish merchant, combined to bring about the innovation which was to revolutionize the Scottish and British fishing industries. In the course of that transformation, the British ice trade was also to grow from a spasmodic cottage industry, first into a major import business and ultimately into a great manufacturing and cold storage operation.

Just how much detail concerning the Chinese system of refrigerating perishable foodstuffs while in transit along the 1,100 miles of the Grand Canal – the oldest artificial waterway in the world – was known to Alexander Dalrymple and how much he in turn communicated to George Dempster is not on record. What we do know is that Dalrymple's story sufficiently impressed Dempster to cause him to write off – on the spot, according to his own testimony – to his salmon supplier in Scotland, a Mr Richardson, telling him of this Chinese custom of preserving fish in ice. Accordingly Richardson, although sceptical (again it is his own story), proceeded to make the experiment of packing freshly caught salmon in boxes filled with pounded ice (the

Scottish lochs no doubt yielded ice in plenty) and sending them to London by sea. Surprise. It was found that the fish, after a six-day journey, were preserved in an excellent state.[6] Thus, belatedly, and 160 years after Francis Bacon allegedly caught his fatal chill collecting snow in order to further his observations on its possible preservative effects on the flesh of a chicken, did the news of the use of ice as a preservative for fresh fish reach the British public.

Yet already fourteen hundred years before Bacon became pre-occupied with the preservative possibilities of extreme cold and its practical application, the Greek physician Galen, in the second century A D, had noted that 'snow preserveth fish from corruption as also flesh from putrefaction', and had remarked on the manner in which human and animal carcasses found among the snows were preserved 'as though embalmed'. For centuries Galen's medical and philosophical writings had dominated European medicine, his works were required study for medical students everywhere, a physician unable to quote his precepts would gain little credence and when in 1571 the Spanish Dr Monardes composed his plea for the greater use of snow in his native city of Seville, he leant heavily on Galen to prove his case.[7] Francis Bacon was, as a matter of course, familiar with Galen's works, quoting him frequently, and from that source appears to have derived his knowledge of the preservative properties of ice and snow, although as an innovative inquirer after truth he declined to take the information on trust, insisting on first-hand observation.

So even if Bacon and his contemporaries had heard that the Chinese had long had a large-scale system of refrigerated transport for easily spoiled foodstuffs such as fresh fruit and fish, they would either have disbelieved it or regarded the story as irrelevant to their own conditions of life – which in a way perhaps it was – and if word of it had reached Mediterranean Europe, where the climate was more extreme in both summer and winter and distances much greater than in England, then it had still been ignored as inapplicable. That is something we must accept, I think, as substantially true.

Less than half a century after Bacon's death in 1626 came many relevant experiments, such as those made in the early 1660s by Robert Boyle and his collaborator Dr Merritt of the Royal Society, on the effects of freezing on eggs, apples, lemons, milk, and a variety of animal carcasses, but these had been treated as academic exercises of no practical application to daily life. In France there had been experiments such as Father Berthier's attempts at preserving fruit and vegetables in jars embedded between blocks of ice in an icehouse, but these again had been regarded as of little practical value.[8] All European countries had long been accustomed to the use of ice to cool wine and water, professional confectioners were familiar with the use of ice and salt in the freezing of ice-creams, the preservative effects of ice and snow on fresh fruit had not gone unobserved. By the 1780s all English country houses of any size and pretension to comfort had their ice house. Yet, when at last it came, the use of ice to preserve fish and to expand its transport potential seems to have struck our fisheries as something in the nature of a blinding revelation.

The success of Richardson's initial consignment of salmon packed in ice had swift repercussions. In a letter published in the *Scots Magazine* of 3 October 1786, Richardson made a public declaration to the effect that the experiment had answered beyond expectation and that 'any benefit which might result from it either to the public or to individuals owes its beginning in this country to that patriotic gentleman Mr Dempster and to none else'.[9] That Christmas Mr Richardson made a gift of £200 to Mr Dempster to buy 'a piece of plate' for Mrs Dempster. The sum was at that time a handsome one, evidence of the importance and financial value to the salmon trade of the newly evolved system of transport. In the previous July the Convention of Royal Burghs of Scotland had already recognized Dempster's services to Scottish trades, manufacturers and fisheries with a presentation of plate worth a hundred guineas.[10] Dempster was indeed a man always open to new ideas. He is credited with innovations such as the building of the first lighthouses on the coast of Scotland, and the installation of a central heating system in his home in Perthshire, so it is in no way surprising that he was farsighted enough to perceive the significance of Alexander Dalrymple's account of the Chinese use of snow and ice in the preservation of fresh fish. To Dempster, therefore, goes the credit of instigating the introduction of a cold storage system, however tentative, to the British Isles. To Dalrymple's part in the innovation nobody gives more than a passing nod, but the value of his report on the Chinese methods of carrying ice both in the fishing boats and in the cross-country river and canal craft should not be underestimated. Without it, our own system of fish carriage in ice might have been delayed many more years.

It should here be explained that prior to the Dempster–Richardson innovation, the carriage of salmon to London from Scotland and other distant places had customarily ended with the approach of warmer weather in April. Carriage had been effected in baskets loaded on to packhorses, or by package in straw in light carts. Only occasionally, given the risks inherent in the vagaries of wind, weather and tides, had sea transport been successful. The use of ice as a preservative changed everything. Sailing delays no longer spelt disaster. Following Richardson's lead, many Scottish fish merchants started conveying salmon from Aberdeen, Montrose, and Inverness, places 500, 600, and 700 miles distant from London. Before long, the salmon trade was transformed and seasonal sales of Scotch salmon at Billingsgate extended far into the summer months.[11]

Although during the first years the use of ice in the fisheries was confined to the luxury trade in salmon, it was not long before the system was extended to the herring fisheries of the Forth. By 1794 Fife fish merchants were dispatching herrings, at that time plentiful in the Forth, in ice-filled boxes loaded in fast sailing smacks from Berwick to London. By 1815 the anonymous author of *The Epicure's Almanack*, a guide to London hotels, clubs, coffee houses, taverns, food markets, provision shops, confectioners and caterers, could write that all first-rate fish dealers had ice stores for the purpose of preserving their fish during hot weather, referring also to the Berwick smacks laden with salmon packed in ice arriving at Billingsgate during the season. Scottish turbot, the *Epicure* recorded, was also occasionally brought to London packed in ice. George Dempster, who lived on until 1818, had cause to be proud of the perceptive action which thirty years previously had wrought such a spectacular change in the fortunes of the Scottish fishing industry.

In 1838, a year after the accession of Queen Victoria, came another great innovation, the inauguration of a regular steamboat service carrying salmon in ice from Scotland to London.[12] In four years the new service had proved so successful that in 1842 2,500 tons of salmon passed through Billingsgate, much of it in the peak summer months of June, July and August. 'Steam navigation has rendered the improvement perfect,' reported J.C. Platt, the enthusiastic contributor of an article on London's famous fish market published in the fourth volume of a collection of essays entitled *London*, published in 1843. Soon the railways would speed up those deliveries beyond recognition.

In the course of the fifty-odd years which had passed since George Dempster and Alexander Dalrymple had met and talked of ice and fish and the China Seas, the whole of the British fishing industry had been transformed, initially by the use of ice, and subsequently by the coming of steam.

The rapid increase in the consumption of ice occasioned by its use in the fishing industry had, necessarily, been followed by the construction of large ice stores at the ports and along the salmon rivers. 'Every salmon fishing is now provided with an ice house for laying in

Ice being unloaded at Great Yarmouth, Norfolk.

a stock of ice during the winter,' reported the *Edinburgh Review* of April 1814. Ice houses, for so long used only by the well-to-do owners of town and country estates, and by a few confectioners and fashionable hotels and clubs, now represented considerable commercial interests. At Berwick as much as 7,600 cartloads of ice – a cartload was about 30 hundredweight or approximately $2\frac{1}{2}$ tons – would be packed away in the course of one winter. In Scotland enough ice to supply the demand could be harvested from the lochs, but in southerly ports local supplies were erratic. It is at about this time, in 1815 or 1816, that we first hear of shipments of ice from Norway and from 'the Greenland seas' arriving in England (see pp. 321–336). Ice from Scotland must surely also have been shipped to London when local supplies failed, although as part of a purely coastal trade such arrivals would not have been recorded. But it was at the fishing port of Barking, on the Thames in Essex, that a firm of fish merchants, founded by the Hewett family in about 1764, eventually created a remarkable ice business comparable in some ways to the operations conducted by the Chinese coastal fish merchants in the seventeenth century, and much akin to what we know of the one at Ning-Po in the nineteenth.

Ning-Po was an important city twelve miles inland from the north-east coast of the Ching Empire, whose association or guild controlling the fishing industry had created a secondary one operated by local farmers and ice harvesters. As already described, the farmers harvested ice from their flooded fields, storing it in ice houses along the banks of the two rivers on the junction of which the city was built. The Hewett operation at Barking appears to have had many similarities with the Ning-Po system, but whether the information had been passed on by Alexander Dalrymple, whether it had come from a later source, or at exactly what period the Hewetts started their ice-making and harvesting activities are points which are far from clear. Samuel Hewett, born in 1797, is usually credited with the foundation of the firm's ice business, and the period given as 'before 1850'. Certainly, the expansion of the Hewett business tallies approximately with the 1845–50 period when reports of the Ning-Po operation by Robert Fortune, Botanical Collector to the Royal Horticultural Society, became public knowledge.

Ice houses near Ning-po, from Robert Fortune's book.

Following the end of the First Opium War in 1842 and the opening up of the Treaty Ports, Fortune had spent three years travelling in Northern China to collect plants and observe the tea-growing and processing industry. While there he had been much impressed by the simplicity of design and the efficiency of the Ning-Po ice houses and had written an account of them to his friend Professor Lindley, who published the letter in *The Gardeners Chronicle* for 1845. Subsequently the same account, in greater detail, appeared in Fortune's book *Three Years Wanderings in the Northern Provinces of China*, published in 1847. The Ning-Po type of above-ground ice houses were not, so far as I know, much adopted in England, but the idea of creating natural ice by the winter flooding of low-lying fields was evidently the one used in the Hewett operation. It was on a very large scale. Samuel Hewett organized the Essex farmers for miles around Barking into flooding their fields in winter and harvesting ice as a regular crop. The Hewett ice house was an underground store 18 feet deep, with walls 8 feet thick and a storage capacity of 10,000 tons. Between 2,000 and 3,000 men, women and children were employed in the cutting, carting,and packing of the ice into the store. Often, according to Charles Cutting, historian of the fish-preserving industry, there were queues of carts outside the ice house, stretching right through the town of Barking, waiting to unload their ice. In 1850 Henry Mayhew, author of the celebrated survey *London and the London Poor*, published two papers in *The Morning Chronicle Survey of Labour and the Poor* in which he included descriptions of this seasonal occupation. Almost the whole population of Barking, he reported, seemed astir collecting ice. It had been the first frost of any intensity or continuance that season, and women and boys were breaking the ice, numbers of men were throwing or lifting it into carts, even into wheelbarrows, every kind of vehicle was in requisition, and some of the roads were all but impassable from the number of ice carriages of every kind. The ice was sent out from the ice houses to the fishing smacks and the fish was all the better preserved. When the English winter is mild, Mayhew concluded, 'the fishing-smack proprietors are at considerable expense, in obtaining ice from Norway or other foreign countries'.[13]

As part of their enterprising scheme, Hewett built special ice-lugs to carry ice from Barking Creek to Rainham where fast sailing cutters, known as carriers, were moored. Each carrier would load up with 18 tons of ice in readiness to join the returning Hewett fishing fleet at their rendezvous at Gorleston near Yarmouth. As the fishing boats came in to port with their catches, the fish, packed in boxes containing about half a hundredweight each and with broken ice spread over the top, were loaded into rowing boats. The small boats, heavily loaded, sometimes perilously so, ferried the cargo of boxes to the carrier vessels and, in the words of a contemporary reporter writing for the *Illustrated London News* of September 1864, 'as fast as the hands can work the boxes and the baskets are struck down into the holds and stowed in tiers, between each tier of which a layer of ice is placed to preserve the fish in good condition'. Each carrier stowed on an average 40 tons of fish, then made with all possible speed for London and Billingsgate market. The fishing smacks could re-load with ice from stores at Gorleston and return to their fishing grounds. It was a well-organized operation, but often a dangerous one, given the speed required for the unloading and re-loading of the catches and the necessity of rushing the fish to market with the least possible delay, regardless of rough weather and high seas. The large-scale use of ice had made such operations feasible, it had enabled the fishing vessels to go much further afield and to remain at sea for considerably longer periods than ever before and still return with fresh – as opposed to salted – fish which would make good profits for the owners of the

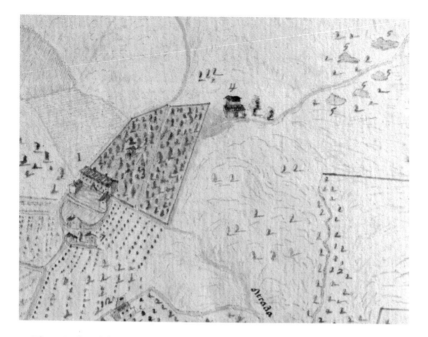

Pl. 1 A detail from a manuscript map of the country estate at Olmo of Santa Maria Nuova in Florence, 1693. In the foreground is the main house on the estate, immediately behind it is the ice house and on the right can be seen the ice ponds.

Pl. 2 Map of the town of Helsingfors (Elsinore), Denmark, published by Braun and Hohenberg in 1580. In the foreground is the thatched ice house of King Frederik II.

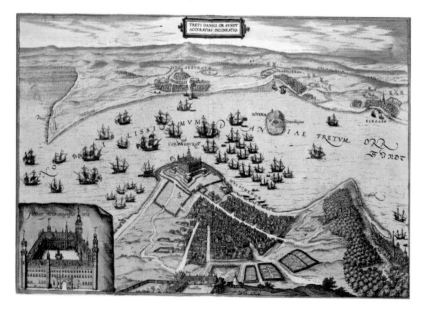

Pl. 3 *Marchands de sorbets à Florence*

Pl. 4 *La belle limonadière*

Pl. 5 An abdar cooling drinks by shaking and turning bottles in a bowl of water cooled with saltpetre. Murshidabad artist, 1790.

Pl. 6 A hokey–pokey man. Unknown Victorian artist.

Pl. 7 A magnificent array
of fancy ices from *Süsse
Speisen und Eisbomben* by
Karl Scharrer, 1907.

1 Trafalgar bombe
2 Pineapple bombe
3 Togo bombe
4 Congo bombe
5 Snowman
6 Bombe Cecilie
7 Basket of oranges
8 Windmill
9 Chess board
10 Turban
11 Bombe Isabella
12 Bombe Marie-Louise
13 Crown
14 Bombe Magnoleskov
15 Othello bombe
16 Champagne cooler

SBOMBEN.I.

1. Crystallized Bouquet. 3. Ice & Flower Centre. 6. Spring Bouquet.
   (for Winter)
2. Fruit & Flowers. 4. Ring of Flowers. 7. Rose Basket.
   (for Summer)
5. Ring of Flowers.

THIS PAGE

Pl. 10 LEFT: A table centre-piece for summer.

Pl. 11 BELOW: A table spread for dinner à la Russe with a plateau of looking-glass and a fountain.

Both illustrations are taken from *The Modern Housekeeper*, ed. Dr Ross Murray, 1872.

FACING PAGE

Pl. 8 TOP: Radetzky bombe taken from *Süsse Speisen und Eisbomben* by Karl Scharrer, 1907.

Pl. 9 BOTTOM: Fancy ices from A. B. Marshall's *The Book of Ices*, 1857. Mrs Marshall ran a cookery school and sold cooking ingredients and kitchen utensils, including moulds for ices.

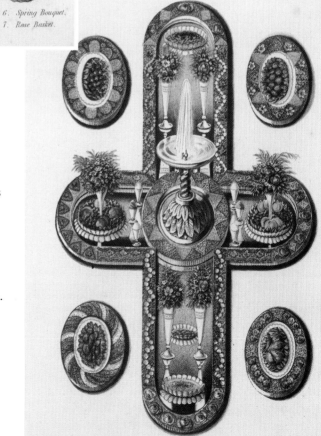

A Table spread for dinner à la Russe with
plateau of looking glass and fountain.

Pl. 12 *The Oyster Lunch* by Jean François de Troy, 1679-1752.
Wine coolers, whether a simple bucket or a huge elaborate gold container,
have been considered a necessity of civilised existence for centuries, at
banquets, in private houses, and even when travelling.

vessels. But ice alone, as today we are all aware, does not preserve fish beyond a limited time. Delays in getting the catches to market meant spoiled fish and damaging financial losses. I fancy that reports of the Chinese ability to convey fresh sea fish far inland and into the very interior of China during the heat of summer tend to be exaggerated, although admittedly Chinese inland transport was highly organized. 'The convenience of inland transit is unrivalled in any part of the world,' Robert Fortune remarked in 1843 while he was at the recently opened-up port of Shanghai.

The country, being as it were the valley of the Yang-tse-kiang, is one vast plain, intersected by many beautiful rivers, and these again joined and crossed by canals, many of them nearly natural, and others stupendous works of art. Owing to the level nature of the country, the tide ebbs and flows a great distance inland, thus assisting the natives in the transmission of their exports to Shanghae [Fortune's spelling] or their imports to the most distant parts of the country . . .

Boats of all sizes were employed in this inland traffic; 'the traveller continually meets them and gets a glimpse of their sails, over the land, at every stop of his progress in the interior'.[14]

How far inland Chinese river and canal boats could reach during seven or eight days, surely the limit for fish refrigerated in ice, it is difficult to estimate, but even given the favourable conditions reported by Robert Fortune, such transport tends to be slow. Fortune himself, in the account of the Chinese use of ice to preserve fish, says they are enabled 'to keep their fish during the hottest weather for a considerable time, and transmit them in this way to different parts of the country', but goes into no further detail. On the other hand John Bell, a very careful observer, had noted even of the frozen fish he had received in Peking at Christmas 1720 that the method of preservation for long-distance transport was practicable only in the coldest season. Had Fortune and Alexander Dalrymple, who is unlikely to have penetrated far, if at all, into the interior, both been misled by over-tall tales fabricated for the benefit of inquisitive foreigners? Robert Fortune alluded several times to the great difficulties experienced by foreigners in obtaining dependable information from the Chinese, and said that he himself made a practice of disbelieving everything they told him until he had seen and judged for himself. That seems to indicate that Fortune was very certain of his story. What is in any case beyond doubt is that it was Dalrymple's revelation concerning the use of ice in the Chinese fishing industry which caused George Dempster's swift and effective action in writing off to his friend Richardson. As James Fergusson, editor of the collection of George Dempster's letters already quoted in this chapter, commented, 'neither Dempster nor Richardson could possibly have foreseen what a vast industry would eventually grow from the initial experiment', but Dempster lived long enough to perceive the significance of the changes which his own and Richardson's initiative had brought to the Scottish fishing industry, and was far-sighted enough to know that there would be many more developments and innovations. Well into his seventies, Dempster was still fostering imaginative schemes and writing – in rhyme – to his old friend Sir John Sinclair about the desirability of equipping all vessels engaged in ferry-crossings with lifeboats. 'I who acquired some small renown, For sending salmon fresh to London town, Now in Fame's temple claim a higher place, For planning safety to the travelling race,' he wrote.[15] Today that renown seems, indeed, a great deal too small for the man who brought such far-reaching innovation to the fishing industry of these islands.

Eighty years after that first Richardson/Dempster experiment, the Samuel Hewett fishing business was supplying Billingsgate market with the bulk of its fresh fish. Conveying those supplies from the fishing boats to the market was still, however, a cumbersome exercise, and the carrier vessels which had seemed so modern and rapid in the 1840s, by the 1860s were inadequate to their task. Accordingly the Hewetts replaced them with steam-powered carriers and another era was inaugurated. By 1879 John Gamgee, a prominent refrigeration engineer, who created the earliest artificial ice rinks, was reporting that Hewett's steamers were carrying about 35 tons of ice each, that they were built of a size small enough to drop into the trough of the sea with the fishing boat, and that 'the two hug each other, without danger of a crushing collision . . . were they large, the difficult process of transferring the fish from the boats would be attended with even

The basement vaults of the old Billingsgate fish market, which closed in January 1982. The stores also sold crushed ice, used by merchants to keep newly-arrived fish at the peak of freshness.

greater danger than it is at present'. It was in this way, Gamgee added, that England and especially London and the fishing ports of Great Yarmouth and Grimsby had become the centres of the expensive and lucrative ice trade from Norway.[16]

Before long the railways would carry fish packed in ice throughout the length and breadth of the British Isles. In the huge ice stores of our ports, Norwegian ice was packed in hundreds of thousands of tons. From Grimsby, Hull, Yarmouth, Aberdeen, Berwick, Glasgow, Leith, Newcastle and Cardiff, to every lesser fishing port around the coast, no town was without its commercial ice houses. Seaside resorts, naval ports, spa towns, the great brewing centres, all had their ice companies.

On 15 September 1899, *The Cold Storage and Ice Trades Review*, a monthly London journal launched in April of the previous year, reported that in the five years ending with 1898, nearly 2,200,000 tons of ice had been imported from Norway and that the value was £1,316,185. No comparable figures exist for ice harvested in Britain

and used by fishmongers, confectioners, caterers and private individuals, but these were certainly peak years for the Norway traffic.
The falling off after 1900 was marked. Manufactured ice was gradually
replacing natural ice in a number of trades. The breweries which had
consumed great quantities for the cooling of their wort in the summer
months were installing their own refrigeration systems. The first mechanically refrigerated ships had brought frozen meat from South
America to France in 1877, and in 1880 and 1882 respectively Australia
and New Zealand had sent their first cargoes of frozen lamb and
mutton to England in sailing ships equipped in Glasgow with Bell-
Coleman refrigerating apparatus. In June 1898 *The Cold Storage Review*
reported a novel experiment. Five thousand dozen New Zealand
oysters, shelled and frozen into blocks of eight dozen, had arrived by
S.S. *Perthshire* and were selling at 8s. per block. A fish dealer named
Tabor reported that they were certainly equal to the best English sauce
oysters, and were very plump and white. In the following December
Tabor took delivery of another 65,000 frozen New Zealand oysters
and was selling them at 5s. to 5s. 6d. per hundred. The equivalent
English deep sea oysters, known as 'commons', were fetching about
8s. per hundred open, so the New Zealands were good value. The
imports, of which we hear little more, represented an interesting piece
of enterprise of the kind which George Dempster would have enjoyed
and approved.

The British sea fisheries, meanwhile, although still consuming large
quantities of natural ice – for lack of it the Irish mackerel fisheries of
Peel had to throw overboard £1,000 worth of fish in the summer of
1898 – were also beginning to construct their own ice factories and
to build steam trawlers with insulated fish rooms and self-contained
ice-making apparatus. In December 1898, *The Cold Storage Review*
reported that the Provost of Aberdeen was expressing his opinion that
the role of ice in the transit of fish was only in its infancy. Mechanically
made ice would, he believed, be largely used even in the transport of
herrings.

By 1902, the building of cold stores and ice factories, already
common in the United States for three decades, was enjoying an
extraordinary boom in England. The Imperial Lager Brewery, of

Tottenham, which had built its own ice plant, now found that ice was more profitable than brewing, disposed of its beer trade, extended its ice plant to produce 500 tons per week, and announced that during May the price of ice to the trade would be only 3d. per block of 56 lb, increasing to 5d. in June and July. This company was also renting cold storage rooms for meat, fish, and other perishable produce of all kinds.[17] Given the competitive prices of manufactured ice, and the necessity for the Norway ice importers to reduce their prices in accordance with the competition – in the 1860s and 70s their ice had been retailing at about 4s. for 56 lb – it is perhaps surprising that the Norway trade continued so long, indeed until well after the First World War. The prejudice against manufactured ice, public distrust of the ammonia used in the factories, and the amount of coal they consumed, were all factors which contributed to keeping the natural ice trade alive.

A curious little footnote to the story of Chinese ice technology, from which Britain and Europe had in the eighteenth century learned such valuable lessons, was contained in a brief report which appeared in *The Cold Storage Review* of 21 September 1911. The Chinese were now lagging far behind the West in the refrigeration technique. In the whole of Northern China there was only one ice-making plant, and this, unsurprisingly, was in the grounds of the American Legation Guard at Peking. It was operated by a Lieutenant of the Marine Corps and produced ice for the Legation and the members of the Guard. It was not that the Chinese had by any means abandoned the use of ice. On the contrary, it was extensively used, being cut from rivers and ponds, and piled up in large rectangular heaps on shore. These stacks were then covered with several feet of clay, yet another variation on ice preservation technique. This natural ice was presumably regarded with suspicion by the Americans, but then the Chinese, as the report pointed out, never introduced ice into any drink. In that respect, as in so many others, the ancient tradition of China still obtained. To put it into a drink even in the hottest weather was going altogether too far in the pursuit of achieving balance through opposites. To the Chinese the sound of ice tinkling in tumblers of water, whisky, and long mixed drinks, so attractive to American and European ears, must have been quite alien, even improper. There had, it is true, been times when Chinese physicians had found it necessary to warn people, just as European doctors had so frequently warned their readers and patients, that the eating of ice in summer was dangerous and a potential cause of illness:[18] but such occurrences must have been rare. Ice-chilled fruit, on the other hand, seems to have escaped censure, and in fact many ice-cooled foods and dishes were, and long had been, appreciated by the Chinese; it was the direct presence of ice in drinks and indeed anything icy which they found distasteful. That in the twentieth century the Chinese took to eating American-style ice-cream was one of the most notable food revolutions in the history of China, although it was just a little local happening when compared to the importance of the ice revolution effected in the eighteenth century when those perspicacious Scotsmen turned their information concerning the Chinese methods of preserving fresh fish to such good account. I wonder if the Chinese themselves ever became aware of it.

In November 1909 the American trade journal *Ice and Refrigeration* carried an item condensed from a report received from the United States Consul in Canton, to the effect that crowds had been gathering to watch a street vendor in the city operating his ice-cream freezer, and that as a result of the upper classes having taken to the idea of serving ices in their homes there was now a much increased demand for the freezing churns. There was even talk of starting an ice factory. The Chinese were really taking to the use of ice, the Consul had said. He hadn't realized that in China the use of ice was hardly new, although what certainly was new, or recently acquired, was the Chinese taste for ice-cream. So was the notion of manufacturing ice by machinery.

In 1930 came China's first American-style ice-cream factory. In Peking alone sales were soon reaching 1,000 tons a year. Some clever public relations person seems to have succeeded in putting it about that the eating of ice-cream promoted the increase of male children. Of that same period in Peking Cecilia Chiang, a remarkable lady who founded what became one of the most successful restaurants in San Francisco, wrote in her autobiography, *The Mandarin Way*, 'we made ice cream ... by the old fashioned method, churned in a wooden barrel ... and it tasted infinitely better than the commercial kinds today'. Mrs Chiang also records that although hot tea was regarded as much more cooling than any cold drink, she and her sisters, on holiday with an aunt and uncle in Peking, refreshed themselves between meals with imported grape juice, and crab apple juice, poured over shaved ice. So by the 1930s it had become acceptable to put ice directly into fruit juice drinks. A concoction of red beans cooked and ground to a paste (shells included) with brown sugar, and cooled likewise over shaved ice, is also mentioned by Mrs Chiang.[19] That sounds like, and probably was, one of the traditional delicacies which had so long been a speciality of those Peking restaurants where only iced foods were served. As so much in the story of the uses of ice in China, the cooling dish of ground red beans and brown sugar enjoyed on sultry summer days in Peking is alluring and strange. It would be agreeable to know more of it.

To India's Coral Strand

Ice by Elephant, Ice by Tribute

Knowledge of how to chill beverages in saltpetre-cooled water is said to have reached Europe via merchants returning from India in the days of the early colonists, probably the Portuguese, perhaps the Dutch. India, particularly Bengal, is very rich in saltpetre, and the method certainly seems to have been commonly known to the Moghuls in the days of Akbar the Great, who reigned from 1555 to 1605, almost exactly contemporary with Queen Elizabeth I.

A precise account of how the drinking water was cooled at Akbar's court is recorded in the famous *Ain-i-Akbari*[1] or *Institutions of Akbar*, written at the Emperor's order by Abul Fazl Allami and completed *c.* 1590, and there is little doubt that the system had for long been known. 'Saltpetre,' says the chronicler, 'which in gunpowder produces the explosive heat, is used by his Majesty as a means for cooling water, and is thus a source of joy for great and small. Saltpetre is a saline earth.' A brief description of the boiling and crystallizing process now precedes the instruction to pour a *se'r*[2] of water into a long-necked, pewter, silver, or other metal flagon, and stop it up. Two and a half *se'rs* of saltpetre and five *se'rs* of water are then to be thrown into another vessel and stirred round for a quarter of an hour, when the water in the flagon will become cold. The word used by the nineteenth-century translator of the *Ain-i-Akbari* to denote flagon is *goglet*, a corruption of the Portuguese *gógoleta*, but it is unlikely that Abul Fazl, writing in Persian, would have used that term. In central India the word for the long-necked globular water bottles, usually made of earthenware, was *surahi*. It was this long-necked flagon, copied from

Persian or Moghul Indian models, that was used in Italy when saltpetre was introduced as a cooling agent for wine and water. The stirring gesture was the one still familiar today to anyone who has ever watched a waiter setting a bottle of wine to chill in an ice bucket.

In 1586 Akbar abandoned his palace at Fathipur Sikri near Agra and moved his capital to Lahore in the Punjab. It was from that date, according to Abul Fazl, that the use of saltpetre for cooling water was replaced by ice and snow brought from the northern mountains.

Since the thirtieth year of the Divine Era [AD 1586], when the Imperial standards were erected in the Punjab, snow and ice have come into use. Ice is brought by land and water, by post carriages and bearers from the district of Panham, in the northern mountains, about forty-five *kòs*[3] from Lahor. The dealers derive a considerable profit, two or three *se'rs* of ice being sold *per rupee*. The greatest profit is derived when the ice is brought by water, next when by carriage, and least when by bearers.[4] The inhabitants bring it in loads, and sell it in piles containing from 25 to 30 *se'rs* at the rate of 5 *dame*.[5]

At this stage of the journey south, the ice was sold at three different prices, according to the distance it had been brought, and was then loaded on to boats or carriages.

Out of the ten boats employed for the transport of ice, one arrives daily at the capital, each being manned by four boatmen. The ice bundles contain from six to twelve *se'rs*, according to the temperature.

A carriage brings two loads. There are fourteen stages, where the horses are changed; and besides one elephant is used. Twelve pieces of ten to four *se'rs* arrive daily.

The record now goes into minute detail concerning the price of ice during different periods of the year. It would be tedious to quote the passage in full, since we have such scanty means of relating either the prices or the weights to those of today. The main distinctions between the seasons, however, were first, winter when the ice was at its cheapest; second, during the rains when it was nearly five times as much; and third, 'the intermediate time', when it was only twice as much as during the winter.

When brought down by bearers, there were fourteen stages, requiring altogether twenty-eight men. Every day one load, containing four parcels, was brought. The cost in winter (the beginning of the year) was nearly twice as much as when it was brought by horse and cart; in the mid-season three times more, and during the end of the season a little more again.

Unfortunately we are not told by the compiler of the *Ain-i-Akbari* how or where the ice was stored – presumably it was in trenches or in pits – but we do get an illuminating note to the effect that 'all ranks use ice in summer; the nobles use it throughout the year'.[6]

Akbar's grandson, Aurungzeb, whose fifty-year reign, from 1657 to 1707, was contemporary with that of Louis XIV in France, was not so enlightened about the use of ice at his court and by his subjects. From Niccolao Manucci, a Venetian who spent over forty years in India, many of them at the Moghul court, we learn that Aurungzeb exacted tribute in the form of ice from the mountain rajahs. 'Near Kashmir there are several other rajahs, of whom some also pay tribute,' wrote Manucci.[7]

In one of the mountains, the nearest to Dilhi [Delhi], one of these rajahs pays one hundred and fifty rupees in tribute, besides some boat-loads of ice that he sends down by the Jamnah river during the hot season. This rajah asked Aurungzeb to exempt him from this money tribute, when he would undertake to send him every year enough ice for the whole city of Dilhi, if he were empowered to sell it. But the king refused his consent for three reasons. The first was that much coin would be exported from his court. The second was that the rajah would become wealthy. The third was he did not want anyone to use ice, except those to whom he should deign to accord such a favour.

This rajah, Manucci's translator tells us, was the ruler of Nahan or Sirmur in the outer hills, who still in the eighteenth century retained the nickname of Baofi Rajah, or 'Snow King', owing to his sending of ice to the Delhi court.

Ice by Evaporation, Ice by Absorption

A detailed description of the method of making ice in Calcutta and Allahabad was written in March 1775 by Sir Robert Barker, Fellow of the Royal Society and an officer in the army at that time maintained by the British India Company.

For three months in the year, Sir Robert wrote,[8] from December to February, it was usual to collect ice every morning before sunrise and carry it to special ice pits where it was stored for the summer. Since natural ice is scarcely ever known in Bengal, where the thermometer never or extremely rarely sinks to freezing point, the ice was artificially induced, by a method which shows much ingenuity. As was the case with the ice produced and stored outside the city of Isfahan in the seventeenth century (see p. 189), the method could only have been practised in a country where there was almost unlimited and barely paid, not to say slave, labour.

The ice pits at Allahabad from Fanny Parks' *Wanderings of a Pilgrim in Search of the Picturesque*, 1850.

The ice-maker belonging to me at Allahabad (at which place I principally attended to this inquiry) made a sufficient quantity in the winter for the supply of the table during the summer season. The methods he pursued were as follows: on a large open plain, three or four excavations were made, each about thirty feet square and two deep; the bottom of which were strewed about eight inches or a foot thick with sugar-cane, or the stems of the large Indian corn dried. Upon this bed were placed in rows, near to each other, a number of small, shallow earthen pans, for containing the water intended to be frozen. These are unglazed, scarce a quarter of an inch thick, about an inch and a quarter in depth, and made of an earth so porous, that it was visible, from the exterior part of the pans, the water had penetrated the whole substance.

Towards the dusk of the evening, they were filled with soft water, which had been boiled, and then left in the afore-said situation. The ice-makers attended the pits usually before the sun was above the horizon, and collected in baskets what was frozen, by pouring the whole contents of the pans into them, and thereby retaining the ice, which was daily conveyed to the grand receptacle or place of preservation.

Half a century later, an Englishwoman provided us with a very similar account of ice-making near Calcutta. Emma Roberts had lived in the Upper Province of India with her sister and brother-in-law, Captain and Mrs McNaghten, from 1828 to 1830, and there contributed articles to the *Asiatic Journal*. Following the death of her sister she settled in Calcutta, where she became editor of the *Oriental Observer*.

At the principal stations in the Mofussil, there are regular ice-harvests; the night-frosts during a certain number of weeks being always sufficiently strong to congeal water exposed to their influence, if of an inconsiderable depth. A piece of ground commensurate to the concern, is laid out for the purpose of collecting a sufficient quantity of ice to last through the hot season; shallow pans are provided, of convenient dimensions, and these are placed in rows, close to each other. After sunset, they are filled with water by superintendents, whose business it is to remove the cakes when sufficiently frozen, and to replenish the pans; an operation which is performed several times in the course of each night. The cakes of ice are deposited in excavations made according to the principles observed in England, and with proper care may be preserved during the rains. The least neglect, however, is fatal in the damp season; the ice melts in an instant.[9]

A notable point in Miss Roberts's account is her assertion that the ice pans were replenished several times during the night. This detail occurs in no other account I have come across (there is, for instance, a much longer account by Fanny Parks, written at Allahabad in 1828 but not published until 1850), and one wonders whether it does not relate more to her experience in the Upper Province: the original article was evidently written at Berhampore.

The *Encyclopaedia Britannica*★ is a little more technical in its note on Bengal ice-making:

Pits are dug about 2 ft deep and filled three-quarters full with dry straw, on which are set flat porous pans containing the water to be frozen. Exposed overnight to a cool dry gentle wind from the north-west, the water evaporates at the expense of its own heat, and the consequent cooling takes place with sufficient rapidity to overbalance the slow influx of heat from above through the cooled dense air or from below through the badly conducting straw.

Much the same had already been said by Sir Robert Barker:

Other factors governing the formation of ice were the porous clay of the vessels which made them well qualified for the admission of the cold air internally; the spongey nature of the sugar-cane, or the stems of Indian corn placed under the pans and giving passage to the cold air which, acting on the outside of the vessels, carried off by evaporation a proportion of the heat; and the placing of the vessels a full foot beneath ground floor level protected the surface of the water from being ruffled by any small currents of air, and thereby preserved the congealed particles from disunion.

It is hard for us today, accustomed as we are to take a plentiful and continuous supply of ice for granted, to appreciate the necessity of explaining the process of actually using it to freeze other fluids during the severe heat of the summer season, which Sir Robert Barker goes into at some length. Since he uses 'creams and sherbets' as examples

★ 11th edition, 1910, article 'Ice'.

in his dissertation, it is interesting to learn what he had to say. 'The sherbets, creams, or whatever other fluids are intended to be frozen,' we learn,

are confined in their silver cups of a conical form, containing about a pint, with their covers well luted on with paste, and placed in a large vessel filled with ice, saltpetre, and common salt, of the two last an equal quantity, and a little water to dissolve the ice and combine the whole. This composition presently freezes the contents of the cups to the same consistency of our ice creams, etc. in Europe; but plain water will become so hard as to require a mallet and knife to break it. Upon applying the bulb of a thermometer to one of these pieces of ice, the quicksilver has been known to sink two or three degrees below the freezing point: so that from an atmosphere apparently not mild enough to produce natural ice, ice shall be formed, collected, and a cold accumulated, that shall cause the quicksilver to fall even below freezing point.

'The promising advantages of such a discovery,' Sir Robert told his fellow members of the Royal Society,

could alone induce the Asiatic, (whose principal study is the luxuries of life, and this may well be called such, when I have often been regaled with ices when the thermometer has stood at 112) to make an attempt at profiting by so very short a duration of cold during the nights in these months, and by a well-timed and critical contrivance ... they have procured to themselves a comfortable refreshment as a recompense, to alleviate in some degree the intense heat of the summer season which in some parts of India would be scarce supportable but by the assistance of this and many other inventions.

What Sir Robert did not say, and perhaps had not discovered, was whether the 'well-timed and critical contrivance' by which ice was produced and stored in Bengal was a very ancient method or a comparatively recent one introduced by Europeans. The Portuguese, first European colonists of the region, may have been responsible, since they themselves were familiar with the cooling properties of the porous clay vessels of their own country[10] – by all accounts those used in India for making ice were very similar. Or was it in fact from the Indians that the Portuguese had learned the method? The point is one calling for research.

A significant point in Sir Robert Barker's account is his mention of the conical silver cups in which the Indian ices were frozen. (His reference to ices as 'sherbets' was, I think, an anglicism: in India sherbets are fruit juice or other non-alcoholic drinks, usually cooled with ice, but not frozen, whereas the traditional Indian ice-cream – or rather milk ice – is called a *kulfi*, apparently of very ancient Persian origin, the word being a popular corruption or reversal of *kufli*, a lock – in other words, a mould in which the preparation to be frozen is enclosed or confined.) Those moulds described by Sir Robert are still used in India today. They are usually made of aluminium, and are much smaller now, holding only about 5 oz rather than a pint – but the shape and the cover are exactly as described by Sir Robert. The *kulfi* mould is in fact almost identical with the tall conical ice-cream mould which in Europe became known as a bombe mould. Did European confectioners take it as a pattern from the Persians and Indians? Or was it a seventeenth-century Indian imitation of the European ice mould? And did the familiar form of the sugar-loaf have some bearing on the design?

Emma Roberts provides us with more than just an account of indigenous ice-making, she takes the story to the brink of mechanical ice production. 'Artificial ice,' she says,

made by the assistance of an air-pump and other machinery, has been found too expensive, and is seldom or never resorted to in India: upon the first introduction into Bengal, the novelty proved very attractive, and a rich and luxurious native, it is said, expended seven hundred pounds in the single article of ice at an entertainment given to a European party.

It is of interest to note that no refrigeration historian that I know of, and equally no historian of social life in British India other than Miss Roberts, has mentioned ice-making apparatus actually on the market and in operation at this time, i.e. between 1828 and 1832 or, at the latest, 1835, when her book was published.

Whose invention was 'the air-pump and other machinery' introduced into Bengal? Somewhere in the Bengal newspapers of the period there must surely be a reference to the introduction of the mystery machine and its inventor. As described so sketchily by Emma

Roberts, it could have been the apparatus for which a Brighton brewer named John Vallance took out two patents, one on 1 January 1824, and the second on 28 August of the same year.[11] Vallance's machine was an improved version, to be made commercially, of the invention of Sir John Leslie, the famous Scottish physicist or natural philosopher of Edinburgh University, whose paper *Experimental Inquiry into the Nature of Heat*, published in 1804, had earned him the Royal Society's Rumford Medal. The practical possibility opened up by Leslie's system of absorbent cooling (the forerunner of all the absorption machines later used in the industry) was the production of cheap ice in all climates, and John Vallance in his elaboration on what was purely laboratory apparatus had clearly had that point in mind. That the Bengal climate defeated Vallance's machine – if indeed it was his, and the fact that it was 'described by *some* as an evaporative cooling method similar to the Hindu processes of making ice',[12] although somewhat misleading, seems to confirm this – was perhaps predictable. Eighty years later C.H.B. Forbes of the Bombay Ice Producing Company patiently explained to critics of his doubling the price of ice from a quarter to half an *anna* (about a half pence) per pound that 'it must be borne in mind that it is much more difficult to make ice here than in Europe. The temperature of the water and the atmosphere are much higher in Bombay than in London and it stands to reason that a greater number of thermal units of heat must be extracted from the water before it will solidify and become ice.'[13] He was also describing new ice-making machinery recently installed by the old established British engineering company Messrs J. & E. Hall of Dartford, for whom the inventor Richard Trevithick had been working at the time of his death in 1833. It was Trevithick (see p. 337) who had predicted that ice would one day be made very cheaply by means of steam power.

Calcutta's Crystal Palace

India – ice. The one does – and yet does not – suggest the other, remarked Mr George Cecil in a report on the Indian ice business as he saw it in 1901.[14] In my own mind India and ice are just about inseparable, and this is due to an incident, in itself totally trivial, but which has nevertheless stuck in my mind for nearly forty years. Somehow that little incident was a typically Indian one. As I remember it, I see the Indian barman making great play with the cocktail shaker, in the approved manner of barmen all over the world. It is midday and we have just arrived in the grandest hotel – after so long its name escapes me, but I remember that its grandeur was very relative – in the famous hill station of Darjeeling. It is June 1946. We have escaped from New Delhi temperatures of 112 degrees and the city's non-functioning air-conditioning. Travelling by the night train to Calcutta, we have done the second part of the journey via the astonishing mountain railway to Darjeeling. Still a bit dazed from that dizzy ride, I become aware that Tony, my husband, is talking to the barman in Urdu. 'What's it about?' I ask. 'Just that there's no ice in that shaker. It turns out he hasn't got any. The hotel's refrigerator has broken down.' So here in Darjeeling, at the very feet, so to speak, of Kin-chinjunga and the mightiest range of mountains in the world, our cheerful charming barman is giving us a brave show in the hope that perhaps we won't notice that while whenever we look out of a window we see ice and snow, inside the hotel there is none, and the Colonel sahib and his lady must make do with lukewarm martinis.

This absurd but touching episode came to my mind once more when not so long ago I read in Jacquetta Hawkes's biography of Sir Mortimer Wheeler, the celebrated archaeologist, of something which must have happened at about the same time I was lying sweltering on my bed in our New Delhi apartment praying for the electric ceiling fan to start working again, or perhaps packing our life-saving portable ice box for the overnight journey to Calcutta, or loading it up for a Sunday picnic in the ruins of one of Delhi's seven old cities. Sir

Mortimer was on a dig at the site of Taxila, high up in north-western India. Students from all over the sub-continent had flocked to offer their services. So many and various were these young people, Jacquetta Hawkes remembered, that one never knew quite what to expect next. On one occasion a boy from a southern province was seen putting a lump of ice in his pocket. His parents, he said, had certainly never seen such a thing, and he was going to send it home to them.[15]

Small wonder then that when, in 1833, Calcutta, at that time the capital of British India, headquarters of the East India Company and official residence of the Governor-General, witnessed the first arrival in the port of an American ship carrying ice from Boston, its citizens were galvanized – and the citizens of Calcutta were on the whole slow to galvanize. True, the cargo was a small one, no more than 40 tons. The quantity, however, was irrelevant. It was the astonishingly beautiful quality of the ice itself, clear, pure, and cut in great blocks weighing as much as two Bengal *maunds*, or 160 lb, and the fact that it had survived a voyage of 16,000 miles, taking four months and involving two equatorial crossings, that sent the European residents and the civic dignitaries of Calcutta into action.

The story of the beginnings of the Boston to Calcutta ice trade is a curious one, and as in all things to do with India, accounts are conflicting. The version I have was written by a man called Longueville Clarke, a distinguished Calcutta advocate and the prime mover in the setting up of the Boston to Calcutta ice trade. Clarke's account, however, was written some years after the event, at the request of Lord Dalhousie, Governor-General from 1848 to 1856. Inevitably there are discrepancies between his story and that told in Richard Cummings's *American Ice Harvests* (1949) and the British National Maritime Museum's monograph on the *Ice Carrying Trade at Sea* (1981). Those accounts are based, like several others, on Frederick Tudor's diary and papers now housed in the Baker Library at Harvard Business School. Given the discrepancies, it is only right to warn the reader that while to me Longueville Clarke's story, representing as it does the reactions of people who were to be on the receiving end of this much desired and most attractive commodity, has more human detail and immediacy than Tudor's records, which chiefly concern the economics and mechanics of the venture, I cannot help feeling that in Clarke's account there may be inaccuracies as well as gaps. There are equally, I believe, omissions and perhaps exaggerations in Tudor's story. In both versions, discrepancies and conflicting dates, it seems to me, are of minor importance, and are not particularly relevant to the main drama of the very extraordinary saga of the East India ice trade. About that extraordinariness there can be no disagreement.

The story starts, not with Frederick Tudor of Boston, but with an unknown, unnamed American apothecary who had had the idea of bringing that very first consignment of ice from Boston to Calcutta. As a result of the excitement caused by the shipment and in the hope that its arrival would not remain an isolated or unique event, a subscription was organized by the Right Reverend Daniel Wilson, Lord Bishop of Calcutta, and with the money contributed a silver cup was presented to the ice-importing apothecary. As a stimulus to further exertion in the matter of ice for Calcutta this silver cup proved a non-starter. Promptly converting his gift into dollars, the apothecary set himself up as a boarding-house keeper, practising dentistry as a sideline. This character now vanishes from the cast of the Calcutta ice drama. Next to appear on the scene is Longueville Clarke, star of many a committee and instigator of numerous movements aimed at the improvement of the city's amenities. The provision of ice and a suitable place for its storage – a necessity which the American apothecary had apparently failed to take into consideration – were without doubt amenities greatly to be desired in the Calcutta of the 1830s. Longueville Clarke, undaunted by the defection of the shadowy apothecary and confident now in the knowledge that the shipping of ice from Boston to Calcutta was a feasibility, decided to write to 'the great Boston ice-importer', as Clarke called Frederick Tudor. Putting to Tudor the proposition that since many American ships came to Hooghly in ballast, the cost of carrying the ice would be trivial, Clarke suggested that provided the citizens of Calcutta were prepared to pay for the construction of the essential ice house, the retail price they would have to pay would be half what it was currently selling for in London, and it would be available all the year round. Tudor wrote accepting the deal.[16]

The next move for Longueville Clarke was to call a meeting at the Town Hall. The prospect of a supply of purest ice at a cost equivalent to three halfpence a pound all the year round in place of the so-called 'Hooghly slush' (meaning ice made by the evaporation and radiation process, described on pp. 249–252 by Sir Robert Barker, Fanny Parks and others), obtainable only for about six weeks during the hottest season and at the much higher cost of fourpence per pound, was one not to be resisted. Within three days a grant of riverside land on a site considered suitable for the construction of an ice house was made by the government and 25,000 rupees* had been raised by a committee of prominent citizens headed by Longueville Clarke himself. Terms were quickly agreed with Tudor, the ice house was built, and the first large cargo of Boston ice, amounting, according to Longueville Clarke, to about 700 tons,† was safely landed. An unfortunate setback now occurred. The capacity of the ice house was found to be too small. Longueville Clarke set to work once more. Calling another meeting, he obtained a further grant of government land – the speed with which these events appear to follow each other is no doubt due to a telescoping of time in Clarke's account – and raised another 25,000 rupees.

At this stage, Henry Meredith Parker, an eminent member of the Bengal Civil Service, enters the scene. His written appeal for more funds was based on humanitarian grounds. Addressing those citizens of Calcutta whose first concern was the welfare of the sick rather than the comfort of the healthy, Parker enlisted the support of two local medical practitioners who sent in certificates stating that ice was among the first remedies in the hospitals. Accordingly Parker's fund-raising plea was addressed primarily to the women of the community, an astute move resulting in the raising of a further 3,000 rupees, and the heading of the subscription list by the Misses Emily and Fanny Eden, sisters of the new Governor-General, Lord Auckland, who had

---

* Approximately £2,500.

† Tudor himself recorded that he had sent 180 tons to Calcutta in 1833, and that about 120 tons had been landed. This cargo was not mentioned by Longueville Clarke.

arrived in Calcutta in 1836. The piece of ground granted for the second ice house was formally handed over to Longueville Clarke in his capacity as President of the Committee by Lord Auckland himself.

The second Calcutta ice house, described by Cotton as a 'strangely-shaped globular building perched on the summit of a flight of steps challenging the attention of every passer-by',[17] proved adequate to its task. For nearly fifty years the American ice ships plied their improbable trade to British India carrying their 500 ton, 600 ton, and even, in peak years, 1,000 ton burdens of blessed comfort to Calcutta, Bombay, Madras, and Galle, the shipping port of Ceylon. Profits to Tudor were

The Bombay ice house, built in 1843.

of course variable. Much depended on the length of the passage. Sometimes Tudor's ships would sail first to Bombay, discharge part of their cargo, and proceed thence right round the sub-continent to Calcutta. On one occasion in 1835, early in the history of the India trade, a brig took half a year to reach Calcutta from Boston, whereupon Tudor presented her master with a goblet for having demonstrated that ice could be preserved for six months at sea. In 1837 Tudor sent out a new and youthful agent named Caleb Ladd to Calcutta. 'There is lots of money to be made in this country with ice,' he wrote to his master. 'Send me the ice, I will take good care that you get the money.'[18] Tudor duly got it. His ships returned from India carrying cotton goods, muslins and silks, jute, saltpetre and linseed. As Longueville Clarke had reasoned, prior to the setting up of the ice trade the ships had sailed to India in ballast, and to Tudor the ice business did indeed represent almost pure profit. Again, as predicted by Longueville Clarke, Tudor was enabled to sell his ice at very low prices, and when in the 1850s the rival ice ships of the Gage Hittinger Company of Boston appeared on the Calcutta scene and undercut him he reduced his price to three farthings a pound. By threatening to bring it down still further if his rivals persisted in their price-cutting war, Tudor eventually succeeded in shaking them off.

To the inhabitants of Calcutta, the cost of ice was of relative unimportance compared to the fact of its arrival, whatever its source. Colesworthy Grant, an artist who spent some years in Bengal at that period, and who kept – and eventually published – lively records, written and pictorial, of the domestic manners, customs, trades, and products of the province, noted the acute need for ice in Calcutta's unhealthy, fever-ridden climate. Like Henry Meredith Parker he stressed its medical value and the anxiety concerning its arrival. 'Our English mail is not more anxiously expected than that of an American ice-ship when supplies run low,' he wrote. 'Neither money nor mails are of equal value with life, and the ice has frequently exercised a vital influence upon patients on whose fevered and burning heads I have seen large lumps of it applied continuously for hours together, with the most important and happy results.' Revealing that a certain quantity was now regularly held in reserve in the ice house for medical purposes, Grant remarked that 'the stoppage of the Bank of Bengal could hardly exceed the excitement of a failure during our hot weather of the Ice!'[19]

To those familiar with the discomforts, not to say miseries, of the hot season in India, Colesworthy Grant's exclamatory prose will come as no surprise. Indeed, his expressions of the joy, the comfort, the benefits, the luxury, the solace, which the Boston ice trade brought to India seem decidedly on the restrained side. It should not, by the way, be supposed that the servants of the East India Company and the sahibs to whom the tinkle of ice in a glass at sundown or the relief of an ice-bag laid on a fevered brow were such welcome amenities were the exclusive beneficiaries of the new trade. 'Even Hindoos,' Colesworthy Grant reported, 'otherwise so scrupulous in the matter of what they eat and drink, do not hesitate to mix the frozen waters of America with the sacred stream of Ganges,' and even the strictest Moham-medans could not resist the temptations of American ice. They used it 'with unlimited freedom ... and little children' – anticipating the ice lolly – 'continue eagerly to seek and to suck it as though it were a sweetmeat'. It was entirely understandable that Colesworthy Grant should talk of nectar, invoke Elysium, and revere the Calcutta ice house as 'our Crystal Palace', even whimsically suggesting that at its door some Moore-ish couplet might declare that if there be a luxury 'IT IS HERE, IT IS HERE'.[20]

Tudor's ships brought other luxuries to India, small ones compared to ice, and extraordinarily expensive. American apples, packed in barrels filled with the same sawdust with which the ships' holds were insulated, fetched as much as 50 to 75 cents each, and later, when the China ice trade had been established, New England apples sold in the Treaty Ports 'for their weight in silver'. That in countries where oranges, pineapples, melons, mangoes, fresh dates, and all manner of tropical fruits were to be had in plenty, apples which had spent three or four months in barrel could command such prices can be explicable only by homesickness on the part of the English residents. Or was it the novelty of the idea, the innovation, that was the attraction? Caleb Ladd wrote to Tudor in 1837: 'the gentlemen are willing to pay a good price for a good article ... never send me nothing but the very best . . . and one half of the quantity will pay double the profit', going on to tell his employer that as the ice house was right on the Strand, where 'all the first cut', as he called the gentry, passed on their regular twice-daily rides, he had decided to have a small room stylishly fitted up for the retail of apples.

A community short of excitement in the way of social entertainment and always avid for even four-month-old news also found the arrival of the ice ships a pleasing diversion. In the 1850s Mrs Caleb Ladd came out to Calcutta on the *Elizabeth Kimball*, a 1,200-ton half-clipper. The Chief Mate, Captain John Whidden, wrote that while discharging her cargo the ship was 'a popular resort for all the officers of the surrounding ships. Iced drinks were concocted in every shape.' The apple barrels were brought ashore and opened in the ice house, and when found to be in good condition sales of the fruit were brisk. The Tudor ice ships had become a Calcutta institution.[21]

American butter packed in ice, oysters, clams, and sensibly enough, ice pitchers, were other tempting items brought to India in Tudor's cargoes. Until the ice ships came the ancient saltpetre-cooling method had been used for butter and milk, wine and water. In the houses of rich Calcutta merchants and high-ranking East India Company officials, 'silver vases' containing the butter and milk were enclosed in vessels filled with saltpetre and gave their breakfast tables 'a princely air', said Miss Emma Roberts,[22] who in the pre-Tudor days had spent four years in India, two of them in Calcutta. If there was anybody qualified to describe and comment on the domestic lives of British officials in the India of the 1820s and early 1830s it was Emma Roberts, who had edited a Calcutta journal called *The Oriental Observer*, contributed many articles on Indian life to the *Asiatic Journal*, and in 1835 had published three volumes of them under the title *Scenes and Characteristics of Hindustan*. Staying at Parel, residence of the Governor of Bombay, on her return to India in 1839, Miss Roberts noted, a trifle plaintively, that the tables of high officials in Bombay, while handsomely enough appointed, lacked the splendours prevailing in Bengal. In particular she missed those silver cooling vessels to which she had become accustomed in Calcutta.[23] Having left India in 1832, she had missed the excitement of the first American ice ships and perhaps was not even aware of the newly developed double-jacketed ice jugs, pitchers and wine coolers with improved methods of insulation which were encouraging an increased demand for ice and boosting Tudor's sales in the great seaports of India. Poor Miss Roberts did not live to record the changes, nor even to see the Bombay ice house, for it was built only in 1843, and she died at Poona in September 1840, without completing the year she had planned to spend in India editing a new journal, and without ever seeing in print the immensely successful revised edition of Mrs Rundell's famous *New System of Domestic Cookery*, the 64th edition, published in 1840, which she had completed for John Murray before leaving for India. She had not even had the chance to arrange for the publication in book form of her account of her *Journey through France and Egypt to Bombay in 1839*, which appeared only five years later.

In the early years of the Boston to India ice trade, only the citizens of Bombay, Madras and Calcutta and those outlying settlements situated within a radius of about thirty miles of a main city benefited from the American shipments. Further inland, or up country as the rest of Bengal was known to Calcutta, transport to British trading stations such as Allahabad, Cawnpore and Benares, whether by land or water, was far too slow and cumbersome to allow of the delivery of ice from the port. In those districts the making of ice by evaporation continued far into the nineteenth century, even into the twentieth if the *Encyclopaedia Britannica* of 1910 is to be relied upon, the article on 'Ice' in that famous 11th edition describing the system in the present tense (see p. 251), but the railways were gradually opening up the possibility of relatively fast and regular deliveries of American ice to up country stations. Already by 1862 the railway from Calcutta had reached Benares,* and the Bombay line was servicing at least part of Western India.

The blessing of American ice was now in turn leading to the installation, in the houses of residents in British India, of heavy mahogany or teakwood ice chests, lined throughout in zinc, fitted with

---

* Formerly the journey, a distance of 400 miles, had taken about ten weeks by river boat and eight or nine days by road.

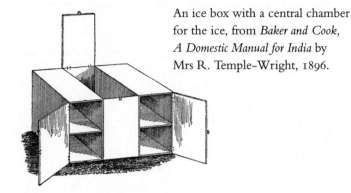

An ice box with a central chamber for the ice, from *Baker and Cook, A Domestic Manual for India* by Mrs R. Temple-Wright, 1896.

reservoirs for water, compartments for bottles, decanters, butter pots and milk jugs. With their central chambers for ice and their flannel and green baize padding, these ice chests now formed, according to Colesworthy Grant, 'handsome items of domestic furniture, as common and as indispensable as the sofa and the sideboard'. In time the ice chest did indeed become an institution inseparable from the domestic life of every European household in India, but that desirable state of affairs took rather longer to achieve than Grant implied. For some little while the traditional ice baskets, padded inside and out with *numdar* (a kind of felt about half an inch in thickness), and when filled wrapped in double or treble *cumlies* or blankets large enough to envelop the whole contraption, remained in common household use – common, that is, in districts where ice was to be had – for there were still many of the more isolated stations where the ancient methods of saltpetre-cooling were the only ones available to men such as indigo planters, living and working in the *mofussil*, or far out, isolated settlements. Even then, much exertion was required on the part of the *abdars*, the menservants in charge of the care, the cooling and the serving of drinks who were then employed in nearly every household of any standing, whether European or Indian. It took an hour or so of continuous shaking of bottles enclosed in containers made of hollowed-out bamboo, or of vigorous turning of long-necked bottles immersed in pails or tubs of water cooled with the chosen salt – Glauber's salts were much recommended for the purpose – before an acceptable degree of cold was achieved (see pl. 5).

By the mid 1840s a few lucky people might have one of the newly developed hand-operated machines in which small blocks of ice could be produced by means of freezing mixtures containing salts and mineral acids. One of these devices had been patented in 1843 by Thomas Masters, confectioner to the Royal Zoological Gardens and to the Royal Polytechnic Institution, who was well known in London for his demonstrations of ice-making and for his *Ice Book*, the work which publicized his invention. This book, published in 1844, and the Masters domestic ice-making machine, were both sufficiently well known in India by 1850 for the author of *Indian Domestic Economy*, who in that year published a second edition of his book,* to go into some detail as to its workings, and to pronounce upon its efficiency. The conclusions of the author, Dr R. Riddell (he did not reveal his name on the title page of the 1850 edition) were that the apparatus required a great deal of attendance, that the process was extremely slow and laborious, that the salts made much dirt and that they corroded everything. The mineral acids were quicker to produce ice, but they were dangerous and even more destructive than the salts. In short, Masters's much-publicized apparatus does not appear to have stood up to conditions in India.[24] Dr Riddell's findings must have been mortifying to Masters, who had strongly recommended his machine to 'gentlemen in the East or West Indies, or in any other place where ice cannot be procured'.[25] He had even gone to the trouble of including an inserted copy of a handwritten testimonial dated from 'East India Rooms, 8 St Martin's Place, Charing Cross, 18th May 1846' and signed by half a dozen East India Company army officers. This letter attested that one of the rooms at the St Martin's Place premises had been heated to 104°F and that at this temperature, using one of his Masters freezing machines and his new freezing mixture *containing no acids* (my italics) the gentlemen had produced a solid block of ice in sixteen minutes. As for their dessert ice, it had frozen, they asserted, in two minutes. Who was right? The gallant officers of the Madras Cavalry and the Bombay Fusiliers who signed the testimonial or the painstaking Dr Riddell, who appears to have conducted his trials without bias either way?

* The first had appeared in Bombay in 1849.

Better Than a Doctor

When natural ice was obtainable it was still, for a while, cheaper and infinitely less troublesome than ice made by artificial means. Refrigerators, or rather ice chests, were still, however, far from being the routine piece of domestic furniture optimistically described by Colesworthy Grant in 1862. In a big city like Calcutta an ice chest was perhaps common equipment, but in up-country stations things were different. Flora Annie Steel, a resolute memsahib who in 1868 arrived in India as a twenty-year-old bride and in later life became a best-selling novelist – for the authenticity and power of her Indian background material her works were favourably compared to those of Kipling – also produced a comprehensive housekeeper manual for English residents in India. Working in collaboration with a friend, Mrs Grace Gardiner, Mrs Steel put the book together, entitled it *The Complete Indian Housekeeper and Cook*, and published it in 1887. In this quite remarkable document, setting forth the tribulations to be expected in every branch of domestic management in India and supplying advice on how best to triumph over them, Mrs Steel laid it down that after punkahs and thermantidotes – an air-cooling device resembling a winnowing machine* – 'the next luxury is an ice-box. In this again stinting is *no* economy ... a large refrigerator is better than a doctor.'[26] A warning that 'the refrigerator requires scrupulous cleanliness and the personal attention of the mistress' was considered necessary by Mrs Steel. After twenty years in India she had good enough reason to remain unimpressed by the prowess of Indian servants in the matter of cleanliness, as also of the capacity of Europeans to survive in the gruelling conditions to which so many were at the time subjected. Chilling, and alas all too truthful, observations abound in her book. 'Life is very uncertain' and 'It is useless to take more than

---

* The invention dated from the 1830s. It is said to have been the brainchild of Dr George Green Spilsbury, who came to India in 1823 as surgeon to the Saugor Political Agency.

six months supply of clothing' were fair samples of her warnings. If not discouraged right from the start from investing in such items as 'a real large refrigerator', the youthful memsahib of the mid nineteenth century surely did begin to discover that her ice-box was among her best friends, providing as it did cold drinks, the means of keeping her milk and butter cool, and medical aid in the ever-likely eventuality of sudden and devastating illness.

Flora Steel and many of her contemporaries must have been familiar with the story recounted by Fanny Parks – her book, published in 1850, was well known in British India – of how in 1828 a combination of three ice packs draped over his head and iced towels round his neck had restored her husband, Major Parlby, to health when stricken at Allahabad with a fever which threatened to be fatal. A diet of claret and strawberries had greatly assisted the cure.[27]

The comforts to be derived from the ice bag and from cool drinks, one has the impression, came before the 'avoidance of the mere waste of provisions' which the refrigerator also provided, and it is easy to see why. Ice boxes were not yet very efficient, and the preservation of the ice rather than that of the foodstuffs being still the primary concern of those who managed them, spoilage of meat and fruit in the hot weather would be delayed only a day or two, if as long. The servants had to be taught that it was not a good idea to wrap the ice in blankets before putting it into the chest – the old ways with the ice basket described by Doctor Riddell in 1850[28] evidently still persisted – and it was most definitely unhygienic, Flora Steel warned, to 'stuff the box with indiscriminate provisions wrapped in dirty dusters'. In the circumstances it was no doubt preferable to relegate meat and poultry to second place and fill the ice box with iced milk and soda water which to Mrs Steel was 'as good as anything' in the way of a hot weather beverage – I don't think she would have recommended Major Parlby's claret cure for fevers. She believed in 'not drinking whenever you felt thirsty' and advocated acquiring 'the habit of only drinking at certain times' as being the more wholesome. As for the ice for drinks, 'it should not be taken on trust and should not be put into them unless it is known to be made in a machine from pure water'.[29]

No domestic ice-making machine is mentioned by Mrs Steel or Mrs Gardiner, and it is unlikely that either of them, more especially the former, would have advocated the use of a potentially dangerous device such as the Masters apparatus with its corrosive freezing salts and acids. In fact, by the time they published their book for the benefit of 'the English girls to whom fate may assign the task of being house-mothers in our Eastern Empire', as they put it in their dedication, they appear to have taken it for granted that ice was generally available at out-stations as well as in the cities.

By 1887, factory ice was indeed becoming fairly common in India, but when Flora Steel first arrived there in 1868 the natural ice trade was still flourishing and factories were scarcely heard of. During their early years in India, from 1871 to 1878, the Steels had been stationed at Kasur in the Punjab, where Mrs Steel was the sole European woman at the station. There they 'received ice daily by special post from Lahore'. This detail Flora recorded in *The Garden of Fidelity*, the autobiography she wrote when she was eighty.[30] Kasur was thirty-five miles distant from Lahore on the Firozpur road and the 'special post' appears to have been a courier who brought the ice from the city. One terrible day when the flooded Sutlej river brought devastation to Kasur the Steels learnt that 'our ice-bringer had been swept away on the highroad and drowned'. Where did the ice come from? Not yet, surely, from a factory. Was it still brought down from the northern mountains as in the days when Akbar had made Lahore his capital 300 years earlier? Mrs Steel gives no hint as to its provenance. Nor does she make any reference to the saga of ice carried 16,000 miles in wooden sailing ships from New England bringing comfort and solace to those young house-mothers of Old England's Empire to whom she and Grace Gardiner addressed their housekeeping manual.

The Ice Was Here, the Ice Was There

Flora Steel must surely at least have heard of Frederick Tudor the Ice King. True, when she arrived in India in 1868 Tudor had already been dead for four years. The trade which was almost entirely his invention was, however, still flourishing, and among the very first buildings Flora and her husband would have seen was the ice house situated on the Strand at Madras, where they landed briefly from their passenger steamer on a visit to Flora's brother before re-embarking the same night for Calcutta. The story of Tudor the Ice King and the million-dollar fortune he left when he died at the age of eighty, which we today find so remarkable a tale, might not have made any impression on young Flora. It was said of Tudor after his death that, having exchanged Indian goods such as cotton, molasses, silver and gold for frozen water packed in sawdust, he had turned on its head the old mercantile dictum according to which any nation exporting goods of lower value than it imported was on the road to ruin.[31] But it was really the years of the American Civil War of 1861–5 which had brought the Tudor Company its most phenomenal prosperity. Those were the years of the frenzied cotton boom in India, a boom brought about by the North's blockade of the Southern ports and the consequent unprecedented demand for cotton as a replacement for the raw material the South was now unable to export. Tudor himself, by that time retired, did at least live to see the spectacular success of the latter years of the trade he had created. In 1850 the total value of ice exported to British India was recorded in the United States Foreign Commerce Reports as having been 50,296 dollars. By 1860 it had risen to 82,550 dollars.[32] In the following three years the Calcutta ice business alone was taking an annual average of some 125,000 dollars. Tudor, retired though he was, was still known throughout the tropical countries where his chartered vessels had operated as the Ice King of Boston, and in the judgement of the American maritime and naval historian Samuel Eliot Morison, 'Mr Tudor and his ice came just in time to preserve Boston's East India commerce from ruin. Our carrying trade between Calcutta and Europe had declined almost to extinction . . . For a generation after the Civil War, until cheap artificial ice was invented, the export trade increased and prospered.[33]

Giving an account of Tudor's involvement with the tropical ice trade in an article published in *Scribner's Monthly* in July 1875, F.H. Forbes reveals how, after the end of the war of 1812, the British government had made overtures to Tudor suggesting the establishment of an ice depot at Kingston, commercial capital of Jamaica, and of how there was nothing of fancy or mere speculation that induced him to embark on this experiment and how, having made the subject a study, 'this eccentric citizen of Massachusetts had effectually vindicated the soundness of his theories'. Although he had been sending ice to Martinique since 1805 and had thereafter built up quite a trade in the West Indies, Jamaica had been the turning point. At the time the richest of all British colonial possessions, the island became the first prominent and permanent point of Tudor's tropical trade. The British had granted him the monopoly of the Jamaica trade – there was nothing Tudor appreciated more than a legal monopoly – and also waived port dues which at that time were very heavy. This was an important concession. Later the Bengal government was to do the same for Calcutta, and in due course Bombay and Madras followed suit. When that time came, Tudor's trade already embraced Havana, Cuba, Martinique, Barbados, Trinidad, St Thomas, and Demerara on the mainland. His domestic shipments were mainly to Charleston in South Carolina and to New Orleans, later to become the largest consumer of ice in the United States south of Philadelphia. By 1833, when his first tentative Indian shipments launched out on their 16,000-mile voyages, Tudor was fortified with the experience of an already extensive trade and the certainty that even if there were initial setbacks his East India ventures would eventually prosper.

As Forbes commented, Tudor was not in the least deterred when setbacks in due course occurred. The inadequacy of the original Calcutta ice house no doubt contributed to the financial loss of his first shipment, and quarrels with Austin and Rogers, with whom he had set up the venture, inevitably followed. It was only two years later that Tudor managed to re-establish his Calcutta business. The result of his perseverance was, Forbes recorded, 'the establishment of a trade which ... enables Boston to hold the key to the rich and extensive commerce between Calcutta and the United States'.

The Calcutta and Bombay ice trades, both initiated in 1833, were soon followed by the establishment of depots in Madras and in the port of Galle in Ceylon, where by the 1840s the company was selling ice to passenger steamers. Further east, Tudor was before long supplying Rangoon, Batavia, Singapore, Hong Kong and Yokohama. In 1834 Rio de Janeiro added another link to Tudor's extraordinary chain of ice depots, and other South American ports followed. It was with justification that Tudor had now come to be known as the Ice King of the World, but in his sparkling crown the three most brilliant jewels were undoubtedly Calcutta, Bombay and Madras.

In 1875, Forbes, who had been well acquainted with Tudor, and who seems to have had some close connection with his company, expressed the opinion that the ice trade was still only in its infancy. Every year, he said, it was attracting more attention. But too much of the ice shipped, from one-third to one-half, was being wasted in handling and transportation. He looked forward to the day when progressive science would introduce some method of reducing the great margin of waste. Meanwhile, he recognized the vital role which would soon be played by fast steamships built with airtight compartments, which alone would save so much waste that the cost of building them would be covered. As for the future of the ice trade to the Orient, Forbes opined that it would soon be transferred to the Pacific coast. He expected that with the opening up of ports in Alaska, California, and Oregon, spacious ice houses would be established to supply India, China and Japan. 'Parties' were already prospecting for that area, he revealed.

In view of the future which Forbes had forecast for the American ice trade to the East, and in particular his reference to the vital role of steam-powered ships, it seems odd that only two years after his article was written, and at a moment when the ice cargoes sent to India and the Far East were falling to an average of 50,000 tons annually, the Tudor Company took the decision to build three new sailing ships for the East India trade. To build their own ships was in any case a new departure for the Company, Tudor himself having always used chartered vessels. Now, in 1877, came these three expensive Boston-built ships. By sailing ship standards they were fast, and they were proudly named *Ice King*, *Iceland*, and *Iceberg*. Very properly the *Ice King's* figurehead was a representation of Frederick Tudor. These three fine vessels were the last of the American East Indiamen. In 1870 the value of ice exported from the USA to India had amounted to nearly 100,000 dollars. By 1880 it had dropped to just over 5,000 dollars. Although the trade for the British West Indies continued at least until 1910, and to the Dutch West Indies and Dutch Guiana until 1900, to British India and British Far Eastern ports it was virtually finished.

Forgotten Things

As was happening in other tropical countries, in India an increasing awareness of the benefits of refrigeration and the resulting demand for ever more ice, so vigorously fostered by Tudor himself, was to be the undoing of the great overseas trade he had created. From being regarded as a sensational innovation, ice was becoming almost a necessity.

Already in June 1837, Miss Emily Eden, whom we have met before at the head of the subscription list for the new Calcutta ice house, was writing home of the miseries inflicted by the failure of the ice. Dining at Bishop Wilson's, she tells a friend, 'we are all in a horrid way about the ice, which oozed out yesterday; and no signs of an American ship ... the water we drink would make very good tea as far as warmth goes, but the Bishop had persuaded the ice-managers to give him the last little scrapings of ice, on the plea of our dining there'. Again a few days later, on 4 July, 'in the absence of ice, great dinners are so bad. Everything flops about in the dishes' – how well she puts it – 'and the wine and water is so hot, and a shocking thing is that a great ship was seen bottom upwards at the mouth of the river, supposed to be an American, and consequently the ice-ship.'★[34] When in 1850 Bombay was in a similar predicament, again owing to the non-appearance of an ice-ship, there was a more public outcry. The newspapers carried angry protests and demands for the adoption of measures 'to preserve us from the recurrence of the present evil'. There were references to King Tudor having laid down his ice sceptre and calls for 'agitation pervading high and low, great and small, against the abominably sudden and inexplicable cutting off of our supply of ice'. Quite what the newspapers had in mind or what the 'agitation spreading over the ghauts to Dapoorie and Poona' would achieve they did not say, only alluding acidly to that lack of public spirit in Bombay which could allow the occurrence of a disaster such as the current ice famine.[35]

The truth was that already in 1850 inventors and scientists had for many years been grappling with the problem of ice production by artificial means on a commercially useful scale. We know, and probably the ice-deprived journalists of Bombay knew, that inventors such as Richard Trevithick (1771–1833), Jacob Perkins (1766–1849) and Oliver Evans (1752–1819) had all worked in England on the development of ice-making machinery, and that on a domestic scale some success had been achieved. (The Thomas Masters apparatus described on p. 341 was by no means the only such device to have been put on the market, but Masters was a more skillful publicist than most inventors.) Hand operated ice-makers for the household and for cafés were now at last about to be superseded by large-scale machinery.

In 1850, the very year of the Bombay ice famine, an American inventor named Alexander Catlin Twining (1801–84) was granted a British patent for a refrigeration machine for the compression of ethyl ether which would make 400 kilos of ice per day. The following year Twining published his brochure *Manufacture of Ice by Mechanical Means on a Commercial Scale (By Steam and Water Power)*. In November of

---

★ Longueville Clarke mentions an ice ship wrecked at the Sandheads, the dangerous, ever-shifting shoal in the Bay of Bengal, notorious as the graveyard of ships making for the entrance to the Hooghly river and anchorage at Garden Reach in the port of Calcutta. Another ice ship was burnt at sea in those early years.

1853 his US Patent (No. 10,222) was granted and he then set up a plant in Cleveland, Ohio, which would manufacture 2,000 pounds of ice every twenty-four hours. It was not a vast amount, but Catlin Twining had achieved an important breakthrough. 'It is to Alexander Catlin Twining that goes the honour of making the first commercial ice by vapor refrigeration,' writes Woolrich, the American historian of industrial cold.[36] Unfortunately for Twining, he had built his plant in a locality where there was abundant natural ice. The advantages of manufactured ice over lake ice as announced by Twining were the uniformity of manufactured blocks, the abolition of ice houses – away in Boston Tudor must have fumed at the very idea – the decreased losses on delivery of ice, the direct loading of ice at the factory, and the elimination of the heavy manual labour involved in the cutting and stowing of natural ice. The inducements spelled out by Twining left Cleveland as it were cold. In the northern states of America the same story was to be many times repeated. What was wrong with God's ice? How could the stuff made in the factory compete with it? In Twining's case it couldn't. After operating his plant for six years he had to concede defeat.

In the tropics and the Southern States of America the attitude to man-made ice was very different. Only two or three years after the failure of Twining's ice factory, the Civil War of 1861–5, which created India's great cotton boom and brought unprecedented prosperity to Tudor's East India trade, was to become perhaps more than any other factor responsible for the arrival of manufactured ice. The blockade which cut off the South's cotton outlets also meant the cessation of shipments of Boston ice to New Orleans, Charleston, Savannah and all the southern ports. With a view to obtaining the ice for which their hospitals now had a grave need, the Southern States turned to France, where Ferdinand Carré had recently developed and patented an ammonia-and-water absorption process. Carré's machine had been granted an English patent in 1859 and an American one in 1860. In 1863 a 500 lb Carré absorption machine was shipped safely through the blockade to Augusta, Georgia, and a second one, routed via Mexico, reached Brownsville, Texas, where it was set up at the King Ranch. It was to these French ammonia-absorption machines installed during the Civil War that the long tradition of ice manufacture in Louisiana and other Southern States owed its beginnings.

By now other ice-making plants were being set up. Among the great pioneers of ice-factory machinery was a Scottish-born printer named James Harrison, who in 1837 had been sent by his employer on a mission to Australia and had decided to stay there, eventually becoming editor and subsequently owner of the Geelong *Advertiser.* His interest in refrigeration aroused through his conviction that Australia's economic salvation lay in the marketing of her colossal meat resources, Harrison applied himself to the study of the subject. He had heard about Twining's Cleveland venture and its failure, he had realized that the extreme climate of Australia presented special problems, and accordingly he set about developing a refrigeration compressor which in high temperatures would produce cold for industrial uses with unfailing reliability.

By 1855 he had had a compressor machine constructed in Geelong. Using sulphuric ether as his refrigerant, Harrison found his machine unworkable, probably owing to faulty engineering. Undeterred, he sailed for London and commissioned a second machine to be built by the well-known firm of Siebe in Denmark Street, Soho. In May 1858 the *Illustrated London News* reported that Mr Harrison's large ice-making machine had been erected in premises at Red Lion Square for the purpose of testing its efficiency prior to its exportation to Australia. Although the arrangements were only of a temporary nature, the machine could produce ice at the rate of from 5,000 to 6,000 lb per day, and when permanently fixed and regularly worked it was expected that the inventor's estimate of 8000 to 10,000 lb of ice per day would be accomplished.

James Harrison had made a wonderful breakthrough. The *Illustrated London News,* in the course of its fairly detailed report, forecast that although the whole expense of making ice in London, including interest on capital, etc., would be considerably less than ten shillings per day, it would be in hot climates that the full value of the invention would be felt.

Ice within the tropics will soon be looked upon as a necessary of life, as much so at least as fuel is necessary in the winters of temperate regions ... perhaps the most beneficial application of the process will be the cooling of rooms in hospitals etc. in tropical regions ... it is evident that buildings can be cooled in the same manner as that in which they are now warmed – by circulation of water in pipes ... the mortality arising from the prevalence of fevers in an atmosphere ranging from 80 deg. to 100 deg. can only be checked by treating patients in cool apartments. The cooling of the water for this purpose will be only a few pence per barrel...

How enlightened was this reporter compared to those American critics of Dr John Gorrie when some dozen years earlier they had derided the very ideas of manufactured ice and the artificial cooling of hospital rooms.

James Harrison's subsequent part in the development of the Australian seaborne meat trade to the British Isles is not related here. It is the relevance of his ice-making machine to India and its tropical

Harrison's ice-making machine, reproduced in *The Illustrated London News*, May 1858.

climate that concerns us. At the time of the installation of Bombay's first ice factory, which appears to have been built in 1867 by the old-established private banking firm of Forbes & Co. – an article on the Bombay ice trade published in *The Cold Storage and Ice Trades Review* of 15 May 1902 refers to the Forbes factory as having been in existence for thirty-five years – there were few machines available or suitable to commercial ice-making in tropical conditions. Firm information relating to the installation of the Forbes ice plant is lacking, but of the two main options one would have been Carré's machines which, after much modification and adaptation by Daniel Holden, a celebrated figure in the early history of Texas and New Orleans ice factories, had by 1866 proved sufficiently satisfactory to be providing Texas and Louisiana with manufactured ice. Of Mr Holden's enterprise, the San Antonio, Texas, *Daily Herald* reported on 4 July 1866: 'our city is under the greatest obligation for the establishment of this factory as one of the permanent institutions of San Antonio – furnishing our citizens with one of the greatest luxuries of civilisation'. The price was then 5 cents per pound delivered, 'a cost much below what would ever have been imagined previous to this time', and the factory was producing 'a beautiful chunk of ice weighing twenty pounds every four minutes'. The second option would have been Harrison's machines. By 1862 Harrison had evidently gone into business with Siebe Brothers, now of Mason Street, Lambeth, for the production of his machines, and one was shown in action at the International Exhibition that year. The *Illustrated London News* correspondent noted that of all the mechanical wonders crowded into the western annexe of the Exhibition, the machines for making ice took precedence in the eyes of the general public. As usual with ice-making dem-onstrations, this one savoured somewhat of a conjuring show.

Describing the visitors crowding round the machine, looking on in amazement as miniature icebergs rose up before their eyes, the *Illustrated*'s correspondent reported that many thought they had been tricked. One visitor asserted that the transparent square blocks, 18 inches square and $1\frac{1}{2}$ inches thick, continually being extracted from Siebe's magical box, were actually being handed to the operator of the machine by a man hidden somewhere at the back. Another onlooker was of the fanciful opinion that for every 1 lb of clean, clear ice produced, 3 lb of dirty ice had been devoured by the machine. The reporter conceded that it was after all very hard to credit that the miniature icebergs were the results of the labours of a powerful steam engine (it was ten horse-power) and a quantity of very hot-looking apparatus, and that not only was the refrigerator, as he called it, exposed to the direct influence of the rays of the sun, but was surrounded by other steam machinery at work, with admiring spectators crowding round it, watching the process. 'Yet still the blocks of ice were drawn forth with wonderful rapidity, to the infinite delight of the lookers on.'

A defect which had not gone unnoticed when Harrison's machine had first come to public notice in 1858 had been the opacity of the ice produced, which had then made it look more like frozen milk than pure water. This fault had now apparently been overcome, and the ice blocks when broken produced pieces as clear as naturally formed ice. To those Londoners who since the mid 1840s had become accustomed to the sight of great blocks of pure clear Wenham Lake ice being transported through the streets of the capital, that clarity of the ice was a prime point, and the *Illustrated*'s reporter had appreciated its public appeal. He had also understood that the Harrison machines, 'by equalizing the temperature of different seasons, were commercially of the first importance'. Significantly, his report concluded with the announcement that the Indian government had ordered one of Siebe's largest ice-making machines for the use of Her Majesty's troops in India, and a prediction that the machine would be generally adopted for a like purpose in all tropical climates.[37]

Whether, following the successful demonstration of the Siebe–Harrison ice machine at the 1862 International Exhibition and the official order from the Indian government, the Forbes Company of Bombay followed suit and installed a Siebe-Harrison ice-making plant, or whether they preferred a Carré machine, we can only conjecture. What appears certain is that once set to work, the Bombay plant operated efficiently enough to compete with, and within ten years, to supplant the trade in natural ice.

By 1875 Bombay's Marine Street ice *khana* fell into disuse,[38] but in

The Siebe-Harrison ice-making machine, shown at the great Exhibition in London in 1862. Reproduced in *The Illustrated London News*, August 1862.

the same year F.H. Forbes wrote in his *Scribner's* article that about 50,000 tons of Boston ice was still being exported annually to Calcutta, the China ports, Batavia, and Yokohama. He also mentions Marseille as having received shipments from Boston, but such shipments must have been rare and were probably confined to years of acute shortage in the Mediterranean. Neither Bombay nor Madras are mentioned by Forbes as taking Boston ice shipments at that time, nor does Galle figure in his lists for 1872, 1873 and 1874. There may possibly have been shipments from the ports of Maine, and even from New York – the Tudor Company did not at any time obtain a monopoly in the British East Indies – but since ice entered Indian ports duty free records are hard to come by, and after 1880 exports of ice to the British East Indies cease to figure in the United States Foreign Commerce Reports.

In 1882 it was the turn of the citizens of Calcutta to allow their precious ice house, their revered 'crystal palace', to be razed to the ground. In 1907, recording that no vestige of it now remained, H.E.A.

Cotton remarked that 'the memory of Calcutta is proverbially short, and the Ice House has passed into the category of forgotten things'. With more than a hint of reproach, Cotton added that Calcutta was more iconoclastic than Madras, where at least the shell of the ice house had been preserved.[39] That shell still stands today. Described as an elegant Palladian villa-style building, it has been adapted as a home and school for orphaned girls. An account from the days when the Madras ice house was in its heyday, and when landing an ice cargo at that port presented difficulties unique even to that strange and hazardous trade, will serve I think as an appropriate valediction to Frederick Tudor, the man who had believed 'that ice is so beautiful a thing in countries where it has never been seen before that even penny-saving Martinique creoles cannot help buying'[40] and had been proved right so far and away beyond anyone's expectations but his own.

It should here be explained that hazards to all cargoes and passengers landing at Madras were of a special order. As Captain Alexander Hamilton, the old seventeenth-century trader, had put it so long ago, 'Maderass is a Colony and City belonging to the English East India Company situated in one of the most incommodious Places I ever saw.'[41] Built on an exposed point of the Coromandel coast, Fort St George, as Madras was originally called, had no harbour proper and was no more than an open roadstead inadequately protected by a couple of breakwaters. 'The shore is flat, the buildings mean in comparison with Calcutta', reported Captain Mundy, ADC to Lord Combermere, Commander-in-Chief of India in the 1820s, 'and Madras is a full half century behind the sister Presidency in the luxuries and conveniences of life.'[42] Passengers were obliged to transfer from their ships into light native craft called *masulahs*. Propelled often as far as two miles from ship to shore in these craft, passengers then jumped ashore, often getting a good wetting in the foaming surf as they scrambled up the beach. Descriptions of landing and embarking at Madras are not uncommon in Anglo-Indian chronicles of the nineteenth century, and particularly lively ones are to be found in the late eighteenth-century *Memoirs of William Hickey*, edited by Peter Quennell (1960), but the account written in 1868 by an American sea captain, Andrew Curtis, master of the Boston ice ship *Eastern Star*, is concerned with the hazards to his cargo rather than with any to his own person. On that occasion his cargo included, along with the ice, no fewer than 200 barrels of the apples which had come to be so much appreciated in British India:

There is always a heavy surf on the beach and the boatmen are very skilled scarcely wetting their cargoes. The boats are large and sewed together no nails or spikes are used and capable of carrying from six to ten tons. When we began to discharge our cargo one of these native boats would come alongside and receive her load and pull ashore and through the surf landing her on the beach, where the natives would take a cake of ice in a hand-barrow and carry it a couple of hundred yards up the beach of hot white sand to the ice house, and then up a stairway on the outside to the top, where it could be lowered into the ice-well. If the ice was wet by salt water in coming through the surf it was spoiled except for immediate sale as the water went right through it, but this rarely happened. I do not remember that I ever got wet but once, and then only slightly, but I would not pay the boatman . . . so it never happened again.[43]

Describing Tudor's India venture as the most spectacular of his career, the American social historian Daniel Boorstin sums up his character as 'flamboyant, defiant, energetic, sometimes reckless, imperious, vain, contemptuous of competitors and implacable to enemies'. More kindly critics have written of Tudor's personal mag-netism, of his capacity to make others follow where he led, to persuade men to do whatever he asked of them, whether it was sailing a cargo of ice half-way round the world in a 'discovery ship' (the description he applied to the *Tuscany*, the very first of his East India ships to carry ice to Calcutta in 1833), whether it involved attacking an iceberg with picks and crowbars, or supervising the safe conduct of 500 tons of ice through the thundering surf of the Madras beach, across the burning sands and into the storehouse so incongruously camouflaged as a Palladian villa.

Tudor's spectacular had lasted for forty-five years. He had never had cause to regret the tenacity with which he had conducted his East India trade. But had he been told, before he died, that what he had really done for India was to create so urgent a need for ice that it would hasten the coming of mechanical refrigeration and factory-made ice to the tropics by several decades he would have been incredulous. Man of vision though he was, could he have accepted that the time was coming when all the natural ice of North America would not be enough to satisfy the needs of his own continent, let alone another one half a world away? I think he would have sought rather a method of taming and harnessing and utilizing those fabulous ice mountains and ice islands continuously forming and reforming up in the Greenland seas and floating so temptingly down towards the coast of the Labrador peninsula.

Ices in a Cold Climate

.

Winter's Dark Prisons

We need not really be surprised at the taste shown by people who live in cold climates for very cold food and drinks. Geographically the Russians and Scandinavians were so placed that appreciation of the charms of iced wines and half-frozen fruit juices came early in their histories because a plentiful supply of ice for the summer had always been accessible to them. In Europe the Spaniards and the Italians of the sixteenth century had no monopoly of organized systems of storage for the ice and snow they needed for hot weather comfort. One of the earliest views we know of an European ice house is to be seen in the town map of Helsingfors – better known to us as Elsinore – published by Braun and Hogenburg in 1580. In the centre of this very clear perspective map is the high hill with the King of Denmark's great citadel-palace of Kronberg towering above the waters of the Sound, busy with great sailing ships. In the foreground behind the little city of Elsinore lies Frederik II's country manor of Lundhove and its pleasure gardens. Clearly visible in the grounds is his thatched ice house, encircled by a palisade of fencing and situated close to what appears to be a specially made ice pool or reservoir, shaped like a swimming bath. To the east of the ice house enclosure are three smaller rectangular spaces marked out in neat patches, denoting formally laid out gardens and walks (see pl. 2).

King Frederik had his ice house constructed in or about 1564, when he wrote from his castle of Koldinghus to his agent at Frederiksborg informing him that a man was being sent along to stock up his ice cellar with the requisite quantity of ice. In the same letter the King requested his agent to supply all necessary help and to ensure that the functionary known as 'the King's corn-measurer' – the equivalent of a quarter-master, it would seem – was instructed in the proper way of keeping ice. In that same year of 1564, we find among workers in Danish royal service 'carpenters making ice-boxes', or more literally 'ice-coffins', and by 1585 the King had appointed an official, Hans von Han, to take charge of his several ice cellars – the Danish counterpart of that James Frontine who appears on the English scene as Charles II's Yeoman of the Icehouses some eighty years later (p. xv).[1]

As was to be the case with James Frontine, Hans von Han soon found himself with ample work supervising the construction and filling of the royal Danish icehouses. Frederik II and his son and successor, Christian IV, appear to have had at least as many ice cellars or ice caves as their contemporaries the Grand Dukes Francesco I and Ferdinand I of Tuscany. Had Frederik perhaps initially borrowed the idea from the Florentines? At any rate, when in 1588 Queen Elizabeth I of England sent a delegation to Denmark to condole with the nine-year-old Christian IV on the death of his father, a Frenchman called Josias Mercer, who was a member of the party, noted in his journal, not without surprise, that there were ice cellars at Frederiksborg and at all the other Danish royal castles.[2] Though perhaps not known to Mercer, yet another was about to be added to the list by Frederik's widowed queen, Sophia Magdalene, who had decided to move to Nyking Falster Castle on the island of Falster. Her order to Hans von Han to build her an ice cellar close to the castle is still preserved, as is a letter written in July 1590 by her son Christian IV from Koldinghus to his Lord Chamberlain in Copenhagen, informing him that Hans von Han is leaving for the capital to build an ice house (there is now a change of Danish usage from ice cellar or cave to house) for his castle there. The King requests his Lord Chamberlain to make sure that the stone, timber and other materials necessary are available to his ice-master.[3] The Danish royal family were certainly ensuring that wherever they were in residence there would always be ice to cool their wine and their beer.

It was about 1575, it will be remembered, that the refinement of iced wine was first appearing at the court of Henri III of France, second son of Catherine de Medici and Henri II, so it is interesting to find that in 1588 the Frenchman Mercer was apparently unfamiliar with the practice of storing ice for the summer until he visited Denmark. Possibly he was of a Huguenot family settled in England as refugees after the St Bartholomew's Day massacre of 1572. Describing how the cellars were insulated with wooden boards, how water was poured over the pieces of ice in the cellar so that all would weld together, and how in summer the ice was chopped from the solid block to cool the wine, Mercer's notes are a little reminiscent of Pierre Belon's description of the building of Turkish snow stacks as he witnessed the process in the 1550s (see p. 41).

To pinpoint the moment, the year 1588, when Mercer visited Denmark, was also that of the defeat and destruction of the great Spanish Armada by a combination of the fury of the elements and the skill of Queen Elizabeth's sea captains, Drake and Frobisher, Howard and Hawkins. In 1588 Galilei Galileo and William Shakespeare were both twenty-four years old. There was no *Hamlet* to quote, nobody had said 'And still it turns.' On 9 August 1588 Giambattista Della Porta, the celebrated chemist-alchemist-philosopher of Naples, was granted approbation for the publication of his enlarged version of *Magia Naturalis*, the work in which he gave the first printed directions for the freezing of wine and water by means of snow and saltpetre. In 1589 the book was published, and in that year died the seventy-year-old Catherine de Medici, for nearly thirty years Queen-Regent of France, to whom legend so firmly and so erroneously attaches the introduction of ice-cream to her husband's kingdom. A few months later her last surviving son, Henri III, also died, bringing to its end the era of the Valois kings of France, and in the person of Henry of Navarre ushering in that of the Bourbons. Nine years later, with Henry's signing of the Edict of Nantes in 1598, came the long period of religious tolerance and equality of civil rights for the protestants of France, which was to end with its revocation in 1685 by Henry's grandson, Louis XIV. In 1605, seven years after the signing of the Edict of Nantes, Francis Bacon, aged forty-four, in mid-career as a political and legal luminary, published his *Advancement of Learning*, the work which foreshadowed the methods of scientific experiment and investigation upon which the great Royal Society of London was founded over half a century later. According to tradition, it was in putting his own precepts into practice that in March 1626 Bacon, collecting snow on Highgate Hill, contracted the chill which ten days later led to his death at the age of sixty-five from the illness we now call bronchial pneumonia.

The story is a good enough one, originating apparently in John Aubrey, who said he got it from Hobbes, the eminent philosopher who was tutor to Charles II when Prince of Wales. According to Aubrey, Bacon and Dr Witherborne, one of Charles I's physicians, were 'taking the air in a coach toward Highgate, snow lay on the ground, and it came in my Lord's thoughts, why flesh might not be preserved in snow as in Salt'. Resolving to try the experiment on the spot, the two gentlemen alighted from their coach, 'went in to a poor woman's house at the bottom of Highgate Hill, bought a hen from her, made the woman exenterate it and then stuffed the body with snow, and my Lord did help to doe it himselfe. The snow so chilled him that he immediately fell so extremely ill, that he could not return to his Lodging but went to the Earle of Arundel's house at Highgate.' It was there that some days later Bacon died.[4]

The tale, like many so beguilingly recounted by Aubrey, may be taken with a few of the proverbial pinches of salt. For one thing, Bacon was already suffering from bronchial troubles, and for another the nature of cold had for some while been one of his preoccupations. Living in semi-retirement at Gorhambury, the Hertfordshire estate to which he had retreated following his dismissal from office and banishment from Parliament and the court in the summer of 1621, it would surely have been more logical to have an ice house constructed in his own grounds and thus ensure a supply of ice or snow at any time when the mood took him to experiment than to set about making observations in the haphazard fashion described by Aubrey. To use Bacon's own words, 'whosoever will be an enquirer into Nature let him resort to a conservatory of Snow or Ice', lines written in the work which was to become his posthumously published *Sylva Sylvarum*.[5] Whether he did have a conservatory of snow and ice at Gorhambury, or in the grounds of Verulam House, the 'ingeniosely contrived little pile', as Aubrey put it, that he had himself designed for summer use, is no more than speculation. According to Aubrey, the gardens at Verulam were splendidly laid out with 'walks, stately trees, ponds, and variegated verdure, resembling the workes in Irish-stitch', and in the house were 'Two Bathing-roomes wither his Lordship retired afternoones as he saw cause'. At the time John Aubrey visited Verulam in 1656, it was thirty years since Bacon's death and if a snow conservatory had been built in the grounds it would have been overgrown with trees and shrubs and most probably be in a state of disrepair. Visitors would have been unaware of its existence, but in a house with such unusual features as two bathrooms and with an owner of a mind so inquiring and a character so open to innovation, what more appropriate than that his garden should have had a snow conservatory? While Bacon was Lord Chancellor there had been a royal precedent. In the winter of 1619–20 the nineteen-year-old Prince of Wales, later Charles I, had had a 'conserve of snowe' constructed in Greenwich Park and had followed it up with a second one a year later. The Prince's innovation was one the Chancellor can scarcely have failed to hear about. The projected marriage of the heir to the throne with the Spanish Infanta had been preoccupying the King's ministers since 1617, and other domestic events would have brought the young prince and his father's administrators into close contact. Early in March 1619 the Queen consort, Anne of Denmark, had died at the age of forty-five, and her building activities at Greenwich under the direction of Inigo Jones, already suspended owing to lack of money, had looked like coming to a permanent halt. Shortly after the Queen's death however, King James had assigned Greenwich Palace and its park and gardens, given to his wife in 1612, to his son. There Prince Charles, a young man who liked quiet and a country life, had spent part of the summer following his mother's death. My own surmise is that the snow conserve made in the grounds during the winter of that year was an amenity already planned by the late Queen for her new little riverside palace. As a daughter of Frederik II of Denmark she had been brought up to expect such aids to civilized living. What more natural than that she should discuss the matter with Inigo Jones, who was familiar with the Danish royal palaces from the years he had spent early in his career at the court of her brother Christian IV?[6] As for Chancellor Bacon, it was predictable enough that he should castigate the use of snow and ice repositories simply as a means of enabling the rich and frivolous to cool their wine, and as 'a poore and contemptible' use 'in respect of other use that may be made of such conservatories'.[7] In other words, snow and ice preserved for the summer should be put to work for the benefit of 'enquirers into Nature' such as himself.

Cutting the Solid Pond

While yet it is cold January, and snow and ice are thick and solid, the prudent landlord comes from the village to get ice to cool his summer drink; impressively, even pathetically wise, to foresee the heat and thirst of July now in January, – wearing a thick coat and mittens! when so many things are not provided for. It may be that he lays up no treasures in this world which will cool his summer drink in the next. He cuts and saws the solid pond, unroofs the house of fishes, and carts off their very element and air, held fast by chains and stakes like corded wood, through the favoring winter air, to wintry cellars, to underlie the summer there. It looks like solidified azure, as, far off, it is drawn through the streets. These ice-cutters are a merry race, full of jest and sport, and when I went among them they were wont to invite me to saw pit-fashion with them, I standing underneath . . .

To speak literally, a hundred Irishmen, with Yankee overseers, came from Cambridge every day to get out the ice. They divided it into cakes by methods too well known to require description, and these, being sledded to the shore, were rapidly hauled off on to an ice platform, and were raised by grappling irons and block and tackle, worked by horses, on to a stack, as surely as so many barrels of flour, and there placed evenly side by side, and row upon row, as if they formed the solid base of an obelisk designed to pierce the clouds. They told me that in a good day they could get out a

Ice cutting at Spy Pond, near Cambridge, Massachusets. Reproduced in
Gleason's Pictorial Drawing-Room Companion, c. 1854.

thousand tons, which was the yield of about one acre. Deep ruts and 'cradle
holes' were worn in the ice, as on *terra firma*, and the horses invariably ate
their oats out of cakes of ice hollowed out like buckets. They stacked up the
cakes thus in the open air in a pile thirty-five feet high on one side and six
or seven rods square, putting hay between the outside layers to exclude the
air; for when the wind, though never so cold, finds a passage through, it will
wear large cavities, leaving slight supports or studs only here and there, and
finally topple it down. At first it looked like a vast blue fort of Valhalla; but
when they began to tuck the coarse meadow hay into the crevices, and this
became covered with rime and icicles, it looked like a venerable moss-grown
and hoary ruin, built of azure-tinted marble, the abode of Winter, that old
man we see in the almanac, – his shanty, as if he had a design to estivate with
us. They calculated that not twenty-five per cent would reach its destination,
and that two or three per cent would be wasted in the cars. However, a still

greater part of this heap had a different destiny from what intended; for, either because the ice was found not to keep so well as was expected, containing more air than usual, or for some other reason, it never got to market. This head, made in the winter of '46–7 and estimated to contain ten thousand tons, was finally covered with hay and boards; and though it was unroofed in the following July, and a part of it carried off, the rest remaining exposed to the sun, it stood over that summer and the next winter, and was not quite melted till September, 1848. Thus the pond recovered the greater part.[8]

When Thoreau wrote this, ice was harvested on many lakes and rivers on the Atlantic seaboard of the United States. The largest and best documented sites were on the Hudson to serve New York, on Spy Pond, Fresh Pond and Wenham Lake to serve Boston and the export trade, and on the Kennebec and Penobscot rivers in Maine. He could speak of ice being divided into cakes 'by methods too well known to require description', but since his time the ice-harvesting techniques used throughout New England in the early and middle decades of the nineteenth century have largely been forgotten. *Scribner's Monthly* of July 1875 carries a long article on the American ice industry and the manner of harvesting on Fresh Pond near Cambridge. It was here and on Spy Pond, very close to the city of Boston, that ice was first cut commercially; the ice was renowned for its purity.

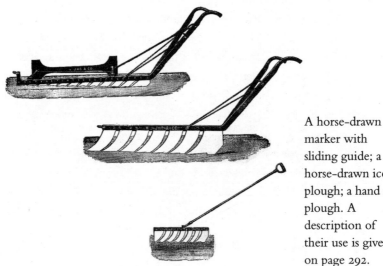

A horse-drawn marker with sliding guide; a horse-drawn ice plough; a hand ice plough. A description of their use is given on page 292.

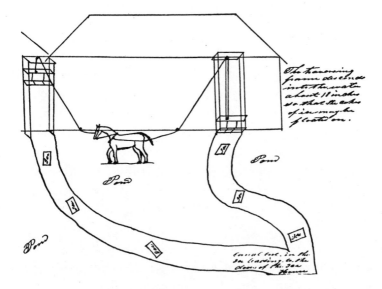

Drawing from Tudor's manuscript diary of ice harvesting at Fresh Pond, Cambridge. Blocks of ice, floated through channels cut in the frozen surface of the pond, were raised by horsepower to the top of the ice house and then slid down an inside chute for storage. The hand-written text on the right explains; 'The traversing frame descends into the water about 18 inches so that the cake of ice may be floated on'.

A little more than forty years ago, Mr Tudor employed as his foreman Mr Nathaniel Wyeth, of Cambridge, a man of remarkable ability. Up to this time [no reliable data are at hand to fix the year] ice was housed in subterranean vaults, generally excavated on the slope of the bank and removed some distance from the shores of the pond. Mr Wyeth conceived the idea of erecting buildings without cellars and handy to the shore. These buildings were of wood, *battened* from the base, and were double-walled, the space between the inner and outer being filled with tan or sawdust. These were capable of holding from three to ten thousand tons each.

The next progressive move was in the direction of cutting. When the entire crop hardly exceeded five thousand tons per annum, the original method of scraping the pond answered well enough; so did the method of 'shaving' the ice and sawing it into blocks. The scraper was a rudely constructed machine moved by hand; the shaving off of the porous or snow ice was done with broad axes; the cutting was done by means of a common cross-cut saw, one handle being taken off. One can imagine the laborious work thus entailed.

Mr Wyeth at once put his ingenuity to work and produced the tools that are now in use throughout the country, and which have reduced the cost of cutting to a mere nominal figure. Under the old process, one season would not suffice to secure a year's supply. Now, the cutting and housing seldom occupy more than three weeks, and the average daily work by one concern of housing six thousand tons is not considered remarkable.

It is seldom that clear ice is secured, that is, ice without a fall of snow upon it. With the modern improvements, this coating of snow is not regarded as detrimental. In fact, the thin layer of snow ice is regarded as a preservative of the clear ice.

As soon as the pond is completely closed the ice, with the atmosphere at a temperature of ten degrees above zero, forms very rapidly. If, after it has attained the thickness of say three or four inches, capable of bearing a man, a fall or two or three inches of snow follows, then the workmen begin to 'sink the pond', as it is termed. This is done by cutting holes an inch or two in diameter, and at three or four feet apart, thus admitting the water to the surface and submerging the snow, which forms the snow ice. With a steady temperature of ten degrees above zero for a week or ten days, the ice will have formed to the desirable thickness, say an average thickness of fifteen inches.[9]

By then the ice will bear the weight of horses and workmen. An area of the pond's surface of around 600 feet is marked out, surface snow is scraped away and the pond is lined into squares. As in surveying, two lines are run, at right angles, and marked on the ice with the side of a plank. Then the harvesting tools come into their own. First a horse-drawn marker cuts into the line already set out, to a depth of 2 or 3 inches. Then a sliding guide with a smooth-edged blade is attached and this follows the cut just made as the marker moves across the field cutting a new line, usually 22 inches (in some places 44 inches) from the first. Once the field has been lined and marked in one direction, the process is repeated at right angles until the surface resembles a huge chessboard.

Following the marker come the cutters or plows with sharp teeth measuring from two inches in length to ten or twelve, and used according to the

The ice blocks were hooked out of the water with giant tongs.

thickness of the ice. Then comes the snow-ice plane, which shaves off the porous or snow ice, it first being determined by auger-boring how many inches of snow ice there are. The ice is now ready for gathering. It is broken off into broad rafts, then sawed into lesser ones, then barred off in sections and floated into the canal. The calking operation consists of filling the groove lines or interstices with ice chips to prevent the water from entering and freezing; this is only necessary in very cold weather. The rafts or sheets of cakes are generally thirty cakes long by twelve wide, frequently longer. The ends have to be sawed, but every twelfth groove running lengthwise of the raft or sheet is cut deeper than the other, so that one or two men can, with one motion of the bar, separate it into strips ready for the elevator canal.[10]

The 'rafts' are pulled by teams of horses, or poled along by an ice cutter walking on the blocks, using a long wooden tool fitted at one end with a double-sided metal tip – a hook for pulling and a spike for pushing, in other words, an ordinary boat-hook. When the blocks arrive at the ice house they are cut into single cakes or into squares of four cakes, and then hoisted into the ice house by means of a conveyor belt set at an incline to the house.

The ice-houses contain from three to five vaults or bins, corresponding to the several stories in a warehouse. A single range of buildings will contain five or more. The elevator is arranged so that one flat or story containing these five bins or vaults can be filled simultaneously; that is, as the ice leaves the elevator and is passed off on the wooden tramway of the platform, a man stands at the entrance of each vault to turn the cakes of ice in, the first cake from the elevator going into the farthest opening, and then in regular rotation till the first or lower flat in the range is filled . . .[11]

None but the most experienced workmen are employed in storing the ice, as this requires a quick eye, a steady hand, and good judgment. As each flat or story is completed, the openings at either end are securely and tightly closed, and when the whole building is filled up to the bed-plate, the space between that and the hip of the roof is filled with hay, thus providing a sure protection against waste by shrinkage, which seldom exceeds one foot during the season.[12]

Ten Thousand Ice Cellars

In March 1902 the British Ice Trades journal *Cold Storage* reported that in Russia the consumption of ice in restaurants was great, and that in its love for iced drinks, puddings and creams, that country appeared to be closer to the United States than to England.[13] *Cold Storage* also remarked that in Russia every private house, small as well as large, had its cellar. According to the British journal the floors of these cellars were covered with straw and the ice, packed in snow, was laid on top. That was not quite how Georg Johann Kohl, a Viennese artist and writer, had described the packing of ice houses as he had observed the procedure at St Petersburg in the 1830s, but methods of ice house packing vary a good deal from place to place and undergo change with the passage of the years. Kohl's descriptions, however, of the whole process of breaking, cutting, transport, and packing of the

Neva ice into the cellars of St Petersburg is so detailed and so vivid that it deserves to be quoted in full:

The Russians have accustomed themselves to use a prodigious quantity of ice for domestic purposes. They are fond of cooling all their beverages with ice; indulging themselves freely in the frozen juices which are sold all the summer in the streets of all their towns; and drink not only ice-water, ice-wine, ice-beer, but even ice-tea, throwing into a cup of tea a lump of ice instead of sugar.* Their short but amazingly hot summer would render it difficult to keep all those kinds of provisions which are liable to spoil, if their winter did not afford them the means of preventing the decomposition accelerated by heat. An ice cellar is therefore an indispensable requisite in every family, and is to be met with not merely in towns but very generally among the peasants in the country.

In Petersburg the number of ice cellars is nearly 10,000. It may be conceived that the supply of these cellars is no unimportant branch of business. It is certainly not too high a calculation if we assumed that each of those 10,000 cellars requires 50 sledge-loads for its share. Many of the fishmongers, butchers, kwas-dealers, etc., have such large cellars as to hold several hundred loads. The breweries, distilleries, etc., consume enormous quantities of ice. Accordingly, 500,000 loads must be annually obtained from the Neva, and this amount can only be considered as the minimum, for every inhabitant of the city may fairly be reckoned to consume one sledge-load in the course of the year. Ice is the commodity with which most traffic is carried on in the middle of the winter. Long trains of sledges laden with ice are then seen coming from the Neva, and thousands of men are engaged on all the arms of the river in collecting the cooling production.

In his next long paragraph Kohl records how the Neva ice was harvested. From his very precise account it can be seen that the Russian method of marking out the ice before attempting to cut and remove it achieved the same aim as the horse-drawn ice plough invented by Nathaniel Wyeth in 1825 and subsequently used by all the American

---

* Kohl might have added that the Russians were also much addicted to iced soups. In another chapter he does in fact give a detailed description of the iced summer soup called *botwinya*.[14]

ice companies. The Russian system clearly pre-dated the American one, possibly going back to the founding of St Petersburg in 1703, and was based on cheap manual labour on a massive scale, whereas Wyeth's invention was designed both to economize on labour and to increase its efficiency.

In breaking the ice, the process is this. In the first place they clear away the snow from the surface, that they may mark the more exactly the pieces to be broken. They then measure a large parallelogram, and mark it out with the axe upon the ice. This parallelogram they divide by parallel longitudinal lines into long narrow stripes,* and these stripes again by cross-lines into a number of small squares of a size suitable for the sledges. After these preliminaries they fall to work to separate the entire parallelogram from the mass of ice upon the river, by cutting a deep trench round it with the axe. As the ice is in general three or four feet thick you at last lose sight of the men while stooping to their work in the trench. They take care to leave beneath them a sufficient thickness of ice to support their weight, and this is afterwards broken down from above. When the parallelogram is thus detached, it is easy to split it into the stripes as marked. A row of labourers place themselves on each stripe and, keeping time, all at once strike their heavy iron crows into their respective lines. After this has been repeated several times, the violent shock given by the simultaneous descent of the crowbars on the same line at length effects separation. A single labourer upon each of the floating stripes then cuts them with less trouble into the small parallelepipedons required.

For the convenience of landing the floating blocks an inclined plane is formed in the thick ice. A couple of holes are hewn in the surface of the block; strong iron hooks are inserted; and with an hurrah, the transparent mass is dragged out of the water. The ice of the Neva is emerald green, at least so it appears in winter when it lies on the white snow, and at the same time extremely compact without bubbles or cracks.

The blocks are placed in long rows about the quarry, and delivered to the sledge-driver who placing two or three of them on his sledge, and seating himself on this cold throne, posts off singing to the city. It is not a little amusing to visit the numberless ice-quarries on the Neva and to watch the Russians at this employment in which they feel quite in their element.

* In the original German, Kohl used the word *streifen*.

About the packing of the ice cellars, both theoretically and in common practice, Kohl is equally precise:

In the cellars the slabs of ice are piled regularly and one upon another, and great walls are built with them on either side. In these walls are then hewn benches, shelves, niches, so that meat, milk, and other things, may be conveniently set in these cool receptacles. Such is the usual practice in well regulated cellars.

Such indeed may have been the ideal tidy and orderly Russian ice cellar, but as contemporary English critics remarked, 'tidiness and order do not always preside over Russian arrangements' and in Kohl's own words 'the national Russian usage is merely to throw the blocks into the cellar, to break them in pieces with the axe, and to spread the whole level on the floor'.

It might be supposed that so careless a procedure would have been wasteful of the ice and result in rapid melting, but according to Kohl that was by no means the case. On the contrary, the ice, thus broken and rammed down, 'freezes after a while from its own coldness into one solid mass on which the articles to be preserved are placed. In these cellars the ice does not easily melt; indeed it loses more by evaporation than by fusion.' The popular system can scarcely have made it easy to hew out small quantities of ice for daily domestic consumption, whether it was for icing the *kwas*, the tea, the soup, or was destined for the freezing tubs of the confectioners and the street vendors of ices, but again, in Russia labour was cheap and plentiful and the use of ice in summer so universal that nobody thought twice about any unnecessary work arising through haphazard packing of the ice cellars. 'So accustomed are the Russians to their ice cellars,' Kohl wrote, 'that they cannot conceive how it is possible to keep house without them; and their wives are in the greatest distress when they perceive that they have not laid in sufficient stock of this necessary during the winter and that it is likely to run short. It may be assumed that the consumption of ice in St Petersburg, the packing in the cellars included, costs the inhabitants from two to three million roubles a year.' In contemporary English terms that meant £300,000 to £450,000 sterling.

The water of the Neva, we learn from Kohl, was well known to be one of the purest of all river-waters. So highly prized was it to the citizens of St Petersburg that on returning from a journey they always congratulated themselves on once again having Neva water to drink, and according to Kohl, when the Emperor Alexander travelled he always had a supply of it sent after him in bottles. It made admirable tea and coffee, and beer brewed from it was exported all over the Russian empire. It is likewise excellent for washing, Kohl reported, and 'the English here are quite delighted with the good qualities which it imparts to their linen'.[15]

At the time when Kohl was resident in Russia there was still an important English mercantile colony settled in St Petersburg. English ships accounted for about half the 1,700 or so foreign vessels trading with St Petersburg, and during the summer months, that is from April to September, to be found lying at anchor in its harbours. The most important and grandest shop in the city, offering luxury goods of all kinds and of all provenances, was founded in the 1780s by an Englishman and was thereafter always known as the English Magazine. An English merchant named Beart controlled a porcelain manufactory, an iron foundry, sawmills, and a sugar refinery, the product of which was much sought after because no ox-blood was used in the refining process, thus making it acceptable to those whose religious scruples would otherwise have forbidden sugar during the rigorous fasts of the Russian church.[16] Beart was also owner of ten passenger steamers plying between Cronstadt and St Petersburg and had established his own private dock for the landing and lading of raw materials and manufactured goods. To all the English colony, which in those days included many English governesses and children's nurses, as also to the members of the large German and French communities of St Petersburg, the prodigious consumption of ice in the brief but baking summer months would have been a familiar phenomenon, the sale of street ices and iced drinks equally so, and reports of these customs must inevitably have been circulating in Britain and Germany long before Kohl's detailed accounts were published, first in German in 1841, and in the course of the following two years in English translation.

In England at that time the days of Wenham Lake ice and the company's delivery carts circulating in London and the great fishing ports were yet to come. So were those of London street ices, although their time was approaching. By 1850 they had been spotted by Mayhew,* and in 1851, as the Great Exhibition was drawing visitors from every part of the globe, the early English itinerant ice-cream vendors were getting into their stride, Thomas Masters was demonstrating his apparatus for simultaneously making ice and churning ices within the precincts of the great Crystal Palace, and before the Queen herself, and in mid-August of that year a lengthy article entitled simply 'Ice' appeared in *Household Words*, the popular weekly journal (price 2d.) edited by Charles Dickens. From that article, published anonymously, as was everything in *Household Words*, but in fact written by a regular contributor named Henry Morley with the collaboration of W. H. Wills, Dickens's sub-editor, a wide public was able to learn about the importance of ice to the modern Romans, the Americans, the Latin Americans, the Sicilians, and above all, the Russians. Messrs Morley and Wills had made a careful study of Kohl's book, and acknowledging their debt to him, they had adapted – rather than quoted – his descriptions of the cutting of the Neva ice and the packing of the St Petersburg ice cellars. There was something for several categories of readers in the Morley–Wills essay, including a homely little dissertation on the nature of ice, a reference to Wenham ice and the expense of importing it, and some sensible propaganda directed at dairy farmers, urging them, if they couldn't afford to build ice houses, to make use of local English ice or snow and build it up into ice stacks, which were cheaper to construct than an ice house proper and just as effective. Careful and detailed instructions, probably derived from a gardening journal, followed. According to the *Household Words* article, the method described was the one which had recently been found successful at Chatsworth. Taken both as an essay in general information about ice and as propaganda for its increased domestic use in Britain by the poor as well as the rich – 'I would be an ice missionary,' declared one of the authors – the article must have been quite a revelation to many of the readers at whom it was directed.

* The first London street ices and their vendors were described by Henry Mayhew in 1851 (see p. 304).

It was a pity, though, that the writers made so little attempt to appeal to the imagination of their readers by describing some of the conditions of a St Petersburg winter, the backdrop, as it were, to the harvesting of the Neva ice. The strange spectacle of the frozen animal produce – everything from whole reindeer to swans, hares, partridges, poultry of all kinds, fish, large and small, oxen, piglets, brought to market on sledges and displayed for sale as in life, complete with fur, skin, antlers, as described by Kohl would surely have made a most memorable impression on the public of *Household Words*. So too would his evocation of the brilliance of a calm midwinter's day in St Petersburg:

with a cold of 30 degrees, the sky is clear, the sun shines brilliantly, and the more brilliantly as his rays dart through millions of minute glistening crystals of ice with which the atmosphere is filled as with diamond dust. From all the houses, and likewise from the churches, which are heated too, whirl thick columns of vapour, which appear as dense as if there was a steam-engine in every house, and reflect all sorts of colour. The snow and ice in the streets and on the Neva are white and pure as though all were baked of sugar. The whole city is clad in a dress of the colour of innocence and all the roofs are coated with a like stratum of sparkling crystal dust. Water freezes as it is poured out; and the horse-troughs, the vehicles engaged in carrying water and their drivers, the washerwomen at the canals, are all encrusted with ice; for every drop is instantly changed to stone, and contributes to form about them the most fantastic icicles and wrappers. In the streets everything displays the most active life in order to escape the clutches of death; and all scamper in such haste as if he were literally at their heels. The snow, as you tread on it, crackles and howls the strangest melodies; all other sounds assume unusual tones in this frigid atmosphere: while a slight rustling or buzzing is continually heard in the air, arising, probably, from the collision of all the particles of snow and ice that are floating there.[17]

A winter-piece indeed. Like one of those wonderful white landscapes the Dutch artists of the late sixteenth and early seventeenth centuries were so fond of painting, Kohl's icily gleaming word picture is as alive as though we were seeing it on television, listening to that crunch and crackle of snow as it is trod underfoot, even hearing the faint and distant buzzing in the freezing air.

February: men cutting ice in a town, by the Dutch artist Jacob Cats,
1741–99.

Moscow and London

In 1675 Dr Pierre Barra, a Lyon physician, published a book on the
usage of snow and ice and the custom of drinking chilled beverages in
various European countries.[18] It was a good 100 years since the medical
men of Europe had started arguing the pros and cons of such usages.
The ferocious condemnations of the earlier days had somewhat abated.
Faced with the use of ice to cool wine, fruit, and all manner of sweet
beverages, as established practice not only by royalty and the rich and
fashionable but, in many countries, by the general public, the medical
profession now contented itself with fairly mild warnings. Remarking
that Ferdinand, Grand Duke of Tuscany (who had died in 1670), used
to put ice made from snow in his glass and drank it without ill effect,

301

Barra thought it 'all the same dangerous', adding that the King of Spain's physician 'prefers fruit with snow to drinking iced beverages'. Doctor Barra had gathered information from several European countries. Quite apart from snow being 'publicly sold all over Italy in Summer' and his reference to a great ice house in Lyon from which everyone could buy, there were some less familiar items of information. In Denmark there were seaside ice reservoirs for the use of the Court, in Hungary the peasantry made snow trenches for their own use, covering them with pyramid-shaped straw roofs, and even in Moscow, where the snows melt in May and return in September, says Dr Barra, they keep ice for the months of June, July, and August. He expressed some wonderment that the Russians should bother to store ice for such short summers, or indeed use it at all in so fiercely cold a climate.

In terms curiously similar to those used by Dr Barra, modern travel and food writers, bemused by the Russian addiction to ice-cream in and out of season, note that 'an abiding memory of Moscow in November is of people eating ice creams in the streets with snow falling',[19] that 'ice cream was selling in huge quantities even when snow was thick on the ground', that 'there are fantastic sales of ices by Moscow stalls when the hardened snow is high on pavements and roads and the temperature many degrees below freezing point'. The last comment, written in 1968 by the very individual editor of what was at that time a no less singular little trade journal called *Ice Cream Topics*, surmised that the Russian public flocked to buy ice-cream in freezing conditions because it was by contrast warm.[20]

I have never myself visited Russia, and having no first-hand experience, am in no position to judge the quality of the ice-cream to be found there, but would hazard a guess that what makes it so sought after, whether in icy winter or summer sunshine, is quite simply that it is both good in itself and good value for money. The well-known Russian love of sweet things apart, ice-cream parlours and street stalls are as popular as they are in Russian cities because they sell a high-class product, 'exceptionally rich and delicious', reported the late Philip Harben, television cook of the fifties and sixties, when in the winter of 1965 he returned after a visit to Russia in company with a group of British ice-cream manufacturers. That visit, described by Harben in a television talk, must have been quite an eye-opener to our own manufacturers of Dolly Maid, Snowball Dairy Delights, Iceberg Dreams, Creamofreez Velveto Choc Bars and the like. The ice-creams they enjoyed in Moscow were, it is true, churned out in a great factory forming part of a government co-operative for dairy products. Strangely, however, it was not Soviet skill with additives, stabilizers, emulsifiers, hardened palm oil, and millac powders, nor even any mastery in the high art of overrun which so impressed the English visitors. It was simply that Russian factory ices were made with pure cream and eggs. Only those and nothing more – save, of course, sugar and flavouring, vanilla being the most popular.

The standards have not deteriorated. Lesley Chamberlain, author of *The Food and Cooking of Russia*, published in 1982, uses almost the same words as did Philip Harben in 1965: 'The product sold is of a purity and creaminess that constantly astounds Western visitors.' Mrs Chamberlain also reveals that the famous Moscow ice-cream factory, the first of its kind in Soviet Russia, was set up in the 1920s by Anastas Mikoyan and was 'an immensely popular move'. It was certainly an imaginative one. Mikoyan, on his appointment as Minister of Trade in 1926, at once turned his attention to the food industry and the improvement of Russian standards of living. For him, the dairy co-operative and its concomitant ice-cream factory must have been something of a dream come true. Mikoyan's name reveals his Armenian origin and hence a hereditary interest in the good things of life. The Russian love of ices was also a tradition dating far back into the past. Georg Johann Kohl, long resident in Russia, described as long ago as 1841 how every year, and in every Russian town, the vendors of ices appeared on Easter Sunday and from that day until the end of the summer carried ices about 'for sale in the public places and streets'. This custom, Kohl remarked, 'to which we in other countries are strangers, is greatly promoted by the cheapness of ice and of the sweetened juices of fruits in Russia'. So struck was Kohl by the street vendors of ices in St Petersburg, Moscow, Odessa and Russian cities in general, that he noted their customs in detail and in St Petersburg struck up a acquaintance with one in order to record his patter. In

Petersburg in Bildern und Skizzen (Dresden and Leipzig, 1841), Kohl, with all the attention of a Mayhew to popular speech, provided his readers with a lively and picturesque recreation of the performance of a Russian itinerant vendor of ices tempting his potential customers to buy: 'Ice! Ice! the freshest and the coolest; Chocolate, vanilla, coffee, rose ice, and, best of all, flower-blossom! Flower-blossom, poppy-blossom, vanilla-blossom, coffee-blossom, chocolate-blossom! Who will taste my delicious ice?' When in 1842 Kohl's book was published in a two-volume English translation entitled *Russia and the Russians*, readers must have been startled to learn that the citizens of the northern city of St Petersburg were able to buy ices in the streets and that the vendors carried them about in 'tin jars standing in a wooden tub, covered up to the necks with natural ice' and thus 'their cooling commodity' remained frozen even in the hottest sunshine. It was to be seven or eight years, as Mayhew himself tells us, before London street and park life was enlivened with itinerant ice-cream vendors with their decorated carts and their tempting offers of a sample taste, just as their Russian counterparts had been doing for so long: 'Who buys my beautiful ice? Now, mother, what are you looking for? Does it not make you long? Just taste!' cries Kohl's St Petersburger, and holds out a morsel at the tip of a wooden spoon. The customer takes the bait, and buys an ice. It costs her eight kopecks. *Moroschnije ssami ssladkija moroschnije!* Ice, the sweetest ice in the world! and the Russian hokey pokey man keeps up his unbroken stream of sales patter until sunset.

Anastas Mikoyan's achievement in providing the post-Revolution citizens of Moscow with the joyous luxury of unlimited ice-creams of wholesome quality probably superior to those they had known before 1917, and now to be available all the year round instead of only in the summer months, was one of his personal triumphs. The factory he established is still referred to as 'the Mikoyan ice-cream factory'. Not after all such a bad way of being commemorated by his people.

How reputable in comparison to the factory ices of Russia are the products of our own commercial ice-cream producers? They too, that is to say, the two best known among them, started production in the 1920s, Walls in 1922, Lyons in 1923, a few years therefore before

Mikoyan's scheme was set up. Well, in the Year of Grace 1982 Walls celebrated their Diamond Jubilee, and in May of that year the BBC broadcast a discussion on ice-cream in the Sunday Food Programme. The two events were not necessarily connected, other than by coincidence, but it was certainly interesting to hear what had happened to British ice-cream in the sixty years since the first Stop Me and Buy One tricycles wheeled off from Acton to London with their cargoes of chocolate-covered ice-cream bars. Joyful the news was not. Within a few minutes a Dr Swindlehurst, technical director of the Walls factory at Acton, came on the air to answer questions put by Mr Derek Cooper, the Food Programme's guiding spirit. When we buy an ice-cream, what are we actually eating? Mr Cooper asked.

Without precise knowledge of what goes into the famously delicious Russian ice-creams it would hardly be fair to reproduce in detail the exchange which ensued between Mr Cooper and Dr Swindlehurst, but the gist of the matter was that Walls ice-cream could be defined as a frozen aerated emulsion of which the principal ingredients were fats, sugars, milk solids (not milk or any other dairy fat), locust bean gums (a homogenizing or stabilizing ingredient), emulsifier, flavouring – and 50 per cent overrun, in other words air. There was of course, Dr Swindlehurst said, a certain amount, about 25 per cent of the factory's output, which was superior, and called dairy ice-cream, and by law dairy ice-cream must contain a minimum of 5 per cent of milk fat or cream, only Walls didn't use cream, they used butter. The overrun or air percentage was apparently the same as for non-dairy ice-cream.

At this stage the programme was beginning to sound increasingly like an exchange between Beachcomber's immortal Mr Justice Cocklecarrot and Lewis Carroll's Mad Hatter. 'You're getting the air for free,' said Dr Swindlehurst reproachfully. 'In places like Australia [how many places *are* there like Australia?] it goes as high as 140 per cent.' 'Ice-cream isn't treated as a food here, is it?' suggested Derek Cooper, or words to that effect. 'It's a fun thing. Is that why there's VAT on it?' Dr Swindlehurst thought the VAT was because it's eaten frozen rather than thawed.[21]

If any Russians were listening they must have been laughing their heads off. For that matter, so were a good many other people. The possibilities opened up by the Swindlehurst–Cooper exchange were boundless. It would scarcely be relevant to enlarge upon them here. But I think I can go a little way to explain Dr Swindlehurst's reasoning concerning the levying of VAT on ice-cream. He would know what many of his listeners, and his interlocutor, perhaps didn't and don't, which is that if you leave a portion or a scoop of the frozen aerated emulsion under discussion – for the moment we will call it ice-cream – to melt completely, all that remains to show for it is a very small pool of indeterminate liquid. There isn't, you find, any appreciable substance to justify a tax. In that context, in the early years of Value Added Tax, a ruling concerning water given in one of the bulletins issued by Customs and Excise laid it down that both ice and steam were in general zero-rated but ice made from distilled or other demineralized water was taxable at the standard rate.[22] Dry ice, which is frozen carbon dioxide, is equally a manufactured and taxable article, although when it evaporates there is nothing you could pin a tax on. So British commercial ice-cream, which is 50 per cent frozen air – it must be said that I have come across brands of French commercial ice-cream which are in no respect an improvement – is logically taxable because it is frozen, and Dr Swindlehurst was at least partially correct in his surmise that that is the justification for the tax.*

Traditionally, however, ice-cream, whether commercial or otherwise, is classed as confectionery, and it was ostensibly on that basis that in 1962 Purchase Tax was imposed on it. Increased over a period of six years from 15 per cent to 22 per cent, the tax was abolished in

---

* A closely related problem of definition arose for the excise officers when in 1984 Chancellor Nigel Lawson imposed VAT on fish and chips and other hot takeaway meals. The finance bill authorizing the new tax classified hot food as 'food which has been heated for the purpose of enabling it to be consumed above the ambient air temperature and is, at the time of supply, above that temperature'. That the taxed food would probably, if not certainly, be cold by the time the customer consumed it was irrelevant to the tax collector. Bread and pies which *happened* to be warm when freshly baked but weren't sold 'to enable them to be consumed hot' were to remain outside the scope of VAT. Effectively, this meant that in the case of fish and chips it was the cooking process which was taxed, just as in the case of ices it was really the freezing process which attracted the tax.

1973, when the Chancellor announced that for purposes of the newly introduced VAT, which replaced Purchase Tax, all kinds of confectionery, ice-cream, crisps, soft drinks and so on would be zero-rated. Only a year later a newly-elected Labour government reversed the 1973 ruling and reimposed the tax on the exempted confectionery and ice-cream in the shape of the then $8\frac{1}{2}$% VAT.[23]

Perhaps more relevant in the Cooper interrogation of Dr Swindlehurst was the latter's reply to the suggestion that the main ingredients of commercial ice-creams were really air and water. 'Oh yes – Oh yes,' said Dr Swindlehurst. 'As in a very large number of things we eat.' He had a point there.

At the end of 1982 a description of Russian ice-cream was written to me from Moscow by Miss Darra Goldstein, an American student of Russian literature who was then collecting material for her book *A Taste of Russia*. There appeared to be a startling contrast to the standards of British commercial ice-cream. 'Russian ice-cream *is* delicious,' Miss Goldstein confirmed. In view of the poor quality of the milk in Russia, due to the very skimpy diet of Russian cows as compared to that in Western countries, she found it strange that ice-cream was so good. Their cream ices, *slivochnoye*, contain 10 per cent butterfat and 16 per cent sugar; their milk ices, *molochnoye*, only 3.5 per cent butterfat and as much as 20 per cent sugar (figures quoted from a contemporary Soviet cookbook), which latter, it has to be admitted, do not to me sound all that tempting. By a long way the favourite Russian ice-cream, Miss Goldstein told me, is *plombir*, which contains 15 per cent butterfat – rich beyond the dreams of British mass market ice-cream manufacturers. *Plombir*, I take it, is the Russian version of the French *plombières*, that favourite ice of nineteenth-century Europe, composed of a very rich egg and cream custard, with the addition of ground almonds, raisins and small pieces of glacé fruits, and no doubt it travelled to Russia via the French and Italian pastrycooks and confectioners who were so highly regarded there in the days of the Grand Dukes and the lavish entertainments of the foreign embassies and imperial palaces of St Petersburg. Today *plombir* is the most expensive of all Russian ices, while the most commonly sold variety at kiosks is vanilla. It comes in cones, briquettes, sandwiched between soggy waffles, or in cylinders, horns and tubs. At home and in ice-cream parlours, Miss Goldstein told me, vanilla ices are almost always topped with sweet runny jam, fruit syrup, liqueur, or even sweet wine. The *omelet syurpriz* or baked Alaska, chocolate ices (containing 6 per cent of chocolate or 2.5 per cent of cocoa powder), eskimo bars, which are vanilla encased in chocolate – presumably real chocolate as opposed to the substance (a form of chocolate made without cocoa butter and therefore not legally chocolate) used by the Walls factory for their choc bars – and something called *crème brulée*, a caramel-flavoured ice-cream, are less successful, another informant tells me, than the vanilla.

To English and other Western visitors, the Russian addiction to ice-cream remains puzzling, and so, given the generally poor quality of the food in Moscow, does the high quality of the ices sold from street kiosks. There is no synthetic taste in these ices, another friend reported to me in February 1983, and you see almost more adults than children walking along the streets with their cornets or other kiosk ices. That might be accounted for by the price, which seems fairly high in comparison with other daily expenses. A scoop in a cup-shaped cornet, for example, cost 20 kopecks (at that time 20p by the artificially fixed exchange rate) as compared to 12 kopecks for a large loaf of excellent black bread, to 15 to 20 for a finer-quality loaf and 2 kopecks for the flat rate bus fare.[24] Bread, however, was subsidized and so presumably was public transport, and when you find that an un-subsidized luxury such as a bottle of vodka cost from 9 roubles (£9.00) up, and in a bar a single drink of it 1 rouble, ice-cream would seem to represent excellent value nutritionally as well as in enjoyment, and in the contrast, and supplement, to the rather monotonous and stodgy daily diet of the average Russian.

I would myself much like to learn the reaction of Russian visitors to English street ices. In June 1983 Richard Owen, a *Times* correspondent in Moscow, described how he and a Russian friend queued at an ice-cream kiosk. The friend commented on how many Russian products like Fiat-type cars, and buildings such as shopping centres, modern hotels and airports, never really worked properly, they were illusions, the form without the content. They were Russian adaptations of a quite different tradition, made because the West has them and the Russians think they should have them too. However, as the two men reached the head of the queue, Owen's Russian friend remarked, 'Mind you, our ice-cream is better.' If he intended his comment to apply specifically to British ice-cream, it was a mild enough one. Richard Owen's explanation of the excellence of Soviet ice-cream is that the formula originally brought from America in the 1920s by Anastas Mikoyan was for a product much superior to that commonly found today in the States, and that in Russia the original quality has been maintained. 'Muscovites are therefore eating honest-to-goodness American ice-cream circa 1940,' says Owen, and much of it is still made in the Mikoyan ice-cream factory.[25]

The London Confectioners

All Sorts of Ice

When Hannah Glasse remarked, in her *Compleat Confectioner,* published *c.* 1760, that ice-cream was 'a thing us'd in all deserts [her own spelling] as it is always to be had at the confectioners', she was not, I think, exaggerating. By the second half of the eighteenth century cream ices – as they were then usually called – had become quite a craze in fashionable London. Already in 1749, and as early in the season as 25 April, the Earl of Chesterfield was reporting that a masquerade in the Venetian manner was to begin at Ranelagh (the fashionable pleasure gardens close to the Thames at Chelsea) the following afternoon, and all the boxes were to be transformed into shops for toys, lemonades, ices and other refreshments. Next day there were to be fireworks. Twenty years later, in 1769, an Italian confectioner called Domenico Negri founded a business in Berkeley Square premises destined to become famous for the delicious ices sold there. His shop was at the Sign of the Pineapple – an emblem much used by confectioners – and his trade card announced that he made and sold

all Sorts of English, French and Italian wet and dry'd Sweet Meats, Cedrati and Bergamot Chips, Naples Diavolini and Diavoloni, All sorts of Biskets & Cakes, fine and Common Sugar Plums, Syrup of Capilaire, Orgeate and Marsh Mallow, Ghimauve or Lozenges for Colds & Cough, all Sorts of Ice, Fruits, & Creams in the best Italian manner, Likewise furnishes Entertainments in Fashions, Sells all sorts of Desarts, Flower-frames & Glass-work at the Lowest Price.[1]

During the second half of the eighteenth century Negri was undoubtedly the king-pin of London confectioners. With his list of Italian and French specialities, his syrups, his candied fruits, his citron and bergamot orange chips, his cakes and biscuits, his decorative table furnishings for desserts and his fruit and cream ices, he could supply the grandest households in the land. A man who had trained at Negri's, subsequently Negri and Gunter, and later still Negri and Witton, Wetton or Wetten, had a reference for life. Several men who published books on confectionery and ices during the second part of the eighteenth century and the early decades of the nineteenth acknowledged a debt to Negri and his partners, implying of course that this was in itself sufficient proof that the writer in question was thoroughly versed in all branches of his profession.

One of the confectioners who invoked his apprenticeship with Messrs Negri and Gunter as a recommendation for his book was Robert Abbot, whose *The Housekeepers Valuable Present* appeared without a date but possibly before 1780, when Wetten had replaced Gunter as Negri's partner, and certainly by 1791, when an owner of the book, Anne Jones, dated her signature in a copy acquired by a later collector, Mrs Pennell. In the Preface to his modest little work, Abbot revealed something useful as publicity for his former masters and of some interest to posterity. During the course of his apprenticeship with Messrs Negri and Gunter in Berkeley Square, Abbot explained, 'many housekeepers to noblemen and gentlemen were frequently present in order to observe our peculiar method of preparing confects'. By allowing those housekeepers into their pastrycook's and confectioner's workshops, Messrs Negri and Gunter must have achieved a good deal of extra business and at the same time aroused much curiosity. Robert Abbot, who had gone on from his apprenticeship to engagement in 'the service of several noblemen', had evidently been plagued for 'receipts and information respecting improvements and additions to this art' but had understandably been too busy to comply. Now, as a man who 'has devoted the greater part of his life to the pursuit of the art under consideration', he felt that it was time something new should appear on the subject ... 'all the treatises I have seen contain only old and exploded Receipts'. His, on the other hand, 'are the result of my own practice and experience' and he hopes that 'it might supply the place of personal application'. Further, he hopes that those who buy the book will also present copies to their friends and that his treatise will indeed be considered a Valuable Present. Having served an apprenticeship to 'men of such eminence in the line of Confectionery, and such respectability in their connections as Messrs Negri and Gunter', Abbot reiterates his assumption that this will be considered a recommendation. Abbot sounds like a good and modest man but for all his promises of new techniques, he did not, so far as I can see, provide anything particularly original, his book was not reprinted, and to me the information contained in his Preface remains his most interesting contribution to our knowledge of practices current in the confectioners' shops of his period.

Now it was one thing for the confectioners to let the gentry's housekeepers into their workshops and to provide them with recipes and instructions, quite another when someone outside the profession took to publishing books on the subject. When in 1789 Frederic Nutt, who like Abbot had served his apprenticeship in the Negri establishment (by this time Negri and Wetten, Gunter having left Negri to set up on his own at 31 New Bond Street), published his *Complete Confectioner*, he took a hefty swipe at Hannah Glasse's book on confectionery. He had seen the book, he said in a note prominently printed opposite the opening of his Preface, 'entitled *The Confectioners and Housekeepers Assistant*, written by a Mrs Glass', and this had obliged him to change the planned title of his own book 'lest the Public should consider it the same, or some such spurious Production'. His assertion was odd, to say the least. In the first place the title he gives as that of Mrs Glasse's book was not hers, or anything like it. Nor, so far as can be discovered from the bibliographies, was it that of any other contemporary work. As for changing his own title in order to eliminate the possibility of confusion, he appears to have ensured it by choosing – give or take an *a* and an *e* in the spelling – the identical one. There is certainly some mystery here. By the time his fifth edition appeared in 1808 the note had disappeared, and so had his Preface. In place of both was an *Advertisement*, in which Nutt observed that 'It is very extraordinary that only one work except the present was ever presented to the Public on the Art of Confectionary; that production has already met with the contempt which it justly deserved'. In case any reader missed the point, 'Mrs Glasse's Confectionery' is named in a footnote. This summary and manifestly absurd dismissal of all previous works on confectionery, from the much plagiarized translation of Massialot's book on the subject which, incorporated under the overall title of *The Court and Country Cook*, had appeared in 1702, to that of Menon's *Les Soupers de la Cour*, published in translation in 1767 as *The Art of Modern Cookery displayed, Consisting of the most approved methods of Cookery, pastry and confectionary of the present time*, and by 1776 already in its third edition, was perhaps motivated by Nutt's anger at Hannah Glasse's amateur meddling in professional matters. Mrs Glasse herself had died in 1770, but two more editions of her confectionery book had been published before Nutt's own work appeared, the latest in 1787, and in 1800 two rival editions of a new version 'with considerable additions and corrections by Maria Wilson'. This had been advertised as due to appear in ten weekly parts in the previous year.[2]

If Nutt had seen those new versions he would have been further infuriated, and in 1806 had presumably taken the first opportunity he had had since 1790 to amend his note concerning Mrs Glasse. By 1807, when Nutt first identified himself by name, his contempt for the lady's confectionery work had in no way abated. What it was in that book that had so particularly aroused his scorn it is hard to say, but he must have felt that in some way it represented competition. Alternatively the explanation may lie in a spurious version of Hannah Glasse's confectionery book published under the title *The Whole Art of Confectionary* and giving the author's name as Mrs Eliz. Glasse. This book was apparently copied from the real Mrs Glasse by a Mrs Elizabeth Price of Berkeley Square, signatory of its Preface, and author of two previous publications, *The New Book of Cookery* and *The New Universal, and Complete Confectioner*, both undated but *c.* 1760 and 1780 respectively. *The Whole Art of Confectionary* was also undated, and appeared without a publisher's or printer's name. The title of this fraudulent version of Hannah Glasse's confectionery book still doesn't tally with the one given by Frederic Nutt in his first edition, but he appears to have been subject to confusion in the matter of book titles, so perhaps there was something in this impudent piece of deception which had particularly riled him. If so, what it was may emerge when, as it surely will, a copy of the Price/Glasse book comes to light. At present, as explained by Virginia Maclean in her *Short-title Catalogue of Household and Cookery Books, etc. 1701–1800*, no actual copy has so far been located.

To return to Frederic Nutt's own work, which was a well-printed and well-ordered book, supplying ten copper plate engravings of arrangements for desserts, and plenty of up-to-date recipes, all carrying the implied guarantee that they were those used by one or other of the three finest confectioners in London. Ices in particular were offered in impressive variety. There were thirty-one different ice-creams – called so, unusually for the period – many made with fresh fruit, others with jams or fruit jelly, some with a basis of fruit syrups and a flavouring of some potent essence such as bergamot orange. Ginger, chocolate, coffee, pistachio were other flavourings used by Nutt, and he had a good mixture of Naples and ratafia biscuits with cream and a sugar syrup, another with brown breadcrumbs – an ice-cream which later became a much-loved Gunter speciality – one consisting of perfectly plain cream very lightly sweetened, and a Royal ice-cream of dense richness in which 10 egg-yolks and 2 whole eggs were made into a custard with 1 pint of cream, the whole mixed with pistachios and three kinds of candied citrus peels. There was even an ice made with a cream custard and syrup and a strong flavouring of Parmesan cheese. In short, by 1800, the London confectioners were making, in somewhat primitive form, nearly all the ice-creams we still love today and some others which have disappeared, such as one called prunello ice-cream, an egg, cream, and syrup mixture flavoured with prunello spice, a mixture assumed by Nutt to be known to everyone.*

Nutt's water-ices are based on much the same ingredients as his cream ones, the cream being replaced with syrup and plenty of lemon juice. He suggests freezing his pineapple water-ice in a pineapple mould, and of his barberry water-ice, made with one spoonful of barberry jam, the juice of one lemon and a pint of water, he says, 'be

* Perhaps some preparation of dried prunes?

very careful it freezes thick and smooth like butter before you put it in your moulds', a tall order for an ice made of such unpromising ingredients. Had he inadvertently omitted a key component? One way and another Nutt's water-ices were not as convincing as his cream ones, and in the decade following the publication of his book they were much improved upon by the next generation of London confectioners.[3]

Besides all the usual products of the confectioners, the wet and dry preserved fruits, the marzipan, the comfits, the wafers, Nutt offered some fruit cheeses such as damson, cherry, and apple, and some rich buttery puddings. Lemon pudding is a mixture of melted butter, sugar, lemon peel, lemon juice and eggs cooked in puff pastry with pieces of candied lemon peel, and a carrot pudding not quite so rich in eggs and butter, but with the addition of brandy, and equally baked on a base of puff pastry. From Frederic Nutt may be derived a good idea of the kind of sweet things to be had from the high-class confectioners' and pastrycooks' shops at the turn of the eighteenth century and of the desserts which would have been served in the well-to-do houses of the day.

By the time Nutt published his third edition, in 1806, the firm of Negri and Wetten, with whom he had trained, had changed. Wetten & Sons were now established in Bruton Street, and Gunter had returned from New Bond Street to the old Negri premises in Berkeley Square. Negri had either retired or had been bought out by Gunter, or perhaps had died. At any rate, from now on it was Gunter whose reputation dominated that of all other confectioners and caterers in the capital. There was, of course, plenty of competition. Since about 1760, when James Gunter was a young lad – he was born in 1745 – there had been fashionable confectioners' shops in the neighbourhood. At one time there had been Edward Lambert, whose shop was in St Alban's Street, Pall Mall, and who had written a small treatise on *The Art of Confectionary*, published in 1744, and had also been the joint author with Mrs Penelope Bradshaw of *Bradshaw's Valuable Family Jewel*, published in 1748. On the title page of this book Mrs Bradshaw described her collaborator as 'the late ingenious Mr Lambart, confectioner'. Edward Lambert had evidently been succeeded by Talbot

Waterhouse, his apprentice, who advertised on his trade card that 'he makes and sells all sorts of fine Sweet-Meats, Harts-Horn, Jelleys, Creams, sherbets, Lemond Ice'. In Leicester Square there had been a confectioner named Johnson who offered ices, jellies, fruits, and to make it clear that he was just as conversant as the next man with French and Italian usage added that he also supplied '*Gelati d'ogni sorta* and *Glace Toujours Prêt*'. There was no shortage, then, of confectioners who could have supplied Ranelagh and the other London pleasure gardens with ices for their festivities in the 1740s.

In the 1750s there had been Thomas Street, confectioner to His Majesty (George II), whose business was in Old Bond Street, and two other confectioners in the area, William Smith at Ye Kings Arms, Old Bond Street, and Robinson, Harper, and Hoddle of New Bond Street, were flourishing in the 1760s. Both of them announced 'Ice Sold Here' on their trade cards. By ice, did they mean ices or just plain ice? At this period, when people often referred to eating or buying ice when in fact they meant ices, it isn't always easy to determine, but there is no ambiguity about Richard Perry at the Sign of the Pheasant at 60 Oxford Street, who about 1790 had a card announcing that 'he continues making ... ice creams, whips and jellies, all kinds of sweetmeats and Brandy Fruits, trifles, and blanshmanges, lemonade and orgeat'.[4] So Hannah Glasse had been perfectly justified in writing that ices were easily obtainable from the confectioners, although Londoners did not enjoy the café life of their contemporaries in Paris, Naples, Palermo, Venice and Vienna, cities where ices were always to be had in those now multiplying establishments. To be sure, sherbets could be ordered in some London coffee houses, but so far as I know, there has never been any hint or suggestion that these were frozen, although they may well have been cooled with ice.

James Gunter, founder of the firm which so long and so famously bore his name, came from a family said to be of Norman origin and owning estates in Wales, at Tregunter, between Talgarth and Brecon, at Gilston near Talybont, and, after the Reformation, Abergavenny Priory. There were also Gunter properties in Glendwr and Glasbury near the Herefordshire border.[5] At what date James Gunter entered the confectionery trade or whether he had served an apprenticeship with Negri before becoming his partner in the 1780s we do not know, nor do we know what his early circumstances were, but we do know that by the early years of the nineteenth century his business in Berkeley Square was flourishing. His shop was frequented by the royal dukes whom he had served when they were children – George III and Queen Charlotte had nine sons and six daughters – and when in August 1805 the Marquess of Buckingham entertained the Prince of Wales and his brother the Duke of Clarence, future William IV, at his magnificent house at Stowe, it was Gunter who was invited to supply the confectionery and organize some of the catering for the five-day visit.

For the great occasion fifty house guests were assembled at Stowe, and early in the evening of the arrival of the royal party there was an imposing formal dinner. Next night there was a late out-of-door entertainment, music playing from a bandstand in the centre of the ornamental lake, morris dancers, crowds of the local populace strolling in a part of the grounds suitably roped off but close enough to cheer the passing royals, supper for the princes and the house party in the famous grotto, the great house illuminated, a magnificent display of fireworks, and not even a shower to mar the evening. The visit appears to have been organized with great efficiency and with little of the suffocating ceremony which came to prevail in Queen Victoria's day. At Stowe that week breakfasts were served at noon, there were afternoon drives in the grounds, Lady Buckingham conducting the Prince in a horse-drawn 'garden chair', Lord Buckingham escorting the royal party to visit local worthies, in the evening much informal dancing, singing, flirting and jollity, the whole glorious week culminating in a ball for 400 guests and a 4 a.m. supper for all of them, with tables laid in the library, the Grenville Room, and in the Music Room for the Princes. The younger guests were tireless and the party broke up only at six in the morning. Save for a violent storm and incessant rain which rather marred the evening of the ball, the weather had been kind all week, and the Prince in gracious humour, on at least one occasion rather more so indeed than a Prince should be, confided the irrepressible Harriet Wynne to her diary, but preoccupied with their chatter, their strolls in the grounds, their flirtations, their exchanges of confidences, the younger members of the house party were quite relieved when on the morning after the ball the royals departed, leaving the remaining twenty-five members of the house party to their own devices. The son and daughter of the house, Lord George and Lady Mary Grenville, together with Harriet Wynne and Lady Mary's beau, promptly made for 'Mr Gunter's room' and with much merriment proceeded to raid his biscuits and pastries. One way and another, Harriet summed up the whole week on that second evening of the visit, when the fireworks, the music, and the illuminations had been 'totally surpassing my greatest expectations'.[6]

The Stowe festivities of 1805 must have been a highlight in Gunter's career, and his presence there a great boost to his business. It would be interesting to discover what staff he took with him, and how many of the ornamental wax and gum paste baskets, *assiettes montées* and other such decorative paraphernalia were transported from London to Stowe – a distance of about fifty-five miles – and how much made on the spot. Presumably there was a fully equipped pastry kitchen in the house, and we may also assume that Lord Buckingham had an amply stocked ice house, and a large coolroom or spacious pantry – or a dairy in the grounds – where the freezing of ices on a large scale could be operated. True, neither Harriet Wynne nor her sister Betsey Freemantle, who was also in the house party, make any mention of ices, and neither does John Simpson, the Buckinghams' head cook, who the following year published a book in which he embodied the bills of fare for all the dinners served during the Prince of Wales's visit, plus those for the suppers on the night of the ball, but the lord of the kitchens would not in any case have meddled in such matters. Ices came into the category of confectionery and, as John Simpson very properly remarked in the brief introduction to his book, 'cooks, if they study their own profession, will not have time to attend to this department'.[7] Ices, however, there must have been during the royal visit to Stowe. It would have been unthinkable in the middle of August, and with Gunter in attendance, not to have had them. Most probably they would have appeared at the end of the supper, served in the grotto to the princes and the house guests, probably also on other outdoor occasions during the week. It is sad that no records of the Gunter business of the period and of his personal involvement in the royal visit to Stowe survive, and that the only reference Simpson makes to Gunter is when he gives a cursory sketch of the 'Chantilla Baskets made of Wafers' which were created for the dessert course at dinner on the evening of 19 August. Quantities more were made for supper, for it was the night of the great ball, and these, along with wax baskets filled with shellfish, gum paste baskets filled with pastries, and caramel baskets filled with more pastries, would all have been the work of Gunter's men. Simpson, however, merely explains that to make Chantilla baskets the wafers are stuck round a dish and the basket filled with cream, etc. 'The wafers are to be had of the confectioner. The best that I have had are made by Mr Gunter, Berkeley Square.' One senses that the resident master-cook and the visiting caterer-confectioner had not hit it off too well. When it came to recommending a man for supplying wax baskets and other ornaments, John Simpson ignored Gunter and advised his readers to go to Mr Hickson of Duke Street, Grosvenor Square, 'who is remarkably clever at that and all other cold work, such as ornamenting tongues, hams, etc. and cold work in general'.[8]

Mr Hickson of Duke Street was one of Gunter's many rivals at this period. By 1815 he had moved to 134 New Bond Street, and is mentioned by the anonymous author of *The Epicure's Almanack*, published that year, as maintaining 'a Pastry Shop of the first class'. Bond Street was still popular with confectioners. Barker's Repository of Confectionery was at 106 New Bond Street, and had a royal warrant for supplying their Majesties and the royal family. At the Oxford Street end of New Bond Street was Owen and Bently's, a luxury fruiterer where jellies, ices and liqueurs were served on the premises and who supplied desserts for fashionable dinners at a cost said by Captain Gronow (see below) to have been at least £1 0s. 0d. per head.

Woods Pastry-Shop at No. 43 specialized in turtle soup and dressed turtle as well as pastry of every sort. Mr Waud, in neighbouring premises, was 'a part proprietor in almost all public masquerades and undertakes to supply the suppers and refreshments and the Prince Regent and Duke of York have honoured Mr Waud with an appointment to serve them with *bon bons*, and have thus placed him in the via lactea of preferment'. At 19 Old Bond Street was Chapman's, 'a celebrated Fruit-Shop where jellies, ices, marmalades, cakes, liqueurs, and other delicious things are sold in the highest state of perfection', and at No. 4 there was Lyne the confectioner, 'who supplies routs and balls'. The highest praise is reserved by the *Epicure* for Monsieur Parmentier at 9 Edward Street, three doors from Duke Street, near Hickson's old premises. Parmentier was 'the celebrated confectioner to the Prince Regent and the Dukes of York and Kent [father of Queen Victoria]'. Here you could find

eau de cologne, pâte de guimauve [marshmallow], rose, orange and violet cachous, papillotes avec devises [presumably sweetmeats wrapped up in papers containing mottoes] and conserves of every sort, jellies, jams, fruit dried or preserved in French brandies, comfits, lozenges, drops of every colour and flavour, superior macaroons, and rout cakes of the most fanciful forms, with ices and creams.

Another French pastry-cook, Monsieur Farrance, had an establishment at the corner of Spring Gardens, St James's Park. 'This long celebrated shop has no superior, perhaps, in the world,' asserts the *Epicure*. 'Here are exquisite soups, highly flavoured tarts, savoury patties, and delicious pastry and confitures. Fruits and ices throughout the whole extent of their season, are good and in great variety.' The *Epicure* was quite carried away by 'this temple of Pomona and Ceres', 'holding daily a levée of beauty and fashion'.

In comparison, his verdict on Gunter is reserved.

We could not, if we would, leave Berkeley Square without paying a tribute to the merit of Mr Gunter, as a cook, confectioner, and fruiterer, if not the first, as Goldsmith says of somebody else, in the very first line. Mr Gunter has had for many years the high honour of supplying the Royal Family with articles from his shop. Some of the Royal Dukes condescend occasionally to give Mr Gunter a call for the purpose of tasting his pines, as if in gratitude for the many sweet repasts furnished to them from Mr Gunter's shop during their juvenile days.[9]

Perhaps the royal visits consoled Mr Gunter for not being in quite the same class as Messieurs Parmentier and Farrance. All the same, it is significant to find that about the year of publication of the *Epicure*'s implied criticism of Gunter's products, or shortly afterwards – it was 1815, and as we have to remember, the year of Waterloo – his son Robert went to Paris to study the art of making Italian ices. This we have on the authority of that splendid society gossip Captain James Gronow, who in his old age wrote the *Reminiscences and Recollections* of his days as a Regency dandy who kept company with all the legendary wits and beaux of those boisterous years. It comes in fact as quite a shock, after all the flowery good-food-guide praises of the *Epicure*, to learn that prior to the peace of 1815 and the second restoration of the Bourbons, 'our London ices and creams were acknowledged, by the English as well as by foreigners, to be detestable'. Accordingly, says Gronow, 'Gunter, the eldest son of the founder of the house in Berkeley Square' arrived in Paris – Gronow was already resident there – to work at Tortoni's in the boulevard des Italiens, at that time the most prosperous and fashionable café in the capital.[10]

Robert Gunter's spell at Tortoni's certainly paid off. After his father's death in 1819 Gunter's fame grew ever greater, and as a London institution the firm endured for a century and a half. Parmentier and Farrance, Mr Hickson of Duke Street and all those other confectioners who had ministered to the apparently insatiable appetites for sweet-meats and ices of the Georgian royal dukes and their companions have long been forgotten. Gunter's ices became the yardstick by which all others in London were judged. They too, alas, have entered the realm of legend. But it is a legend which lives on.

From Greenland's Icy Seas

By 1815, the year of publication of the *Epicure's Almanack*, James Gunter was already a very prosperous man, living in a large house in what was then the village of Earls Court, Kensington. There he owned acres of nursery gardens, fruit orchards and greenhouses. From those gardens came much of the produce which kept his shop supplied with the basic materials needed by his cooks and confectioners. In his greenhouses grew the pineapples so much appreciated by the royal dukes and indeed by all the fashionable world of the time, and from his fruit gardens came strawberries, raspberries, red currants, white currants, black currants, and apricots, of which enormous quantities went into the Gunter ices and creams, used fresh in the summer, in the winter preserved in the form of jellies, syrups, jams, and by 1819 bottled without sugar according to the method evolved by Appert and made public in his book.★

The scale on which the Gunter business was then operating may be judged by Guglielmo Jarrin's statement, in his book *The Italian Confectioner* (1820), that the previous year he had preserved more than 2,000 bottles of fruit by the Appert system, and that was only a first trial. Jarrin was 'Confectioner and Ornament Maker at Mr Gunter's', as he proclaimed beneath the portrait of himself which served as the frontispiece to the book. A young, handsome, elegantly dressed man, Jarrin reveals elsewhere in his text that he had worked in Paris in the days of the Emperor, and on the occasion of a dinner given by the city of Paris to mark his triumphant return from Germany, had made a gum paste group two feet high representing Napoleon himself, led by Victory, and attended by a retinue of allegorical figures. This was made for the centre of the table. The Emperor, according to Jarrin, rarely noticed anything which ornamented the table but on this occasion observed his portrait and was pleased to encourage the artist by his appreciation. It seems likely that Robert Gunter brought Jarrin back to London with him from Paris after his spell at Tortoni's.

Although Jarrin's main preoccupation was the creation of table

---

★ *L'Art de Conserver, Pendant Plusieurs Années* ... (Paris, 1810). Appert was himself a confectioner and distiller. In later editions of his own book Jarrin revealed that he had had some trouble with fruit preserved according to the Appert system, particularly with regard to fermentation. The large bottles advocated by Appert were also wasteful. Once opened, the whole contents of a bottle had to be used up immediately. In his 1837 edition, p. 247, Jarrin gave supplementary instructions for packing the fruit in bottles of small capacity. Soda water bottles were the best. In Italy he had discovered a corking machine which would cork 300 bottles an hour.

Guglielmo Jarrin

ornaments of every kind, edible and inedible – a *pièce montée*, he pointed out, was an ornament to be eaten and was not to be confused with an *assiette montée*, which was made of pasteboard or wire work, or partly of both, and might represent anything from a temple to a great urn to be filled with sweetmeats – he was also thoroughly versed in the art of making ices and made some useful comments on the subject. He warned that there were many defects to be guarded against. In ices that are badly made the sugar sinks to the bottom and they have necessarily a sharp unpleasant taste. Another very general defect is their appearing full of lumps. They are also often of a disagreeable dirty red colour – Dubuisson, it will be remembered, had laid it down that to obviate that defect red fruit ices be frozen in silver *sorbetières* – and there are few houses in London where ices are to be found entirely free from such faults. The mixing of the salt with the ice must be particularly attended to, as upon this circumstance depends the freezing power, and consequently in a good measure the goodness of the ice. Unfortunately Jarrin omits to tell his readers precisely how this should be done or in what proportions, saying no more than that the pounded

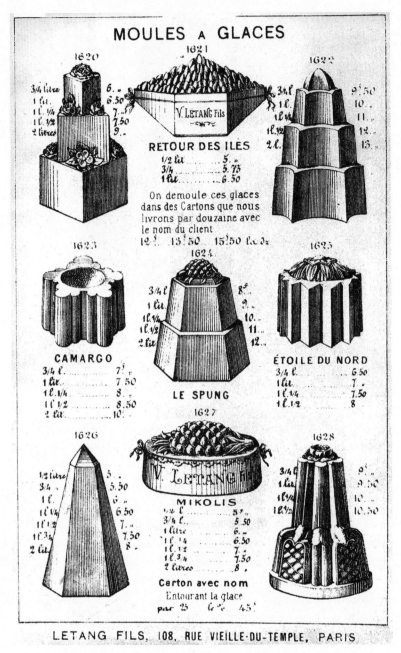

These moulds from the 1912 Letang catalogue would seem to derive from those used by Fugoli's operators to make the decorative centre pieces he described (see p. 60).

(see p. 60).

ice may be mixed with salt, or salt nitre, or soda. He gives a good description of the technique of moulding ices in fruit shapes and of how to colour and conserve them. He notes that fruit preserved without sugar on the Appert system 'is extremely valuable for ices'; of a strawberry water-ice he says that the chief recommendation of all ice is to be smooth and soft. Things have changed a good deal since the days of Redi's crackling *sorbetto* (see p. 19). The fruit jellies which were one of the great features of the Gunter ball suppers of the nineteenth century – the family house in Earls Court was known to the children of the neighbouring mansion as 'currant jelly hall' – were made on a basis of calf's foot jelly clarified and strengthened with the addition of isinglass. They were set in copper moulds placed in 'a box full of pounded ice, quite to the edge of the mould', and, protected with tin or other thin covers upon which more ice was placed, the jellies would be ready for turning out after three hours.[11]

The consumption of ice for cooling and freezing in an establishment such as Gunter's was clearly very considerable. When the author of the 1815 *Almanack* listed all those fashionable confectioners – and many more in less aristocratic quarters of London – one begins to wonder where, at that time, all the ice came from. It was not until the mid 1840s that the American Wenham Lake Ice business started sending its cargoes to Britain, to be superseded within a very few years by regular Norway shipments on an increasingly massive scale. A quite large proportion of the ice used in the early days was obtained by the caterers, the confectioners and the fish trade – all first-rate fish dealers have ice stores for the purpose of preserving their fish during hot weather, reported the *Epicure*[12] – from lakes, ponds, man-made re-servoirs, and purpose-flooded fields or ice farms, but ever since the 1780s when George Dempster and his fish dealer on the Tay had initiated the sea transport of salmon packed in ice from Scotland to London, the demand for that latter commodity had been on the increase. What happened to the confectioners, the fish dealers, the landed gentry, when in a mild winter the ice harvests failed and by midsummer the country's ice houses were empty? Probably the first source Londoners turned to when there was a shortage were Highland lochs, from which a supply of good thick ice could usually be relied upon, even in a relatively mild winter. Further afield there was the Baltic, there was Norway, and there was a scarcely known region, a kind of El Dorado of ice, the home of the iceberg and the whale, known to the English as 'the Greenland seas'.

It may have been the Prussians who initiated the collection of ice for commercial purposes from those Greenland seas. They would have derived the idea from returning whalers who were in the habit of picking up large blocks of ice which were stowed on deck or broken up to be stored in casks and melted down for drinking water. As those who studied the sciences would also have known, the renowned Flemish chemist van Helmont had long ago in the seventeenth century noted that the whalers in Greenland used ice to freeze out the watery element of wine and thus concentrate its alcoholic content.[13] Given the gear to hoist whale carcasses on board, a ton or two of ice at a time was scarcely a problem to the crew of a whaler. How long a commerce in ice from the Greenland seas had already been in existence in the eighteenth century we do not know, but that it was so is clear from a note made by Johannes Beckmann some time between 1793 and 1805 when he was writing his paper on artificial cold. 'Some years ago,' Beckmann then added in a footnote, 'as no ice could be procured on account of the great mildness of the preceding winter, the merchants of Hamburg sent a ship to Greenland for a load of it by which they acquired a considerable profit.'[14]

The next we hear of a trade in Greenland ice is in 1815, in *The Epicure's Almanack*. No more than hints to us but possibly quite well-known facts at the time, the *Epicure*'s remarks nevertheless begin to add up to what seems like solid information: 'Neither a native Greenlander, nor a Highlander from the remotest part of Caledonia, nor yet a Norwegian would calculate the value of the ice in Mr Gunter's cellar.'[15] A few years later, in 1822, an article in a Danish journal, *Handels-og Industrie Tidende* (The Trade and Industry Times), related the sad story of a cargo of ice brought from the Greenland seas to London six years previously. When the ship arrived in the Thames the Customs officers promptly turned up. But given that 'on the iceberg from which the ice had been taken there was no customs house to give clearance documents, no bills of lading or other papers could be produced'. The Customs officers were unable to decide whether ice should be listed as Products or as Manufactured Goods (one sees them scratching their heads over the problem), but at any rate it was a foreign product and duty was chargeable. After further delay it was agreed that it was 'a foreign relict', which attracted *ad valorem* tax. This amounted to a hefty 20 per cent, but the owners had the right to estimate. None too easy with your cargo visibly diminishing as everybody adds up their sums. Eventually a settlement was reached and what was left of the precious cargo was hurried off to the ice cellars. The writer of the report had received his information from a London correspondent who had been prompted to send the story by the recent occurrence of a heavy frost which, he hoped, come the summer, would save the London confectioners from the necessity to resort to a repeat performance of this risky and expensive enterprise.

Asked recently whether it was not very dangerous to hack icebergs about, the old colonial manager of a Danish company operating on the West Greenland coast several decades ago said that in his day, in the summer it had been quite customary to use iceberg ice for drinking water. It was the purest water obtainable, and getting water on shore was difficult. So they simply sailed out to an iceberg and chopped down as much as their vessel would hold. He dismissed the idea of danger. 'If you know icebergs, you know which ones are going to tip round. You sail right up to the side of the iceberg and simply chop at it.'[16]

The heavy freezing of 1822 reported by the Danish journal's English correspondent must have been of brief duration. It did not, as things turned out, save the London confectioners from an ice shortage in the following summer. Among the very few surviving records of the Gunter firm in the nineteenth century is an announcement published in *The Times* of Friday, 5 July 1822:

> Messrs. Gunter respectfully beg
> to inform the Nobility and those
> who honour them with their commands
> that, having this day received one of
> their cargoes of ice by the Platoff,

from the Greenland seas,

they are able to supply their

CREAM and FRUIT ICES, at their

former prices. – 7, Berkeley Square.

This was good news for fashionable London. An ice famine at the height of the season was a great inconvenience. Even in a small seaside resort such as Weymouth* in Dorset, visitors expected to find ice available and were annoyed if it was lacking. In September 1804 Cassandra Austen had written from Weymouth to her sister Jane, who was staying in Lyme, along the coast on the Devon border, complaining that among the many inconveniences she was experiencing was a lack of ice, to which Jane replied with characteristic irony: 'your account of Weymouth contains nothing which strikes me so forcibly as there being no ice in the town. For every other vexation I was in some measure prepared ... but for there being no ice what could prepare me?'[17]

Mr Gunter and his cooks and confectioners must have been more relieved even than their customers when the ice ship from the Greenland seas came into the Thames that first week of July 1822. Without ice how could they set the gallons of jellies and aspics needed for their ball suppers, how cool the champagne and punches which were drunk in such lavish quantities, let alone freeze their cream and fruit ices?

Greenland seas ice was in any case something very special, of great purity, hardness and long life, in every way very much superior to the local English pond, marsh, and reservoir ice. There was also something rather mysterious and romantic about cargoes of ice 'from the Greenland seas'. Just where those seas were was known to few people other than the crews of the whaling ships, and as for Greenland itself, the place was more of an abstraction, a great inaccessible mass of land consisting of nothing but ice mountains, and situated somewhere close to the Pole, than an actual country. The *Encyclopaedia Britannica* of 1810–11 had stated that Greenland was

---

* At the time, Weymouth was a fashionable resort, made popular by George III and his son the Duke of Gloucester.

a general name by which are denoted the most easterly parts of America, stretching towards the north pole, and likewise some islands to the northward of the continent of Europe lying in a very high latitude ... West Greenland is now determined by our latest maps to be a part of the continent of America, though upon what authority is not very clear ... In a great many places however, on the eastern coast especially, the shore is inaccessible by reason of the floating mountains of ice.

In the British public consciousness the Greenland seas in those days were as undefined as Greenland itself, which was nominally Norwegian territory. The *Britannica* was right to express doubts about the authority of the latest map-makers, but in general terms 'Greenland seas' could cover not only that vast stretch of water between the west coast of Norway and the east coast of Greenland, on some modern maps called Norwegian sea, but also the 500-odd miles of water between Iceland and East Greenland later rechristened Denmark Strait. (In 1814 Greenland and the Faroes had passed to the Danish crown.) To add to the confusion, from the mid sixteenth century until the 1820s, the far northern island deemed by the whaling industry of western Europe to be East Greenland or just plain Greenland was actually Spitsbergen, where the early whalers had established blubber-boiling and oil-extracting depots, while the ice-blocked east coast of the real Greenland was held to be West Greenland.[18] In early nine-teenth-century terms of reference, then, 'the Greenland seas' implied the northern Arctic waters in general, and in the context of the ships collecting ice for sale to British confectioners and fish merchants almost certainly indicated that the provenance was either somewhere off the west coast of Iceland or that of northern Norway.

Only in 1818, when reports of the breaking up of the ice barrier blocking the coast of East Greenland proper reached the newspaper-reading public, was it realized that there was a huge icy Greenland a long way to the west of the islands hitherto known, at any rate to the whaling industry, by that name. The same public also learned that vast ice mountains from the coast of East Greenland proper were drifting south and menacing Atlantic shipping far from polar waters.

Reading Captain William Scoresby Jr's engrossing *Journal of a Voyage* to the Northern Whale-Fishery, published in 1823, it is impossible not to come to the conclusion that, in spite of my Danish informant's dismissal of the hazards of attacking icebergs to obtain ice for drinking water, an ice-collecting voyage to the Arctic was beset with danger, and required at the least a very high degree of skilled seamanship. When in 1818 the master of one of Frederick Tudor's ships ran out of ice for Martinique he sailed north to attack a Labrador iceberg. His crew, working with picks and crowbars, were in constant fear that the mass might topple, and one roll of the iceberg lifted the ship six feet before the cargo was finally secured.[19] Captain Scoresby, an immensely experienced whaler, was of the opinion that a Greenland voyage was 'perhaps one of the most arduous of all maritime adventures'.

A ship setting out for the Greenland seas to collect ice rather than to hunt whales would not have faced so many hazards and would not have required so much expensive specialist equipment as a whaler, but would still have needed ice-breaking and ice-lifting gear, and the ice-anchors described by Captain Scoresby as large iron hooks, nearly the shape of the letter S. One extremity of the ice-anchor is inserted in a hole drilled into the ice, and to the other the rope for mooring is attached. In this manner the whaling ships anchored to ice-floes while the whale-hunters were out in their boats, and when Arctic gales blew and moving ice put his ship in imminent peril, Captain Scoresby relates how 'we are driven from one refuge to another, by the accumulation of ice setting in, until we scarcely had room to wear ... it was now no longer possible to keep underway in safety'. At the crucial moment he was able to grapple to a large mass of ice, ropes were fastened by ice-anchors to two or three of the heavier pieces of ice, which preserved the ship during the gale in safety. Next morning, Sunday, 26 May 1828, a calm succeeded the gale. The ship was warped into a more commodious situation, 'and again moored to a small sheet of ice and had our usual devotional exercises. A large whale came up near us, and appeared three times in the same spot; but being the Sabbath day, we did not pursue it.'★

★ Scoresby was a devoutly religious man who on the sabbath declined even to buy much-needed fresh vegetables, eggs, fowl and milk proffered by the islanders of

In the land of icebergs, fog, as is known to everybody familiar with the story of the *Titanic*, is an ever-present danger to ships, and one of its special hazards in the days of sail was that in freezing temperatures 'the fog was deposited on the rigging in a thick coating of transparent ice. At every movement in the rigging, this was dislodged in hard sharp masses of several pounds, which came down in such showers as to render it dangerous to look up.' On another occasion, as the *Baffin* at last approached land and Scoresby was about to set foot for the first time on a coast entirely unknown to Europeans and totally unexplored, 'an extraordinary quantity of ice that had formed in the rigging during the morning of the day was soon dislodged by the warmth of the sun. It fell in large transparent rods, several pounds in weight. Some of the men who were so imprudent as to look upward were cut on their faces.'

An ice-collecting ship would not of course have spent two to three months in the iceberg-infested Greenland seas as did the whalers, and if the *Platoff* had been lucky in that summer of 1822, she could probably have lifted her cargo of ice within a few days and made with all speed for the Port of London. In fact she is entered in Lloyd's List that year as having arrived at Gravesend from Iceland on 29 June, so would have been making her way back through the Greenland seas by the first week of the month. She would therefore have been conducting her ice-lifting activities during the last week of May, just about the time when the *Baffin* had captured a very young narwhal and at the same time 'picked up and hoisted on board a block of fresh water ice weighing between two and three tons'. It was 22 May, and Captain Scoresby reported that the ice was 'remarkable for its purity and transparency' and that he had tried out that well-known experiment of 'making a small lens of this ice and using it to ignite inflammable substances, by the concentration of the sun's rays', and it had of course worked 'readily'.

Captain Scoresby contacted several of his fellow whaling ships that summer, including his father's, the *Fame*, but he did not sight the *Platoff*,

Rachin, who had put out in a boat to reach the *Baffin*. In 1824, having completed his last whaling voyage the previous year, Scoresby went into the Church.

or he would have reported her in his journal. She was probably a long way from the *Baffin*, but she would certainly have been picking up the same kind of ice. Captain Scoresby's freshwater ice meant ice-mountain ice, ice-mountains being icebergs, in those days called polar glaciers, and also 'ice islands'. This ice is a different matter from ice-field ice, which is salt. There was also calf ice, described by Captain Scoresby as 'a portion of ice beneath a large mass, but not frozen to it, which shews itself on one side, and is apt to be disengaged by a slight motion'.[20]

In 1822, the crew of the *Platoff* would have found an ice-collecting mission easier to accomplish than did the men on earlier voyages made with the same objective. Since 1815 extraordinary changes had been occurring not only off the east coast of Greenland, but in the seas for many hundreds of miles around. The London *Times* of 22 July 1818 reported the breaking up of the ice on the Greenland coast in dramatic words quoted from a letter received from Copenhagen. 'Four hundred and fifty square miles of ice has recently detached itself from the eastern coast of Greenland and the neighbouring regions of the Pole. It was this mass which during four hundred years had rendered the province at first difficult of access, and afterwards inaccessible so as even to cause its existence to be doubted.' The account went on to refer to continuous changes in the North Pole seas reported by whalers ever since 1786, 'but at the present time so much ice has detached itself, and such extensive canals are open amidst what remains, that they can penetrate without obstruction as far as the 83rd degree'.

It was the breaking up of the ice and the opening of the channels described by *The Times* which in 1822 had enabled Captain Scoresby to sail the *Baffin* right into the sound which he christened with his own name – in honour of his father rather than himself – and to achieve his landing on the unknown East Greenland coast. The floating masses of ice were drifting south, *The Times* reported, and a packet from Halifax had fallen in with one of these islands in a more southern latitude than the situation of London; it appeared about half a mile in circumference, and its elevation above the waters was estimated at 200 feet. Only a few weeks earlier, on 12 May 1818, *The Times* had been reporting an 'island of ice', or 'iceberg stranded upon the island of Foula [in the Shetlands], said to be the Ultima Thule of the ancients'. The iceberg was three miles long and one and a half broad. No wonder the population of the island was, according to *The Times*, 'in a state of terror'.

With such dramatic events taking place in the polar seas and even so near home as the Shetlands, and with the ancient quest for a north-west passage to India now, as a result of the breaking up of the Greenland ice, once more being pursued by the British, it might have been supposed that ships arriving with cargoes of ice from those Arctic seas would have aroused some comment or occasioned the publication of an account or at least a *Times* report of one of these ventures. So little, however, can be discovered of the imports of Greenland seas ice at the time of the Gunter announcement of 1822, or indeed at any other period, that it has proved impossible to establish how ships set about their ice-collecting missions in the polar regions, what routes they took, what their methods of collection and stowage were.★ Of the arrival of the ice cargo of 1816 there appears to be no surviving official record, and we learn of it only from the account given in the Danish journal quoted above. It was Robert Gunter's announcement in *The Times* of 3 July, 1822 which sent me to Lloyd's list for that year and eventually to the confirmation that the *Platoff*, her master one Smith, had indeed arrived from Iceland and docked at Gravesend on 29 June. Of her date of departure for the Greenland seas no trace is to be found in the Lloyd's List for 1822, so we do not know how long she spent on her ice-gathering mission. From the 1821 List, however, we learn that she had arrived at Gravesend from St Petersburg on 21 September of that year. At the time the *Platoff*'s owners were W.H. Hobbs and Son, listed in Kent's *Directory* of 1813 as shipowners and lightermen to the Russia Company.† In the 1822 *Directory* the same

★ In 1982 the then Director of the National Maritime Museum, Dr Basil Greenhill, told me, in reply to my inquiry, that nothing whatever was known at the Museum about ice being brought from the Greenland seas at the period in question.

† An ancient trading company better known as the Muscovy Company, incorporated under that title by an Act of Elizabeth I. In 1610, under James I, the Muscovy Company made a serious attempt to exploit the whale fishery in Arctic waters and in 1622 the Greenland (meaning Spitsbergen) section of the Muscovy Company's trade was put to auction and the purchasers formed a separate concern known as the Greenland Adventurers. At the period concerned here, the Russia Company's principal agents were the British consuls at St Petersburg and Elsinore.

owners were entered as having premises at Globe Street, Wapping, so in all probability the *Platoff* came up the Thames from Gravesend and at the Hobbs wharf unloaded her ice into lighters to be towed by barge to the ice houses serving the confectioners of central London. It all tallies with the Gunter announcement of 5 July.

Where there appears some discrepancy in the story is in the customs records. Their ledgers of imports for 1822 list only two arrivals of ice in that year, neither of them dated. One is noted as having arrived via 'the Greenland whale fisheries', and the second one as coming from Norway. Both cargoes were valued at £700. On the first, duty paid was £140, in other words, 20 per cent, the same charge as had been made in 1816 on the occasion described in the Danish journal already quoted. Of the cargo from Norway only £400 worth had been destined for London, and the 20 per cent duty, amounting to £80, had been duly paid. The remaining £300 worth of ice had been landed at an unspecified port and had come in duty free because it was destined for the fisheries.[21]

That either of those two recorded ice cargoes of 1822 was the one brought by the *Platoff* appears improbable. She was not, we know, a whaling ship,[22] so the first option is ruled out. The ship bringing the Norway ice to London seems to be an equally unlikely candidate. She had already discharged part of her cargo at an unnamed British fishing port, so her master would not have recorded, as Captain Smith did of the *Platoff*, that she had arrived from Iceland. It should be explained here that from other entries of the relevant period in Lloyd's List it emerged that the *Platoff* was regularly employed by Hobbs in his Russia trade. Her summer ice-collecting voyage of 1822 completed, the ship sailed from Gravesend on 19 July bound for St Petersburg, where she arrived on 23 August, returning to Gravesend on 1 October. There she was probably laid up for the winter, unless Hobbs used her in some other trade such as coaling, It was certainly too late that year for a further voyage to St Petersburg.

The most likely explanation of the absence of any recognizable Customs record of the ice brought by the *Platoff* in the summer of 1822 is simply that the relevant entry has been lost – the records of the period are by no means complete – although it is not impossible that the cargo was wrongly recorded as coming from the 'Greenland whale fishery'. Given the confusion as to the actual whereabouts of the Greenland seas and the impossibility of knowing whether Captain Smith of the *Platoff* had actually collected his cargo off the coast of Iceland as the record of his ship's arrival at Gravesend would seem to imply, who can say what the Customs officer may have decided was its technical provenance? It is worth noting, though, that for some reason ice brought from Iceland and the Faroes was not so highly prized as that brought by the Greenland whale fishery vessels. The comparative values were presumably worked out by an assayer and based on the quality, thickness, clarity, hardness and staying power of the ice.* Since imported ice attracted *ad valorem* duty of 20 per cent, it was of some importance that its quality be carefully assessed, and that this was so is revealed by mentions here and there in the Customs records of the tonnage of ice landed as well as of its estimated value. In 1832, for example, a foreign vessel of the Greenland whale fishery brought in 500 tons of ice valued at £950, making the cost per ton, not counting duty charged, £2 0s. 0d. From Iceland and the Faroes, however, a cargo of 150 tons brought the same year was valued at £200, amounting to only 25 shillings per ton. Calculated on the basis of the first 1832 entry, the £700 cargo which had arrived in 1822 via the Greenland whale fishery would have amounted to about 400 tons. Of the comparative price of ice from Norway at that time no record has yet come to light, although we do fortunately know the explanation of the exemption from duty of ice brought in specifically for the use of the fishing industry. It was earlier in that very year of 1822 that the Treasury had granted the ice and fishing trades this important concession. In the wording of the Customs records, 'such ice as was intended solely for the purpose of the British Fisheries' was to be allowed in duty free, whether imported in British or foreign vessels, and the decision was duly reported to Customs officers at the ports of Berwick, Carlisle, Yarmouth, Harwich and London.[23]

---

* As the basis of investigation of the intrinsic value of ice an article in the *Journal of the Institution of Civil Engineers* for November 1848 cited the example of ice from Lower Canada being much colder than that from Upper Canada, which is colder than that from Wenham Lake, the ice from the latter being much colder than that formed in England.

It was an enlightened move on the part of the Treasury to exempt from duty ice imported for the fisheries, belated though the decision might seem, in view of the fact that it was over thirty years since Sir George Dempster and the Scottish fish dealers had proved the value of ice in the transport of fish. One may also speculate as to whether the concession was not a fairly easy one to abuse. Was it possible to ensure that ice landed into the fishing industry's ice houses was not on occasion resold at a profit to other tradespeople – confectioners, dairymen, club and hotel owners and the like? Or for that matter to private individuals? Was it perhaps from this time that it became customary for fishmongers to supply private customers with ice for the kitchen and the pantry?

Given the scarcity of records relating to the ice industry during the 1820s and 1830s, we can have no means of knowing whether or not the system of exemption solely for the fishing industry really worked, but it does appear that their Lordships of the Treasury may have realized that the rule was difficult to enforce, for from the figures available for 1825, 1828 and 1832, it emerges that they had halved the temptation to cheat by reducing the 20 per cent *ad valorem* tax to 10 per cent. Only one small import of ice is recorded for 1825, £150 worth attributed once more to the Greenland Whale Fishery, and £15 duty charged. When we come to 1832 there were the two cargoes already noted above, neither of which paid duty, plus £430 worth from Norway, with £43 duty paid.[24]

There the story of ice from the Greenland seas brought in specifically for the London confectioners appears to come to an end. We hear no more of the *Platoff* and must leave that curiously elusive vessel knowing no more of her ice-collecting voyage of the summer of 1822 than the few sparse facts I have set down. But at least we know that when Robert Gunter announced that he had received a cargo of ice from the Greenland seas he was not, as might easily have been supposed, romancing. We can see, too, that he was paying much less for Iceland ice which nominally did come from the Greenland seas than for the same commodity brought in by a whaler from further north, and which in any case would not have arrived until the end of the whaling season and the return of the ships to their home ports in late August or early September. So we know why he did not need to raise the prices of his fruit and cream ices that hot July.

The Inventors versus the Wenham Lakes

Those few cargoes of ice arriving spasmodically from the Greenland seas, from Iceland, the Faroes, and regions of Norway unspecified, constitute one of the most curious episodes in the whole saga of the growth of natural refrigeration and of the use of ice in the food industries of Britain. A footnote to the story, the sole part of it ever to be mentioned by the historians of refrigeration, is a letter written on 29 June 1828 by Richard Trevithick, the Cornish inventor, to his friend Gilbert Giddy, who had changed his name from plain Gilbert. In his letter, Trevithick, who had built the first working steam locomotive in Great Britain and had spent most of his working life on projects involving steam power, remarked that he had recently been in company where he had heard that £100,000 per year was being spent on ice brought by ships from the Greenland seas, and 'a thought struck me at the moment that artificial cold might be made very cheaply by the power of steam engines'.[25]

It was not the first time someone had been struck with that thought. In November 1823 the unnamed writer of an article published in *Blackwoods Magazine*, observing cartloads of Norway ice moving from the below-bridge wharfs in the early hours of the morning, reflected that 'perhaps an improvement or two as to the application of steam' might 'turn the seasons out of doors altogether'.[26] On Trevithick the effect of the exaggerated estimate of the value of the current ice imports – not questioned by Woolrich or others who have quoted the story – was to set him working on the practical possibilities of artificial refrigeration. Later in the year he lectured on the subject of *The Production of Artificial Cold*, and in this dissertation foreshadowed the design of a machine for simultaneously making ice and cooling air such as was later, in the 1840s, patented by Dr John Gorrie of Apalachicola, Florida, a man in his own time derided, but posthumously glorified as the pioneer of American air-conditioning. At the time Trevithick was employed by the engineering company J. & E. Hall, and although privately much preoccupied with refrigeration had little opportunity, beyond writing reports and making sketchy designs, to apply himself to the matter in a practical way. In 1833 he died. Ironically, a year later, the American-born but British-domiciled Jacob Perkins took out a pioneering British patent (No. 6662, 1834) for a vapour compressor refrigerator. Perkins, who had probably corresponded with, if he had not actually met, Trevithick, may well have discussed his invention with the latter, but other inventors, notably Oliver Evans, had long preceded Trevithick and Perkins in their dreams of manufacturing ice on a commercial scale, and the Greenland seas story was no more than a trigger which set off yet more unsuccessful attempts to make the replacement of natural ice by a machine-made product a feasibility. The ice-making capacity of Jacob Perkins's machine, built on a small scale in 1830 by John Hague of London, set up on a barge moored on the Thames somewhere west of the City, and driven by water power, was successfully demonstrated, but proved to be yet another of the mechanical ice inventions which was never followed up. Rather as Cornelius Drebbel's air-cooling apparatus – whatever it was – of two centuries earlier had been treated as something between a conjuring trick and black magic, the Perkins machine was evidently regarded as little more than an ingenious machine-driven toy. The mistake had perhaps been John Hague's, in building only a small-scale version of the invention which would not be taken seriously. Perkins, disillusioned, abandoned his inventor's drawing board and, although he lived until 1849 and was aged eighty-three when he died, invented nothing further.

Real ice, natural ice, meanwhile, was increasingly in demand in England, and supplies were soon forthcoming from a somewhat un-expected source. We hear no more now of ice from the Greenland seas, whether brought in by whalers or other vessels, and it was from the United States that in 1842 ice ships began to arrive. These were not Frederick Tudor's ships but those of two of his rivals in the ice business. The first cargo, brought over by the Gage, Hittinger Company of Boston which had so infuriated Tudor by its competitive price-cutting during the early years of the India trade, proved, as things turned out, a notably dismal flop. Quite why is not clear, given that there was a proven demand, but in spite of advance advertising in *The Times*, the approach seems to have been inept, and an attempt to sell American-style iced beverages to a gathering of middle-class British males met with a particularly hostile response. Without persevering, Gage, Hittinger and Co. for the time being abandoned any further attempt on the British market. Within two years, however, the newly formed Wenham Lake Ice Company of Boston, making a lively bid where their predecessors had failed, arrived with two cargoes of ice, one for Liverpool, one for London.

Establishing their London headquarters in premises in the Strand, with an underground vault to be used as an ice store, the manager of the company was astute enough to dispatch a large block of Wenham Lake Ice to Queen Victoria and Prince Albert at Windsor. The royal couple were much struck by the clarity and purity of the ice, and publicly expressed their intention of arranging for a regular supply. With that useful piece of publicity the company got off to a promising start. A massive block of their ice, frequently replaced from their store beneath the Strand office, was displayed in the window and this appeared, to the wonderment of the regular passers-by, to be indestructible. The simple and harmless deception helped to spread the fame of this remarkable product. It was the New Look ice. Advertisements for the company's own refrigerators or 'miniature ice houses' were placed in the London *Times*, and the required accolade for any innovation in English domestic custom was duly forthcoming from *Punch*, whose writers enjoyed several field days making fun of the whole enterprise, affecting not to understand 'the object of the company' or 'whence the profit is to be derived'.[27] The *Illustrated London News* meanwhile had already, on 17 May 1845, published a lengthy and informatively illustrated account of the ice-harvesting operation on Wenham Lake, the main substance of which was reproduced by the editors of the 1846 edition of Johannes Beckmann's widely read *History of Inventions and Discoveries* as an appendage to his already well-known paper on artificial cooling.

Altogether a great deal of interest had been aroused in the Wenham Lake venture, and in a relatively short space of time. The manager of the company had even contrived to bring Wenham Lake and its ice to the public notice of Sir Robert Peel, the Prime Minister, with a letter written early in 1845 asking if the remaining duty on imported ice could be abolished. Through his secretary Sir Robert replied that in his opinion there ought not to be any duty on imported ice and 'trusted to be enabled to include it among those articles to be exempted'. It was on 14 February that Peel's new budget, described as a massive exercise in tariff reduction, was presented to Parliament, and 430 of the remaining 813 articles in the Book of Tariffs exempted from duty.[28] While no specific mention of ice was made in this list, it has to be assumed that for some while already Customs Officers had been including it in a category known as 'Goods unenumerated, not being either in part or wholly manufactured, not enumerated or prohibited'. Duty on this category was abolished in the Peel budget of 1845.[29]

Whether it was the repeal of the import duties on ice or whether it was due to an increasing demand created by the Wenham Lake Company's clever publicity, the years between 1845 and 1860 were a period of rapid growth in the ice trade. It is perhaps not irrelevant that in his day – he died in 1850 – Sir Robert Peel was nicknamed the Refrigerator, owing, it is usually said, to his allegedly icy temperament but more probably, I believe, because of his support of the ice trade. At the time the term refrigerator, as applied to an icebox or ice chest, although familiar in the United States and already introduced by Frederick Tudor to British India, was comparatively new to Britain, and it was via the Wenham Lake Company that it was disseminated. It is notable that Thomas Masters, in his often quoted *Ice Book* of 1844, did not use, and seems to have been unaware of, the American term. He called his various patented ice chests Ice Preservers and Ice Safes, advising potential buyers that 'ice can be kept in these preservers for months, by continually adding a small quantity of ice every second day. By those who are in the habit of using ice, this may be employed to great advantage, as they would, by having a preserver, require to open the ice-house but seldom.'

The logic of the claim seems a trifle shaky. If you were to top up the ice in your safe every second day, where were you to obtain it from except by opening the ice house? Presumably, the idea was to convince those who had bought Masters's ice safe that they also needed his freezing machine.

As already mentioned on p. 174, Masters was confectioner to the Royal Zoological Gardens and the Royal Polytechnic Institution, at which establishments he demonstrated various apparatuses of his invention. One of these, it was claimed by the *Mechanics Magazine* of 10 February 1844, was 'little larger than an ordinary teapot but in less than four minutes manufactured two quarts and a half of ice cream, and in an hour would have produced full thirty quarts, more than enough for the largest private party'. The *Mechanics Magazine* writer, referring to sources of ice, mentioned that 'the cadger providers of our Gunters and Verreys continue, as in the days of Pepys, to lay every suburban pond from Stratford Marshes to Willesden Bottom under contribution'. He asserted that ice from Rotterdam was exported to Naples, and from New York to Calcutta and Hong Kong, and was aware that the ice trade between North America and the East Indies employed 'of itself, several ships'. Of the 1842 ice shipment from Boston to London the *Mechanics* writer had evidently heard nothing. To him the Masters machine was not so much about to revolutionize the ice trade as to abolish it altogether. 'We anticipate nothing less from it than the speedy and entire abandonment of the present traffic in natural ice.' His optimistic prediction referred, it should be explained, to the Masters method of freezing blocks of ice in conical moulds filled with water and immersed in a simple freezing mixture of snow and salt or pounded ice, in the proportion of three or four of ice or snow to one of salt. Hence 'the ice-wells of noblemen and gentlemen might be filled with the purest ice, without the trouble of skimming ponds'. A dozen moulds, made of zinc or galvanized iron, and measuring about 3 inches thick, 16 to 22 inches deep and 20 inches in length, could be immersed at one time in a wooden tray say 6 feet long, 2 feet wide and 18 to 24 inches deep, and great stress was laid by Masters on the advantages of the ice thus procured over ordinary ice from ponds and fields. A word of warning to the readers very slightly spoiled the effect of Masters's own confident eulogies. 'We still think it necessary to impress upon our readers how much depends upon the charging of it; if that is not effectually done, in nine cases out of ten, the operation must partially fail.' In other words, when the freezing didn't take, the operator had only himself to blame. The *Mechanics Magazine* writer, who watched a successful demonstration of the Masters freezing machine, saw 'a large circular tub or pail' weighing about 10 lb and about 1 inch thick, frozen into ice within half an hour. This, he revealed, was intended to serve as a wine cooler, an ingenious trick in that Masters used a container in which, as he explained, the water was frozen into a shape resembling a castle turret. It was another manifestation of the old ice goblets and bowls of the seventeenth century.[30]

The printers' ink can hardly have been dry on Thomas Masters's *Ice Book* when the Wenham Lake Company's very first consignments of their ice were landed on British shores. It must have been galling for Masters, not to mention for the *Mechanics* writer, with his confident prediction of the imminent extinction of the natural ice trade, when the very points in favour of artificially frozen ice which both had been at such pains to make were now taken up as selling points for natural ice imported from a foreign source and endorsed by the highest in the land.

The Wenham Lake Company advertised widely and made strenuous claims to support the quality of their ice over that of other importers. Many fishmongers and dealers in common rough ice 'profess to supply American ice to their customers, but it is only to be obtained from the Company's advertised agents, no other American ice than theirs being now in the country'. There had been a shortage of ice in the United States that summer and none was to be had for export. Explaining that Wenham Lake ice was frozen from pure mountain lake water, its promoters claimed that it was suitable for table use, could be put direct into drinks, placed in contact with jellies and other provisions, and owing to its solidity was very long-lasting. A half hundredweight weekly, it was suggested, would 'furnish a provision safe in which wines also could be kept always ready for use, and without the slightest deterioration'. Packed in hampers or blankets ice could be dispatched to the country in large or small quantities. In addition to the Strand depot there was a second London one in Oxford Street, and in the provinces there were Wenham Lake stores in Manchester, Liverpool, Birmingham, Hastings and Dublin. With a fleet of horse-drawn delivery carts sent out twice daily, at eight o'clock in the morning and three o'clock in the afternoon, the London depot of the Wenham Lake Company appears also to have been highly efficient. Anybody who sent in an order one hour in advance of either delivery would receive his ice by that very morning or afternoon van.

That other ice-importing ventures had rapidly been launched in the wake of the Wenham Lake Company's success, as has been assumed by ice historians,[31] was perhaps true, but two shipments which arrived from Norway in April 1846 may well have been simply a continuation of the earlier enterprise involving ice for the fisheries and the confectioners. Now, however, that arrivals of ice from Boston had attracted so much public notice, *The Times* had taken to reporting such shipments. On 23 April the paper announced that 'arrivals of ice from the kingdom of Norway continue ... two importations into the port of

The Wenham Lake Ice Company cart used for local deliveries.

London took place on Monday, one at Deptford, by the ship *Little Caterina* ... and the other by the *Johanna Margaretta* ... which arrived in the Regents Canal, having a cargo consisting solely of ice', amounting to 250 tons.

From *The Times* report it emerges that the winter of 1845–6 had been another exceptionally mild one such as those in the 1820s which had occasioned the import of ice from the Greenland seas and other northern regions to supplement supplies for the confectionery and fishing industries. In 1846 *The Times* remarked that these arrivals of ice from the continent of Europe must be 'a great source of convenience to the confectioners and others, to whom a supply of the article is considered an absolute necessity'. The report further explained that the Regent's Canal greatly facilitated the distribution of the ice from the Thames docks and, via barges, to the northern and north-western districts of the metropolis. There was also mention of carts having been observed issuing from Paddington in the neighbourhood of the Canal, loaded with ice for removal to the persons' private stores. 'At this advanced period of the season' the reporter thought that 'the ice-loaded carts presented a very novel and remarkable appearance'.

Oldest of the ice stores in the vicinity of the canal was a very large one belonging to William Leftwich, who had come from Aldford in Cheshire in 1795, aged twenty-five, to join relatives in London who made ship's biscuits. Around 1810 he set up independently as a confectioner at 162 Fleet Street, soon opened a similar business in Kingston-upon-Thames, and by 1882 had a shop in Throgmorton Street as well. In that year, after the hot summer of 1821 and the mild winter that had followed it, Leftwich chartered a vessel called *The Spring* [Yarmouth, Captain Clare] to bring about 300 tons of ice, in blocks of 20 cwt, gathered some hundred miles north of Trondhjem on the Norwegian coast. The ship and its load arrived in the Thames on 8 May 1822, and the particulars of load and duty paid make it clear that this was the second mystery ship referred to on p. 334. Having made a handsome profit on this rather speculative venture, Leftwich decided to go into the ice trade for good. In 1825 he had an ice well constructed at Cumberland Market, close to the new canal. 'Shaped like an inverted pear', 82 feet deep and 34 wide, the ice house could hold 1500 tons. Subsequently known as Arctic Wharf (James Street – now Jamestown Road – Camden Town) it took in both Norwegian and Greenland ice.

William Leftwich died in 1843, but the firm continued under his six children. A second ice well was constructed in 1857, during the fruitful reign of the youngest of the three sons, George, who had trained as an architect but took over the running of the ice business in 1852 and greatly expanded it until his own death in 1885. In 1910 ownership passed to the North Pole Ice Company, who continued to use the Leftwich name (a Royal Warrant of Appointment was issued in 1911 to George Leftwich & Co.) and the by then familiar green carts. When the importing of natural ice became unprofitable the company tried making refrigerators but without much success. All the same, the Leftwich name was still in use when in 1955 the first ice well was rediscovered (and promptly filled in) during work on the Piccadilly Line underground railway – the other one also briefly came to light and is now buried under a block of flats.[32]

The reporting in *The Times* of ice arrivals in the Thames resumed briefly in March 1848, but covered now by a different reporter. Recording an importation of an entire cargo of ice by a vessel arrived in the river from Leer, in Hanover, the new man remarked that this was 'the first arrival of ice from any European state, although there has already been one of considerable extent from the United States of America'. The Hanover one was 'the first of its kind as far as *The Times* could recollect', he repeated, referring to ice as 'this singular article of merchandise' and 'this novel arrival, giving the assurance of a probability of future supplies of the article from quarters whence we have not been accustomed to receive or expect them'. After so much wonderment on the part of *The Times* reporter, the cargo from Hanover appears to have been negligible – 'something less than 100 tons weight in bulk'. Three days later, however, on 31 March 1848, there were two arrivals from Wolgast in Prussia,[33] amounting in all to 200 tons, landed at St Katherine's Dock, 'where the U.S. ice used to be landed'. This was 'the first ever arrival from Prussia', *The Times* concluded.

The small cargoes from Wolgast on the Baltic coast of Prussia and from Leer in the Duchy of Hanover would hardly have made a dent in the Wenham Lake Company's British trade, but possibly, as *The Times* implied, there had been a hiatus in American deliveries to London. Back in Boston there were certainly signs that all was not well with the business. Ownership of the original company had already changed hands. In 1850 it suffered the indignity of being bought out by Gage, Hittinger & Company, the rival Boston firm which had so signally failed, in 1842, to sell its experimental cargo of ice to Britain.

Forced by the increasing demand in the United States, the Gage, Hittinger Company began to turn its attention more and more to the supply of ice for the domestic market, while Norway now began to take over the trade to Britain, France and Germany. Records at this stage are vague as to dates, but it is certain that Norwegian ice merchants had quickly learned the American methods of harvesting, storing and shipping lake ice originally evolved by the pioneers Nathaniel Wyeth and Frederick Tudor, and that trade in their ice to

Loading ice at Kristiania, Norway, 1900; from *Norge i det 19. aarhundrede.*

Britain very soon superseded that from Wenham Lake. What had happened, however, was that initially the directors of the original Wenham Lake Company negotiated the right, for commercial purposes, to rechristen the Norwegian Lake Oppegaard, near Kristiania, Lake Wenham, so that the ice harvested and exported from it still legally retained the name which in Britain had so quickly acquired a great reputation. Not all the Norway ice exported to Britain came from that one lake, but by association Wenham Lake had become almost a generic name, just as in the 1930s all mechanical refrigerators were known as Frigidaires and all vacuum cleaners as Hoovers.

By the 1860s the age of manufactured ice was at least in sight, and in 1870 the Sheryheton Ice Company set up a factory in Upper Ground Street, Blackfriars. It was London's first ice factory and its initial impact was small. For two more decades at least the Norway ice trade to Britain increased rather than diminished. The 'remarkable purity, cheapness and abundance' of Norway ice formed 'irresistible recommendations', or so at least was the opinion expressed by the unnamed author of an excellent article on ice and its storage which appeared in the very first issue of a newly launched trade publication, *The Caterer and Refreshment Contractor's Gazette*, dated 6 April 1878. The Norway ice ships were then carrying 500 tons or upwards and were unloaded at the Surrey Docks or Limehouse Basin, whence the ice was conveyed to the ice stores, still mainly, as in the 1840s, by canal barges. In the 1870s many of the ice ships were Carlo Gatti's – he is said to have owned twenty-four – and of the sixteen large London ice stores mentioned by the *Caterer's* reporter some half-dozen seem to have been his. The reporter may have miscalculated, for the 1862 *Trades Directory* listed sixteen ice dealers, several of them owning more than one store. At that time Gatti, listed for the first time as an ice merchant in the 1860 Post Office *London Directory (Commercial)*, had only two stores, one under Hungerford Market demolished two years later to make way for Charing Cross station, and the second in the New Wharf Road, Caledonian Road. An Innocenta Gatti of High Street, Notting Hill, is also listed as an ice dealer of that time.

Carlo Gatti's original enterprises, established by 1852, were a pastrycook's and confectioner's business at 33, 34 and 65 Great Hall,

Hungerford Market, and by 1856 also as an ice maker (meaning confectioners' ices) at 122 Holborn Hill, 90 Whitechapel High Street, and 254 Oxford St, plus a partnership with Agostino Gatti – his father or brother perhaps – and one Bolla, as chocolate manufacturer at 129 Holborn. The fact that Hungerford Market, now Villiers Street, had been built with ice cellars below for keeping both vegetables and fish may have influenced Gatti in his choice of premises. They were by the steps leading down to the steamboat pier below the market, and there he sold, in addition to confectionery and cakes, penny ices, wafers, cold soft drinks and hot coffee. His business must have been extraordinarily prosperous, for when Hungerford Market was demolished in 1864 he was paid the very large sum of £54,000 in compensation, or so it was reported in the *Illustrated London News*.

The building of Charing Cross station completed, Gatti reopened his establishment under the station arches, where it later became famous as the Charing Cross Music Hall. The equally famous restaurant in the Strand known as Gattis, was not, incidentally, part of Carlo's empire. It was opened in 1862 by two of his young nephews and was a café-restaurant, where according to Colonel Newnham Davis, writing in *The Gourmet's Guide to London* (1914), they made a feature of chips, a notable novelty at that time. The enterprising Gatti family came from the Italian-speaking Swiss canton of Ticino. Do we owe them that phenomenally popular culinary institution too? If so, that makes two innovations brought to London by the Gattis, for it seems certain that it was Carlo who popularized the ice-cream cart (see pl. 6) and penny ices sold in the streets, known as hokey pokey, a name which was simply a corruption of *ecco un poco* or 'here's a little', the phrase used by Gatti to persuade potential customers to try his ices.

Carlo Gatti the great ice tycoon was only sixty-one when he died on 8 September 1878, but his ice business endured and continued to expand for almost a century. By 1900 the London ice trade had become almost a monopoly operated by Carlo Gatti's successors, Carlo Gatti, Stevenson and Slater, later United Carlo Gatti. At that time the main Gatti ice depot was at Ransome's Dock, Battersea. Until the 1970s the firm's yellow lorries, which had replaced the original horse-drawn delivery carts, were still to be seen in London. In 1974, it was recorded

Inside a Gatti ice well.

These black and yellow Gatti ice carts were in use in London until
the 1950s.

by the editor of the journal *Ice Cream Topics* that the annual sales of Gatti's manufactured ice had reached 15,000 tons.[34] The quantity was no more than a fraction of the firm's past imports of natural ice from Norway. In 1896, one of the peak years of Norway exports, Gatti's successors had not only imported 204,490 tons, but owned ice stores adjacent to the Norway lakes from which 30,000 tons could be drawn out should an emergency arise. In addition, large-scale dealers such as Gatti often kept ships loaded with their ice cargoes lying in the fjords long before they sailed in March, and a ship could be dispatched within twelve hours. Ice-laden ships were even kept waiting in the Thames. It was during unloading and carriage to the stores that rapid melting of the ice often occurred, but so long as it was safely stowed in the holds of the ships there was little danger of wastage.

The author of the 1878 *Caterer* article recounted how he had recently boarded an ancient sailing ship, a privateer of the American war of 1774, but still sound and strong and loaded with a cargo of 300 tons of ice, as she was lying off Billingsgate. The captain's cabin had been like a refrigerator, he reported. 'Hot grog,' said the captain, 'is the only game to keep one's toes from falling off here.'[35] The ice vessel in question was not named by the *Caterer* writer, but he revealed that she had formerly been a whaler – one of those very ships, perhaps, which fifty years earlier had come to the rescue of the ice-starved London confectioners and fish dealers, bringing their livelihood-saving cargoes from the Greenland seas.

A bomba or sugar loaf ice mould.

Bomba

In the bleakest days of food rationing towards the end of the 1939–45 war, a Hertfordshire village greengrocer receives, for the first time in years, a quota of oranges. A local writer, Joyce Cunningham Green, with her family, is allotted twelve large shining fruit. 'Could we ever bear to eat the lovely glistening spheres? And how to spin them out?' There is prolonged discussion, nostalgic digressions about the crisp juicy orange sections covered with a thin toffee mixture that were served with *glaces pralinées* at the Arts Theatre Club in happier days, and memories of Gunter's tangerine ices.[36]

Like everybody else who had been taken to tea at Gunter's or eaten their ices at a ball supper, I too remembered, in the immediate post-war years, those wonderful smooth creamy delicacies. There had been also a rare warm summer afternoon in 1934 or 1935 at the Open Air Theatre in Regent's Park, when one of the leading ladies, Miss Margaretta Scott, as I remember, treated the cast of *Midsummer Night's Dream* to ice-cream ordered from Gunter's and sent from Berkeley Square in huge pots which were circulated among the company in pails of ice. What an inspired treat. Rich, creamy, pale pink strawberry ice-cream and slightly crunchy, grainy, bisque-coloured brown bread ice came out of those pots in a seemingly endless supply of voluptuous scoops. The women's dresses in that *Dream* production were Motley-designed, romantically pale pink, billowy, begarlanded with white flowers. The becoming dresses, the magical singing of Leslie French as Puck, the presence on that day, I think, of the legendary stage idol Henry Ainley, all combined with the Gunter's ices to create an absurdly idealistic memory of just one early evening between the matinée and the evening shows in Regent's Park. A rare occasion.

It was a distinctly less successful day, some fifteen years later, when I took a schoolboy godson to tea at Gunter's, then long since removed to Curzon Street, to find that the years of rationing had done – were still doing – their deadly work. In place of pale, fragile creams, coffee, strawberry, orange, apricot, vanilla, praline, so smoothly frozen they seemed like melting marble, were hard, crude ices smelling falsely of vanilla essence, dabbed with jam and mock cream. It had been foolish of me, in an England in which eggs, cream, milk, butter and sugar were either strictly rationed or totally unobtainable, at least legally, to expect anything else. My godson tells me he has no recollection of the occasion. That is perhaps fortunate for both of us.

It was at about this time, the early 1950s, that I began to harbour the delusion that when cream and eggs came back in plenty I would be able to discover how Gunter's had made their ice-creams in the great days. Accordingly, I bought any book which seemed to have bearing on the subject. The 1837 edition of Guglielmo Jarrin's *Italian Confectioner* was an early find, although it was some while before I tumbled to the fact that Jarrin had been one of Gunter's men, and that his book had initially been written under the aegis of James Gunter, founder of the firm, and published in 1820, just a few months after James's death. Jarrin, it turned out, had left Gunter's and Berkeley Square by the time the third edition of his book appeared in 1827, announcing himself on the title page that year as 'Confectioner, New Bond Street'. Already his book had become the English classic on the subject. Jarrin himself was careful to keep it up to date, adding supplementary material as necessity arose, and as the years passed having a new portrait and new plates engraved. According to the bibliographers, *The Italian Confectioner* was still being reprinted, in what must have been at least the twelfth edition, in 1861. In that same year appeared a different book, although one still based on Jarrin's work, entitled *Gunter's Modern Confectioner*, by William Jeanes, Chief Confectioner at Messrs Gunter's, Confectioners to Her Majesty, Berkeley Square.

William Jeanes dismissed Jarrin's book on the grounds that his recipes were no longer those in current usage at Gunter's, that many of the utensils he described had been superseded (some of them had been Jarrin's own patented designs) and that processes such as the making of pasteboard and of gold and silver paper, the spinning of glass, the art of engraving on steel and wood, were fully described, to the exclusion of more important matter. It is indeed the explicit directions for making and using the more elaborate paraphernalia of his trade as it was in the early nineteenth century that today make Jarrin's work so fascinating. How stucco moulds were made, how sugar was prepared for moulding, how gum paste figures were constructed, how different coloured golds for gilding wax and sugar ornaments were mixed by the gold-beaters, are detailed chapters which now make highly instructive reading, filling out as they do many gaps in our knowledge of Italian and French confectionery techniques, and describing skills now long forgotten and all but lost to us.

When, over thirty years ago, I bought Jarrin's book, it was, however, his ice-cream recipes which I found of primary interest. His basic custard was composed of 8 egg-yolks to a pint of cream and 6 oz of sugar. Even had there been any question of lavishing four weeks' egg ration on one single pint of illicit cream, this sounded a bit too rich, but using 4 yolks and one of those precious pints as a basis I managed a modified version of Jarrin's exquisite white coffee ice-cream, in which freshly roasted coffee beans were infused in the hot, sweetened cream, thickened with the egg-yolks to make, when strained, a most delicate coffee custard. This to me is the basis of one of the finest ice-creams in the world and in varying versions I still make it. Ironically, it is now the fine pale aromatic Java coffee beans I used to buy for this ice which have become almost unobtainable. Cream and eggs may be a financial problem, not to mention a health one, but at least they can be bought. Brown bread ice-cream in Jarrin's 1837 version – I discovered only later that it had not appeared in his 1820 first edition – was simple and successful, although I have improved it since, and his strawberry ice-cream recipe embodied an intelligent reminder that 'the mixture must be so managed as to be equal, neither the taste of the strawberries or of the cream must be predominant'. That may seem obvious enough, but the balance of ingredients in ice-creams and water-ices, just as vital as in sauces and fine consommés, is easily forgotten, and subtlety thereby sacrificed.

Undoubtedly there *was* something special about Gunter's establishment and Gunter's ices, or they would not already have achieved such fame that long before the mid nineteenth century a young man was apostrophizing a Gunter ball supper in terrible verse: 'Gunter, great man! had done his glorious best To warm the chilly heart of cold

A bomba Trinacria from Ciocca's *Dolci freddi e rinfreschi*, 1913.

December . . . his cailles aux truffes, his soufflé au gingembre, his Paniers de Chantilly' – this was in 1837, over three decades since James Gunter had made Chantilly baskets for the Prince of Wales's visit to Stowe – 'For the rest So glittering all and sweet I can't remember, Gelées and tourtes and cremes ad finitum, 'Twas easier far to eat than write 'em, Light airy things . . . But soft, the supper. Well, despite the weather, we sipped on ice and flirted with a trifle.'[37] After all, not such a bad evocation – and I have quoted only a fraction of it – of a fashionable ball supper in the year of Queen Victoria's accession to the throne. Nearly half a century later we find a more specific testimonial from Major L., author of *The Pytchley Book of Refined Cookery and Bills of Fare* (1885) – 'My only remark on the making of ice is that it should be quite smooth and not too much frozen. I do not think you ever get ice better than at Gunter's shop, where it is taken out of the freezing pot and put into no shapes.' Explaining that to retain the shape of a moulded ice-cream over-freezing is necessary, Major L. advised the ladies and gentlemen of the Pytchley Hunt that unless they had very good cooks they would do better to scoop all ices out of the freezing pots just before they are sent to table, and put them into a glass dish in spoonfuls as they are taken out. 'Ice should be quite smooth and soft enough to cut with a spoon.'[38] Note, in passing, the usage, still common at the time, of referring to ices as ice in the singular.

Major L. had probably hit the nail on the head. It was indeed difficult to gauge the exact moment to turn out a moulded ice. How to be sure that your guests would be faced with neither an intractable ice mountain all chips and icicles or a sadly flopped sprawl? Nevertheless ice *bombes* were evidently fashionable at the time. William Jeanes mentions 'bomba moulds' with a capacity of 4 to 6 pints, no doubt used for grand suppers, and intended for spectacular entrances at private parties, not for use in the Berkeley Square shop. In fact Jarrin had long since, in his original 1820 edition, published a recipe for a *bomba* ice which seems to have been a large-scale version of Lorenzo Magalotti's *candiero* or zabaglione (see p. 26), although without the perfumes of lemon leaves and jasmine petals. Sixteen egg-yolks, a pint of spring water, a glass of noyau or maraschino and a sugar syrup 'to your liking' were whisked over the fire as if you were whisking whites of egg, and 'when it is nearly up on the boil take it from the fire, continue to whip it until it becomes a light froth, then pour it into the freezing pot'. Turned out whole on to a dish insulated with a folded napkin, you had the option of scooping out the centre of the *bomba* and refilling it 'with cream ice of any other kind or colour'. By the time William Jeanes came on the scene forty years later the Gunter *bomba* had grown. Twenty-five egg-yolks, $1\frac{1}{2}$ pints of clear water, 1 pint of sugar syrup and 2 glasses of maraschino or noyau were now specified. One appreciates the necessity for moulds of 4 to 6 pint capacity. The method of freezing was crude. The mould, with top and bottom cover, was left untouched in the ice for three hours.

This zabaglione type of ice appears to have existed in Italy from the

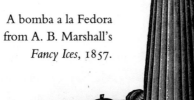

A bomba a la Fedora
from A. B. Marshall's
Fancy Ices, 1857.

The standard equipment and work place of the ice cream maker. From
Grifoni's *Trattato di Gelateria*, 1911.

very first, and was still much in evidence in 1914 when several different
versions of it were given in a modest book of family desserts, Adolfo
Giaquinto's *I Dolci in Famiglia* (Bracciano, 1914). It was then no longer
called a *bomba*, but simply *zabaglione gelato*, just as it still is in Italy, and
for that matter in London restaurants which bring in ices from one or
other of the Italian ice-cream factories operating in the capital. Curiously enough, I don't remember ever having come across a sabayon
ice in France. In the chic menu-speak of the 1980s, a sabayon was not
so much a dessert as a quite ordinary egg-thickened, lemon-flavoured
sauce which came on a plate underneath scallops or some other costly
morsels.

Another category of ice once highly thought of by fashionable
society in London as well as in France, Italy, Sicily, no doubt also in
other European countries, and one which was certainly among Gunter's particular specialities in the 1820s and 1830s, was the moulded
fruit ice. Of those complex confections, which relied rather more on
the arts of the mould-makers and the colourists – who finished off the

demoulded ices with the fine painting and brushwork required for the realistic representation of peaches, apricots, plums, oranges, bunches of grapes, pomegranates, figs and the like – than on that of the confectioner who made the foundation ices, William Gunter, younger son of James, founder of the firm, wrote proudly, 'these are among our triumphs, and deservedly. A summer dessert, at Windsor, would speak volumes on this subject.' That note appeared in William's *Confectioner's Oracle*, published in 1830 and obviously written before the death of George IV in June of that year. It provided further proof to the public of Gunter's services to the Royal household.

What had prompted William Gunter to exchange his ice spaddle for his pen? Could it have been at the urging of his friend Dr William Kitchiner, author of *The Cook's Oracle*? Certainly Gunter appears to have modelled his style as well as his title on that of Kitchiner, and with all too much success. Having apparently been given a classical education, he had subsequently, according to his own testimony, participated actively in the confectionery business, claiming that his

receipts for desserts in 'the most Economical Plan for Private Families' were founded on 'the Actual Experience of Thirty Years'. The lengthy experience was not very evident in *The Confectioner's Oracle*, a sketchy little book larded with Latin tags, and heavily besprinkled with caterer's French. Whenever possible and very often when not so, an italicized French word replaces a plain English one. A piece of pastry becomes 'a delicious *morceau* of confectionery', which same confectionery is 'no edulcorated Bauble but perfects the *jouissances* of life'. A dish is inevitably a *plat*, a fork is a *fourchette*, the Greek philosophers aren't much use in revealing the history of confectionery, Aristotle is too vague when he talks of a Macedonian dessert, but Suetonius tells him that *biscuits*, *compotes* and preserved fruits were known in the time of Augustus. I think William Gunter envisaged the bakeries of classical Rome as something like a Paris confectionery in the days of Louis XIV or Louis XV in whose times 'our art reached perfection'. One must hand it to Mr Gunter, however, when he decides to let Herodotus off a charge of yielding no useful information concerning 'the history of cates or beverages' on the grounds that the founding father of all historians did provide a story of 'one of the Ptolemies, who having conveyed his bevy of beauties up the Nile as far as the Island of Elephanta, entertained them and the Nobles of his Household with a collation served in double vessels lined with ice brought from the hills of Wady Halfa'. One would like to have had chapter and verse from Mr Gunter.

A quick canter through the year offers month-by-month advice and comment on the season's ingredients and entertainments. In June 'the strawberry, the raspberry and cherry are in perfection; the pale-faced and interesting cauliflower, with its powdered head, submits without a murmur to our gastrological caresses'. In July 'a dinner is out of the question. Now it is that *my* art is felt in all its enchanting influences: now the dessert *is* the dinner, and the guests have an air truly Homeric; – they are demi-gods and Hebes – feasting on pine-apples and candied orange-chips'. August is 'a month *de rien*; everybody buries him or herself in the country', and September is still a month *de rien*. By December things are looking up. 'Meat and vegetables are all excellent during this month; and on Christmas-day, the cup of abundance is emptied in sublime confusion on millions of tables.' In January, Mr Gunter reflects that this is 'of all the months in the year the most favourable to the enjoyments of the table provided of course that your host is RICH, and that the guest himself is also opulent, for he will have to play the Amphytrion in his turn'. 'A gastrologist without money,' Gunter reminds us, 'is one of the most pitiable creatures existing.'

It isn't difficult to make fun of the pompous style adopted by William Gunter in this *Companion to Dr Kitchiner's Cook's Oracle*, nor of the relentlessly smug and snobbish attitude of the prosperous British tradesman on hobnobbing terms with the Countesses, Duchesses and Honourables who flit in and out of his pages as though calling into the Berkeley Square shop to buy a pound or two of strawberry jam, or discussing in their own drawing-rooms the flavour of the ices for the next week's ball supper or the size of the bridecake for the Honourable Adelaide's wedding breakfast in June, but the truth is that he has singularly little solid information to offer. The odd assertion that the Spaniards are famous for their ices and that '*Agras*, or Green-Grape ice is the favourite' lingers in my mind. So does his advice to 'Always employ a journeyman gilder' and his rule that for a dessert for four persons 'you should have beside the plateau eight dishes around it, containing fruits, ices, biscuits, and preserves'. A recipe entitled 'Indian Ice' is notable because it turns out to be none other than our friend the egg-yolk *bomba* again. 'Whip up the yolks of 20 eggs with two glasses of any liqueur; pour it into a pan; add syrup: let it *just* boil; (stirring *well* with the whisk) take it off; put it in the freezing pot, which line with muslin. Turn it out of the freezing-pot *whole*, after having placed the last for an instant in warm water.'

The reason given by William Gunter for calling this confection 'Indian Ice', totally inconsequential as it is, is one of the most pleasing things in his book. 'This may appear contradictory,' he says in a footnote, 'but we are to recollect that some of the higher mountains in the world are in torrid India, and are perpetually capped with snow and ice. The beautiful Mrs Palmer, of Calcutta, at a table of extraordinary magnificence, is remarked for the quantity and tasteful varieties of ices which she introduces.'[39]

Thus abruptly is William Gunter's static and ungainly prose suffused with the scents of cardamom and cinnamon, of rose and jasmine essences distilled by Moghul perfumers. Saffron-coloured ices flecked with gold and silver leaf and powdered with pale green pistachios, frozen in tall silver cones, as in the days of General Sir Robert Barker, rise before our eyes as we visualize the magnificent table presided over by the beautiful Mrs Palmer. Who was she, and what did William Gunter know of her? William Palmer, Private Secretary to Warren Hastings, who died at Berhampore in 1816, had married an Indian princess, daughter of the ruler of Delhi. Was she the beautiful Mrs Palmer? Or was William Gunter alluding to the wife of John Palmer, second son of William and the Princess of Delhi, who had become a famous figure in Calcutta, known throughout the British India of his day as Prince of Merchants, and renowned for the magnificent scale of his hospitality? Whichever lady it was, she must have employed a good confectioner, one who knew how to make the best of such ice as was available to him in the days before the arrival in India of the first Tudor ice cargoes in 1833. The soft slushy ice created by induction on the old ice farms of British India was successful enough when used in the freezing of ices, provided you had plenty of it. Normally it was rationed to so much per household per week, but the Palmer family, who were prosperous bankers, may well have operated their own ice farm. As for Fanny Parks, whose husband, Major Parlby – she wrote under her maiden name – was in charge of what she called 'the ice concern' at Allahabad in 1838, long before the railway brought American ice up country, she asserted that their ices, made with cream from their own cows, were as good as any in England, mentioning incidentally that Gunter's jam was used as a flavouring for the ices made by her *abdar*. When her book was published she quoted Jarrin's recipes as her authority.[40]

The reputation of Gunter's products had travelled a long way from Berkeley Square. So well known was Gunter's catering that Captain Mundy, ADC to General Lord Combermere, C-in-C of the East India Company's armed forces 1827–8, alleged that young gentlemen newly arrived in Calcutta after a four- or five-month voyage from

England would discuss the merits of 'the last Gunter's dinner' during the early morning rides on the Strand. Poor young men, they must have been very homesick.

Shapes of Crystal

James Gunter, founder of the firm, and his elder son Robert were shrewd businessmen and property investors. James's market and nursery gardens in the villages of Earls Court and Brompton were enlarged by Robert. As London spread westward the value of the Gunter estates as building land brought the family a second fortune. In 1831 Robert was able to buy for his own eldest son, also Robert, a Yorkshire country house, Wetherby Grange, and an estate to go with it. In due course James, the younger son, was also established in a Yorkshire mansion bequeathed to him by his father. So it was that when the Earls Court and Brompton market gardens came to be built over, many of the new streets, gardens and squares were given Yorkshire names. Wetherby, Collingham, Gledhow, Courtfield, Barkston, Bramham, Knaresborough, Drayton, Redcliffe and a dozen more are localities familiar to anyone who has lived, worked in, or even driven through Kensington. Those places really had been gardens, fields, and groves, and their conversion to residential properties had largely been planned by the first Robert Gunter before his death in 1852. For other parts of the development, in contrast, the Gunters chose names recalling their Welsh origins. Tregunter Road, Gunter Grove, Gilston Road, named after an allegedly ancestral Gunter property near Brecon, and Talgarth Road, known to everyone who has driven from central London to Heathrow airport or vice versa, were all Gunter property. So were Edith Grove and Edith Terrace, close to Chelsea Embankment. The name commemorates a daughter of Robert the elder's second marriage who had died in infancy.

By the time the Boltons development – it was on the site of Bolton's Field, a property bought by the first James Gunter from the Boulton family – was completed in 1875, George Godwin, surveyor to the Gunter estate and editor of *The Builder*, was able to write 'Lo! The wand of Midas touched the soil, and up rose mansions instead of cabbages.'[41] The land investments made by the first two Gunters of Berkeley Square and Earls Court had certainly turned to gold. The second Robert and his brother James were now fine gentlemen and professional officers in the 4th Dragoon Guards who had both seen service in the Crimean war. James, Colonel of the regiment, was eventually promoted to major-general, and lived at Boston Hall in the West Riding, the property bought by the first Robert for himself and left to his younger son. The second Robert, who had transferred to the 3rd Battalion of the Yorkshire Regiment, was also promoted Colonel and in 1884 entered Parliament as Member for Knaresborough. From 1885 until his death in 1905, Robert sat for the West Riding of Yorkshire, and on 9 March 1901, Queen Victoria conferred a baronetcy on the eldest son of the confectioner whose sweetmeats and cakes she had known in her childhood at Kensington Palace and who had supplied so many of the suppers and collations she had attended during the early years of her reign. It was one of the last public acts of her sixty-four years as Queen.

Evidently neither Robert nor James Gunter the younger took an active part in the running of the Berkeley Square business and from 1853, the year following the death of Robert I, it is listed in the Post Office London Directory under the name of Thomas Gunter. There was also a Richard Gunter who concurrently had a confectioner's business at 23 Motcomb Street and 15 Lowndes Street, Belgrave Square. Whence their fruit and vegetables, their eggs and poultry, their cream and butter, had been obtained since the disappearance of the farms and gardens of Brompton, Earls Court and Chelsea, we do not know, but the coming of the railways, steamships, and by the 1880s even refrigerated ships, had eliminated many of the problems of supply which had confronted caterers such as the Gunters in the early decades of the century. By the 1860s Covent Garden market was bursting at the seams with cheap home-grown and imported fruit and vegetables, in and out of season. Although early peas and hothouse grapes and peaches might be only for millionaires, exotic fruit from the colonies was plentiful. It was easier and cheaper, for example, to buy pineapples at the London fruit market than in their places of origin in the Far East,★ so caterers such as Gunter had no difficulty in buying for their trade.

One thing we know for certain about the Gunters is that their business continued to flourish, and that that useful gift of getting its name into print without apparently advertising, with which the first James and the first Robert had been so amply endowed, had not failed the third generation. Gunter still carried the royal warrant. The name was still one that implied excellence in its own line, just as it had in the days when the famous Lord Alvanley, the charming chivalrous idol of the Regency clubs, bosom friend of the Duke of York, loved by all society from the King down to the least ensign of the Guards, automatically went to Gunter's when he wanted the best food and wines for an entertainment, and the devil take the cost. Once, in the 1820s, deciding to give a water party on the Thames, Alvanley turned over the organization of the whole event to Gunter, who hired the largest available boat and had it carpeted, canopied, and manned by twelve boatmen. Together with Gunter's dinner and Gunter's waiters, the bill came to 200 guineas. The occasion was reported in *The Times*, and if Gunter had to wait for his money, well, Alvanley's doings were always first-rate publicity. Another story related of his extravagance was of the intention he expressed to his *maître d'hôtel* of having a cold apricot tart every day of the year. 'Just go to Gunter's the confectioners and purchase all his preserved apricots,' he is supposed to have instructed his worried *maître d'hôtel*, 'and don't plague me any more about the expense.'[42]

As we know from Jarrin, the preserving of apricots and other fruit from the Gunter orchards at Earls Court and the putting into practice of the Appert system of bottling had been an innovation during the

★ According to Mayhew's *London and the London Poor*, the cheap West Indian pineapple trade dated from 1844, when pines were first cried in the streets 'a penny a slice'.

last years of the first James Gunter, and there was probably more significance in the Alvanley story concerning Gunter's preserved apricots than would appear to our modern eyes. At the time they were novel luxuries. Whether or not Gunter allowed his famous client to buy up his whole stock of them, or whether the story was an apocryphal one illustrating Alvanley's generally reckless spending, it was another one which made good publicity for the business. The royal dukes and their patronage helped. When graciously pleased to express appreciation of his home-grown hothouse pineapples, their compliments were returned by Gunter in the form of long-term credit. When the Duke of Sussex died in 1828, he appears to have owed Gunter nearly £700.[43]

It was not, however, just any nobleman who got away with indefinitely outstanding debts to Gunter and his fellow tradesmen. There had been a notable occasion back in the days of the French wars in 1798 when James Gunter, at the time a captain in the St George's Volunteers, banded together with some of his fellow officers, including 'Major Harrison the coal merchant', and refused to pay the landlord his rent for ground they were using for drilling until their demands upon his Lordship were paid. The Lordship in question had been the Earl Grosvenor of the day.[44] A pleasant piece of improvised justice exercised by the Mayfair tradesmen.

Gunter's business was already over a century old when in 1887 the nation celebrated Queen Victoria's Golden Jubilee. Evidently timed to coincide with that event appeared yet another book by an ex-employee of Gunter's, Samuel Hobbs, who called his work *The Kitchen Oracle* and announced himself on the title page as the author of *One Hundred and Sixty Culinary Dainties* and Late Chef to Messrs Gunter & Co., Berkeley Square. (The publishers were Dean and Son of Fleet Street, 'Publishing Office of Debrett's Peerage', who for some reason chose not to print a date on the title page. From internal evidence, however, it is clear that the year of publication was either 1886 or 1887.) Was Samuel perhaps a grandson or other relative of the W.H. Hobbs who in the 1820s had been lighterman to the Russia Company, owner of the *Platoff*, and clearly in some ways a business associate of the Gunter firm?

In a business-like Introduction Hobbs explained the plan of his work, which was an unusual one, indeed, so far as I know, unique for his time. Recherché dinners in the style known as *à la russe* were the main theme. A Bill of Fare for a dinner of eighteen to twenty persons was suggested for each month of the year. Each menu was followed by what Hobbs called a Requisition List, showing every item needed for each dinner. Then followed a detailed description of the preparation and cooking of every dish 'and its belongings; also how to serve each dinner, and when to commence its preparation'. The scheme was a very ambitious one, and it must be said that Hobbs did fairly carry out his promise. That the book on which he lavished such infinite pains remained obscure and appears never to have been reprinted was perhaps due to the very conscientiousness with which Hobbs had performed his self-appointed task. For the chef or the female head cook employed in 'every nobleman and gentleman's household' at which the book was directed, and in which Hobbs believed it would be 'a welcome visitant', study of this work must have been daunting. As might have been expected, given Hobbs's own career, it was more of a manual for the professional freelance caterer and chef than a book of instruction for the cooks of the Debrett world of country houses and great town mansions, however large the staff employed in those establishments. The food Hobbs described was very much caterer's food, elaborate presentations for ball suppers and wedding breakfasts, public celebrations, official banquets.

Three points particularly emerge from Hobbs's lists. One is the remarkable number of tinned and bottled foods he uses. Pineapples, peas, peaches (American) in tins. Tins of fat livers, pint bottles of truffles, pint tins of the same, quart cans of preserved American tomatoes, pint tins of champignons, pint canisters of apricot purée, Ponson's preserved apricots (preserved in Portugal – he mentions this firm several times), preserved gooseberries to be bought from the confectioners, *ragoût* in pint bottles, *pied de veau* gelatine bought by the $\frac{1}{4}$ lb, quart cans of preserved French artichoke bottoms. As against these rather dispiriting items there are frequent demands in the shopping lists for 2 lb each of fresh and salt butter, 30 eggs, 2 quarts of fresh cream and 2 of milk (the cream to be the best double cream, and very fresh), 24 lb of soup meat, half beef and half veal, without bones, 2 lb of gravy beef, 6 calves' feet, 1 ox-tongue, 4 young fowls of best quality, 2 old hens for soup, and so on. Your banquet or ball supper might offer bottled truffles and canned tomatoes in the sauces, canned peach mousse or a *compote* of bottled gooseberries among the desserts, but meat extracts, gravy colouring, custard powders, there were not. Nor did flavouring essences appear in the requisition lists. Vanilla beans were pounded with sugar; orange and lemon zests for custards, creams, and ices were scraped off on a 2 lb hunk of sugar from the loaf; there was no stinting on the sherry, maraschino and brandy for the kitchen; the cheese used in the cooking was invariably parmesan.

Two more of the points which strike a modern reader of the Hobbs manual, the first to a great extent dependent upon the second, are the quantities of elaborately moulded set creams and jellies described, and the very large amounts of ice called for during the summer months. The common belief that in pre-refrigerator days cool dry larders had adequately supplied the deficiency is evidently erroneous, or at any rate is so where London houses were concerned. According to Hobbs, writing as a freelance cook, he had encountered so many *bad larders* (his italics) that he considered a good refrigerator – by which he meant an ice chest – as necessary as a good bain-marie case. Since a Hobbs dinner usually involved the preparation of two soups, eight to ten different sauces and assorted small garnishes such as button mushrooms, quenelles, *ragoûts à la financière* and the like, all to be kept hot in their separate saucepans, the importance he attached to the bain-marie case is understandable. Indeed, Hobbs laid it down that the host or hostess lacking that essential piece of equipment should hire one from a confectioner or a coppersmith, while in the absence of a refrigerator rough ice should be kept in a tub or in a turbot kettle – another utensil taken for granted – in the larder.

Ice was still carried from Norway mainly in old wooden sailing ships, but Sir Robert Peel's abolition of the import duty on ice in the 1845 Budget and the scale on which it had since been brought into the country and distributed had resulted in progressive price reductions. In 1858 the retail price of Wenham Lake Ice had been 2d. per pound, but in twenty years it had fallen, provided you bought enough, to just over $\frac{1}{4}$d. a pound. In 1878 a Sunderland firm of importers, W.B. Harrison, was advertising fine Norwegian block ice in 2 to 3 hundredweight blocks at 2s. 6d. per hundredweight, 1 to 2 hundredweight at $\frac{1}{2}$d. per pound, and under 1 hundredweight at 1d. per pound. The ice was dispatched by the first passenger or goods train after receipt of an order by telegram or post. Packing and mats for the blocks were supplied free, and 3d. each allowed on the mats if returned in good condition.[45]

With ice at such a low price it was not surprising that during the summer months Hobbs would think nothing of calling for 2 hundredweight of rough ice for just one dinner party, with the occasional additional hundredweight of Wenham Lake Ice, from the fishmonger, brought in on the day of the dinner. As compared with the 15 lb per week reckoned a quarter of a century previously to have been the amount required to keep a large ice chest, 4 feet by 2 feet 8 inches by 3 feet 2 inches, properly charged, it seems a lot, but Hobbs was using rough ice for the kitchen, which was less than a third of the price of imported block ice★ but also melted more quickly, and was unsuitable for the table. 'Most pastry-cooks in the country have icehouses,' wrote Dr J.H. Walsh, FRCS, in 1856, 'and retail coarse and dirty ice, which serves tolerably well to freeze creams etc. but not for actually putting into beverages.' Dr Walsh had been a great advocate of Wenham Lake Ice, and was already then doing his best to explain to his readers that the temperature of ice could show wide variations and that it was cheaper in the end to buy Norway ice, even if it cost 4d. per pound, than to spend a quarter that amount on the local rough product which melted more than twice as quickly. Hobbs, however, adhered to the tradition of his calling and preferred on the whole to use 'pastrycooks' ice. Possibly he even owned an ice house. At any rate he was specific about its delivery. For a dinner to be given on 4 August a $\frac{1}{2}$ hundredweight was to be in the kitchen on the 2nd, another $\frac{1}{2}$ hundredweight on the 3rd, and on the day itself 1 hundredweight. By that time about two-thirds of the dinner was already

★ In the 1870s Carlo Gatti had been paying 14s. a cartload of about 30 hundredweight to the codgers or cadgers who brought ice to his stores. One hundred of these cartloads were needed to fill an icehouse 18 feet deep by 12 feet in diameter.

prepared. A quart of aspic jelly, a clear consommé of leveret, fillets of fowl for coating with the aspic, cream of salmon, sole fillets to be moulded in darioles and sauced with jellied mayonnaise, a boiled ox tongue, and a wondrous concoction of chopped cooked macaroni and béchamel enriched with a quantity of eggs which Hobbs called macaroni soup *à la reine* were all in the larder, each item surrounded with ice. The soups were in containers lowered into oval fish kettles with half a pail of ice packed around each. This, said Hobbs, would guard against the effects of a thunderstorm should one arise. He was certainly taking a risk with all those quarts of aspic and consommé. Even the ice might fail to save them from the effects of a violent storm or sudden heatwave.

The number of sweet dishes, and the quantity of each, is not the least remarkable feature of a Hobbs dinner. For this August spread, he specified two second course Removes, a peach ice pudding (fresh peaches this time) and a *gâteau diplomatique* with apricot sauce. The ice pudding requires 3 pints of cream, a glass of maraschino, 8 peaches and a glass of brandy for the sauce. The *gâteau* is made in a quart capacity *charlotte* mould and consists of a kind of jellied trifle made with sponge cakes, custard, mixed ratafias, cherries, brandy and angelica. This of course also required ice for the mixture to set, and would involve one person's attention for several hours on and off. In the intervals the dessert cooks could be attending to the four sweet entremets to be served after the Removes, two *macédoine* jellies and two *bavaroise* creams. These were to be succeeded by a cheese entremets, *croûtes au parmesan*. Then came ices, a cherry water-ice and a raspberry cream ice, to be brought into the dining-room on china or glass dishes, with two plates of ice wafers to accompany them. 'And thus the dinner has ended,' says Hobbs.

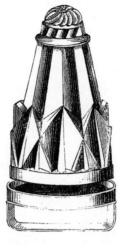

In its way this Victorian feast is no less awe-inspiring than a seven-teenth-century Medici banquet, particularly in the manner in which the desserts were presented. It was the heyday of the decorative mould, and the Hobbs school of cooking revelled in those crenellated, betow-ered, beswirled and colonnaded creations of the coppersmith's art and the porcelain manufacturer's skills. Minareted like the mosques of Stambul, many-domed as the Brighton Pavilion, as variously bespired as Ludwig of Bavaria's neo-gothic palaces, the jellies and creams, the *chartreuses* and *bavaroises* and *charlottes russes* of the Victorian age grew ever more fanciful in presentation (see pls. 7–9).

Looking at the displays of copper and china moulds often to be seen in country houses open to the public and museums devoted to the do-mestic arts, I have often wondered if the cooks and confectioners of the time really used those tortuously designed moulds, and if so, how any-thing set in them actually came out whole unless quite unacceptably stiffened with gelatine. The lavish use of ice during the setting period was a requisite. Saucepan after saucepan filled with rough ice and cold water was called for by Hobbs during the making of two quart-sized jellies *à la Victoria* made for a July dinner expressly designed with the Golden Jubilee celebration in mind. For this occasion $2\frac{1}{2}$ hundredweight of ice was ordered, 1 hundredweight of it to be the best Norway Wenham Lake product from the fishmonger, the remainder rough local ice. Gold leaf – six leaves of it – was blown into the maraschino-flavoured jelly in its liquid state, the leaves being broken up into tiny particles with a plated fork and, together with a couple of ounces of split or shredded pistachio nuts, distributed evenly throughout the jelly. If successful the gold- and green-flecked jellies would have been charmingly decorative. But, Hobbs makes it clear, no amount of gold leaf and jewel-like effects, such as whole bwhite grapes, strawberries and other small fruit embedded in the jellies, would compensate for lack of perfect brilliance in their appearance. Where jellies were concerned, a shining clarity was the very pitch of attainment. They should appear 'like shapes of crystal', Hobbs said.

The skills required for the successful confection of those shapes of crystal, those glassy sparkling spires, gold-flecked domes, pistachio- and strawberry-studded turrets, obelisks and columns, were those of craftsmen, and they are long since extinct. The *charlottes*, the *bavaroises*, the *chartreuses*, wondrous mixtures of layered creams, fresh fruits, variously coloured jellies and blancmanges built up in stages, each necessitating hours of finicky work and the use of not less than 28 lb of ice per mould during the prolonged setting process, were works of industry and of infinite patience. They ended up resembling small versions of fairytale palaces, mosaics of pink, white, lemon, ruby red and jade green, and as fairytale palaces do, they too have vanished, dematerialized. Only the moulds remain, dumb witnesses to the terror of many a kitchenmaid and confectioner's assistant called upon to judge whether the jelly round the strawberries were sufficiently set to allow of the next layer of gelatine-stiffened, rose-tinted cream being superimposed without danger of it seeping into and shamefully clouding the sparkle of the jelly beneath.

Studying Hobbs's extraordinary step-by-step directions for the construction – one can use no more appropriate word – of two *chartreuses* of strawberries *en surprise* to be presented at his Golden Jubilee dinner, it came into my mind that this meal was first cousin to one memorably satirized by Sybille Bedford in *A Legacy*. When I looked it up it turned out to be rather more opulent than anything Hobbs had described, an ostentatious bourgeois celebration in the Berlin of the 1890s: 5 lb tins of caviar afloat in silver coolers, Strasbourg terrines large as band-boxes, hot-house asparagus as thick as pillars, 50 plover's eggs in a nest of bronze twigs ... plumes of massed heads of pineapple ... a buffet displaying Supremes and Fondants, Velours and Claires, Masques and Glazes, en

Bellevue, en Chartreuse, en Savarin, en Bouquetière ... Richelieus, Figaros and Maintenons, Niagaras and Metternichs and Miroités ... en Sainte Alliance, en Belvedère ... en Demi-Deuil and Demidoff, Gramonts, Chimays, Souvaroffs, Albufera and Tivoli.[46]

In Paris, in Berlin, in Vienna, in London, in St Petersburg, the ceremonial food of the rich really was as Mrs Bedford described it, as Samuel Hobbs and the successful caterers, chefs and confectioners of the day bought and cooked and served it. The ice puddings, the Nesselrodes, the *soufflés glacés à la vanille* which in Hobbs's view were 'the best and most recherché of all the ice Removes sent to table', were the culmination of

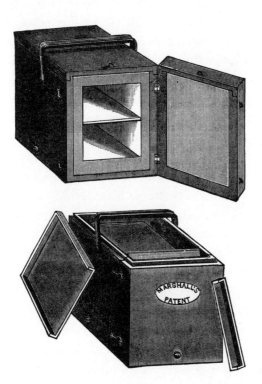

Ice cave from A.B. Marshall's *Book of Ices*, 1857 edition. 'Remove the lids and fill in between the metals with a mixture of 2 parts broken ice and 1 part salt; shake it well down so that the mixture goes underneath the cupboard of the cave, and fill well up so that the lid will just slide over the ice and salt. Replace the lids ... Place the mould (of frozen cream) for $1\frac{1}{2}$ to 2 hours in the cave.'

371

the long feasts of the late nineteenth-century upper classes. Towering 5 inches above the rims of silver or plated linings of soufflé cases – these were deep oval dishes, very unlike today's round white china ones – the ice puddings were presented in the containers in which they had been frozen in ice caves, the familiar small chests with double walls and door, the cavities packed with a freezing mixture of ice and salt. When poured into the case for freezing, a protective paper collar tied around the inside to the height of 5 inches, the soufflé was enclosed in its cave, and this in turn embedded in a large tub containing about 28 lb of crushed ice mixed with 2 lb of salt, more ice and salt – probably as much again – piled over it to the height of at least 6 inches. The freezing was begun at three o'clock in the afternoon and at half past five the cave was removed from the ice, the meltwater poured off and the tub repacked with fresh ice and salt. Back into the tub went the ice cave, there to remain until, as dinner neared its end, it was time to serve the iced soufflé. Divested of its paper collar, its top surface strewn with a handful of ratafias crushed to powder, the soufflé and its dish were set on a folded napkin in the centre of an oval silver charger and brought to table. Since Hobbs's dinners were timed to start at eight o'clock sharp, it would be well after nine o'clock before the ice pudding stage was reached and the *soufflé glacé* had been in the ice cave for six hours. Hobbs warned that a third charge of ice and salt might be needed, and that supplies of both commodities should not be spared. He remarked also that it was not given to every Tom, Dick and Harry of a confectioner to possess the art of producing a light and delicious *soufflé glacé* of the kind he described, and cautioned that 'many vile imitations are made to take its place'.[47] That one may readily believe. His recipe was a very difficult and ambitious one. Escoffier, in his 1934 *Ma Cuisine*, advised powdered gum tragacanth to help set his iced soufflés and mousses, he whipped the mixture over ice rather than over heat, and specified that it should rise only $1-1\frac{1}{2}$ inches above the rim of the dish. As compared with the 5 inches demanded by Hobbs, Escoffier's effort was rather modest.

To Cool the Air:
Ice Pillars and Lily Pools

A feature of London society dinners of the three final decades of the nineteenth century which had much changed since the 1830s, when Queen Victoria came to the throne, was the decoration of the table, the arrangements of the flowers, the centrepieces and the desserts. Now service *à la russe*, with each course handed round successively by footmen, firmly supplanted the old fashion when most of the dishes had been placed on the table simultaneously and the dessert had been almost a separate meal in itself. The new fashion required a tall, standing centrepiece of choice fruit flanked by lower and smaller dishes filled with sweetmeats and bonbons, alternating, if the table were large enough, with vases of fresh flowers. All remained on the table throughout the meal. The display of silver and cut-glass dishes, the variety of the sweetmeats and the novelty of the flower arrangements for the table had now become the subject of keen competition among hostesses (see pl. 11).

In the great country houses it was still the head gardener who dictated which flowers and fruit were to adorn the dinner table and the dessert, and often it was his responsibility to create the whole effect, trimming the table with trails of vine leaves, ivy or ferns which in the candlelight threw attractive shadows on the tablecloth as the guests settled into their places for dinner. At a time when pre-dinner drinks – other than the surreptitious swig while changing into dress clothes – were unheard of, the provision of some such ice-breaking gambit was very necessary. In London, the task of decorating the table was increasingly being taken over from the upper servants by professional florists or, as the 1891 edition of *Household Management* put it, 'by people who devote their time to this pleasant occupation'. Hence the revival of the table fountains of seventeenth-century Italy, the miniature lily pools and the mirrors of the Louis XV era as parterres, with low curved glass vases filled with massed small flowers and bright green moss forming borders which were reported as being popular in Diamond Jubilee year. Predictably, the flowers that year were red roses, white daisies, blue forget-me-nots.

It was at about this period, too, that amateur flower arrangers began to take up this occupation, at the same time genteel and artistic, which admitted them into the confidence of the rich and great almost on the same terms as those of a Gunter arranging a ball supper, or of a Samuel Hobbs organizing a dinner. It was the privilege of moving freely in and out of the homes of 'people whose names are in the papers', as Henry James wrote when he cruelly caricatured the pathetic pretensions of such a personage in his 1898 novel *In the Cage*, that was the great attraction of what he called 'this new profession'.

Mrs Jordan – 'I *do* flowers you know' – a clergyman's widow with 'extraordinarily protrusive teeth', is friendly with the young girl behind the wire screen in the Mayfair sub-post office who takes in the telegrams which in pre-telephone days were society people's most effective means of rapid communication and their favoured method of conducting their social lives. By telegram they issued and declined invitations, made appointments with their milliners and dressmakers, placed their racing bets, carried on their illicit affairs. The younger woman is not entirely impressed by Mrs Jordan's boasts, but the lady presses on gamely. 'If you were to see me some day with a thousand tulips' (at a shilling each), she throws out. She was made free of the greatest houses, she did the dinner tables, often set out for twenty, she explained. 'The great people were waking up to the gain of putting into the hands of a person of real refinement the question that the shop-people spoke of so vulgarly as that of the floral decorations. You know the look they want it all to have? – of having come, not from a florist, but from one of themselves.' Alas for her aspirations, Mrs Jordan never does become 'one of them', never, in fact, Henry James implies, gets much beyond creating the effect of a vicarage dining-table or perhaps of the parish church decked out with spring flowers. So much, poor lady, for those thousand tulips. In the end Mrs Jordan gets engaged to Mr Drake, 'a person who, flanked by two footmen, opens the door'. In other words, a butler.

In spite of his acute eye for the movement of fashion, Henry James missed describing one which nevertheless he must often have seen in London, one which had been imported from his own native America. This was the decorating of dinner tables with small blocks of ice and the cooling of reception and ballroom with very large ones. The idea had reached London in the mid 1840s, following the early shipments of Wenham Lake ice from Boston to Britain. Already in the summer of 1845 the *Liverpool Times* was reporting, in a long article on the subject of the new American import, that even the cooling of large crowded rooms could be effected by placing a block of the Wenham Lake ice in a passage where a current of air could pass over it ... and hence its introduction at the routs and *conversaziones* of the nobility of London, especially the Foreign Ambassadors ... [1] By the fifties the Norway ice trade had supplanted the true Wenham Lake product, but one of the Norwegian ice lakes had been formally renamed Wenham Lake, so that the ice on fashionable British tables, however Scandinavian its origin, could still legitimately be called Wenham Lake ice. The writer of the 1845 *Liverpool Times* article had reported that 'merely as decoration of a dinner table this beautiful ice, its crystal-like transparency reflecting and refracting the lights of the chandeliers' was already becoming quite a feature of London society entertainments. By 1860, when Surtees published his novel *Plain or Ringlets*, the fashion was well established in the provinces. When Mr O'Dicey, one of the chief protagonists of that novel, gives a slap-up dinner at the Dolphin Hotel, Roseberry Rocks, a well-patronized seaside resort, the table is laid in the latest *à la russe* manner and sports an impressive table centrepiece consisting of 'a splendid vine-wreathed-pillared A.B. Savory epergne full of cut flowers, with four thickly cut glass side-dishes filled with transparent Wenham Lake ice'. The ice in the cut-glass dishes was evidently intended for precisely that decorative purpose described by the *Liverpool Times* in 1845. At any rate, although the wines were plentiful and ostentatiously varied – Bordeaux, Johannisberger, Steinberger, old dry Sillery and creaming champagnes, ending with a Clos Vougeot presented 'in a cradle with all the pomp and circumstance peculiar to Babies and Burgundy'² and accompanied by 'some nice fresh Parmesan Cheese', the ice is never again mentioned. Had it been destined to cool the wine rather than merely to refresh the eyes of Mr O'Dicey's guests, Surtees would certainly have let his readers know. His detail in such matters was always revealing, particularly so of the social niceties and current eating and drinking fads.

By 1872, when Frederick Warne's *The Modern Housekeeper*, compiled and edited by Doctor Ross Murray, was published, the use of ice for table decoration had progressed rather beyond its simple appearance in cut-glass dishes and was being used in far more conspicuous forms. A novel table centre for the summer, fully described in *The Modern Housekeeper*, was a towering three-tier glass stand, the base shaped into a deep bowl with a wide rim on which small flower heads and leaves were arranged, while inside the bowl were arranged a few fine water lilies. On the second tier were more water lilies and on the third a small block of clear ice, wreathed with little bunches of violets and charmingly crowned with another little bouquet of the same. The delightful coloured plate illustrating this ingenious contraption shows the melting ice cascading softly down like a transparent veil into the basin below, floating the beautiful cool water lilies to the surface (see pl. 10). Very properly, the caption writer warned that the ice must be in exact proportion in size to the volume of water which the lower basin would contain. One hopes that the device was sold with an instruction leaflet giving the correct dimensions of the block of ice to be poised on the summit, otherwise some sadly watery dinner tables must have resulted.

Water lilies and ice – an obvious enough combination perhaps, and certainly a very decorative one – recur when it comes to a spectacular method of cooling the stifling ballrooms of the London summer season. An extension of the simple blocks of ice mentioned by the *Liverpool Times* in 1845, this was described in the editorial pages of *The Modern Housekeeper* as the most novel and 'delicious mode of decorating a ballroom' and had been introduced during 'the last season

... Pillars of solid blocks of Norway ice, clear and sparkling like diamonds, were placed at intervals down the room on each side'. Standing in great pans in which water lilies had been placed, the ice pillars slowly melted in the heat and as they dripped into the huge stone tubs the lilies floated on the water. 'The coolness of the air produced by this device can scarcely be conceived if not felt,' wrote the delighted Dr Ross Murray.[3]

The new fashion evidently caught on, no doubt happily abetted by the Norway ice importers. The celebrated Carlo Gatti, of music-hall and hokey-pokey fame, was at the time one of the most flourishing of those ice merchants, operating a fleet of twenty or more ice ships, massive ice stores in Battersea and Hackney and several more in North London, plus a land fleet of horse-drawn delivery vans. Gifted with a singular flair for publicity, Gatti may well have been behind the newest craze for air-conditioning by means of massed blocks and pillars of ice. Cumbersome and messy though they were, ice blocks used in such formidable quantity were obviously effective enough as a cooling device, and for well over a quarter-century after Ross Murray had introduced a wide public to the novelty of 1871, the system was still in fashion. In the summer of his mother's Diamond Jubilee, on 20 July 1897, the Prince of Wales gave a great dinner and reception at St James's Palace. The occasion was the celebration of his appointment as Grand Master and Principal Knight Grand Cross of the Order of the Bath. Between seventy and eighty members of the Order were present. The centrepiece on the principal table was the Prince's great silver bowl with a fountain spraying rose water, surmounted by a second bowl filled with roses. Massive silver candelabra of the same service, brought from his residence in Marlborough House, provided the lighting. The picture gallery had been converted for the evening into a smoking saloon – it was the Prince of Wales who had introduced after-dinner smoking, at the time regarded as a welcome relief from the heavy drinking of former days – and all the apartments contiguous to the banqueting hall, including the Council Chamber and the Throne Room, were opened up so the guests might stroll around and admire the sumptuous ornamentation, the portraits, the floral displays, and the cooling ice blocks placed along all the corridors. The account

of the entertainment, published in *The Epicure* of August 1897, concluded with the observation that the Prince had not needed to draw
upon the great gold pantry at Windsor to bedeck St James's Palace but
had had the rooms decorated with the collection of silver trophies he
had accumulated during half a lifetime of representing the Queen in
all parts of the world.[4]

As the ice extravaganza of the time went, however, it must be
admitted that the Prince of Wales's blocks of ice standing like sentinels
among the roses in the corridors of St James's Palace, and even the
crystal-ice pillars rising from water-lily pools in the ballrooms of
fashionable London, were rather upstaged by the Paris Ritz when one
hot summer night the garden of the hotel was tented over and turned
into a gorge 'apparently somewhere near the North Pole'. The scene
was described by Colonel Newnham-Davis in his *Gourmet's Guide to
Europe* of 1903. Blocks and pillars of ice were everywhere, the Colonel
recorded, but 'the anteroom was a mass of palms, and the idea of the
assemblage of the guests in the tropics and their sudden transference
to the land of ice was excellently carried out'.[5]

To many an old traveller, to a Della Valle, a John Fryer, a Thévenot,
a Tavernier, a Bernier, a Jean Chardin, the theme of the Ritz fantasia
would have been a reminder of wearisome rides across the parched
deserts of Persia as at last they came in sight of the snow-capped
mountains beyond Tabriz, or of terrible sufferings as they all but
succumbed to heat and thirst on their journeys from the burning
plains of India to the icy passes of the Himalayas. To an African
explorer both palms and pillars of ice would have been a desert mirage
made manifest. And the men who sailed to the Greenland seas, men
like the crew of the *Platoff*, who had steered their vessels safely
through deadly peril by fog and iceberg in order that the caterers
and confectioners of Western Europe might not go short of ice at
midsummer – would their reactions have been entirely those of delight
when they saw the garden of a luxury hotel in Paris transformed, as
though in a pantomime, into a polar palace with crags of real ice
dripping on the grass? But in France, by the turn of the century, those
pillars and crags and floes had most probably not been transported
from the frozen lakes of Norway nor hewn from an Alpine glacier or

some ice-bound mountain cavern but quite simply delivered by horse-drawn carts from a Paris factory.* Now that really would have impressed the early inventors, the chemists, the scientists, the Della Portas and Cornelis Drebbels of the sixteenth and seventeenth centuries who had dreamed of and experimented with air cooling as well as with artificial freezing but who had certainly not envisaged being able to make ice on a scale large enough to turn a whole summer garden into one great ice palace. But frolics such as the Ritz occasion were short-term experiments, entertainments for the privileged few, and transient as those snow mountains which early in the third century AD the Emperor Heliogabalus is supposed to have had built up in the grounds of his villa near Rome.[6]

* In France it was about 1895 that natural ice, either imported or from domestic sources, began to be substantially supplanted by manufactured ice. Before that time considerable quantities of Norwegian ice were brought into Paris and other cities of the interior via the port of Dieppe, but fifteen years later France was producing 150,000 tons of factory ice per year and using only 50,000 tons of natural ice.

ICE PYRAMIDS

FOR DANCES,
RECEPTIONS, &c.

WE retain the services of an expert for the above purpose. These Pyramids form an ideal addition to the decorations, and are effective in keeping the rooms cool. Carefully decorated with flowers and placed in the corners of a room, they reflect the numerous lights and present an indescribably attractive appearance. Orders received in the morning can be executed for the evening.

Stands, as illustrated, for supporting Pyramids and receiving the water as the ice melts, supplied FREE OF CHARGE.

Style B.

Style A.

High - Covered with Red Baize and finished with Gold Braid.

Style B.

Low - Japanned Green and finished with Gilt Line.

Style A.

Notes

[The notes are not always complete, because in some instances it has proved impossible to find full details of Mrs David's sources.]

Introduction

1. Sylvia P. Beamon and Susan Roaf, *The Ice-houses of Britain*, London, Routledge, 1990, p. 7.

2. ibid., p. 8.

3. Athenaeus, *The Deipnosophists*, with an English translation by Charles Durton Gulick, 7 vols., London, William Heinemann, 1927, vol. 6, p. 129.

4. ibid., vol. 2, p. 77.

5. Plutarch, *Symposium*, VI, Quaest. 6.

6. Alexander Henderson, *The History of Ancient and Modern Wine*, 1824, pp. 107–8.

7. Margaret Newett, *Canon Pietro Casola's Pilgrimage to Jerusalem in the Year 1494*, 1907, p. 229.

8. *Voyages du Père Labat en Espagne et Italie*, 8 vols., 1730, vol. 3, p. 343.

9. Andrew Lumisden, *Remarks on the Antiquities of Rome and its Environs*, 1797, p. 464.

10. Beamon and Roaf, op. cit., pp. 15–16.

11. Elizabeth David, *Fromages Glacés and Iced Creams*, in *Petits Propos Culinaires*, 2, London, 1979.

12. Philip Miller, *The Gardener's Dictionary*, 8th edition, 1768.

13. *The Gardener's Journal*, quoted in Spon's *Household Manual*, c. 1887, p. 115.

14. J.B. Papworth, *Rural Residences*, 1818.

Florence

[References carrying the initials [S.B.] are those so generously supplied to me by Dr Suzy Butters of Manchester University.]

1. *The Complete Works of Montaigne, Essays, Travel Journals, Letters*, translated by Donald M. Frame, London, Hamish Hamilton, 1965, p. 1006.

2. ibid., p. 929.

3. *La Cronica Domestica di Messer Donato Velluti, scritta fra il 1367 e il 1370, con le addizioni di Paolo Velluti, scritta fra il 1555 e il 1560.* Florence, G. C. Sansoni, 1914, xxx, 179. *Folgore da san Gemignano*, 13th–14th c. Translated Dante Gabriel Rossetti (1828–82), *Complete Poems*.

4. Guardaroba 77 (Debitori e creditori della Guardaroba del Serenissimo Gran Duca di Toscano, Segnato A), 1570–74 [S.B.]. Mediceo del Principato 5125, register of Cardinal Ferdinando dei Medici's letters, 1570–77, c.10 verso [S.B.].

5. M. Piero Nati da Bibbiena, Medico & Filosofo. *Breve Discorso Intorno alla natura del Popone, & sopra il cattivo uso del ber fresco con la Neve*, 10–14. Published together with a treatise on vinegars by Antonio Donato d'Altomare, Medico & Filosofo napoletano, translated from the Latin into vulgar Florentine, and under the main title *Modo Facile et Ispedito da Conservarsi Sano Ne Tempi Pericolosi Della Pestilenza.* Al Serenissimo Don Francesco Gran Duca di Toscana. Florence, Giorgio Marescotti, 1576. The treatise on the safeguarding of health in times of plague appears to be anonymous.

6. Capitani di Parte, Numeri Neri 1466, no. 244 [S.B.]. Mediceo del Principato 247, Grand Duke Francesco to Benedetto Uguccioni, cc.74 verso 75, 21.xi.1577 [S.B.].

7. Mediceo del Principato 1189, inserto 12, Benedetto Uguccioni to Cavaliere Serghuidi, 12.11.1582 [S.B.].

8. P. Letarouilly, *Edifices de Rome Moderne* ..., Liège, 1849–53, 421–70, Planches vol. 2, Pl. 221.

9. Mediceo del Principato 5125, register of Cardinal Ferdinando dei Medici's letters, 1570–77, c.10 verso [S.B.].

10. Mediceo del Principato 247, cc.8 verso–9 recto, Grand Duke Francesco dei Medici to Signor Mafio Veniero, 10.viii. 1577.

11. Dott. Cav. Alberto Cougnet, gastronomic historian, in a Preface to the third edition of G. Ciocca's *Il Pasticciere e Confettiere Moderno*, 1921, p. lxx: 'the secret of making sorbetti was for many years retained in the Medici family. The chronicles of the French court record that the first *gelati* served at the Louvre date from 1533; but since the Florentine confectioners and *gelattieri* [ice-cream specialists] of the Louvre gave away none of the secrets of

their art, the Parisians had to wait another century before tasting ices.' Dottore Cavaliere Cougnet gave no documentary evidence to support his tale. It is of course a fairytale. Elsewhere in the same Preface (p. xliii), Cougnet asserts that 'the art of freezing and condensing to a succulent snow those juices prepared by the sherbet-makers of the East was practised from remote times'.

12. G. E. Saltini, *Tragedie medice domestiche, narrate su documenti*, Florence, Barbera, 1898, 299–302. Letter written by Gianvettorio Soderini to Silvio Piccolomini on the deaths of the Grand Duke Francesco and Bianca Cappello. Quoted in Della Stufa's *Pranzi e Conviti*, 1965, 118 and 190 n. 79.

13. Michelangelo Buonarroti il Giovane. *Descrizione della felicissime nozze della Christianissima Maesta Maria Regina di Francia e di Navarre*, Florence, 1600, 16.

14. John Evelyn's *Diary*, Oxford, Oxford University Press, 1949.

15. Ascario Condivio, *The Life of Michelangelo*, trans. A. S. Wohl, Baton Rouge, 1976, p. 15.

16. Mediceo del Principato 1257. No pagination. Bernardo Buontalenti to Lorenzo Usimbardi, 14.vi.1598 [S.B.].

17. Capitani di Parte, Numeri Neri 1473, n. 6 [S.B.].

18. ibid., nn. 230, 231 [S.B.].

19. Dott. Giovanni Gaye, *Carteggio inedito d'artisti*, Florence, 1840, iii, 536.

20. Capitani di Parte, Numeri Neri 1476, n. 455 [S.B.].

21. ibid., nn. 445, 3111 [S.B.].

22. Manoscritto (Spoglio Mariti) c.50, Palchetto 106, Filza 1617.1618; c.58, Palchetto 106, Filza 1621.1625 [S.B.].

23. Francesco Redi, *Bacco in Toscana*. Composed 1666 and 1685. *Collected Works*, Milan, 1809, vol. I, p. 10.

24. The *cantimplora* of Spain and the *chantepleure* of France, although related in name and appearance, were only distantly so in fact. For example Cotgrave (1611), like Covarruvias, gives the meaning of *chantepleure* as a gardener's watering pot and makes no suggestion that it was ever a special vessel for chilling wine or water, while its main modern meaning, according to Harrop (1940), is a 'wine funnel (pierced with holes)' and its alternative 'a long-spouted watering-can, sprayer'.

The *cantinplora* of Italy has also undergone further changes. The modern *Grande Dizionario* goes into the history at some length. Among interesting points are that the Spanish word derived from the contraction of two Catalan verbs, *canta i plora*, to sing and to cry, and that it reached Italy from Spain in 1543. According to Corominas the word first appeared in Catalan in 1460. A variation in the same language was *chanaplora*. Rigutini is quoted (from his *Dizionario dei Sinonimi*, Milan, 1957) as saying that at present it is a large pewter (*stagno*) flagon with a big, low, flattened body and a long neck wide enough to put a fist in. It is used solely for chilling water and is placed in a wooden tub which it almost entirely fills, and when filled with water the body and neck of the bottle are surrounded with ice. Cassell's *Italian-English Dictionary*, 7th edition 1967, gives the original Spanish spelling *cantimplora* and renders it as ice-pail, wine cooler.

The modern *cantimplora* of Spain, according to Cassell's *Spanish-English Dictionary*, 1970 edition, is a siphon, alternatively water-cooler and water bottle. A French variation I have come across is *champoreau*, a stoneware vessel with a hermetically sealing stopper, two big handles, and a pouring tap. This was a kind of coffee urn designed to be placed inside another vessel made of metal which, filled with hot water, acted as a bain-marie, and in summer could be filled instead with ice. The device appears to be a descendant of Scacchi's japanned calidarium cum frigidarium.

25. Richard Lassels, *The Voyage of Italy, corrected and set forth by his old friend and fellow traveller S.W.* Printed at Paris by Vincent du Moutier 1670, I, 2. Lassels, *c.* 1603–68, made five prolonged journeys into Italy, between 1638 and *c.* 1662, conducting young gentlemen on the Grand Tour.

26. Francesco Redi, *Arianna Infirma*, 2, 103–15, 117–52.

27. ibid., 1, 293–5.

28. Published in *Saggi di Naturali Esperienza*, Florence, 1667, translated into English by Richard Waller, FRS, under the title *Essayes of Natural Experiments*, London, 1684. The Cimento was disbanded in 1667, after only ten years of existence.

29. Redi, *Arianna Infirma*, 1, 293–5.

30. ibid., 1, 25; 2, 108; 2, 134.

31. *The Travels and Memoirs of Sir John Reresby, Bart ... During the Time of Cromwell's Usurpations . . .*, 3rd edition, London, 1831, p. 101.

32. Lassels, op. cit., 1698 edition, 14.

33. *Le usanze fiorentine del secolo xvii descritte del Cav. Tommaso Rinuccini*, Florence, 1868, 20–21.

34. Redi, *Arianna Infirma*, 2, 138.

35. Lassels, op. cit., 1670 edition, 1, 2.

36. *Agaricus pruneolus*, the delicate little woodland mushroom which appears with the early spring rains and continues into summer and autumn. The Italian name, meaning little plum, refers to the bloom on the young mushrooms. In English the *prugnolo* is called the miller's mushroom, from its supposed scent of meal, and in French *mousseron*. In Italy *prugnoli* were artificially cultivated from an early date.

37. *Piegatura*, the decorative pleating and folding of napkins, and making them into *trionfi*, was a whole art form, in which the butlers and their aides were required to be proficient. A famous work illustrating the art is Mattia Giegher's *Tre Tratatti*, three treatises dealing with carving at table, the duties of stewards, and linen-folding. Mattei often directs that there be four *trionfi* for the table, two each of sugar work and *piegatura*.

38. Marguérite-Louise despised her humourless, unattractive young husband, took against all things Florentine, and was resolved to return to France almost from the day she landed in Italy. After the births of three children and fourteen years of domestic strife and rebellion, the Princess, by that time Grand Duchess, was given permission by Louis XIV to return to France on condition she retire to the Abbey of Montmartre. Her second son, Gian Gastone, succeeded as Grand Duke in 1723. He was the last Medici ruler of Tuscany.

39. Gaetano Pieraccino, *La Stirpe dei Medici di Caffaggiolo*, Florence, 1924, 2, 2.

40. Also *capirotada*, *capirote* and other variations. Battista and Alessio, *Dizionario Etimologico Italiana*, Florence, 1954, say that the name may derive either from the Catalan and Provençal *capirote*, a kind of hood or cowl, or from *capirotto*, one with a broken head. In one of Scappi's three versions of the dish, roasted capon breasts were minced and recooked with cheese, egg-yolks, spices, sugar and broth, and the resulting composition poured over fried sweetbreads, breast of veal, or small birds spit-roasted. Scappi's *Opera* was published in 1570.

41. In the English translation of this book, published in 1685, the author's name was erroneously given as Nicolas Lémery, 'Apothecary to the French King', a well-known and much respected apothecary who was quite certainly not responsible for this ancient hodge-podge of curiosities. Although Lémery had indeed been one of Louis XIV's official apothecaries, he was a Huguenot who by 1685 had been obliged to give up his practice. The Wellcome Institute Library Catalogue gives the correct name of the author of *Recueil de Curiositez* as Antoine Joseph D'Emery.

42. Lassels, op. cit., 1670 edition, 2,367.

43. The saga of Marguérite-Louise is told in minute detail by E. Rodocanachi in *Les Infortunes d'une petite fille d'Henri IV*, Paris, Flammarion, c. 1903, and in part by Harold Acton in *The Last Medici*, London, Faber, 1932. A newly revised and splendidly illustrated edition of the latter work was published by Macmillan, London, and Thames & Hudson, USA, in 1980. Madame de Sévigné frequently alluded to Marguérite-Louise in her letters, always as '*la duchesse de Toscane*'.

Ice Houses and Sherbets

1. Pierre Belon, *Les Observations de Plusieurs Singularitez et Choses Memorables . . .*, 1553, pp. 417–19.

2. Pierre-Jean Baptiste Le Grand d'Aussy, *Histoire de la Vie Privée des Français*, 1782.

3. Nicolas Monardes, *Tratado de la Nieve e del Bever Frio*, 1571.

4. Abraham Hayward, *The Art of Dining*, 1853 edition, p. 6.

5. Isabella Beeton, *Household Management*, 1861, p. 112.

6. Lefeuve, *Histoire de Paris Rue par Rue, Maison par Maison*, 1875.

7. Belon, op. cit.

Perpetual Snow

1. Fernand Braudel, *The Mediterranean and the Mediterranean World in the Age of Philip II*, London, 1972.

2. The first part of Monardes's work, originally published in 1569, was concerned mainly with medicinal plants and herbs and spices brought to Spain from the Spanish West Indies, Florida, Mexico, and Peru. The second part, which appeared in 1571, treated of tobacco, sassafras, pineapples, guavas, ginger, cinnamon, cardoons, cashews, cassareep and many other imports, some of them then quite new to Europe. A curious dissertation on the virtues and medical uses of iron follows the main parts of the work, which ends with the *Tratado de la Nieve y del Bever Frio*. In 1574 both parts of the book were published in one volume. It was from this edition that John Frampton made his translation. In the same year an Italian translation called *Trattato delle Neve e del Bere Fresco* was published in Florence. Another translation appeared in Venice in 1589, and I have taken my quotations from this translation. The plaint of the faire and white snow quoted from Frampton does not appear in the Italian translation.

3. *The Boke Which Treateth of the Snow.* Published in vol. 2 of *Joyfull Newes out of the Newe Founde Worlde*. Written in Spanish by Nicholas Monardes Physician of Seville and Englished by John Frampton, Marchaunt, 1577.

4. Roger Thévenot, *A History of Refrigeration throughout the World*, translated by J.C. Fidler, Paris, International Institute of Refrigeration, 1979.

5. *The Travels of John Sanderson in the Levant 1584–1602*, edited by Sir William Foster, London, 1931.

Icemen of the Seventh Century

1. *Barclay his Argenis or the Loves of Polyarchus & Argenis. Faithfully translated out of Latin into English by Kingsmill Long Esquire. The Second Edition Beautified with Pictures, Together with a Key Prefixed to unlock the whole Story.* London. Printed for Henry Seile at the Signe of the Tygres head in Fleet Street near the conduit, 1636, pp. 612–15. In Barclay's original Latin the passage occurs on pp. 577–80 of the 1630 edition and pp. 471–5 of the 1650 edition, both published by the Elzevier Press. The key to the characters in Kingsmill Long's translation is signed by William Haywood, printer of the book. It is more discursive than the one in the Latin version but omits the reference to the *Vigna di Madama* in Rome.

2. J.R. Partington, *The History of Greek Fire and Gunpowder*, Cambridge, Heffer, 1960, p. 268.

3. No description of the creation of ice-encased fruit pyramids is given by Frugoli or by any of the numerous seventeenth-century Italian stewards whose works I have studied. Directions, from which my own are condensed, appear in L. Audiger's *La Maison Réglée*, Paris, 1692, p. 202. See *Ices for the Sun King*, p. 77.

4. See Elizabeth David, *Savour of Ice and of Roses*, in *Petits Propos Culinaires*, 8, 1981.

5. *The Epicure*, London, August 1898, p. 319.

6. Giuseppe Ciocca, *Gelate, Dolci Freddi e Rinfreschi*, prefazione di A. Pettini, Milano, Ulrico Hoepli, 1913, pp. 85–87.

7. Mark Twain, *Life on the Mississippi*, 1883, ch. 39.

8. *De Augmentis Scientarum*, 1628, is Bacon's own translation of *The Advancement of Learning*, which had originally appeared in 1605. It was in the Latin translation, revised and enlarged, that Bacon alluded to the artificial freezing experiment. See J. Spedding's *The Works of Francis Bacon*, 1857–9, vol. 5, p. 2. *Sylva Sylvarum* was Bacon's last work, posthumously published, in English, 1627. The quotation is from p. 22 of the 1628 edition.

9. W.B. Rye, *England as Seen by Foreigners in the Days of Elizabeth and James I*, 1865, pp. 232–4; Lynn Thorndyke, *A History of Magic and Experimental Science*, New York, Columbia University Press, 1958, vol. 11, p. 496; J.R. Partington, *A History of Chemistry*, Macmillan, London, and St Martin's Press, New York, 1961, vol. 2, pp. 321–4.

10. Francis Bacon, *Novum Organum*, 1620, edited with notes by T. Fowler, Oxford, 1889, 3, 5.

11. O.E. Anderson Jr, *Refrigeration in America*, published for the University of Cincinnati by Princeton University Press, 1953, p. 22, n. 30.

12. *The Secret Miracles of Nature in Four Books. Written by that Famous Physitian Laevinius Lemnius*, London, 1631, 2nd edition, p. 176.

13. Dr Baldassare Pisanelli, *Trattato della Natura de Cibi et del Bere*, 11th edition, Treviso, 1611, p. 179.

14. J.R. Partington, *A History of Chemistry*, vol. 2, p. 21.

15. In the English translation: *Natural Magick by John Baptista Porta A Neapolitane in Twenty Books*, London, 1658, p. 324 (facsimile reprint, New York, 1957).

16. ibid., p. 398.

17. Latinus Tancredus, *De Fame et Siti*, Venice, 1607, book 3.

18. See note 8 above.

19. Auguste Escoffier, *Ma Cuisine*, Paris, Flammarion, 1934, pp. 636, 677.

20. *Philosophical Transactions of the Royal Society*, vol. 18, 1666, 1, 255, no. 15. Abridged edition, 1809, vol. 1, p. 86. Boyle used 1 lb of sal ammoniac to 3 pints (48 oz) of water. Thomas Birch, *History of the Royal Society of London*, 1758, 4 vols., vol. 2, pp. 105–9 (Experiments July 1666). *Philosophical Transactions of the Royal Society*, vol. 40, 1737, 1738, pp. 307–10. *New Experiments upon Ice: taken from Abbé Nolet FRS at Paris*. J.B. Dortous de Mairan, *Dissertation sur la Glace*, Paris, l'Imprimerie Royale, 49, p. 356.

21. John Nichols, *The Progresses, Processions and Magnificent Festivities of King James the First*, London, 1828, vol. 14, p. 1042.

22. Johannes Beckmann, *Beyträge zur Geschichte der Erfindungen 1783–1805: A History of Inventions, Discoveries and Origins*, translated from the German by William Johnston, 4th edition, revised and enlarged by William Francis and J.W. Griffith, London, 1846, 2 vols., vol. 2, pp. 142–60.

Ices for the Sun King

1. L. Audiger, *La Maison Réglée*, Paris, 1692, préface, 15 unnumbered pp.

2. *Le Grand Condé et le Duc d'Enghien, Lettres inédites à Marie-Louise de Gonzague, Reine de Pologne, sur la Cour de Louis XIV (1660–1667)*, ed. Emile Magne, Paris, 1920.

3. Gourville, *Mémoires*, I, p. lxx.

4. Madame de Sévigné, 30.11.1688, vol. 9, p. 120.

5. Mercier's *Mercure Galant*, January 1680, supplément p. 65 and fn. Quoted by Alfred Franklin in *La Vie Privée d'Autrefois: Variétés Gastronomiques*, 1891, p. 82.

6. Duc de Saint-Simon, *Historical Memoirs*, vol. 1, 1691–1709. A Shortened Version. Edited and translated by Lucy Norton, London, Hamish Hamilton, ch. 8, 1698, 111–12; ch. 22, 1707, 330.

7. Audiger, op. cit., pp. 165–86.

8. Alfred Franklin, *La Vie Privée d'Autrefois: Comment on Devenait Patron*, Paris, 1889.

9. Audiger, op. cit., 233.

10. *Neige de fleurs d'orange*: 'You must take sweet cream, and put thereto two handfuls of powdered sugar, and take petals of Orange Flowers and mince them small, and put them in your Cream, and if you have no fresh Orange Flowers you must take candied, with a drop of good Orange Flower water, and put all into a pot, and put your pot into a wine cooler [*carafons*]; and you must take ice, crush it well and put a bed of it with a handful of salt at the bottom of the *carafons* before putting in the pot, and there must be room to put a finger between the pot and the sides of the *carafons* so that they do not touch: and you must continue putting a layer of ice and a handful of salt, until the carafons is full and the pot covered, and you must put it in the coolest place you can find, and you must shake it from time to time for fear it will freeze into a solid lump of ice [*glaçon*]. It will take two hours.' François Pierre La Varenne, *Nouveau Confiturier, qui Enseigne la manière de bien faire toutes sortes de Confitures, tant sèches que liquides, et autres delicatesses de bouche.*

11. *Sorbec d'Alexandrie*: This curious recipe appears in *Le Confiturier Royal*, a treatise which was one of six which made up *L'École Parfaite des Officiers de Bouche*, published in Paris by Jean Ribou, 1662. No authorship is given for any of the works, but the *Confiturier* is evidently an early version of a well-known treatise on the same subject, subsequently published by Ribou in 1667 and written by La Varenne. (Vicaire, p. 501, says that La Varenne's name is given under the *privilège* or licence to publish, granted on 6 December 1666, but a previous version entitled *Le Confiturier François* had been published in 1650.

The Alexandrian sorbet or sherbet consists of a veal broth, sweetened with sugar, boiled to a syrup, and bottled for keeping. 'Take a large fillet of veal, take off the fat, beat it well on a block, with a rolling pin: put it in a very clean pot, with six pints [48 oz] of water; let it reduce to one *chopine* [16 oz]; take two pounds of good sugar, put it in a skillet with the broth which has come from the Veal, after having taken off the fat and passed it through a clean white cloth; boil all well together, & after it is skimmed, boil it to the large pearl; pour it into a glass bottle and cork.'

It is interesting to find that a derivation of this *sorbec* was still going the rounds in England about sixty years later. The *École Parfaite* was translated into English by Giles Rose, one of Charles II's master cooks, in 1688. (Was Giles perhaps the brother of John Rose, one of the King's gardeners, who appears presenting him with a home-grown pineapple in the famous painting at Ham House?). So Rose's version was perhaps responsible. At any rate, the recipe took the fancy of John Nott, a cook who in 1723 published a compilation called *The Cook's and Confectioner's Dictionary*, printed for C. Rivington.

John Nott, who had been cook to a number of exalted personages, among them the 2nd Duke of Ormond, announced on his title page that the recipe was 'revised and recommended'. In his version of 'To make Sherbet', calves' feet are added to the veal, the cooking liquor is a mixture of water and white wine, and when two-thirds is boiled away, it is strained. 'Sweep off all the Fat with Feathers; then put it into a Pan with two or three Cloves, a Stick of Cinnamon, a little Lemon Peel and Sugar, according to your Palate; boil these all together, and clarify it with the White of an Egg whipt; then strain it through a straining Bag. If you design to keep this Liquor a considerable time, you ought to allow two Pounds of Sugar for a Quart of Broth or Juice of Meat, and the former Directions being observed boil the Liquor to the pearled Degree, and put it into Bottles.'

Neither John Nott nor the original source, the *Confiturier*, say on what occasions this odd syrup is to be used. I suspect that it was administered to invalids suffering from fevers and consumptions. Sugar, it has to be remembered, was for long regarded as an important restorative. The more you consumed, the better for your health. Based as it was on the reduced veal broth, the Alexandria sherbet was probably considered to be a doubly strengthening potion.

12. Audiger, op. cit., 227–31.

13. Massialot, *Nouvelle Instruction pour les Confitures, les Liqueurs et les Fruits*, 1702, p. 272.

14. ibid., p. 478.

15. ibid., pp. 276, 277, 268, 245.

16. Maria Kroll (ed.) *Letters from Liselotte* (*Elisabeth Charlotte Princess Palatine and Duchess of Orleans*), London, Victor Gollancz, 1970, p. 116. Maria Kroll's source for this letter, as she very kindly told me, was a German edition of Madame's letters, *Aus den Briefen der Herzogin Elisabeth Charlotte von Orléans an die Kurfürstin Sophie von Hannover*, ed. Eduard Bodemann, Hanover, 1891.

17. ibid., p. 115, 10 August 1704.

The Limonadiers of Paris and the Café Procope

1. A. Bruel, *Bulletin de la Société de l'Histoire du VIe Arrondissment de Paris*, 1, 1898, 155. This is to be found in the Archives Nationales de Paris, p. 2695. It is quoted by Jean Leclant in *Coffee and Cafés in Paris, 1644–1693*, published in *Food and Drink in History, Selections from the Annales, Economies, Sociétés, Civilisations*, vol. 5, edited by Robert Forster and Orest Ranum, translated by Elborg Forster and Patricia M. Ranum, Johns Hopkins University Press, Baltimore and London, 1979, p. 90. The information concerned occurs in an extract from the Chambres des Comptes de Paris for the year 1684 (p. 13), in which it is attested that Francesco Procopio Coltelli was a Sicilian. Unfortunately a fire in the Chambres des Comptes in 1737 destroyed the original text of the naturalization papers. More complete information about Procopio's origins is consequently lacking.

2. Two examples are: (1) Sir John Reresby, *Travels and Memoirs . . .* 3rd edition, 1831, p. 101: 'In summer the meanest person seldom drinks his wine without having it cooled either with ice or snow, which is preserved for that purpose underground, and sold publicly in the markets' (recorded in Venice, 1657); (2) Richard Lassels, *The Voyage of Italy*, Paris, 1670; 2nd edition, 1698, p. 19: 'For their Wines they use Snow, or Ice, which they keep all Summer; they that are much us'd to this way will not in this Country, even in Winter, drink without Snow.' (Recorded during Lassels's five journeys to Italy between 1638 and *c.* 1662. He died in 1668 and the book was post-humously published.)

3. Jean Moura and Paul Louvet, *Le Café Procope*, in the *Bibliothèque d'Histoire Parisienne* series, Paris, Perrin et Cie, 1929, p. 20.

4. Dr Martin Lister, *A Journey to Paris in the Year 1698*, London, 1699, p. 162.

5. Olivier de Serres, *Le Théâtre d'Agriculture*. First published 1600.

6. John Evelyn's *Diary*, Oxford, Oxford University Press, 1949, p. 85.

7. Massialot, *Nouvelle Instruction pour les Confitures . . .*, 1724 edn, p. 257.

8. L. Audiger, *La Maison Reglée*, 1692, pp. 228–9.

9. Dubuisson, *L'Art du Distillateur . . .*, 1779, vol. 1, p. 294.

10. Moura and Louvet, op. cit., p. 41 n.

11. ibid., p. 94, n.

12. Jacques Savary des Bruslons, *Dictionnaire Universel de Commerce*, 3 vols, 1723–30, vol. 1 (entry for *caffez*).

13. *Le Grand Condé et le Duc d'Enghien, Lettres inédités à Marie-Louise de Gonzague, Reine de Pologne, sur la Cour de Louis XIV (1660–1667)*, ed. Emile Magne, Paris, 1920 (letters of 13 February 1665 and 19 February 1666).

14. Lister, op. cit., pp. 175–6.

15. Dubuisson, op. cit., vol. 2, pp. 271–2.

16. Lefeuve, *Histoire de Paris Rue par Rue, Maison par Maison*, 5th edition, 6 vols., 1876.

17. Pierre-Jean Baptiste Le Grand d'Aussy, *Histoire de la Vie Privée des Français*, 1782, vol. 3, pp. 94–6.

Neiges, Sorbets, Glaces, Fromages

1. Dubuisson, *L'Art du Distillateur . . .*, 1779, vol. 1, pp. 70–73.

2. ibid., vol. 2, pp. 287–306.

3. Menon, *La Science du Maître d'Hotel Confiseur*, 1750, p. 166.

4. Dubuisson, op. cit., vol. 2, pp. 271–9.

5. ibid., p. 322.

6. Dr Filippo Baldini, *De' Sorbetti*, Naples, 1775, 2nd edition, 1784.

7. Two typical examples are: (1) Alfred Jarrin, *The Italian Confectioner*, 1820, pp. 124 and 116 of the 1837 edition, custard for ices: 8 yolks to 1 (16 oz) pint of cream, or 10 yolks to 8 oz each of milk and cream mixed; (2) Jules Gouffe, *Le Livre de Pâtisserie*, 1873, p. 408, *glace à la vanille*: 12 yolks to 1 litre (34 oz) of cream, plus 300 g (9 oz) of whipped cream.

8. Dubuisson, op. cit., vol. 1, pp. 69–70.

9. Pierre-Jean Baptiste Le Grand d'Aussy, *Histoire de la Vie Privée des Français,* 1782, vol. 3, p. 96.

10. François Fosca, *Histoires des cafés de Paris,* Firmin-Didot et Cie, Paris, 1934, pp. 81 and 41, quoting *L'Almanac Dauphin* for 1777.

11. Dubuisson, op. cit., vol. 2, p. 272.

Ices under the Volcano

1. Charles de Brosses, *Lettres Historiques et Critiques sur l'Italie,* vol. 2, p. 148.

2. Lady Morgan, *Italy,* 3rd edition, London, 1821, vol. 3, p. 149.

3. Antonio Latini, *Lo Scalco alla Moderna,* vol. 2, 1694, p. 169.

4. ibid., vol. 1, 1692, pp. 484, 485.

5. Joseph Addison, *Remarks on Several Parts of Italy . . . In the Years 1701, 1702, 1703,* 3rd edition, London, 1726.

6. Poullet, *Relations du Levant,* 1667–8, vol. 2, p. 109.

7. Blount, *A Voyage into the Levant,* 1634, in Pinkerton's *Voyages,* 1811, vol. 10, p. 265.

8. Baudier, *History of the Imperial Estate of the Grand Seigneur,* 1635, trans. Grimston, p. 41.

9. *The Manner of Making Sorbet*: 'They made use of an hundred and fifty *Rottes* of Sugar broken into small pieces, which they put into a great Kettle over a Fire, with a little water to dissolve it, when it was ready to boil they skimmed it, and poured in five or six quarts more of water, to make the skum rise better; they put it in by spoonfulls, and wet the sides of the Kettle to cool them. Half an hour after they mingled a dozen whites of Eggs, with four or five quarts of water, and having beat them a little with the water, all was poured into the Kettle at four or five times, and then they began to skim again, till a little after, they strained it through a Cloath, and that they call clarifying of the Sugar. Afterwards they divided that Liquor into three parts, of which they put a third into a great Kettle or Caldron over the fire; and seeing Sugar from time to time was like to boil over, they made it settle, by throwing in two or three Egg-shells full of Milk. When they knew it to be boiled enough, after it had been an hour upon the fire, they took it off; it looked then very yellow, and two men set a stirring of it with wooden peels; so that the more they stirred it, as it grew cold it became thicker and whiter. When it was a little thickened; they put into it about two glass-fulls of the juice of Limon boiled . . . Then they stirred it again to mingle all well together, and a little after they put into it about two spoonfulls of Rose-water in which some Musk had been dissolved, several adding thereto Ambergreass. Then again they stirred it till it became like a Paste, and afterwards put it into Pots;

the same they did with the other two parts. With an hundred and fifty of these *Rottes* they filled twenty nine Pots; therein they spent a little Bottle of Rose-water, with Musk which cost a Crown. When they have a mind to make it of a violet-Colour, after the juice of Limon they put of the Syrrup of Violets into it, which is made by pounding Violets with Sugar, which they clear from the dreggs.' *The Travels of M. de Thévenot into the Levant*, London 1687, vol. 2, ch. 3.

10. Sir John Chardin, *Voyages en Perse*, first published 1711; 1811 edition edited by J. Langlès, vol. 4, p. 44.

11. Addison, op. cit., p. 145.

12. Addison, writing as Isaac Bickerstaff in *The Tatler* (no. 148, 18–21 March 1709).

13. Lady Anne Miller, *Letters from Italy*, 1775, vol. 2, pp. 317–18 and p. 341.

14. Dr Filippo Baldini, *De Sorbetti*, Naples, 1775, 2nd edition 1784, pp. 2, 18, 19, 20, 22–5, 37, 42, 67, 73, 81, 93–6.

15. *Voyages du Père Labat en Espagne et Italie*, Paris, 1730, vol. 2, pp. 301 and 308.

16. Lady Anne Miller, op. cit., vol. 2, pp. 78–82.

17. Dr John Moore, *A View of Society and Manners in Italy*, 1790, vol. 2, p. 311.

18. William Fuller, *A Manual Containing Numerous Original Recipes for Preparing Neapolitan Ices*, n.d. (*c.* 1856).

19. *The Morning Post*, 9 June 1851.

20. Lord Byron, *Letters*, Everyman edition, 1962, p. 144.

21. *Ice and Refrigeration*, New York and Chicago, 3, 1909.

22. ibid., 7, 1910.

23. *Philosophical Transactions*, Royal Society, 1770, 2.

24. Patrick Brydone, *A Tour through Sicily and Malta*, 1776, vol. 1, pp. 50–51.

25. *Voyages du Père Labat*, vol. 5, pp. 142–3.

26. Dr Baldassare Pisanelli, *Trattato della Natura de Cibi et del Bere*, 11th edition, Treviso, 1611, p. 179.

27. George Sandys, *A Relation of a Journey Begun An: Do: 1610*, London, 1615, book 4, p. 245.

28. Brydone, op. cit., vol. 1, 150–51; vol. 2, pp. 46–8.

29. Denis Mack Smith, *A History of Sicily*, London 1969, vol. 3, p. 226.

30. Brydone, op. cit., vol. 1, p. 251.

31. Mack Smith, op. cit., vol. 3, p. 291.

32. Brydone, op. cit., vol. 1, pp. 150–51.

33. *Cold Storage*, London, 15 September 1910.

34. ibid., 19 August 1909.

35. ibid., 21 September 1911.

36. First performed at His Majesty's Theatre on 31 August 1916, *Chu Chin*

Chow ran for a record number of performances and subsequently toured the provinces for many years. Oscar Ashe played the leading part.

37. *Voyages du Père Labat*, vol. 5, pp. 125–6.

38. Giuseppe di Lampedusa. Published in *Two Stories and a Memory*, London, Collins and Harvill, 1962.

39. Giuseppe di Lampedusa, *The Leopard*, translated by Archibald Colquhoun, revised edition, London, Fontana, 1963, p. 187.

40. *Ice and Refrigeration*, New York and Chicago, 7, 1910, p. 20. The article embodies a description of the process and of the machinery used by Cavaliere Hamilton.

A Persian Tale

1. Dr Johnson, on hearing that Goldsmith was writing a Natural History, remarked: 'He will make it as entertaining as a Persian tale.'

2. Pietro della Valle, *Viaggi di Pietro Dalla Valle* ..., Rome, 1658–62, vol. 2, pp. 117–21 (English translation by G. Havers, 1665).

3. Jean de Thévenot, *Suite du Voyage de Mr de Thévenot au Levant*, Amsterdam, 1727, vol. 3, p. 87 (first published 1687; English translation by A. Lovell, 1687).

4. Sir Thomas Herbert, *Some Yeares Travels into Divers Parts of Asia and Afrique*, 3rd edition 1667, p. 162 (earlier editions do not have the quoted passage).

5. J. Chardin, *Voyages en Perse*, Amsterdam, 1711, vol. 2, p. 65, and vol. 4, pp. 62–8 of the 1811 edition edited by J. Langlès, in which there are slight differences in the text. An English translation of Chardin's *Travels* appeared in 1724, reprinted in 1927.

6. Chardin, op. cit., 1711, vol. 3, p. 87.

7. Sir Percy Sykes, *A History of Persia*, 2 vols., 2nd edition 1921, vol. 1, p. 447.

8. Robin Lane Fox, *Alexander the Great*, London, Allen Lane, 1973, p. 245.

9. Chardin, op. cit., 1811, vol. 3, p. 302.

10. Della Valle, op. cit., vol. 1, p. 866.

11. Chardin, op. cit., vol. 2, pp. 404–5.

12. Dr John Fryer, *A New Account of East India and Persia Being Nine Years Travels 1672–81*, London, 1698, p. 228.

13. ibid., pp. 250, 263, 311.

14. ibid., pp. 398, 3, 9.

15. Quoted by Alfred Franklin in *La Privée d'Autrefois: La Cuisine*, 1888, p. 188, from *Etat Général de la Maison du Roy pour 1765*, housed in the Bibliothèque Mazarine.

16. Jean-Baptiste Tavernier, *Les Six Voyages en Turquie, en Perse, et aux Indes*, 3 vols., Utrecht, 1712, vol. 3, pp. 294–5. Tavernier's journeys spanned nearly forty years, ending in 1670.

17. Della Valle, op. cit., p. 751.

18. 'Snow upon the desert's dusty face' is from Edward Fitzgerald's *Rubáiyát of Omar Khayyám*.

19. Fryer, op. cit., p. 295.

20. Elisabeth Beazley and Michael Harverson, *Living with the Desert: Working Buildings of the iranian Plateau*, Warminster, Aris & Phillips, 1982, p. 52.

21. Maxime Siroux, *Caravanserails d'Iran et petites constructions routières*, French Institute of Oriental Archaeology, Cairo, 1949, pp. 131–2.

22. Beazley and Harverson, op. cit., p. 53.

23. James Morier, *A Journey Through Persia, Armenia and Asia Minor, to Constantinople in the Years 1808 and 1809*, London, 1812, p. 123.

24. C.J. Wills, *In the Land of the Lion and Sun*, London, 1883, pp. 240–41.

25. Beazley and Harverson, op. cit.

26. Morier, op. cit., p. 115.

27. Wills, op. cit., p. 241.

28. Tavernier, op. cit., vol. 4, p. 425.

29. Chardin, op. cit., 1811, vol. 9, p. 64.

30. Della Valle, op. cit.

31. Edmond O'Donovan, *The Merv Oasis: Travels and Adventures East of the Caspian During the Years 1879–80–81*, 2 vols., 1882, vol. 2, pp. 79–81.

32. ibid., vol. 1, p. 430.

33. James Fraser, *Narrative of a Journey into Khorasan in the Years 1821 and 1822*, London, 1825, pp. 55–6.

34. R.B.M. Binning, *A Journal of Two Years Travel in Persia*, vol. 2, London, 1857.

35. O'Donovan, op. cit., vol. 1, p. 329.

36. Chardin, op. cit., 1811, vol. 9, pp. 79–89 and 93–4.

37. Lady Shiel, *Glimpses of Life and Manners in Persia*, London, John Murray, 1856, p. 213.

38. C.J. Wills, *Persia As It Is*, 1887.

39. Chardin, op. cit., 1811, vol. 4, pp. 62–8.

Cathay to Caledonia

1. See, for example, Sir Henry Yule's massively annotated two volumes of *The Book of Ser Marco Polo the Venetian* . . ., with further notes and revisions by Professor H. Cordier, 1903 or 1921 edition. Ronald Latham's newer translation, with brief notes, appeared in Penguin Books in 1958. It has a very informative introduction.

2. Quoted by Woolrich, *The Men Who Created Cold*, 1967, p. 32.

3. Edward H. Schafer on T'ang Dynasty food and drink in *Food in Chinese Culture*, edited by K.C. Chang, New Haven and London, Yale University Press, 1979, p. 116.

4. *Memoirs of Wilham Hickey*, edited by Peter Quennell, London, Century, 1984.

5. John Bell of Antermony, *A Journey from St Petersburg to Pekin 1719–22*. Edited with an introduction by J.L. Stevenson, Edinburgh University Press 1965, p. 159 (first published 1763 as *Travels from St Petersburg in Russia to Diverse Parts of Asia*).

6. James Fergusson (ed.) *Letters of Sir George Dempster to Sir Adam Fergusson 1756–1813*, London, Macmillan, 1934, p. 160; Charles Knight (ed.), *London*, 1843, vol. 4, p. 207.

7. Nicolo Monardes, *Libro che tratta della Neve*, 1589, Venetian edition, Proemio (Foreword), and *The Boke which Treateth of the Snow*, 1574, English edition, 162 (see note 2 to p. 385).

8. Pierre-Jean Baptiste, Le Grand d'Aussy, *Histoire de la Vie Privée des Françcais*, Paris, 1782, vol. 1, p. 239.

9. *Scots Magazine*, xxvii, p. 538.

10. *The Epicure's Almanack*, London, 1815, pp. 200, 257–8, 309.

11. Charles Cutting, *Fish Saving*, London, Leonard Hill Books, 1955, p. 216.

12. ibid.

13. ibid., pp. 224–5; Henry Mayhew, *The Morning Chronicle Survey of Labour and the Poor, The Metropolitan District*, vol. 6 (letters lxix, 12 September 1850 to lxxxii, 12 December 1850). First published in book form 1851, reprinted Caliban Press 1982, letter lxxxii, 252–3.

14. Robert Fortune, *Three Years Wanderings in the Northern Provinces of China*, London, John Murray, 1847, pp. 122–3.

15. Fergusson, op. cit., p. 313.

16. John Gamgee, *On Artificial Refrigeration*, Section xx of *Report of Commission of Fish and Fisheries*, Washington 1879, p. 908.

17. *The Cold Storage and Ice Trades Review*, May 1902, advertisement, p. 54.

18. Schafer, op. cit., p. 132.

19. Cecilia Chiang, as told to Alan Carr, *The Mandarin Way*, revised edition, California Living, 1980, p. 125.

To India's Coral Strand

1. *The Ain-i-Akbari* or *The Institutions of Akbar*, by Abul Fazl Allami, translated from the original Persian by H. Blochmann, M.A. Calcutta Madrasah. Printed for the Asiatic Society of Bengal, vol. 1, Calcutta, 1873.

2. A *se'r* or *seer* is now about 2 lb 2 oz. In Upper India in Akbar's day the *se'r* varied between 10 and 33 oz, according to commodity. Ice would have been in the 33 oz to the *se'r* bracket.

3. A *kòs* was somewhat over 2 miles, but varied from district to district.

4. It is curious that in Akbar's India, manual transport was more expensive than water or carriage transport.

5. *Dam* or *damri*, a copper coin of very low value, the fortieth part of a rupee. Hence perhaps the expression 'I don't give a dam', meaning 'I don't give a brass farthing'.

6. *Ain-i-Akbari*, op. cit., p. 56.

7. *Storia do Mogor*, or *Mogul India 1655–1708* by Niccolao Manucci, Venetian, translated by William Irvine, Bengal Civil Service, London, John Murray, 4 vols., 1907, vol. 2, p. 43.

8. In *Philosophical Transactions of the Royal Society*, vol. 65, pp. 252–7.

9. Emma Roberts, *Scenes and Characteristics of Hindostan with Sketches of Anglo-Indian Society*, 3 vols., London, 1835, vol. 1, ch. 5.

10. Johannes Beckmann, *Beyträge zur Geschichte der Erfindungen 1783–1805: A History of Inventions, Discoveries and Origins*, translated from the German by William Johnston, 4th edition, revised and enlarged by William Francis and J.W. Griffith, 2 vols., London, 1846, vol. 2, pp. 142–60.

11. F.T. Woolrich, *The History of Refrigeration*, nos. 4884 and 5001.

12. ibid., p. 153.

13. *Ice and Cold Storage*, 15 May 1902, p. 57.

14. *Cold Storage Review*, 15 July 1901.

15. Jacquetta Hawkes, *Mortimer Wheeler*, London, Weidenfeld & Nicolson, 1982, ch. 9.

16. Tudor's own story differs in that he recorded in his diary (29 April 1833) that the proposition he received came from two East India merchants, Samuel Austin and W.C. Rogers, and that when they offered him a share he accepted with alacrity, and wrote, 'This undertaking it has long been my wish to make . . .' (Cummings, *The American Ice Harvests*, p. 28).

17. H.E.A. Cotton, *Calcutta Old and New, A Historical and Descriptive Handbook to the City*, Calcutta, 1907, p. 190.

18. Tudor's *Diary*, quoted in *Ice Carrying Trade at Sea*, National Maritime Museum, 1981, p. 22.

19. Colesworthy Grant, *Anglo-Indian Domestic Life*, 2nd edition, revised and enlarged, 1862, p. 35.

20. ibid., p. 36–7.

21. *Ice Carrying Trade*, op. cit., p. 23.

22. Emma Roberts, *Notes of an Overland Journey through France and Egypt to Bombay*, with a Memoir, London, 1841.

23. ibid.

24. *Indian Domestic Economy* ... By the author of *Manual of Gardening for Western India*. 2nd edition, revised, Madras, 1850, pp. 263–6.

25. Thomas Masters, *The Ice Book*, 1844. Description of the Masters Patent Freezing Apparatus, unnumbered pages.

26. Flora Annie Steel and Grace Gardiner, *The Complete Indian Housekeeper and Cook*, new edition, 1898, p. 201.

27. (Fanny Parks), *Wanderings of a Pilgrim in Search of the Picturesque During Four and Twenty Years in the East*, London, 1850.

28. *Indian Domestic Economy*, op. cit., p. 27.

29. Steel and Gardiner, op. cit., pp. 201, 202, 204, 172.

30. Posthumous publication, 1929, pp. 74 and 85.

31. *Ice Carrying Trade*, op. cit., p. 26.

32. Richard O. Cummings, *The American Ice Harvests*, Berkeley, 1949, Appendix G.

33. Samuel Eliot Morison, *The Maritime History of Massachusetts*, 1921, pp. 282–3, quoted in *Dictionary of American Biography*, 1936.

34. Emily Eden, *Letters from India*, edited by her niece, 1872, vol. 2, p. 64.

35. *Ice Carrying Trade*, op. cit., p. 22.

36. Woolrich, op. cit., p. 117.

37. Roger Thévenot, *A History of Refrigeration throughout the World*, translated by J.C. Fidler, International Institute of Refrigeration, Paris, 1979, p. 422.

38. Private communication.

39. Cotton, op. cit., pp. 190, 186.

40. Cummings, op. cit., p. 141. From Tudor's *Outline of Proposals Respecting ice*, 1806, printed in full by Cummings.

41. Alexander Hamilton, *A New Account of the East Indies ... 1688–1723*, 1727, 3 vols.

42. Captain Mundy, *Pen and Pencil Sketches Being the Journal of a Tour in India*, London, John Murray, 1833, vol. 2, p. 306.

43. Unpublished account, quoted W.W. Bunting in *Ice Carrying Trade*, op. cit., p. 25.

Ices in a Cold Climate

1. Quoted Morton Lundbaek, *Ishuse*, Institut for Europaeisk Folkelivs Forskning, Brede, Denmark, 1970 (photocopied typescript thesis, lent to author).
2. ibid., quoting Mercer's diary.
3. ibid., quoting Danish royal archives.
4. Oliver Lawson Dick (ed.), Aubrey's *Brief Lives*, London, Penguin Books, 1949, p. 124.
5. *Sylva Sylvarum*, 1628 edition, p. 22 (first published posthumously in 1627).
6. *Dictionary of National Biography*.
7. *Sylva Sylvarum*, op. cit., p. 22. See also Spedding's edition of the *Works of Francis Bacon*, 1887, vol. 11, *Natural History (Sylva Sylvarum)* paras 69–75, pp. 370–71 and para 379, p. 467.
8. Henry D. Thoreau, *Walden*, 1854.
9. *Scribner's Monthly*, July 1875, pp. 468–9.
10. ibid., p. 469.
11. ibid.
12. ibid., p. 470.
13. *Cold Storage and Ice Trades Review*, 15 March 1902, 350.
14. Georg Johann Kohl, *Russia and the Russians*, London, 1842, vol. 2, p. 47.
15. ibid., vol. 1, pp. 42–5, 56–7.
16. ibid., vol. 2, pp. 18–19.
17. ibid., vol. 1, p. 119.
18. M.P. Barra, D. Medecine, Aggrégé au College de Lyon, *L'usage de la Glace, de la Neige et du Froid*, Lyon, 1675.
19. *The Times*, 16 October 1982.
20. *Ice Cream Topics*, Mid-season 1968, 16; Spring 1965, 33.
21. Transcript of BBC transmission, 2 May 1982, *The Food Programme*, presented by Derek Cooper.
22. Customs and Excise Bulletin, *VAT News* no. 12, H.M. Customs and excise, February 1977, 15.
23. *Ice Cream Topics*, Spring 1974, 2.
24. Private communication, Darra Goldstein to author, 7 December 1982; private communication, Jill Norman to author, March 1983.
25. *The Times*, 27 June 1983.

The London Confectioners

1. Ambrose Heal, *London Tradesmen's Cards of the XVIII Century*, 1925, 72.

2. Virginia Maclean, *A Short-title Catalogue of Household and Cookery Books Published in the English Tongue 1701–1800*, London, 1981.

3. A.W. Oxford, *English Cookery Books to the Year 1850*, Oxford, 1913; Maclean, op. cit.

4. *Notes and Queries*, 7 March 1925, 177.

5. Debrett's *Peerage and Baronetage*, 1980.

6. Anne Freemantle (ed.), *The Wynne Diaries*, vol. 3, 1798–1820, London, Oxford University Press, 1940, 187–95.

7. John Simpson, *A Complete System of Cookery*, 1806, pp. 483–90, Intro, vi.

8. ibid., pp. 483, 743.

9. *The Epicure's Almanack*, 1815, pp. 187, 185, 182, 187, 194, 120, 103, 189–90.

10. *The Reminiscences and Recollections of Captain Gronow (1794–1865)*, 1892 edition, vol. 2, p. 284 (first published 1862).

11. Guglielmo Jarrin, *The Italian Confectioner*, 1820, pp. 116, 215, 123, 123–4, 132, 133, 138–9.

12. The *Epicure's Almanack*, 1815, p. 200.

13. J.R. Partington, *A History of Chemistry*, Macmillan, London, and St Martin's Press, New York, 1961, vol. 2, pp. 149, 226.

14. Johannes Beckmann, *Beyträge zur Geschichte der Erfindungen 1783–1805: A History of Inventions, Discoveries and Origins*, translated from the German by William Johnston, 4th edition, revised and enlarged by William Francis and J.W. Griffith, 2 vols., London, 1846, vol. 2, p. 157, n. 1.

15. The *Epicure's Almanack*, 1815, p. 190.

16. Private communication from Jonna Dwinger, 16 August 1983.

17. Jane Austen, *Selected Letters, 1796–1817*, ed. R.W. Chapman, Oxford, Oxford University Press, 1955.

18. J.T. Jenkins, *A History of the Whale Fisheries*, London, 1921, pp. 69, 125–32.

19. The story is told by Cummings in *The American Ice Harvests*, Berkeley, 1949, p. 15 quoting from Tudor's MS diary, 30 January 1820.

20. William Scoresby Junior, *Journal of a Voyage to the Northern Whale-Fishery*, Edinburgh, 1823, pp. 54, 69, 70, 183, 67, 469.

21. CUST 5/11 (Public Record Office, Kew).

22. She was a ship-rigged vessel of 250 tons, American-built in 1807. Her port of survey was Leith. (Information received from Dr Basil Greenhill, the then Director of the National Maritime Museum at Greenwich, 18 October 1982.)

23. CUST 5/21. 1832. CUST 28/47. 15.5, p. 307.

24. Ledgers of Imports (Articles) 1825. CUST 5/14 1828. CUST 5/17. 1832. CUST 5/21.

25. Francis Trevithick, *Life of Richard Trevithick*, 1872, vol. 2, p. 294.

26. *Blackwoods Magazine*, November 1823, article 'The Night Walker', p. 509, col. i.

27. *Punch*, 14 June 1845. *A Cool Project and Cheap Trips Round the World*, followed up 30 August 1845 with *Wonder of the Strand*.

28. *The Caterers and Refreshment Contractors Gazette*, 6 April 1878. Article 'Ice and its Storage', p. 9; Gash, *Life of Peel*, pp. 460–61.

29. CUST 28/172, pp. 1179–80. Minutes 20 March 1845.

30. Thomas Masters, *The Ice Book*, 1844, pp. 83, 173, 170, 172, 163, 165, 167, 173.

31. *Ice Carrying Trade at Sea*, National Maritime Museum, 1981, p. 49.

32. Leftwich Chronicles. A brief account of the family history ... edited and compiled [by Anthony Leftwich, 1979, unpublished].

33. *The Times*, 31 March 1948, p. 5, col. 4.

34 *Ice Cream Topics*, Spring 1974, 28–32.

35. The *Caterer and Refreshment Contractors Gazette*, op. cit.

36. Joyce Cunningham Green, *Salmagundi*, 31.

37. *Frasers Magazine*, 1837. Quoted by Arthur Gray, *Over The Black Coffee*, New York, Baker and Taylor Company, 1902, pp. 45–6.

38. *The Pytchley Cookery Book*, p. 227.

39. William Gunter, *The Confectioners Oracle*, xxvii, xxii, xxvi; Appendix 1, *The Twelve Months of the Year*, pp. 123–46, 72.

40. Fanny Parks, *Wanderings of a Pilgrim in Search of the Picturesque During Four and Twenty Years in the East*, London, 1850, vol. 1, p. 4.

41. *The Builder*, 1875, quoted by John Martin Robinson, 'Mansions in Place of Cabbages', *Country Life*, 10 November 1983, p. 1320. The Gunter estates are dealt with in detail in: *Survey of London*, vol. 40, 1983.

42. *Reminiscences and Recollections of Captain Gronow*, op. cit., p. 23.

43. Gunter papers, in the keeping of Messrs. Payne and Gunter, 1 British Grove, London W4 (1983).

44. *Survey of London*, vol. 39, pp. 42–3.

45. Advertisement in *The Caterer and Refreshment Contractors Gazette*, op. cit.

46. Sybille Bedford, *A Legacy*, 1956, p. 196.

47. Hobbs, *The Kitchen Oracle*, 1887. I have described the menu and some of the dishes given by Hobbs for a dinner of eighteen to twenty persons, for 4 August 1886, pp. 333–59. It is his only dated dinner. All others are simply specified as appropriate to the month in question, starting with January, and culminating in the August feast. Instructions for making and freezing a *soufflé glacé* appear in the July menu, pp. 311–13.

To Cool the Air: Ice Pillars and Lily Pools

1. *The European and Liverpool Times*, 5 June 1845. Quoted in *Ice Carrying Trade at Sea*, National Maritime Museum, 1981.
2. R.S. Surtees, *Plain or Ringlets*, 1860, ch. 28.
3. Warne's *The Modern Housekeeper*, 1878, p. 336.
4. *The Epicure*, August 1897.
5. Colonel Newnham-Davis, *Gourmet's Guide to Europe*, 1903 edition.
6. R.J. Forbes, *Studies in Ancient Technology*, London, E.J. Brill, 1958, vi, p. 113. The snow mountain reference is Lampridius, *Heliogabalus*, ch. 23. According to J. Stuart Hay's *The Amazing Emperor Heliogabalus*, 1911, the text of Lampridius's history of Heliogabalus is at times incomprehensible, and the snow mountain reference appears to be, to say the least, vague.

Index

Note: page references in *italics* refer to illustrations.

...ained under the dominance of inadequate speech forms of barbaric and overripe habituation, peculiarly those proclaiming purportedly ...ulate sense-data.

...hough the name " kennetic " has not heretofore been in use, inquiry ... these suggested lines has already been undertaken, and report ...on has been made, in a book *Knowing and the Known* (22)† by John ...ey and the present writer. To form the name " kennetic," the ...ish " ken " or " kenning " has been preferred to any word in the ...s centering around " cognition," " gnosis," or " epistemology," since ...atter have long since become fixated beyond recall in implications ...ile to present purposes. " Ken " has a further advantage over these ...r roots in recalling the early Teutonic " can," which signified the ac...y of knowing, inclusive of " know-how " and of " be able." Using ...nnetic," we may, with minimum risk of distortion, deal with active ...wings as found among men who are known phases of a cosmos, which ...self in process of being known.

...Ve here proceed to take men as in nature, to take their behaviors of ...atever kind as " natural," and to take all their knowings as naturally ...avioral, along with their other activities. We then strive to discover ...at observation may yield under the employment of such new namings ...we may attain when freed from the interference of the old hostile ter...nologies.

THE KENNETIC PROCEDURE

...Kennetic inquiry, as already indicated, omits from its proceedings all ...cultative action of " mind " or otherwise individuated " knowers " on ...e side of the knowings, and all dogmatically proclaimed or otherwise ...ndividuated " ultimate reals " on the side of the knowns. I have never ...yself made observation of any such " pure knowers " or " pure reals "; ...know no one who has ; and I believe no claim to such observation has ...ver yet been made in a way to conform with modern scientific standards ...ree from linguistic hypnosis. I assert that *it is easier literally to observe — to see — man-in-process with environs,* and to see this full process as ...ne transaction, than *it can possibly be literally to observe a " soul," a " spirit," or a psychic " mind "* (this last, a lineal descendant from the two others), or to see a " thing " as a " real " substratum apart from all our knowing and from conditioning thereby. What we find to observe under our postulation is the organism and its environs in natural presence and

† Parenthetical boldface figures refer to References at end of chapter.

CHAPTER NINETEEN

Muscle-Structured Psychology*

I find today that almost all behavior subjected to psychological inquiry is still approached and studied as if programmed by a Patterner, Maker or Decider, which (or who) is taken as present as an inhabitant or associate of the active human organism. No doubt a fair half of the research workers do not profess belief in such an actor, nor do they introduce one *officially* in their studies. My point is that, belief or no belief, acknowledgment or no acknowledgment, these companionate actors are still distinctively at work inside the terminology through which behavioral research is developed, and that they are still used as border-markers between an alleged physical and an alleged psychological in this subjectmatter. A half century ago mechanistic attempts to replace the human actor gained prominence but proved themselves to be as meager and inadequate as have been the conventional mentalist's attempts to hold the fort permanently and irrevocably for himself. Bowels of mercy, splenetic dispositions, kind hearts, and big brains were no more organically developed than were similar qualities and quantities put in mentalistic terms. The current material and psychical " particulars " are equally non-constructive and disintegrative for modern inquiry. And when the organic process is handled as if within a skin, and not as technically a transaction of the organism and environment jointly, the effect is all the worse.

The human body, anatomists tell us, is about 80 per cent muscle. Inquiries into habit are inquiries directly into muscular patterning, and do not need assignment to powers and capacities developed in other than muscular terminologies. I do not mean this statement to interfere with anyone's belief, or customary method of talk — I am considering only workmanship in research and its needs. But it is just as reasonable, if not as conventional, to refer all the behaviors, so far as they are studied as actions within a skin, to muscular locus as to refer them to neuro-cephalic locus. The value of " intentionality," if one wishes to adopt

* From sketches for a paper on Behavioral Locus (1950).

a strong phrasing for marking off the psychological from the physical, may be assigned to muscle as reasonably as to a mind, a brain, a brain escort, or, for that matter, to an escorted brain. By a turn of a wrist the mental and the mechanistic phrasings alike become unnecessary and the disturbing influences running between individual and social in pompously fictitious terms are on their way toward disappearance.

CHAPTER TWENT

Kennetic Inqui

Kennetic inquiry is a name proposed for org
the problem of human knowings and knowns, wh
that the full range of subjectmatters — all the
knowns — form a common field. Such inquiry is
express postulation, and without specific allegatic
mate factual status. The postulation deals with
knowings and knowns instead of with purported fac
ties; and under it every specific instance of a know
its specific known as a single *transaction* in the fiel
branch, and fruit, the conventional severance of
from detachable knowns. To it the word " epister
historical curiosity, stripped of all pretense to auth
ripe only for the museum. The words " philosophic
ical " become similarly irrelevant to our inquiry: as i
in physical laboratories today when actual research i
the word " knowledge " itself is, at least for the tin
since it is steeped in vagueness, and unable to qua
purveyor of determinable fact. The words " knowin
remain, however, usable, if properly provided with
thus made able to stand for concrete instances of orga
action in behavioral space and time.

Thus organized, knowings and knowns together becon
ess in a cosmos, system, or field of fact, such as postula
anticipates. The inquiry is then on the way, or believes
toward becoming science. It is science in the making, if
understood a procedure of observation and postulation,
tion recognizing that it takes place under postulation, and
lation recognizing that it arises out of observation; and
inquiry is secured through the smashing of the old blo

process together, linguistically still unfractured or otherwise schizo-
phrenic. Permitting observation to run free within its framework of postulation, and putting all the concentrated attention we can behind it, we
secure reports on the unfractured knowing-known events. All such observation and such reports and such events-reported we style *trans*actional,
in contrast with the *inter*actional reports obtained under mechanistic inquiry, and with the *self*-actional reports under conventionally " psychic "
presumptions. In so doing we require the " selves " and the " mechan-
isms," equally with the " transactions," to present themselves in postula-
tory form, free from pretense to underlying authoritative status. We
shall adopt the word " behavioral " [1] to apply to those events involving
organisms and environs which, as events, are not technically physiological
or physical, nor directly covered in physiological or physical inquiry. To
repeat: All behavioral events are by postulation transactions; all knowings and knowns as subjectmatters of inquiry belong among transactional
behaviors.

Before undertaking to locate the knowings and the knowns definitely
among the behaviors, let us briefly characterize the setting of the behaviors themselves as *naturally* viewed within the vastly wider field of
all that is " known-to-modern-science." [2] Many differences in viewpoints
as to the range of scientific inquiry are still offered us, and many different
classifications of the sciences are given. We need here give attention
solely to the three great technical fields recognized as basic under all
classifications, and perhaps best styled Physical, Physiological, and
Behavioral (where Psychological may be used as a possible alternative
for the third, if strongly preferred). We treat the distinctions as those
of subjectmatters of inquiry-in-growth (i.e., of science) and not in the
older way as marking off, or resting on any assured differences in the

---

[1] Anyone who prefers " psychological " may substitute it for " behavioral," provided
he holds it to the given postulation, and adequately rejects the introduction of every form
of disconnected " psyche." Those who prefer the word " cultural " would find it necessary
to make that word expressly include the full range of the " psychological."

[2] An appraisal of the organization of scientific knowing with common-sense knowing
will be found in Chapter X of the book referred to (22). Other recent papers by John
Dewey make further development. A recent comment by E. U. Condon, in which he notes
" the doubtful speculation which has characterized most of the philosophic absorptions
of modern science," speaks of Dewey in the following terms: " One of the rare excep-
tions, one who has in a significant and profound way understood and used both science
and the scientific method is John Dewey. He points out clearly that the growth of ra-
tional thought processes may be considered as a response to the biological necessity of
adaptation to the environment. Its ultimate function, he says, is that of ' prospective
control of the conditions of the environment.' It follows then that ' the function of in-
telligence is not that of copying the objects of the environment, but rather of taking
account of the way in which more effective and more profitable relations with these objects may be established in the future ' " (19).

" kinds " of " materials " that " exist." [3] It is indeed true that " physiological " and " behavioral " belong alike under " biological " when this
is brought into contrast with the " physical," since they both have to do
with the organic. But under present-day observation, and in the status
of current inquiry and for it only, the *differentiation* of *techniques* between physiological and behavioral research cuts as deep as that between
physical and physiological, and this should be technically recognized in
all appraisal as of today.[4] Physical research cannot adequately advance
its own technical form of description and report across the full physiological field, nor can technical physiological research in the general case
be advanced to portray the behavioral field. The " languages " of report
remain for the present noninterchangeable. No examination of brain
or nerves or of muscle or viscera can report that " an election was held,"
nor even that " a cow was seen." The central cores of the three great
regions are natural; the bands of transitional vagueness between them
are to be taken as natural; the inquiry into them is natural. But for
present-day guidance with respect to the knowings of the knowns and
to the knowns as undergoing knowing, the technical differentiation as
above set forth remains in effect.

The Behavioral Background

As between physiological and behavioral subjectmatters, the differentiation can be stated in terms of a comparative directness of process in
the former, which shows itself in contrast with a certain typical indirect-
ness in the latter (22, Chap. VI). Soon after Jacques Loeb at the beginning of this century published his — at that time world-exciting — reports on dominant physical processes within and across the skins of
organisms (28), H. S. Jennings (26) noted a characteristic in low organisms different from that of any immediate direct physical or chemical
excitation and reaction. This was found in the sea urchin, for example,
when an enemy cast a shadow, and the organism moved to evade, not
the shadow itself, but the oncoming, hostile shadow-caster. The present investigators, reporting in *Knowing and the Known* (22), have employed the word " sign " to name this technically characteristic " indirect-

---

[3] The word " exist " occurs in two other passages in this paper but there, as here, it
is set off by quotation marks so as not to involve the writer in any claims conventionally
made with respect to its range of application. If here brought into the discussion, the
word would be treated transactionally within the range of designational behaviors. Signalings are too immediate, vivid, and hard-hitting to pause for existential reference,
whereas symbolings have passed beyond the need for it and are even beginning to overcome the desire. (For this terminology, see the section on " Specific Positions Attained.")

[4] For a strong warning against " biologism," see Bertalanffy (10).

ness," as it is found across the entire behavioral field. They chose this word, not so much despite its enormous variety of current applications, as perhaps on account of them, and because none of these applications has succeeded in ruling the field in which dozens of applications are needed to work in harness. The range of " sign," understood *always* as *trans*actional sign-process, was made coincident with the range most generally of behavior itself. This was to make, in effect, sign-actings (which include sign-knowings) the characteristic technical process in the behavioral field, as distinct from the physiological and, of course, also from the physical processes.

Within the range of sign, the word " signal " was chosen to name the underlying sensori-perceptive level; the word " designation " for the next higher evolutionary level — namely, that of linguistic sign opera-tion; and the word " symboling " for a still higher range in the evolu-tionary sense, to which specific differentiation was given — namely, that of mathematics, inclusive of a comparatively small, but very important, part of modern symbolic logic that is itself rigorously mathematical, rather than a still-confused survival from the older logical attitudes.[5]

The words " know " and " known " are applied in current writing at almost any point across this range of behavior, from protozoa to the purest of pure mathematics. An insect is said to know its way around, and a mathematician (it is said), his technical business. Without object-ing to other uses or attempting to set up a program of naming for others, attention here will be centered closely on the range of knowings that occur in the central regions, those of designation. This knowing is by naming,[6] and its implications are of the general type " knowing-to-exist." Common procedures in these regions are of the type that seem all the more dogmatically satisfied as to *what* they assert to " exist," the less

[5] Fifty years ago a typical classification of the behavioral (psychological) was into sense, intellect, and will — all " faculties." Josiah Royce's sensitivity, docility, and initia-tive, covering physical contacts, social setting, and individual going-power, might have brought a great advance, if factually developed (33). Present-day psychologists' organiza-tions are all, or almost all, " capacitative " — that is to say, merely weakened forms of the " facultative." Our proposed distribution into signaling, designating, and symboling is, we hope, fully freed of the capacitative. In the ordinary conventional organization of behavioral subject-object, where " subject " appears we are to understand " environed organism," and, where " object " appears, " known-named-environs." Lacking, however, in the present exhibit is treatment of emotional events, which, from the crudest to the most refined, are handled by assigning all direct pain components and comparably direct " lik-ing " components to physiological inquiry, stripping out the blurred knowing-naming effects for transactional study, and thus readying oneself for further inquiry into the un-clear physiological-behavioral marginal regions.

[6] For a single instance of temporarily widened application of the word " know," see part (g) of the section on " Specific Positions Attained." For the word " exist," see foot-note 3.

assured they are as to what is meant by the *exist* portion of their assertion.

The word " signal " was adopted for the lowest stratum of behaviors largely because of Pavlov's increasing employment of it as his skill and breadth of vision increased (24, 31, 32). It is used to cover the entire complex of perceivings, inclusive of the sensory, the locomotive, and the manipulative. It covers them as action in living organisms. It covers them — and this must be continually reiterated — transactionally and not otherwise. It presents organisms and environs in process in system. It does not have to do with something organic or superorganic taken on its own. It permits no such fictional " third " item as a " percept " of the kind one finds still accepted in many current texts, despite William James's brilliant identification and rejection of such " intervening thirds " fifty years ago (25). If a dog's bark scares a rabbit, the signal as here viewed is neither a bark in a world of its own, nor is it a dog as such, nor is it a specialized process of rabbit's nerve and brain, but always an aspect or phase of the situation seen in full.

The word " designation " is used as the name for the next higher level of behaviors. It would be better if we could speak always, as is here done occasionally, of " name " directly. " Designation " is substituted only because " name " is still so desperately involved conventionally with presumptive, external, static " things named " — the kind out of which word magic grows — that almost inevitably conveyance of meaning is distorted or destroyed. Designations are subdivided into cue, characterization, and specification, as stages in evolutionary growth; the first of these still in process of emerging from signal behavior; the second, comprising ordinary common-sense naming; the third, demanding ever-increased accuracy and, at its highest level, representing modern science itself — not as static, but as living growth, and with the old expectant certainties gone for good. This great expansion of designation not only arises out of signal, but operates, no matter what slips and falls it has by the way- side, to increase the efficiency of signal. This can be vividly shown under transactional postulation, although under the traditional constructions it is only partially and crudely apparent. In the old form observation breaks into fragments that cannot well be patched together again. In the new form, organisms-environs, knowings-knowns, namings-nameds, can be seen in operation and studied without putative know*ers* or putative *reals* behind them as guarantors or guarantees.

Symbolings evolve out of designatings and operate to increase the efficiency of designatings, much as the latter evolve out of signalings and work to increase the efficiency of signalings. The symbolings have learned in long experience that, for best results, they must forfeit the right to use their own components as names. This forfeiture is no loss; it strips the symbolings down for action. The surviving logics of the past and their reconstructions of today, including most of symbolic logic, still operate under a confusion of symbolings with designatings and even with signalings as well. The struggle, dating mainly from Frege and Russell, to put "logical foundations" under mathematics without seeking any foundations for the reliability of the "logic" relied upon, makes the confusion all the worse. Under the transactional approach a great simplification occurs, with exactness of symbol coming definitely and explicitly to the aid of accuracy of specification.

A Reminder

Let us summarize with respect to observation of behaviors in a scientifically transactional background, within which background, in turn, definite examination of knowings and knowns may proceed. We accept the cosmos as before us in knowings, and at the same time we accept all our knowings as its outgrowth. We regard this cosmos as no better assured in our knowings of it than our knowings are assured by reference to it. We are satisfied with this basis for our research. The cosmos is our realm of fact, where "fact" requires both knowings and knowns, but makes no claim to be either of them by itself, whether today or in extrapolation into the future. Darwin brought first animal life, and then human life, under evolution called natural. Driblets of behavioral interpretation have followed his course, but little more. Efforts are here being made to bring knowings-knowns, as themselves behaviors, into system with the rest of fact in a factual cosmos. They are not in system now. The psychologists toss all such issues to the "dogs of epistemology" they seem to find whining under their banquet table. The epistemologists officiate proudly at a high altar of their own persuasion.

Specific Positions Attained

Kennetic inquiry is still regrettably compelled to spend a good part of its time in delivering itself from old philosophical-linguistic bondage. It has, however, already acquired positively a number of footholds that it regards as safe for future use. However bizarre at first sight some of the reports thereby secured may seem, they will as a body, we believe, establish their reasonableness as acquaintance grows.

For this outcome, however, free development of the extensions and durations of behavioral events must be permitted in behavioral, rather than in Newtonian, forms. To postulate events outside spatial and temporal characteristics altogether, as was the older " mentalist " procedure, would be absurd today. Newtonian clock ticks and foot rules, however, are far from sufficient. When physicists needed greater freedom in this respect, they took it; but even adjustments under Einsteinian relativity will not alone suffice for our needs, nor are the various suggestions of recent physiologies adequate to reach across the behavioral field (8). Behavioral *pasts* and *futures* — histories and goals, habits and purposings — are before us descriptively in behavioral *presents*. Descriptively factual knowings-knowns hold fars and nears together under their own specializations of action. Without at least the beginnings of appreciation for this possible need in behavioral inquiry — without, at least, tolerance for experiment under it — grasp of the following positions will not be gained.

(a) Word-meaning and word-embodying are not separates but occur together as one behavioral transaction. No locus in the cosmos can be found either for verbal " meaning " by itself, or for verbal " embodiment " held in separation. On the one hand, word-meanings as severed from man's linguistic activity are not observable, nor are they attainable as subjectmatters of independent inquiry, despite all the reams that have been written purportedly about them. On the other hand, sounds and graphs apart from their meaningful appearance as man's living activity are not " words " at all for anything beyond a surface inquiry. Physics and physiology are, of course, justified in their special inquiries into their respective aspects of verbal activity, but as aspects only. To use the ancient academic labeling, what they offer is of the character of anatomy and is not an analysis of the full event. For adequate behavioral analysis a full and fair field must be open.

(b) More broadly inspected, no field of events identifiable as " language " can be accurately established and brought separately under inquiry in severance from another field alongside known as the " meanings " of language. Without life-in-process neither language nor linguistic meanings can survive any more than could other behavioral events, of whatever kind.

(c) In the region of designations the namings and the knowings are one process, not two. Where the naming is taken transactionally at its level of behavioral advance, it itself is the behavioral knowing. Knowing through naming is a phase of human organism-in-action. In organism-in-action the knowing is the naming; so postulated; so observed; so investigated.

(d) Once able to see word-meaning and naming-knowing as living processes of organism-in-environs, we may next advance to observation of the knowing and the known as transactionally comprised in common event. An organism, a rock, and a tree remain before us as heretofore, subject to such physical or physiological inquiry as we may wish. Insofar, the scientific situation remains unchanged. But when rock flies and dog dodges and tree is evaded in flight, the situation becomes one in which subjectmatters are on a further level of complexity. Here it is but crude and imperfect presentation, an affair of casual, practical report rather than of scientific procedure, when rock and dog and tree are taken as separates, and when independent initiatives or resistances are attributed to any or all of them separately in the style of the older days, when " actualities " were presumably certified to the scientist as " given " to him in advance of his inquiry. Physicists faced a *similar* transformation in the case of the electron. To say today that the electron is an " entity " known to be such on its own, outside of and apart from the processes of its being known, would be to misrepresent modern scientific report. The electron is " known " under specialized knowings, and in highly specialized technical manners. The electron accepted in physical research is one that " works," not one that claims " reality "; it is dealt with, this is to say, as fact within the frame of existing research, not as assured for eternity. The gene in physiology more and more comes to occupy a similar position (23).

(e) What is the case for the knowing-known is the case also for the naming-named. We have a single event such that without both phases — both the namings and the nameds — we would have no event at all. What here most seriously interferes with full technical observation is the old set of verbal fixations which sunder name, named, and namer. The evil of reliance upon severed name, out of organized contact with manner and named, is illustrated, perhaps at its historical worst, in many of the procedures of professional logics today.

(f) These steps lead to a radical outcome with respect to *what* it is that is *named* by a naming, and so *known* linguistically, within an event of naming-knowing. This " what " no longer enters as if it were a " thing " outside the range of behavioral activity. Instead, " the named " is, in the primary case, itself a behavioral transaction: a signaling or perceiving that requires the joint action of its two presumptive " ends " — roughly, the intradermal and the extradermal — if it is to have any " middle " of factuality at all. This " what " that is named, therefore, neither rests upon some demand made by a " thing " upon an " organism "; nor does it enter as the determination of an " outer " thing by an " organism acting *solo*." The designational processes of organism-environs grasp the underlying signaling processes and bring them into increased behavioral organization. We not only say that a knowing without its known, or a known without its knowing, is an incoherence, but that a knowing-in-naming that pretends to know and name something outside of, or beyond, all signaling — or other organic-environmental contact — is equally an incoherence. The known-in-naming is primarily what is already being perceived or is otherwise in transactional process.

(g) Even more radical may seem a further assertion, again one to be taken strictly under transactional postulation. It is that the character-istic behavioral process is the process of knowing. Knowing — the na-turalistic knowing-contact between organism and environs — is that which must receive basic examination and expression the moment the effectiveness of physiological techniques has been left behind, and the behavioral field has been entered. Its study constitutes the primary behavioral science. Knowing is not some wonder perched on top of organic life; it happens as process in and of the world; it is to behavioral science what radiation and gravitation are to physics, and what blood circulation and neural transmission are to physiology.

In this statement we are temporarily changing our form of expression from the technical manner established above, where " sign " was made the general name for behavioral process, and in which " knowing," as a special form of " signing," was limited to the range of " knowings-by-naming." The present passage is the only one in this paper in which this deviation occurs.[7] The deviation is made deliberately: first, because current uses make the word " knowing " run loosely and irregularly, as previously indicated, over almost all phases of behavioral organic-en-vironmental contact, from the most primitive to the most subtly mathe-matical; and, second, because these same current uses subordinate " knowing " in one way or another to almost every other manner of psychological inquiry. Given this conventional looseness of expression and neglect of fact, which is found as much in professional psychology as in common speech, we accept it for one moment in order to secure the impressionistic report that is lacking at first view under the technical statement in terms of " sign."

In this background of expression, then, the knowing contact is the typically behavioral process; it is what must be inquired into first, in-stead of being evaded and slurred. For such inquiry it must above all things be brought fully into the " natural " frame of scientific observa-tion. Here it is that kennetic inquiry brings the situation out into

[7] See footnote 6.

the light, and literally lays it on the laboratory table for detailed examination. In curt expression we may say, if we wish: " World flows, Life grows, Behavior knows, yet with the knowings and the knowns always components of the flow and of the growth." Most generally, then, the behavioral contact points are know-points in differentiation from physical and physiological contact-points. In kennetic inquiry, under the terminology of " sign," the crude particulate reports are passed over, on the one hand, and the wide sweeping generalizations are passed over, on the other. Transactional presentation is secured as observation gains strength. Translations into " minds," whether of moron or of mage, cease to enter. Use of the techniques of other sciences can be made without forced subordination or pretense of dominance — all of which means that the prospect improves for inquiry and report of the type we today call scientific.

With respect to the above positions (a) to (g), we may recall the various freedoms insisted upon for inquiry at one or another stage of the discussion. These freedoms are indeed at times as much in demand by physiologists as they ever are by behavioral investigators, since the best physics may at times constrict physiological progress, just as the best physiology may at times constrict behavioral; though, of course, in the latter case, protection against the old " psychical " and " mentalist " fixations is the primary need. The freedoms required are: freedom of postulation; freedom of observation under postulation; freedom from conventional speech-forms insistently surviving from prehistoric cultures; freedom for linguistic, as well as for laboratory, experimentation; and, finally, freedom for the establishment of new systems of nomenclature in the open daylight of inquiry.

A general theory of language should become practicable in this framework, perhaps one such as John Dewey has forecast in the preface to his *Logic* (21). No such presentation exists. What we have, instead, is ever-renewed divagation about minds and things, all fictional, with a fictional " language " as hare to both hounds. Leonard Bloomfield's linguistic study (11) is probably the only work to be mentioned as differentiated from the old line, and his construction was hampered by his use of a comparatively early form of psychological behavior*ism*, something not here employed in any phase.

STATES WITH RESPECT TO SCIENCE

The above program of observation and interpretation is not one of speedy recent development, but instead one of slow growth. It is definitely not in favor with — often not even in the field of vision of — metaphysics or other standardizations of the traditional psychological-philosophical terminologies. John Dewey laid the foundation for it in his famous essay " The Reflex Arc Concept in Psychology " in 1896 (20)[8] and has carried it forward through studies in almost all lines of cultural development, culminating in his *Logic, The Theory of Inquiry* (21). The present writer approached it in his study of group pressures in *The Process of Government* in 1908 (4), an inquiry much wider in scope than any study of pressure groups, the " discovery " of which is occasionally attributed to, though emphatically not claimed by, him; and he followed it later with studies of cross-sectional process in society (5), types of linguistic coherence in society (6), and communicational psychology (7, 8). Probably the best sociological construction undertaken from this direction is that of George Lundberg (30). In psychology the earliest and most important effort to see perceptions in terms of interactions between organisms and environs was that of J. R. Kantor (27). The ecologies are well known in all biological lines. Specialized cultural inquiries have in many cases almost reached the transactional form, though without, in any case that I am aware of, having made the necessary generalized formulation.

The greatest strength of the transactional approach at the present time is given it by the advances of physics following the initiative of Einstein, as this rested upon the observation of Faraday and its mathematical presentation by Clerk Maxwell (22, Chap. IV). Newton had achieved the construction of the interactional in its region of greatest usefulness. In the last generation, in place of the interactional, physics has secured envisionments of particle as wave, of mass as energy, and of gravitation as conformation of space-time. All these changes involve widened observation and are transactional in their orientation in the sense of that term as here used. The present procedure falls into line, though at a proper respectful distance, with Einstein's long-concentrated effort to secure a unified field theory for physics.[9] Any physical field theory of most general scope will, we believe, when once soundly secured, show

[8] At the time of the celebration of the fiftieth anniversary of the *Psychological Review*, this paper was judged by a vote of several hundred leading American psychologists to be the most important paper ever published in that journal. Even yet its values are only partially realized.

[9] Although the word " field " has repeatedly appeared in this paper, its use has been casual, and it has nowhere been specifically adopted, despite its apparent superficial advantages. This is partly because certain problems as to its application are not yet standardized by physics, but more because the word has been so widely abused by overly optimistic appropriators in other than physical regions. On this point see a discussion by Ivan D. London (29).

itself to be a process of knowing, as clearly as it shows itself to be a system of the known. The impress of the physical knowing will be upon the physically known, and the status of each will depend upon that of the other. In this case the need of a kennetic theory on the knowing side, as correlate to the field theory on the side of the known, will make itself strongly felt. Einstein's personal attitude, as is well enough known, will not tolerate anything comparable to kennetic theory on the side of the knowing, but the observation of Bohr, and of others, is clearly in line for it. Einstein, amidst the efflorescence of German philosophical terminology — the most resplendent in the world — maintains, largely in the Kantian tradition, all the ancient self-actional treatments, inclusive of the wholly redundant, entitatively personalized know*er*, at the very time that he has been the greatest of all leaders in overcoming the rigidities of the old " knowns " by expelling that sort of reification from the physical range. Bridgman, who has been the world leader in interpreting Einstein's work as human progress (14), holds in his latest discussion that the traditional metaphysical bias in Einstein is now at work where it may be positively hurtful to the results Einstein secures. Bridgman's comment is that " in Einstein's yearning for absolute information and meaning it seems . . . that the ghosts of Newton's absolute space and time are walking again, ghosts which Einstein himself had apparently exorcised in his special theory of relativity " (15, p. 19) ; and again, more specifically, that Einstein " believes it possible to . . . sublimate . . . the point of view of the individual observer into something universal, ' public,' and ' real ' " (16, pp. 349, 354).

RECENT TRANSACTIONAL APPROXIMATIONS

Several papers have appeared in *Science* within the past year outlining scientific development on lines sympathetic to, and in some cases directly comparable with, kennetic treatment. Cantril, Ames, and their associates expressly accept transactional observation and construction under that name for psychology. Bertalanffy proposes regions comparably transactional for physiological inquiry. Bohr sharpens his long-maintained stress on physical complementarity as opposed to the epistemological type of " reality " toward which he, as well as Bridgman, sees Einstein still straining. Dobzansky's discussion of " basic concepts " in the genetic field sees openings for ever-greater observation and research into " system " free from patterns and methods, the enforcement of which earlier workers demand.

Bohr's paper (12) is supplemented by his extended contribution to the volume dealing with Einstein's philosophical cerements in the *Library of Living Philosophers* (13). Where Einstein still holds to man-the-predictor as the test of whatever " element of physical reality " there is to be found, Bohr asserts the rights of verified observations as they come (the issue of " indeterminacy " being central to this discussion) ; he permits the contrasts of observation to stand undisturbed within the system of the known, asserting that in them " we have to do with equally essential aspects of all well-defined knowledge about the objects "; he finds here growth, not confusion; and he insists that " causality " will not be lost, but will in the end be better understood. Outstanding is his demand for the clarification of the many ambiguous terms, ambiguously standard to all the philosophico-scientificoid rummagings. Above all, the word " phenomenon," he declares, should be confined to " observations obtained under specified circumstances including an account of the whole experiment." Such a demand runs side by side with Bridgman's requirement (14) that the " operations " involved in any naming be made known, and with our present insistence that " observation under postulation " should be companion to " postulation derived from observation." With strictly practical intent Bohr quotes the ancient saying that men are both actors and spectators in the drama of existence.

Bertalanffy (9, 10) appraises the intra-integumental organism taken as subjectmatter of general observation and description, and finds it inadequate as a system. He then considers a wider system of organism-plus-environment and develops its import. His attention is not directed to the specialized range of behaviors-in-environment, such as we have been discussing " transactionally " in the still more specialized case of knowings-knowns, but instead covers the underlying field of physiology in general, and covers it in such a manner that, if he so happens to wish, he could readily apply to it the word " transactional " in a sense not in conflict with that in which Clerk Maxwell employed the word three quarters of a century ago, or with that in which we have been using it here. Bertalanffy makes his main differentiation run between " closed " and " open " systems. Most physical systems are closed systems. The organism by itself is an open system. In the technically closed system no material enters or leaves, reversibility is in most cases practicable, and an equilibrium-state in which entropy is at a maximum must ultimately be attained. In the open system, in contrast, there is a continuous flow of components from without, their flow and ratio are maintained constant, irreversibility appears in great degree, growth is characteristic, a steady-state characterized by minimum entropy-production may be approached, and, finally, when disturbance occurs, " self-regulation " operates to restore balance. The status of Bertalanffy's distinction of the physiological from the physical is akin to our present distinction of the behavioral from the physiological in that in neither case are sharp borders set up; in neither case are " existential realities " pretended to; in each case future studies may reduce or eliminate unexplored border-areas; and, more important than all, in each the differentiation rests jointly upon the techniques of inquiry established and upon the main systems of the knowns that appear as the outcome of inquiry. Under this approach Bertalanffy anticipates that biology may advance toward being an exact science, and physics itself will have new pathways open to it. It might comparably be considered assured that, if a sound working basis for the differentiation of knowings and knowns in system is sometime attained, all branches of scientific inquiry will benefit thereby.

Dobzhansky's paper (23) is throughout an exhibit of advancing freedom in genetic research. A transactional attitude, though not in specific development, is seen replacing the earlier interactional stresses deriving from common speech and physical formulation. Priority of research for physics is, of course, maintained here as in the other papers mentioned, and in kennetic inquiry as well. Terminology is not developed, and interactional expression is still largely employed. But whatever components are introduced as particulate quickly reappear in broadened system. The chromosome is an organized system. The genotype (except for viruses) " is an integrated system of many kinds (' loci ') of genes." The genotype is in system with the environment. The environment of the moment " is only a component of the environmental complex that determines the mutation." The development of the individual " is an orderly sequence . . . in which the genotype and the environment are involved." The geneticist's growing freedom from the patterns with which he began is manifest in all this; and it is manifest as widening interconnection of the factors, not as their mechanistic application, one to another.

In three papers under the general title " Psychology and Scientific Research " (18), Cantril, Ames, Hastorf, and Ittelson argue in favor of a transactional approach for psychology, adopting that name as it is established in the book *Knowing and the Known* (22) and believing that they are justified in anticipating revolutionary developments when psychology comes to be investigated from such a viewpoint. The solid strength behind their position lies in the work Professor Ames has carried on for more than twenty years in his laboratory at the Dartmouth Eye Institute, and as elaborated more recently in conjunction with psychologists at Princeton through the Institute for Associated Research. One of his exhibits, that of the distorted room, in viewing which ordinary perceptive processes default, has become well known through widely circulated accounts in newspapers and magazines a year or so ago. An even more startling exhibit, dealing with motion rather than with objects at rest, is that of the revolving windows, the report on which, at the present moment, is still in manuscript (2). A rectangular window of conventional appearance can be seen slowly revolving on its vertical axis. A trapezoidal window, comparable in size, and similarly revolving alongside, cannot be seen to revolve, and cannot even be plainly seen as a trapezoid. Persistent efforts by experimenters to see complete revolutions of the entire frame have failed. Even when a long rod touching the window is used as an aid by the observer, he makes little progress, and that little is lost by the following morning. Headaches and nausea may mark his disturbance. What the observer " sees " — or, perhaps, " seems to see," depending on what meaning one gives the word " see " — is an apparently rectangular window of changing length, oscillating at changing speeds to right and then to left in a total arc of about 100° (if degrees of arc can be injected at all in a case like this), and then returning to its starting point, just as the rectangular window completes its full observed revolution.

Professor Ames's workshops offer some fifty interrelated exhibits of persistent perceptions or, more properly, perceptual processes, that are out of agreement with the commonly accepted approaches to the physiological and behavioral interpretations of vision. We have here not simply illusion in the ordinary sense, but illusion so pronounced that doubt is cast on the apparent " actualities " or " realities " of ordinary visual report, and the need arises for an ever more rigorous inquiry into the conditions under which such observation takes place. This is closely akin to Bohr's requirement, quoted above, for the word " phenomenon ": that its use in physics should be confined to " observations obtained under specified circumstances including an account of the whole experiment " (12). Professor Ames would hardly make as radical a statement as this. Nevertheless, in summary, he holds that perceptions as they come cannot be referred flatly to outer objects, nor to inner capacities as producers; and no more to the latter when neurologically postulated than when taken in the old slipshod form of the " psychic " (2, 3). Perception, to him, tends to become frankly and openly a " transaction " involving organism and environment in union, in the presentation of which both what he styles " assumption " and what he styles " purpose " or " value " must be included; namely, the past history of individual and race, and the advancing objectives of living man and group. " Prognostic directive " is a name he favors as best characterizing this perceptional activity of the organism. He has sketched the organization of the neural processes involved, and has proceeded with patience, ingenuity, and steady attention to openings for further test. In an address to architects a few years ago (1) he summed up: " While in no way denying the existence of the ' external world ' our disclosures apparently show that the only aspects of it man can know anything about are those aspects which are either helpful or thwarting in carrying out his purposes."

In harmony with Ames's work is that of Hoyt Sherman at Ohio State University in which unexpected abilities have been aroused in students by a drawing technique that organizes the total visual field with the muscular requirements of the procedure under way (34).

REFERENCES

1. AMES, A., JR. Architectural Form and Visual Sensations. In T. H. Creighton (Ed.), *Building for Modern Man, A Symposium,* p. 82. Princeton, N. J.: Princeton Univ. Press (1949).
2. ———. *Psychol. Monogr.,* in press.
3. ———. *Am. J. Psychol.,* **59,** 333 (1946).
4. BENTLEY, A. F. *The Process of Government.* Chicago: Univ. of Chicago Press (1908); Bloomington, Ind.: Principia Press (1935, 1949).
5. ———. *Relativity in Man and Society.* New York: Putnam (1926).
6. ———. *Linguistic Analysis of Mathematics.* Bloomington, Ind.: Principia Press (1932).
7. ———. *Behavior, Knowledge, Fact.* Bloomington, Ind.: Principia Press (1935).
8. ———. *J. Phil.,* **38,** 477 (1941).
9. BERTALANFFY, L. VON. *Science,* 111, 23 (1950).
10. ———. *Brit. J. Philos. Sci.,* 1 (2), 134 (1950).
11. BLOOMFIELD, L. Linguistic Aspects of Science. In *International Encyclopedia of Unified Science.* Vol. I, No. 4 (1939).
12. BOHR, N. *Science,* 111, 51 (1950).
13. ———. Discussion with Einstein on Epistemological Problems in Atomic Physics. In P. A. Schilpp (Ed.), *Library of Living Philosophers,* Vol. VII, *Albert Einstein, Philosopher-Scientist.* Evanston, Ill.: Northwestern University (1949).
14. BRIDGMAN, P. W. *The Logic of Modern Physics.* New York: Macmillan (1927).
15. ———. *Rev. int. de phil.,* **3** (10), 479 (1949).
16. ———. Einstein's Theories and the Operational Point of View. In P. A. Schilpp (Ed.), *loc. cit.*
17. CANTRIL, H. *Sci. American,* **183,** 79 (Sept. 1950).
18. CANTRIL, H., et al. *Science,* 110, 461, 491, 517 (1949).
19. CONDON, E. U. *New Republic,* 11. (February 13, 1950).
20. DEWEY, J. *Psychol. Rev.,* **3,** 357 (1896).
21. ———. *Logic The Theory of Inquiry.* New York: Holt (1938).
22. DEWEY, J., and BENTLEY, A. F. *Knowing and the Known.* Boston: Beacon Press (1949).
23. DOBZHANSKY, Th. *Science,* 111, 161 (1950).
24. FROLOV, Y. P. *Pavlov and His School. The Theory of Conditioned Reflexes.* London: Kegan Paul, Trench, Trubner (1937).
25. JAMES, W. *Essays in Radical Empiricism.* New York: Longmans, Green (1938).
26. JENNINGS, H. S. *Behavior of the Lower Organisms.* New York: Columbia Univ. Press. (1906).

27. KANTOR, J. R. *Principles of Psychology*. New York: Knopf (1924, 1926).
28. LOEB, J. *Comparative Physiology of the Brain and Comparative Psychology*. New York: Putnam (1900).
29. LONDON, I. D. *Psychol. Rev.*, 51, 266 (1944).
30. LUNDBERG, G. A. *Foundations of Sociology*. New York: Macmillan (1939).
31. PAVLOV, I. P. *Conditioned Reflexes*. Trans. by G. V. Anrep. London: Oxford Univ. Press (1927).
32. ———. *Lectures on Conditioned Reflexes*. Trans. by W. H. Gantt. New York: International Publ. (1928).
33. ROYCE, J. *Outlines of Psychology*. New York: Macmillan (1903).
34. SHERMAN, H. L. *Drawing by Seeing*. New York: Hinds, Hayden & Eldredge (1947).

Epilogue

It is written: " In the beginning was the *Word!* "
I'm stopped already. Who will help me further?
I cannot possibly rate the *Word* so highly.
I must translate it otherwise,
If I am rightly enlightened by the spirit.
It is written: " In the beginning was the *Thought!* "
Consider the first line well,
Lest the pen write too hastily.
Is it the *Thought* that works and creates all?
Should it not be: " In the beginning was the *Power!* "
Yet, even as I write it down,
I feel I cannot let that stand.
The spirit helps me!   Suddenly I have it,
And confidently write: " In the beginning was the *Deed!* "

Goethe's Faust, translation by MacIntyre

Arthur F. Bentley: A Bibliography

BOOKS

The Condition of the Western Farmer as Illustrated by the Economic History of a Nebraska Township, Johns Hopkins University Studies in Historical and Political Science, Eleventh Series, Nos. VII–VIII. Baltimore: Johns Hopkins Press, July–August, 1893. 92 pp.

The Process of Government: A Study of Social Pressures. Chicago: University of Chicago Press, 1908. 501 pp. Second Edition, Bloomington, Indiana: The Principia Press, 1935. Third Edition, Principia Press, 1949.

Relativity in Man and Society. New York, G. P. Putnam's Sons, 1926, 363 pp.

Linguistic Analysis of Mathematics. Bloomington, Indiana: The Principia Press, 1932. 315 pp.

Behavior, Knowledge, Fact. Bloomington, Indiana: The Principia Press, 1935. 391 pp.

(with John Dewey) *Knowing and the Known.* Boston: The Beacon Press, 1949. 334 pp.

Inquiry into Inquiries: Essays in Social Theory. Boston: The Beacon Press, 1954. 365 pp.

ARTICLES

" The Units of Investigation in the Social Sciences," *Publications of The American Academy of Political and Social Science,* No. 149, June 18, 1895, pp. 87–113.

" Remarks on Method in the Study of Society," *American Journal of Sociology,* Vol. 32, November 1926, pp. 456–60.

" A Sociological Critique of Behaviorism," *Archiv für systematische Philosphie und Soziologie,* Bd. 31, Heft 3/4, 1928, pp. 334–40.

" L'individuel et le social: les termes et les faits," *Revue Internationale de Sociologie,* Vol. 36, March–June 1929, pp. 243–70.

" New Ways and Old to Talk About Men," *The Sociological Review* (London), Vol. 26, October 1929, pp. 300–14.

" Sociology and Mathematics I & II," *The Sociological Review,* Vol. 23, July, October 1931, pp. 85–107, 149–72.

" The Linguistic Structure of Mathematical Consistency," *Psyche,* Vol. 12, January 1932, pp. 78–91.

" The Positive and the Logical," *Philosophy of Science,* Vol. 3, October 1936, pp. 472–85.

" Physicists and Fairies," *Philosophy of Science,* Vol. 5, April 1938, pp. 132–65.

" Situational vs. Psychological Theories of Behavior:
Sights-seen as Material of Knowledge
Situational Treatment of Behavior
Postulation for Behavioral Inquiry."

Journal of Philosophy, Vol. 36, March 30, June 8, July 20, 1939, pp. 169–81, 309–23, 405–13.

" Observable Behaviors," *Psychological Review,* Vol. 47, May 1940, pp. 230–53.

" The Behavioral Superfice," *Psychological Review,* Vol. 48, January 1941, pp. 39–59.

" The Human Skin: Philosophy's Last Line of Defense," *Philosophy of Science,* Vol. 8, January 1941, pp. 1–19.

" Decrassifying Dewey," *Philosophy of Science,* Vol. 8, April 1941, pp. 147–56.

" Some Logical Considerations Concerning Professor Lewis' ' Mind '," *Journal of Philosophy,* Vol. 38, November 6, 1941, pp. 634–35.

" The Factual Space and Time of Behavior," *Journal of Philosophy,* Vol. 38, August 28, 1941, pp. 477–85.

" As Through a Glass Darkly," *Journal of Philosophy,* Vol. 39, July 30, 1942, pp. 432–39.

" The Jamesian Datum," *Journal of Psychology,* Vol. 16, 1943, pp. 35–79.

" Truth, Reality and Behavioral Fact," *Journal of Philosophy,* Vol. 40, April 1943, pp. 169–87.

(with John Dewey) " A Search for Firm Names," *Journal of Philosophy,* Vol. 42, January 4, 1945, pp. 5–6.

" On a Certain Vagueness in Logic: I, II," *Journal of Philosophy,* January 4, 1945, pp. 6–27, 39–51.

(with John Dewey) " A Terminology for Knowings and Knowns," *Journal of Philosophy,* April 26, 1945, pp. 225–47.

(with John Dewey) " Postulations," *Journal of Philosophy,* November 22, 1945, pp. 645–62.

" Logicians' Underlying Postulations," *Philosophy of Science,* Vol. 13, January 1945, pp. 3–19.

(with John Dewey) " Interaction and Transaction," *Journal of Philosophy,* September 12, 1946, pp. 505–17.

(with John Dewey) " Transactions as Known and Named," *Journal of Philosophy,* Vol. 43, September 26, 1946, pp. 533–51.

(with John Dewey) " Specification," *Journal of Philosophy,* Vol. 43, November 21, 1946, pp. 645–63.

(with John Dewey) " Definition," *Journal of Philosophy,* Vol. 44, pp. 281–306.

(with John Dewey) " Concerning a Vocabulary for Inquiry into Knowledge," *Journal of Philosophy,* Vol. 44, July 31, 1947, pp. 421–34.

" The New ' Semiotic '," *Philosophy and Phenomenological Research,* Vol. 8, September 1947, pp. 107–31.

" Signs of Error," *Philosophy and Phenomenological Research,* Vol. 10, September 1949, pp. 99–104.

" Kennetic Inquiry," *Science,* Vol. 112, December 29, 1950, pp. 775–83.

N.B.   Julius Altman has compiled a valuable chronological listing of the writings of Dr. Arthur F. Bentley, published and unpublished, which is available for consultation at the Manuscript Division of the Indiana University Library.

Index of Names

Compiled by Julius Altman

Subject Index

Compiled by Julius Altman

symbiotaxiplasm, 12, 18–23
symbol, 177, 208, 229, 278, 297–298, 300–301, 308–312, 319, 322–323, 341–343; *see also* mathematics and symbolic logic
symbolic logic, xv, 196, 312–313, 319, 341, 343
syntax, 105–106, 112
synthetic, 104, 298
system, 179f., 181, 185–189, 192, 204–206, 213, 225, 262, 291, 315, 342
subjectmatter, 297, 302

temperament, 18
terminology, 55
terms, *see* words
theory, 80, 177
things, 27–28, 56–59, 76–78, 79f., 82, 123, 144, 161, 185–186, 300, 308, 315–316
thirds, 169–170, 251–252, 259, 314, 342; *see also* mental
thought, 137–138, 191–192, 247, 249f.
time, Chap. XII, xiii, 33–36, 44–49, 51, 148, 167–168, 203–204, 207–208, 227–228, 249f., 259, 288, 292, 315, 344
togetherness, 295–296

transactional approach, xiv–xvi, 143, 145, 147, 152, 163, 166, 168, 170, 188–189, 216–218, 222, 229, 260, 283, 285, 293, 296, 299–300, 318, 335, 337–339, 342, 346, 352; early formulations, 20, 46, 52
tropism, 189
true, Chap. XVIII, 262
truth, Chap. XVIII, xv, 23–24, 73, 141f., 235

unification of science, 314
uniformity of knowledge, 167

vagueness, 276, 288–289
values, 3, 23–24
verbal frames of reference, 29f., 83f.
verification, 148, 235–236, 331
visibility, *see* observation
vision, Chap. XV
vitalism, 39–40, 44, 69, 77–78, 165, 180, 183, 185, 190

whole, 86–87, 97–98
words, xiv, 32, 41, 52, 151, 191, 225–228, 247, 298, 301, 309, 344–345, 355